BIOGRAPHICAL MEMOIRS OF FELLOWS, V

PROCEEDINGS OF THE BRITISH ACADEMY · 138

BIOGRAPHICAL MEMOIRS OF FELLOWS V

Published for THE BRITISH ACADEMY
by OXFORD UNIVERSITY PRESS

Oxford University Press, Great Clarendon Street, Oxford OX2 6DP

Oxford New York
Auckland Bangkok Bogotá Buenos Aires Cape Town Chennai
Dar es Salaam Delhi Hong Kong Istanbul Karachi Kolkata
Kuala Lumpur Madrid Melbourne Mexico City Mumbai Nairobi
São Paulo Shanghai Singapore Taipei Tokyo Toronto

British Library Cataloguing in Publication Data
Data available

ISBN 0-19-726393-3   978-0-19-726393-8
ISSN 0068-1202

Typeset in Times
by J&L Composition, Filey, North Yorkshire
Printed in Great Britain
on acid-free paper by
Antony Rowe Limited,
Chippenham, Wiltshire

The Academy is grateful to Professor P. J. Marshall, CBE, FBA
for his editorial work on this volume

Contents

SIDNEY ALLEN

William Sidney Allen
1918–2004

I. Early life and family background

WILLIAM SIDNEY ALLEN WAS BORN ON 18 MARCH 1918 in north London, where his father worked as a maintenance engineer in a printing works, and it was there that he spent his early childhood. He was always known in the family (though not at school) as Sidney, in order to distinguish him from his father, William Percy Allen. Later he chose for professional purposes 'W. Sidney Allen', primarily to avoid confusion with another author in the related field of what was coming to be called in the 1950s applied linguistics: William S[tannard] Allen. The name by which he was known to most of his friends and then more widely when fashions began to change, socially and to some extent bibliographically, in the 1960s was Sidney. Throughout this memoir I will call him Sidney.

His father had been orphaned at an early age and was brought up, initially by his paternal grandfather, a carpenter in Bermondsey, and then by a widowed aunt, a laundress in Lambeth. At the age of ten he was sent to a boarding school for poor children in Oxfordshire, endowed by a philanthropist MP, where he received a sound elementary education and subsequently was apprenticed to the printing trade. Sidney's mother, Ethel Pearce, who was born in Camden Town, was the daughter of a compositor and one of seven children. Printing was thus part of his family background on both sides. Sidney's father taught him to read by the age of three and did what he could to provide him with a good primary education, as well as instructing him at home in such practical skills as carpentry and what would nowadays be called DIY. He sent him to a private school for one year when he was five. Sidney then went on to the local

Proceedings of the British Academy, **138**, 3–36. © The British Academy 2006.

London County Council elementary school, from where, at the age of eleven, he won a scholarship to Christ's Hospital.

It was at Christ's Hospital, as he was to recount later, that he received the kind of education that could be seen with hindsight as having had a major if not wholly determinative influence on his future career. Having come from a school where, as was of course normal at that time, no foreign languages were taught, he immediately started to learn Latin and two years later Greek. From the outset his interests were linguistic rather than literary. Particularly influential was his form master Derrick Macnutt, a demanding but inspiring teacher, who taught his pupils Latin and Greek composition, both prose and verse, and in the sixth form made them read large portions of the main classical authors. It was Macnutt who encouraged him to sit for an entrance scholarship to Trinity College, Cambridge, where he obtained in 1937 a major award. When supplemented with a matching award from the local council and an exhibition from Christ's Hospital, this enabled him, as an undergraduate, to be financially independent of his parents. In later life he was always ready to acknowledge the debt he owed both to the school and to Derrick Macnutt. Macnutt, incidentally, was the person who under the pen name of Ximenes set the notoriously difficult *Observer* weekly crosswords. Sidney himself continued to do *The Times* crossword regularly for the rest of his life and prided himself on the rapidity with which he completed it.

II. Undergraduate at Cambridge, 1937–9

When he arrived in Cambridge for the Michaelmas Term of 1937–8 he found that he had already done most of the work required for the two-year Part 1 of the Classical Tripos as it was then constituted and 'was able to devote most of [his] time (when not rowing) to attending the classes and doing the reading for the Group-E option of Part 2, which [he] was due to take in his third and final year'.[1]

Given his interest in language and languages, it was perhaps predictable that he should have chosen this particular option, which as it was

[1] This quotation is taken from Sidney's own autobiographical contribution to K. Brown and V. Law (eds.), *Linguistics in Britain: Personal histories* (Publications of the Philological Society, 36) (Oxford, 2002), 14–27. As to his rowing, he said that being able to take up rowing, an expensive sport, from scratch (he was a good sportsman and at school had played rugby) was but one of the advantages of being at Trinity, a wealthy college, and coincidentally of having the Senior Treasurer of the Boat Club, (Sir) James Butler as his tutor.

then taught (under the rubric of 'Comparative Philology'), had as its core the study of the phonology and morphology of the Indo-European languages from a historical and comparative point of view, with particular reference to Greek and Latin. It also included a certain amount of what was coming to be called general and descriptive, or synchronic, linguistics, and, given the importance of Sanskrit in the reconstruction of earlier stages of the Indo-European languages by means of 'the comparative method', enough of the grammar of both Vedic and Classical Sanskrit for students to be able to construe selected texts. In addition to doing the Group-E reading, Sidney also attended the relevant lectures, in particular those given by Harold W. Bailey and N. B. Jopson ('Joppie'), the Professors respectively of Sanskrit and Comparative Philology. Both of these, very different from one another in manner and personality, were inspiring teachers who communicated to their students the enthusiasm that they themselves had for their subject. And as far as the youthful Sidney Allen was concerned the content of teaching was admirably complementary. Sir Harold (as he later became) was by then one of the world's greatest authorities over the whole field of the older Indo-Iranian languages. He was also conversant with the more theoretically innovative work in what was still generally seen as the reconstruction of the earliest form of the Indo-European 'parent-language', Proto-Indo-European (PIE). These newer trends could subsequently be seen as originating with Ferdinand de Saussure's *Mémoire sur le système primitif des voyelles dans les langues indo-européennes* (Leipzig, 1879); they had still not come to exert any appreciable influence on the standard textbooks and works of reference. In particular, Sir Harold was thoroughly familiar with the so-called 'laryngeal theory' (relating to the pre-history of the PIE vowel-system). Apart from learning more Sanskrit at his feet than did the average Group-E student, Sidney thus acquired earlier than most an interest in the laryngeal theory and some knowledge of its structuralist underpinnings. If Jopson had any knowledge of the laryngeal theory or of the general principles of structural linguistics, this had no effect on the content of his lectures. On the other hand, his presentation of what was still the generally accepted version of the phonological and morphological structure of PIE and of the prehistoric stages of Greek, Latin and Sanskrit and of the other Indo-European languages (Slavonic, Celtic, etc.) was greatly enlivened by his humorous anecdotes of one kind and another and his own facility in a wide range of modern languages upon which he could draw relevantly at the drop of a hat. In later years, Sidney frequently referred favourably to this aspect of Joppie's teaching.

Predictably at the end of his second year as an undergraduate, he got a first in Part 1, and in the normal course of events he would have come back to Cambridge for Part 2 of the Classical Tripos in October 1939.

III. War service 1939–45

Sidney's career was interrupted by war service, as was that of so many young men of his generation, including several of his future colleagues in London or in Cambridge. In his case the circumstances were unusual. In the summer of 1939 he had gone to Iceland with two college friends. He himself was motivated, in part, by what he was to describe later as a 'marginal interest' in Icelandic which in the 'Group-E' reading he had been doing was reputed to 'have remained virtually unchanged for a millennium'. While they were exploring one of the remoter parts of the island, war was declared. It was with great difficulty that they managed to get back to Britain, via Norway, just in time for the beginning of the Michaelmas Term.

Sidney was already a member of the Officers' Training Corps (OTC) and within a month or so he was called up. In May 1940 he was commissioned and posted to a battalion of the Royal Tank Regiment. It was at this point that his trip to Iceland the previous year proved, in retrospect, to be a decisive factor, not only for the rest of his time in the army, but also, indirectly, for part of his academic career after the war.

As someone with a knowledge of the country and also to a certain degree of the language, he was interviewed about this at the War Office and after a period of training in London was sent as an intelligence officer to Iceland, which had been occupied by the British after their defeat in Norway. He spent the next year travelling around the island on reconnaissance and then, after a further period of special training, as an instructor in 'winter warfare'. In later years he could be quite amusing about his experiences in these two roles. (He could also be critical, whether justifiably or not, of what he regarded as incompetence in some of his superiors.) What is relevant in the present context about this part of his war service is that it confirmed what subsequently became a life-long interest in Iceland and Icelandic: it initiated what I will call the 'Icelandic connection'. It also provided him with some considerable practical knowledge of map reading and cartography.

His knowledge of the principles of cartography was further refined when, having returned to Britain in the spring of 1942, he was given command of a photographic intelligence unit involved in the planning of the Normandy landing. Shortly after D-day he himself joined the British Second Army as it advanced through Northern France, Belgium and Holland and, after the hard-fought and critically important 'Battle of the Bulge' in the Ardennes, crossed the Rhine and moved on in the spring of 1945 as far as Lüneburg Heath, where the 'armistice in north-west Europe was signed' and '[his] active war came to an end'. He was demobilised, after six years of war service, just in time for the beginning of the academic year.[2]

IV. Ph.D. research student at Cambridge 1945–8

Back in Cambridge, he was disinclined to resume his undergraduate studies for Part 2 of the Classical Tripos. Instead, with a 'War BA' he registered for a Ph.D. and, with an eye to the future, deliberately chose for his doctoral research a topic 'conveniently on the borders of linguistics/ phonetics and the classical languages [including Sanskrit]'. He did so because, at a time when university posts were few and far between, this kept open for him, as a topic in the field of Group-E comparative philology would not have done, two, if not three, possible points of entry for his preferred future career. At that time a Ph.D., far from being a necessary, or even a desirable, condition for appointment as a university teacher in this country, especially in a non-scientific subject, was widely regarded as un-British (smacking perhaps of German and American professionalism and premature specialisation). He registered as a Ph.D. student because being officially registered for some degree or other was a condition for his obtaining an ex-service maintenance grant. He also had to have an official supervisor. This was A. J. Beattie, a specialist in Ancient Greek dialects, who had little interest in Sidney's research topic and left him largely to his own devices. Beattie, who later became Professor of Greek in Edinburgh, came to be known to the world of classical scholarship, and even to a much wider public, for his rejection of the decipherment by Ventris and Chadwick in the early-to-mid 1950s of the inscriptions on the Mycenaean clay tablets and the discovery that they were written, using

---

[2] 'One of the more interesting of the jobs' that Sidney was given while he was awaiting demobilisation 'was to organise the escorting of sixteen German generals to London for interrogation.' These included, most notably, Hasso von Manteuffel, the charismatic young commander of the 5th Panzer Army in the Ardennes, who had previously distinguished himself in North Africa and on the Eastern Front and then surrendered to the British with all his men.

the syllabic script called Linear B, in an early pre-Homeric form of Greek, and for his obdurate maintenance of his own view, over the years, despite increasing evidence to the contrary.

It may be added at this point that Sidney was from the outset convinced that the Ventris-and-Chadwick hypothesis was, in its main lines at least, correct although their work was peripheral to his own fields of interest. He had, however, enough knowledge of non-alphabetic, syllabic or quasi-syllabic, scripts and of the problems that they pose for the encoding or decoding of languages whose phonological, and morphophonological, structure is typologically different from that of the languages for which they had originally developed to realise that the hypothesis was from this point of view plausible. (He also had the kind of mind—witness his skill with crossword puzzles—which delighted in the cryptographic detail.) When Sidney came back to Cambridge in 1955, he and John Chadwick were colleagues in the Classical Faculty and shared much of the Group-E teaching.

Sidney's thesis, which he submitted in 1948 and for which he was awarded the degree in 1949, was entitled 'Linguistic problems and their treatment in antiquity'. It was examined jointly by the Professors of Sanskrit at the School of Oriental Studies (SOAS) in London and of Humanity (i.e., Latin) in Aberdeen: John Brough and (Sir) Peter Noble. He justifiably took pride in the fact that at the oral examination they had no searching questions to put to him, but congratulated him on the quality of his scholarship. Two of his books had their origins in his Ph.D. research, as did his first major article.

V. University Lecturer at London (SOAS) 1948–55

Meanwhile, he had been appointed to a Lectureship in Phonetics, with effect from September 1948, at SOAS, in the Department of Phonetics and Linguistics, the Head of which was Professor J. R. Firth. It may be noted in passing that Sidney's knowledge of Sanskrit cannot have been irrelevant to his appointment, even though he was to have no responsibility for teaching it. One of those who interviewed him was John Brough, who had co-examined his Ph.D. thesis. And the Director of the School was (Sir) Ralph Turner. What may be called the 'Indian connection' was to be influential at several points in Sidney's career and, like the 'Icelandic connection', was important to him for the rest of his life.

Firth's department was the first university department in Britain to include the term 'linguistics' in its title. The fact that it also included the term 'phonetics' is significant. It reflected the view that linguistics, as an academic discipline, should be associated with, and indeed include, phonetics, since language, it could be said, is necessarily associated with, and indeed inseparable from, speech. This view, though debatable, is one that not only Firth, but most self-proclaimed linguists at the time would have taken for granted. It is a view that Sidney himself explicitly adopted throughout his career.

The importance of phonetics in historical and comparative linguistics had been clearly demonstrated by nineteenth-century comparative philologists, especially in the formulation and explication of the so-called sound-laws which were held to account for wholesale changes, in the course of time, in the pronunciation of languages and dialects and, coupled with changes in grammar and vocabulary, the differentiation of what subsequently came to be identified as separate languages. The importance of phonetics for the study of modern spoken languages taught at school and also, on another level, for investigating and describing previously unrecorded languages had also been increasingly recognised in several countries in the period preceding the Second World War.

In the local context, the fact that the title of Firth's department explicitly conjoined the terms 'phonetics' and 'linguistics' was especially significant. There was already in existence at University College London (UCL) a world-famous centre for the study and teaching of phonetics, headed by Daniel Jones, who had held the Chair of Phonetics (the first and for long the only chair of phonetics in Britain) since 1921. Firth himself had been at UCL in an earlier period of his career. But his views, on phonology perhaps rather than phonetics, had come to differ from those of Daniel Jones. When Firth set up the new department in 1944 he wanted SOAS students to be taught phonetics and phonology by lecturers based there and appointed for the purpose. In this respect, as in others, he was by all accounts a controversially autocratic head of department. It was characteristic of his *modus operandi* that he insisted that all newly appointed lecturers should serve their apprenticeship, as it were, by attending his weekly professorial lecture on general linguistics and also the phonetics classes, including the practical exercises, provided primarily for SOAS students. Although Sidney knew quite a lot about phonetics when he was appointed to his lectureship, he had had no practical training in the subject, and he would have been the first to admit that he was not qualified to teach it at the level required without such training. In the event, and this must have been evident when he was interviewed for the post, he had a very considerable aptitude for both the production and the identification of the subtlest of phonetic distinctions and could hold his own with his colleagues, most of whom were also good phoneticians.

One of Sidney's colleagues at SOAS was Robert H. ('Bobby') Robins, who had also just joined the department.[3] For seven years they shared an office and they became close friends. They were very different in personality, but they had many interests in common, non-academic as well as academic, and they used to spend part of the summer vacations together hill walking in Wales or Scotland. The fact that they had both spent time in the United States (Robins, unusually for a British-based linguist, had done fieldwork on an American-Indian language) meant that they were not as immediately dismissive of the dominant school of American-style structural linguistics as Firth and most of the other members of his department at that time were. For these and other reasons, whilst being then and subsequently always ready to acknowledge the support that Firth had given them and the influence that his ideas had on their own thinking, to outside observers at least they were, and especially perhaps Sidney, less typically 'Firthian' than their colleagues.

Both of them had interests in the history of linguistics, partly overlapping and partly complementary, which they were encouraged by Firth to pursue. This was at a time when the history of linguistics was not generally seen as being relevant to an understanding of contemporary linguistics. Not only was it not taught in university courses or included in textbooks of general linguistics, but also it was far from being a popular research area. It had of course been the area in which Sidney had done his Ph.D. research. One of his earliest articles, 'Ancient ideas on the origin and development of language' (*Transactions of the Philological Society*,

---

[3] Robins, three years younger than Sidney, read Classics at Oxford rather than Cambridge. So too did Frank Palmer (FBA 1975), who joined Firth's department in 1950. This meant that the second part of their undergraduate degree ('Greats') included, in addition to Ancient (Greco-Roman) History and Ancient (Greco-Roman) Philosophy, Modern (i.e. Post-Cartesian) Philosophy. This was taught in many cases by representatives of the then emergent school of Oxford-based 'ordinary-language philosophy' (which over the last thirty years or so, reinterpreted and reformulated, has been assimilated within one or more of the branches of linguistics). I will come back in a later section to Sidney's attitude to this philosophical movement (and more generally to his lack of interest in the philosophy of language). During the three years (1942–5) that Robins spent in the RAF between the first and second period of his undergraduate studies, after a short training course, he was commissioned and became an instructor in military Japanese at SOAS. After taking his degree in 1948, he returned to SOAS as a Lecturer in Linguistics. For supplementary information and bibliographical references see *Proceedings of the British Academy* 115 (2002), 357–64, and Brown and Law, *Linguistics in Britain*, pp. 228–38 and 249–61.

1948, 35–60), derived directly from his doctoral research and, being published in the major British journal of philology and linguistics, did much
to kindle (or re-kindle) an informed interest in the topic. His first book,
published three years later, on *Phonetics in Ancient India* (London, 1953),
also drew on part of his Ph.D. dissertation, but, expanded and revised in
the light of his by then increased knowledge of and practical competence
in articulatory phonetics. It made readily available to interested scholars
and students a reliable and comprehensible account of the highly sophisticated system of phonetics developed by Indian scholars, with particular
reference to Sanskrit, over two thousand years ago. Sidney, unlike Robins,
had no responsibility for teaching the history of linguistics at SOAS and
did not continue actively with research and publication in this field. But
he may certainly be given credit for the impetus that he and Robins gave
jointly at that time to the revival of interest in what subsequently became
a flourishing interdisciplinary area of research and scholarship in which
Robins, throughout his career, continued to play a major role both
nationally and internationally.

Something else from their SOAS days that united Sidney and Robins
was their involvement in the Philological Society. Regular attendance at
meetings (held seven times a year and based in London) and publication
in its journal, *Transactions of the Philological Society*, were strongly
encouraged by Firth. From the 1930s he himself had played an active part
in the Society and in particular had helped to make it the major British
forum for the discussion and promotion of what was by then coming to
be called structural linguistics, with a variety of characteristically distinct
schools. Several of Sidney's most influential articles of the 1950s were
published in *Transactions*. In due course both he and Robins were to serve
as Presidents of the Society. In later years Sidney and Robins were no
longer as close as they had been at SOAS. This was in part a consequence
of Sidney's move to Cambridge in 1955. Also, by then they had both married and therefore did not spend as much of their free time together as
they had done previously.

In 1951 Sidney's post at SOAS had been converted into a Lectureship
in Comparative Linguistics at his own request. Until that time Sir Ralph
Turner had taught this subject to the students in both his own department
and Firth's. He had done so presumably with particular reference to the
Indo-Aryan languages (and, as Jopson was still doing at Cambridge,
without emphasising the more recent developments in historical-
comparative linguistics). In view of the heavy administrative load he was
carrying as Director of the School and in other roles, combined with his

other teaching and research, he was no doubt only too pleased to be able to hand over this part of his teaching to someone who had his full confidence as a properly qualified comparativist (and also as an Indianist): someone whom by then he knew well personally and whose competence he had had every opportunity of assessing for himself.

Among the perquisites of a tenured post at SOAS at that time were the associated research facilities, including the right to fully funded study leave abroad. Sidney took full advantage of these and spent 1952 in India carrying out fieldwork on the dialects of Rajasthan. He was somewhat disappointed that, as he put it later, they provided 'very few really exciting descriptive features beyond what one might expect in a modern Indo-Aryan language'. But he proved to have a talent for extracting from his native-speaker informants reliable and descriptively relevant data. He was able to draw upon the results of his research in the article on prosodic analysis that he contributed to a special volume of the Philological Society, 'Aspiration in the Hārautī nominal', *Studies in Linguistic Analysis*, (Oxford, 1957, 68–86); also in the article he wrote in the same year for the Festschrift for Sir Ralph Turner published by SOAS ('Some phonological characteristics of Rājasthānī', *Bulletin of the School of Oriental and African Studies*, 20, 5–12). He had also made use of his Rajasthani material in the long and important theoretical article, 'Relationship in comparative linguistics', which he published in 1953 (*Transactions of the Philological Society*, 52–108). His year 'in the cities and deserts of "Indian-India" [were for the rest of his life] a source of indelible memories', supplied him with many enduring friendships and confirmed him in his love of the country and its Sanskrit cultural inheritance.

It had the more immediate effect of his receiving an invitation from the Rockefeller Foundation to visit America in the summer of 1957, and, as part of an attempt to encourage American scholars to move into the field of Indian studies, to travel to several of the major universities and meet some of the most influential representatives of American-style, pre-Chomskyan, structural linguistics. Sidney came to know many of these well and kept in touch with them when he returned to Britain. Though he maintained his own 'Firthian', or 'London School', principles, as far as phonology was concerned, he appreciated their emphasis on fieldwork and their descriptive expertise. He also found congenial the link between linguistics and what the Americans called cultural anthropology, which was institutionalised in many universities and was part of the legacy of, most notably, Franz Boas and Edward Sapir. There was a similar link in Britain, going back to the mid-nineteenth century and beyond, between linguistics and what the British called social anthropology, though it did not as yet manifest itself to the same degree either in teaching or in research and publication. What is especially relevant here is the characteristically 'Firthian' notion of 'context of situation', which J. R. Firth borrowed from the great Polish-born anthropologist Bronislaw Malinowski who was based at the LSE in London in the 1930s, and incorporated in his somewhat idiosyncratic theory of semantics. Sidney, unlike some of his SOAS colleagues, did not contribute directly to the development of 'Firthian' semantics (except possibly by his participation in departmental seminars). But certain aspects of it were absorbed into his own version of structuralism and are revealed by the terminology he employs, usually without explication or commentary, in several of his post-SOAS publications, including his Cambridge professorial inaugural lecture.

More challenging, from a linguistic point of view, than his dialect research in India was the 'fieldwork' he did in London with a native speaker of Abaza, Major Huseyin Kumuz, which 'tested one's eliciting and analytic techniques to the limit'. Abaza is one of a group of languages of the North-West Caucasus renowned for (*inter alia*) their phonological and phonetic complexity. Several Indo-Europeanists, including Sidney's mentor and patron Sir Harold Bailey, had expressed an interest in these languages because they were reported to have a very high number of consonantal phonemes, and very few vowels. And this had been hypothesised to have been a feature of Proto-Indo-European by proponents of one or other of the by then different variants of 'laryngeal theory'. The question was how phonetically realistic was the reconstruction of a phonological system of this kind and how plausible was its hypothesised subsequent development into a system with a smaller ratio of consonants to vowels. The answer that Sidney gave to both parts of this question was positive, and was made explicit in a later article 'On one-vowel systems' (*Lingua*, 13 (1965), 111–24). Abaza, as he analysed it, 'turned out to have 64 distinct consonant phonemes, many of them of great phonetic complexity (e.g. glottalised labialised uvular plosives), but only two vowels or by an alternative analysis one'. These results were not universally accepted: some linguists objected to them because of their a priori theoretical commitment to a particular set of typological constraints; others because they themselves lacked the kind of phonetic expertise that he had by virtue of his SOAS training. He was greatly encouraged, and relieved, when his analysis (published in a long article, 'Structure and system in Abaza', *Transactions of the Philological Society,*

1956, 127–76). 'was particularly well received in Moscow and Tbilisi' and 'turned out to agree even in some minute details' with that of the Soviet linguist, A. N. Genko in his *Abazinskij Jazyk: grammatičeskij očerk narečija Tapanta* (Moscow, 1955). Sidney's analysis was based on a hundred hours work with a single expatriate informant. Genko's had been carried out in the 1930s but was not published until 1955. (It was reviewed by Sidney in *Phonetica*, 5 (1960), 212–17). Some years later Sidney published a traditional Caucasian folk-tale, in Abaza, phonetically transcribed and furnished with a grammatical commentary and translation (*Bedi Kartlisa*, 19–20 (1965), 159–72).

Sidney's article on 'structure' and 'system' in Abaza, which uses both of these terms in what by then could be described as their 'Firthian' or 'London School' sense, can rightly be described as epoch-making. Not only was the phonological structure of Abaza, in the broader and more generally accepted sense of the term 'structure', meticulously described. So too was a major part of its grammatical structure, which in various respects is, though by no means unique among the languages of the world, typologically different from the languages with which most linguists, including the majority of Indo-Europeanists, are familiar. Sidney's account is a masterpiece of expository clarity and methodological coherence and consistency. It may be added that Sidney had also done research and published on the phonetics of Ossetic, an Indo-European language spoken in the Caucasus, and knew enough about Georgian, one of the major Caucasian languages unrelated to the sub-family to which Abaza belongs, for him to be able to refer to it in some of his typologically relevant articles in general and descriptive linguistics (notably in his influential article on 'Transitivity and possession', *Language*, 40 (1964), 337–43). Sidney did no further original research on Abaza or any of the other Caucasian languages, but he drew on his own analysis in his Cambridge teaching to illustrate relevant phonological and grammatical features from the standpoint of general linguistics, and in so doing was also able to demonstrate the reality of the phonetic distinctions. It gave him great pleasure that one of his Cambridge students, George Hewitt (FBA 1997), subsequently went to Tbilisi to study Georgian and other Caucasian languages and is currently Professor of Caucasian languages at SOAS.

VI. Professor of Comparative Philology at Cambridge, 1955–82 and Retirement

In late 1954, Sidney was encouraged by Sir Ralph Turner to put in a late application for the Cambridge Chair of Comparative Philology, which was to fall vacant in October 1955 (Professor Jopson having decided to take early retirement). Somewhat to his surprise, given his age at the time, he was elected. Sir Ralph himself was one of the electors, as also was John Brough, who together with Sir Ralph had supported Sidney's SOAS appointment. It may be assumed that Harold Bailey once again strongly recommended his erstwhile student.

It was not until the end of the Lent Term in 1957 when he delivered his Inaugural Lecture (on 8 March) that Sidney proclaimed more widely, *ex cathedra* and *urbi et orbi*, the way in which he interpreted his professorial remit (*On the Linguistic Study of Languages* (Cambridge, 1957)). But he had from the outset adopted a different approach from that of his predecessor. As had been the case for some time, the Professor of Comparative Philology was responsible (together with John Chadwick), not only for the teaching of comparative (Indo-European) philology as such, to the Group-E classicists, but also for the teaching of a certain amount of general linguistics both to them and also to students in three other Faculties (Modern and Medieval Languages, Archaeology and Anthropology, and Oriental Languages) who were taking the optional paper, 'Principles of Language' for Part 2 of the Tripos. Sidney started by giving the basic lectures himself and by including (as Jopson had not) what he judged to be the necessary minimum of phonetics. It was not until much later that it was possible for undergraduates to study linguistics in either the English or the Social and Political Sciences Faculties. It was only a minority of undergraduates that took this particular option, because they were generally not encouraged to do so by their directors of studies, just as classicists were generally not encouraged to opt for Group E: since its several components involved a lot of completely new work which did not follow on from Part 1, it was held to be a more demanding option than others, and there was, additionally, a good deal of anti-linguistics prejudice, even among classicists whose interest in language was primarily literary. Nevertheless, Sidney's lectures were reasonably well attended and had as 'auditors', to use the convenient American term, a few postgraduate students and occasionally members of staff. They were well prepared, well illustrated and well presented and, it is reported, ran perfectly to time. He had a gift for the production of memorable *obiter dicta*, which he used to good effect both in his lectures and in some of his writings. His style was different from Jopson's, but he was no less 'inspirational'.

Meanwhile, Sidney had set his sights on providing for the teaching of general linguistics and phonetics by securing for them two additional university posts. This took some time. He readily admitted later that one of the main reasons why he agreed to serve a term of office (as an elected professorial representative) on the university's General Board was because it gave him an insight into how things were done in Cambridge and perhaps also an opportunity of influencing policy decisions relating to his own ambitions regarding the establishment of linguistics in Cambridge. (One must not forget that he had seen Firth in operation at SOAS: a different kind of operator in a different kind of institution, but one from whom lessons could be learned.) The first of the two new posts was a Lectureship in Phonetics, based in the Faculty of Modern and Medieval Languages (MML), to which John Trim was appointed in 1958. This immediately relieved Sidney of part of his teaching responsibility: the need for such teaching, it is fair to say, had not been seen as existing until he had himself created it by persuading a sufficient number of supporters among his colleagues in MML that the subject must be taught and that he could not be expected to continue giving the lectures himself. He was similarly successful with the establishment of a Lectureship in General Linguistics, to which I was appointed, in 1961, as a member of the Classical Faculty.[4] My appointment had the effect of further lightening Sidney's lecturing load; and he was able to devote more of his time to research and publication. There was still no department of linguistics. But one was eventually created, in 1965, with strong support from an interfaculty committee (a particularly influential and highly supportive member of which was the anthropologist Edmund Leach), and was established in the MML Faculty. John Trim was appointed as Head: he had been appointed to the Lectureship in General Linguistics when I moved to Edinburgh in 1964 and the Lectureship in Phonetics was kept in being. It had been generally assumed that Sidney himself would take on the headship of the new Department. But he decided not to. One of the reasons, no doubt, was that he was reluctant to assume administrative responsibility for either the language laboratory or the Linguistic Computer

[4] For the preceding four years I had held the Lectureship in Comparative Linguistics at SOAS that Sidney had held, but I, unlike John Trim, was, in Cambridge terms, a classicist: as an undergraduate I had done Part 2 Group E, under Jopson and my Ph.D. thesis had just been examined by examiners appointed by the Faculty of Classics.

Centre which had been established in MML (with two tenured posts). He was not interested in running either of what were, at least in origin, two service departments. As to the Chair in General Linguistics, for which Sidney had also been lobbying for some time, once again with support from the special interfaculty committee, as he himself put it later, 'this was long in coming'. He added: 'I suppose I was my worst enemy in this connection, since I had been teaching the subject ever since my return to Cambridge, and it was difficult to persuade the General Board of the difference between traditional comparative philology and modern linguistics (including phonetics)' ('Personal history', 21 ff.). He might also have mentioned that, under the Cambridge collegiate system, much of the teaching of linguistics, and to some extent philology, to Part-2 undergraduates was carried out by supervisors appointed by the colleges who might or might not be university 'teaching officers' (UTOs) and did not necessarily have a college fellowship. John Trim supervised for a large number of colleges for 'The principles of language' option. From 1962 he was elected as a Fellow of Selwyn, not because he was a linguist and phonetician, but because he could also supervise and act as a director of studies in German. Someone else who should be mentioned in this connection is Joseph Cremona, University Lecturer in Romance Philology and Fellow of Trinity Hall. These two between them, and there were others, did at least as much of the teaching of linguistics as did Sidney himself (who, as a professor, was in any case not allowed to do any college teaching).

I have gone into all this explanatory detail because it is relevant to my assessment of Sidney's role in the establishment of linguistics in Cambridge. In the Cambridge context, it is hardly surprising that, independently of a certain amount of deeply entrenched hostility to linguistics, the General Board was not all that enthusiastic about taking on the cost of establishing a new chair. In the event, the Chair of General Linguistics was established in 1980, fairly late in Sidney's tenure of the Chair of Comparative Philology, and its first incumbent was Peter Matthews, who also became the Head of Department.[5] Sidney no longer had even formal professorial responsibility for the teaching of general linguistics in the university, not to mention any associated administrative responsibility. There is little doubt that this suited him. Later, he was

---

[5] John Trim had meanwhile moved from Cambridge to become Director of the Centre for Information on Language Teaching in London, which enabled him to pursue more effectively than he could in Cambridge, and on a wider front, one of his major interests, applied linguistics.

content to note that since the creation of the Chair of General Linguistics, and the appointment to it of one of his own students, 'the subject and the department have flourished' ('Personal history', 22). He was probably right in claiming much of the credit for the eventual achievement of what he had been aiming for when he came back to Cambridge in 1955.

From what has been said above, it will be clear that there were differences of kind and degree in which one might have been taught linguistics or (comparative) philology by Sidney, and this makes it difficult to assess his influence as a 'teacher' of these subjects. Those of us, a relatively small number, who were privileged to have been his students in the fullest sense of this term and to have been befriended by him (I choose the verb with care) can testify to the quality and effectiveness of his teaching and subsequently of his friendship and patronage. Towards the end of his career, he claimed as his 'students' or 'pupils', without distinguishing between these terms or drawing attention to the differences of kind or degree that I have just noted, several who had by then become prominent in the field, nationally and internationally.[6] Among them, he was especially pleased to be able to list, in addition to Peter Matthews and George Hewitt, and the current holder of the Chair in Comparative Philology in Cambridge, Geoffrey Horrocks (whom Sidney identifies as having also been a 'pupil' of both himself and Robert Coleman, who was to succeed him).

Sidney took early retirement in 1982, having been in post for twenty-seven years. The Chair of Comparative Philology was 'put on ice' (Sidney's own expression) until 1985, when he reached the normal retirement age, but, in contrast with other chairs in related 'minority subjects' at Cambridge and elsewhere, it was not suppressed. Robert Coleman, who was appointed to it, had been one of Jopson's students in the early 1950s. Regrettably, he died in 2001 after a very distinguished career as one

---

[6] About one-third of the current members of Section H4 of the British Academy were, in one sense or another, students in Cambridge during Sidney's time. Of the twenty-three contributors to Brown and Law, *Linguistics in Britain*, those who were at one time either students of linguistics or colleagues of Sidney's (or both) in Cambridge include the following: listed in alphabetical order and by family name only, they are Aitchison, Cremona, Gazdar, Hudson, Lyons, Matthews, Smith, Trim, Trudgill. Their 'personal histories' are all relevant to what I have said in this section and are occasionally different in the emphasis they give to certain developments. Also relevant are those of Michael Halliday (who was not at Cambridge but acknowedges Sidney's influence) and of Gillian Brown (for her account of 'English at Cambridge' in the late 1950s and, though this is outside the period in question, for her own role as Director of the Research Centre for English and Applied Linguistics from 1988).

of this country's leading philologists. But once again the Chair was kept in being.

During his time as Professor of Comparative Philology, Sidney published three important books and a number of articles and reviews in the fields of both comparative philology and general linguistics, 'with occasional excursions' into such more 'marginal' fields as 'Aegean cartography and Icelandic bibles'. His publications will be discussed in a separate section. Here I have been concerned with the part he played in the institutional establishment of linguistics in Cambridge and his teaching of both philology and linguistics. During the period in question Cambridge became one of the principal centres in Britain for the study of linguistics in all its branches. As I have made clear, there were many others involved in this process, and many other institutions, some of which I have not mentioned, in addition to the Department of Linguistics. But Sidney's role especially in the earlier years was crucial. I consider this to be undeniable, and it is a point that I will pick up in the final section on his academic 'legacy'. In retirement, he did no teaching, but he kept some of his research interests going and maintained contact with colleagues in Britain and abroad working in the same fields, including some of his Cambridge students.

VII. Personality and personal life

At this point I will say something about Sidney's personality and character and about his personal life from the time that he moved from SOAS to Cambridge in 1955. He was a very private person and did not readily share with others his more intimate thoughts and feelings. He had a somewhat boyish sense of humour, which he retained throughout life, though he had of course long ago abandoned the practical jokes for which he had been notorious as an undergraduate. There could be a sharp edge to his humour, mischievous rather than malicious, and he was not averse from poking fun, in the appropriate company, at the foibles and pretensions of certain well-known Cambridge figures with whom he came into contact. His close friends were few, but those who counted as such valued his friendship and he theirs.

Even as an undergraduate, and possibly at school, he was well aware of his own intellectual gifts; and he knew that he had it in him to have a successful academic career, provided of course that he could gain entry to it in the first place. He did not suffer fools gladly and he could be quite sharp in his rejection of what he judged to be uninformed or uncompre-hending criticism of his academic work. But he was equally ready to recognise what he identified as the high-quality work of others. His reviews were constructively critical and very often helped to establish or bring to the attention of other linguists books whose relevance or impor-tance might otherwise have escaped them. He was also quick to recognise promise in students that he met, even when he himself had not been closely concerned with the supervision of their work.

As I mentioned in the first section of this memoir, in later life if not as an undergraduate or in the earlier part of his career, he made a point of emphasising his working-class provenance. Few, if any, of those who met him could have detected evidence of this in his speech or manner, and sev-eral of those who knew him have been surprised to learn of it. It is clear from what he has written that he was conscious of what he owed to his parents for his upbringing and early education and that he was proud for their sake, and his own, of having successfully established himself in his chosen career and perhaps also socially. His father died in 1948 before he could appreciate the extent of his son's success. His mother died in 1982, aged 89. His brother David, younger by nine years, who had been edu-cated at Christ's College, Finchley, and after national service in the Navy become a local government officer with the Greater London Council, is now retired: his wife, was a school-teacher, and they have four sons. Sidney has no other close family.

Sidney delighted in unexpected coincidences which linked his personal life with his professional expertise and interests. Several of these he explicitly referred to in the material to which I have had access and at times in conversation with friends. Two such may be mentioned. One concerns his first wife Aenea; the other, his second wife Diana; and both may be seen as continuing and perpetuating the 'Icelandic connection'. One of the most striking features of the pronunciation of English in the north-west Highlands of Scotland, where Aenea was born, is the devoic-ing and pre-aspiration of stop consonants (a feature which is readily perceived and imitated by non-phoneticians who might not be able to describe it in these terms) and this too, as it happens, is a well recognised typological feature of Icelandic. One of the things, together with some aspects of the landscape, that made Aenea feel at home when Sidney first took her to Iceland in 1986 was the Icelanders' pronunciation of English. As to the coincidence that concerns his second wife Diana, this is that (as Sidney, ever the amateur vulcanologist, realised immediately) the island of St Helena, where Diana was born, is at almost the extreme other end of the volcanic mid-Atlantic ridge from Iceland, several thousand miles away.

It was at SOAS that Sidney met his first wife, Aenea McCallum. She had recently become the editorial secretary of the School's own journal, the *Bulletin* (*BSOAS*), in which he published three of his early articles. She used to say that when it came to questions of typography and layout he was one of the most demanding, but also one of the most knowledge-able, of her authors. She was 'a daughter of the manse' (as she herself used to put it), her father being a minister of the Church of Scotland in Rosskeen on the Cromarty Firth. Both her parents came from the West and spoke Gaelic as their first language. But she herself was brought up speaking English. She studied English and Modern Languages at the University of Aberdeen and during the Second World War served with a counter-espionage unit. At the end of the war she served with the Control Commission in Vienna. Before coming to SOAS, she had worked on the subtitling of foreign films and in publishing.

Sidney and Aenea got married in 1955, when he was about to take up the Chair of Comparative Philology. They were to be married for forty years. From the outset, they had many interests in common, including hill-walking and alpine skiing. Another, from the 1960s, was travel in Greece. During the summer vacations, they used to spend as much time as possible exploring the smaller Aegean islands, preferably the remoter and less accessible ones, and Aenea, according to Sidney, eventually acquired a greater fluency in Modern Greek than he himself.

For the first few years of their marriage, they lived first of all in one of a block of University-owned flats and then for a few years in a flat that they had purchased. Later on, they bought a house about two miles from the centre of Cambridge, just off the Huntingdon Road, which being on a corner site gave them a sufficiently large garden for them to be able to indulge another of their joint interests and, in the summer, to hold their annual garden-party. On this occasion, to which they invited mainly Cambridge-based friends, not all of them academics, they operated well together and were the perfect hosts, attentive and amusing and success-fully bringing together those of their guests who did not previously know one another.

In 1995, while Sidney and Aenea were on holiday in a remote part of Crete 'it became increasingly evident', as Sidney himself was to put it a few years later, that '[he] needed a new hip'. This was duly fitted in Cambridge and he came out of hospital to be cared for by Aenea. For many years, she had been a familiar figure cycling along the Huntingdon

Road between their house and the centre of town and, to judge from the way she coped with Castle Hill, appeared to be in perfect health. In January 1996 she suddenly collapsed and died a few hours later.

Sidney married for the second time in 2002. He first met Diana Stroud in 1996, three months after Aenea's death. She was one of the part-time carers who looked after him whilst, still on crutches, he gradually recovered his mobility after his hip-replacement operation. Shortly after their meeting he had sold the house (and arranged for the cat, a Russian Blue, to which he was devoted, to be adopted) and moved into a splendid set of rooms in Trinity (G2 Nevile's Court), conveniently situated for the Hall and Fellows' Parlour. Over the next few years, Diana came regularly to visit him as his carer and, with the passage of time, as an increasingly close friend. They both had a love of the countryside and, after a while, Sidney had recovered sufficiently for them to drive out of town and go for long walks in Suffolk and even as far away as Wales. They also spent a lot of time reading poetry and listening to music. When they got married, Sidney's health was failing and he moved out of College. He was taken into hospital, where he recovered sufficiently for Diana to look after him at home, with some assistance from professional carers, until he had to be taken back into hospital, where he died on 22 April 2004. Sidney's friends in Trinity, several of whom became friends of Diana, knew how much he owed to her: they had expressed their pleasure when she and Sidney had decided to get married two years earlier and sent her moving letters of condolence after the very simple, secular, funeral service at the Crematorium, which Sidney himself, together with Diana had had arranged calmly and dispassionately in advance.

Much of Sidney's personal life was based in College. He was intensely loyal to Trinity and grateful for what it had given him as an undergraduate and postgraduate student. As a professorial fellow he was not permitted to engage in college-based undergraduate teaching. Nor could he be a tutor or hold any other college office. It was primarily on the social, rather than the administrative or educational, level that his loyalty and involvement were manifest. He was a staunch supporter of the Boat Club. He lunched regularly in College and was a familiar and popular figure in the Fellows' Parlour after lunch. He did a certain amount of his entertaining in College. He particularly enjoyed taking to College feasts, as his personal guests, visiting scholars, as well as Cambridge-based friends and colleagues and some of the friends with whom he had kept in touch from earlier days. He was in his element at College Reunions presiding at one of the tables in Hall. He knew a lot about the history of Trinity and enjoyed showing visitors the Wren Library and other gems of Trinity's material patrimony. He was proud, too, to be a senior member of the college that could lay claim to both Bentley and Porson, the two great eighteenth-century classicists. Incidentally, he was also proud to have been, as an undergraduate, the holder of the university's Porson Prize for Greek-verse composition, and in later life it pleased him that some of his original work on Greek metre and accent had the subsidiary effect (this was not its primary intention) of explaining away some of the many exceptions to 'Porson's Law' in Greek poets of the classical period. This could be seen as another of the coincidences, in which he delighted.

VIII. Publications, theory and methodology

It is convenient to deal with Sidney's publications and with his views on linguistic theory and methodology in the same section. The former provide us with the best evidence that we have for our knowledge of the latter; and some understanding of his theoretical and methodological principles is a prerequisite for our interpretation and evaluation of his published works

By the standards of many of his contemporaries, Sidney was not a prolific writer: his written *oeuvre* comprises six books, some forty articles and rather fewer reviews. But the range of more or less distinct areas of research and scholarship in which he worked is certainly greater than that of many of those who have published more than he did. These areas include general and descriptive linguistics, historical/comparative linguistics (and philology), phonetics, metrics, Classical Latin and Ancient Greek, Indian and Caucasian languages and Aegean cartography. I have referred to these as 'more or less distinct' areas because the boundaries between them are not always clearcut and also because, in so far as they are distinct, several of Sidney's works may be assigned to more than one 'area'. It should also be mentioned that the titles of many of his articles ('Notes on . . .', 'Some aspects of . . .', 'Some phonological characteristics of . . .', 'Some observations on . . .', 'Some problems . . .', etc.), which might imply a narrowness of focus and coverage, frequently deal with topics of more general theoretical or typological interest than is immediately apparent. The most important and influential of his publications, some of which have been mentioned in earlier sections, are included in a select bibliography below.

Sidney did not leave behind him an identifiable 'school' of linguistics or group of 'followers' and would probably have been horrified at the thought that he might have done. There is no single 'big idea' in general linguistics that one can associate with him as its inventor or creator, as one can, with due qualification, associate the notion of structuralism with Saussure or, in a later period, generativism with Chomsky. Nor is there in comparative philology (to use the traditional term) any major revolutionary hypothesis, such as the so-called laryngeal theory, that can be seen as his invention or creation.

His approach to linguistics was essentially non-philosophical.[7] He was not really interested in either the philosophy of linguistics, as part of the philosophy of science, or the philosophy of language. He was a theoretically minded descriptivist rather than a theoretician. By this I mean that he was not interested in theory-construction as such, still less in what, in the later part of his career, had come to be called theoretical linguistics: the elaboration of highly formalised models of the structure of languages with at times, he would have said, little empirical control. His role in the promotion of particular theoretical concepts, in so far as he did espouse and promote these, was by demonstrating their utility in the practical business of describing or analysing languages.

The nearest he came to giving an outline of his views on linguistic theory, and it was no more than an outline, was in the professorial Inaugural Lecture that he delivered in Cambridge in March 1957. Inaugural lectures are of course occasional pieces, composed at a particular time in a particular local context, for oral delivery (in the first instance), and with a particular audience in mind. It is not uncommon for the new professor to

---

[7] In his Inaugural Lecture he was rather (amusingly) disparaging about the Oxford-based movement known as 'linguistic analysis' or the 'ordinary-language' movement (referred to in Section V). In that specific context and at that time, this was perhaps understandable, and what he said will have shocked very few of those who heard it. It was doubtful whether any of the Cambridge philosophers who were present (or read the published version of the Lecture later) would have been able to make the connection between the work in the volume to which he referred specifically and what J. R. Firth and his followers (including Sidney himself) classified under the concept of 'the context of situation'. It is possible that Sidney's ex-colleagues, Frank Palmer and 'Bobby' Robins, who had done philosophy as undergraduates at Oxford saw the connection: they were certainly more ready than Sidney was to see the relevance of contemporary philosophy to linguistics (see above, n. 3). Without going further into this question, it may be mentioned that some of the most theoretically productive research that has been carried out since the 1970s in what is now a recognised sub-branch of linguistics, under the rubric of 'pragmatics', has been inspired by the work of the 'ordinary-language' philosophers, John Austin, Paul Grice and Peter Strawson. (Strawson, incidentally, was a member of the Linguistics Section of the Academy from its establishment, and regularly attended its meetings: see below, n. 18).

use the occasion in order to reveal his own personal agenda. This is what Sidney did. What he had to say surprised and shocked many, perhaps most, of those who heard it.

The title itself, 'On the linguistic study of languages', was initially puzzling. It soon became clear, however, that the epithet 'linguistic' was to be interpreted, as meaning 'from the point of view of [a particular approach to] linguistics', and also that the use of the plural, 'languages', rather than the singular, 'language', was significant. The term 'linguistics' itself was defined, implicitly, in the very first sentence, as '[twentieth-century] linguistic science' and contrasted with a variety of non-linguistic approaches to the study of language: on the one hand, philological and, on the other, literary, psychological, logico-philosophical, etc. The new Professor of Comparative Philology turned out to have little to say, on this occasion at least, about the subject for which he was by title responsible (which he referred to as a characteristically nineteenth-century discipline). The whole lecture was a missionary *apologia* for a particular version of Saussurean autonomous linguistics.

The Lecture was published, with notes and references, shortly after it was delivered. It was re-published some years later in two volumes of 'readings', which were widely used for postgraduate courses in some of the principal centres for the study of linguistics (especially, and somewhat surprisingly, of applied linguistics) in Britain and the United States. It therefore had a much wider influence than it might otherwise have done. For that reason, it may be regarded as one of his major publications. There is no evidence in his later publications to suggest that he changed his mind significantly on any of the points of theory or methodology that he revealed in the Lecture.

Like many of the best descriptivists, Sidney had a mathematical turn of mind. By this I mean that his analysis of the structure of particular languages (i.e. of what are referred to pre-theoretically as natural languages and theoretically in Saussurean terms as *langues* or language-systems) was determined by a perhaps intuitive sense of what mathematicians and mathematically minded scientists call elegance: an aesthetic quality that convinces those who have this sense that a conjecture or hypothesis is, if not correct, better than any current alternative, in advance of or independently of its proof or empirical confirmation. Saussure's speculative analysis of the (Proto-)Indo-European vowel system had this quality of elegance, as did Emile Benveniste's *Origines de la formation des noms en indo-européen* (Paris, 1935), to which Sidney was introduced by Sir Harold Bailey as an undergraduate. Of course, linguistics, like the 'hard' sciences, has, or aspires to have, its empirical underpinnings; and it was not until the Polish scholar, Jerzy Kuryłowicz showed, in 1927, that Hittite had some previously unknown consonants where Saussure's *Mémoire* had 'predicted' them to be that the so-called laryngeal theory came to be more widely accepted by Indo-Europeanists.[8] When Sidney himself formulated, in his Inaugural Lecture, the criteria which in descriptive linguistics control the evaluation of a particular (partial) description of a particular language, he listed exhaustiveness, self-consistency and simplicity, noting that these criteria are sometimes in conflict. But the point that I wish to emphasise here is that the aesthetic criterion of elegance, which can perhaps be seen as subsuming self-consistency and simplicity, is probably the one that the best descriptivists implicitly apply. Several of Sidney's descriptive articles, most notably perhaps his article on Abaza (1956), have the quality of elegance (see Section V).

As I have mentioned, Sidney had a gift for the production of memorable *obiter dicta*, which he used to good effect in teaching and lectures, and in some of his writings. One of these, which comes from his Inaugural Lecture, achieved a certain notoriety. It runs as follows: 'There are no facts in linguistics until the linguist has made them; they are ultimately, like all scientific facts, the products of imagination and invention.' As he noted many years later the 'polemical tone of the Lecture [as a whole] was not to everyone's liking' and '[this] one sentence in particular seemed scandalous in some quarters' ('Personal history', 24). Properly understood, however, it should not have appeared to be even controversial. The general context in which the sentence occurred is one in which he had rejected the outmoded positivist ('natural-history') view of science as a theory-neutral observational activity. He may not have been interested in the philosophy of science as such, but he was well aware that by then it was generally accepted that even in the physical sciences, not to mention the social sciences, there is no such thing as theory-neutral observation: that so-called data are selected from, not 'given' in, the phenomena and that their selection by the practising scientist is always determined, to a greater or less degree, by some controlling theory or hypothesis. For him, as I mentioned above, the controlling theory in the case of linguistics, was that of (a particular version of) Saussurean struc-

[8] J. Kuryłowicz, 'ə indoeuropéen et ḫ hittite', *Symbolae grammaticae in honorem Joannis Rozwadowski* (Cracow, 1927), 95–104. Sidney met Kuryłowicz after the war and they became personal friends, he came to stay with the Allens in Cambridge on several occasions, and they kept in touch until Kuryłowicz died in 1977.

turalism. Quoting Firth, he glossed this as 'a *general linguistic theory*' applicable to '*particular linguistic descriptions*, not a *theory of universals* for *general linguistic description*'. This immediately put him on the side of those linguists who reject the notion of 'universal grammar', as this term has been interpreted over the centuries or in any of its modern interpretations, including its Chomskyan post-1960s interpretation.

For Sidney, mid-twentieth-century linguistics was by definition structuralist. As he said elsewhere, in another of his highly quotable apothegms. 'It is as anachronistic to refer to structural linguistics these days as it would be to refer to the talking pictures.' This was by then an eminently defensible view. But there were very many different kinds of structuralism, not only in linguistics, but also in other disciplines, including anthropology. The differences between one version of structuralism and another are quite complex, as also are their historical interconnections. We need not be concerned with these here.[9] For present purposes, it suffices to emphasise just two points. The first is that Sidney (like Saussure in the interpretation of the *Cours* that he adopts) classifies linguistics as one of the social sciences. The second is that, in his view, linguistics can take as its data phenomena which are readily identifiable pre-theoretically as such—spoken utterances (Saussure's *parole*)—and are distinguishable from other phenomena (behavioural and situational) which other social sciences take as their data. It is arguable that in his formulation of this second point he fails to distinguish between the ('behavioural') activity of speaking and the (acoustically recordable, transcribable and analysable) products of that activity. But this does not invalidate the substantial point that he is making. It is the fact that spoken utterances are, within acceptable limits and in normal circumstances, pre-theoretically identifiable as such that justifies the acceptance of the 'autonomy' of linguistics.[10]

---

[9] For a convenient and reliable account of structuralism in linguistics during this period, reference may be made to Peter Matthews, *A Short History of Structural Linguistics* (Cambridge, 2001). This sets the whole movement in its historical context and will clarify what is said in this section about Sidney Allen's adherence to Saussurean (autonomous) linguistics.

[10] To the best of my knowedge, Sidney himself nowhere makes explicit the (more or less Popperian) view of 'the scientific method' that I have attributed to him here, but the passage in his Inaugural Lecture from which I have quoted the 'particularly scandalous' sentence is certainly consistent with the interpretation I have given it. Nor does he seek to justify his affirmation of the pre-theoretical identifiability of what have often been referred to as the primary data of (descriptive) linguistics. In his 2002 'Personal history' (p. 24) he does not dissent from what I say with reference to the 'scandalous' sentence about the ontological status of so-called natural languages and where I claim to 'share [his] view'. Nor does he there, or elsewhere, dissociate

Another of his pronouncements, also taken from the Inaugural Lecture, runs as follows: 'Whatever the informant volunteers about his language (as opposed to in it) must be assumed to be wrong—he is after all not a linguist (or if he is he will be a quite useless informant!).' The methodological principle that this maxim encapsulates was taken for granted by most descriptive linguists in the 1950s. Once again, it is a principle that can be pushed to excess. But it had proved its worth in the description not only of 'exotic' languages, for which 'fieldwork' and 'native informants' were required, but also of familiar well-studied languages, for which grammarians and lexicographers were tempted to use themselves as 'informants'. From the mid-1960s it was explicitly rejected by Chomsky and his followers and lively debate ensued as to the reliability and accessibility of the so-called 'intuitions' of native speakers. Sidney did not engage in this debate, but there is no doubt that he would have rejected, in principle as he did in practice, this kind of 'intuitionism' and the self-validating judgements of 'grammaticality' to which it tended to give rise.

The two books for which Sidney was undoubtedly best known are *Vox Latina: a guide to the pronunciation of classical Latin* (Cambridge, 1965) and *Vox Graeca: a guide to the pronunciation of classical Greek* (Cambridge, 1968), which, incidentally, he was encouraged to write by Michael Black of Cambridge University Press. These were the fruits of his lifelong interest in Ancient Greek and Classical Latin as spoken languages. The obituary published in *The Times* (3 June 2004) commented in this connection: 'It is no exaggeration to say that the pronunciation [of Greek and Latin] that learners are now taught in English-speaking lands has been reformed by Allen's influence.' The two books were unusual in that they combined clarity of exposition with evident authority and meticulous scholarship and were written in a style which made them accessible, not only to those involved in teaching the classical languages at university level, but also to schoolteachers and some of their more highly motivated sixth-form pupils. Sidney took pride in the fact that '[in] subsequent editions both seem to have established themselves as the standard reading on these matters in schools and universities' ('Personal history', 24).

---

himself from my defence of '(so-called) autonomous linguistics' in *Natural Language and Universal Grammar* (Cambridge, 1991). On the other hand, as I have said in the text, Sidney was not really interested in either the philosophy of language, and mind, or the philosophy of linguistics as a branch of the philosophy of science. But very few linguists of his generation were.

Over the years, Sidney had published several articles on the metrical ('prosodic' in the more traditional sense) structure of Greek and Latin in particular. This 'had . . . always had a prominent part in [his] thinking'. When it was suggested to him that he might 'bring together reprints of his "prosodic" writings in both senses of the term into a single volume', he preferred (for reasons explained in detail in the preface) to write a completely new and substantial book, *Accent and Rhythm* (Cambridge, 1973). This work is universally acknowledged for his authoritative treatment of all the interconnected topics that he brings within its purview and might well be rated by fellow-specialists in the relevant disciplines as the most significant part of his scholarly *Nachlass*. *Vox Latina* and *Vox Graeca* were themselves furnished with comprehensive bibliographies, notes and appendices for the benefit of fellow-specialists and those who wished to go further into the topics dealt with. Sidney kept abreast of all the relevant research and made critical reference to this in successive editions. *Vox Graeca* is notable for its inclusion, in Appendix A, of a section in which he gives his own view on the vexed question of the accentuation of words in Ancient (mainly Classical, but also Homeric) Greek: whether it was primarily a matter of tone ('melodic') or of stress; what degree of dialectal variation there was; what changes took place diachronically, etc. This was based on previously published articles, especially the Presidential Address that he gave to the Philological Society in 1966, ('Prosody and prosodies in Greek', *Transactions of the Philological Society*, 107–48), but adjusted to its new context. He developed further the hypothesis he had earlier proposed, reviewed the evidence and provided enough information for interested non-specialists to be able to follow the argument. He himself was to say later that his hypothesis 'provides, if correct, an immediate and simple solution to a number of apparently unconnected restrictions on word-boundaries ("bridges") in a variety of spoken Greek metres' ('Personal history', 25). As to its correctness, not surprisingly, the experts disagree (*Grammatici certant* . . . !). But none of them would challenge its revolutionary nature or the quality of the argument that supports it. Its (incidental) explanation of 'Porson's Law', which was especially gratifying to Sidney, has been mentioned in the preceding Section.

Of Sidney's several articles in the field of comparative philology (to use the traditional term), it is perhaps fair to say that they were, not only not revolutionary, but on the whole rather conservative. In particular, there is very little evidence in them of a characteristically structuralist point of view: this is consistent with his acceptance of the Saussurean view (noted above) that diachronic and synchronic linguistics are two distinct disciplines. The most original feature of his work as a comparativist, as he saw it himself, appears to have been his use of evidence from later stages of related dialects, mainly in the Indian branch of the Indo-European languages, to 'reconstruct' the attested 'parent-language(s)'— rather as one can use the evidence of the Romance languages to 'reconstruct' (non-Classical) Latin—and thus test the validity of 'the comparative method'. This is something which he did in his 1953 paper on 'Relationship in comparative linguistics', and later in his contribution to the Philological Society's special 'Neogrammarian Volume' (1978).[11]

With one exception, nothing further need be said here in detail, in addition to what has been said in general above, about Sidney's publications in the other 'more or less distinct' fields in which he worked. The exception has to do with one of his research projects which engaged several of his interests and specialised knowledge and skills, in his retirement, and was close to his heart. These interests and skills included cartography, vulcanology and the ability to read the relevant ancient, medieval and Renaissance documents in several languages. This project yielded unexpected results and, in due course issued in publication. During one of his visits to Greece, he had been trying to identify various of the smaller islands in the Eastern Aegean referred to on old maps and itineraries with their modern names. One of these, referred to as Kalóyeros, 'allegedly the seat of a small monastic retreat, persisted in eluding identification'. Eventually, he was able to link it with 'a group of volcanic rocks between Andros and Chios, bearing no resemblance to the descriptions or drawings in the early accounts'. What he judged to be 'the probable solution was provided in a report by a 17th-century English traveller of a disastrous eruption there about the middle of the century'. Sidney's 'probable solution' was published in 1977 in *Imago Mundi*, a specialist journal of cartography, a fuller version in Greek having been published the previous year in the *Annual of the Society for Cycladic*

---

[11] 'The PIE velar series: neogrammarian and other solutions in the light of attested parallels', *Transactions of the Philological Society*, 1978, 87–110. There was a sense in which his attitude to (synchronic) descriptive phonology also became more 'conservative' (less 'Firthian') in later stages of his career, when he reformulated some of his earlier analyses in phonemic, rather than 'prosodic' terms. Ironically, perhaps, this was at a time when so-called 'metrical' phonology was giving theoretical recognition to phenomena that had been handled by 'Firthians' in terms of 'prosodies' and some of its proponents were referring to Sidney's earlier work and that of his SOAS colleagues.

Studies. In both cases Kalóyeros was described in the title (interrogatively) as 'an Atlantis in microcosm'.[12]

It suffices, in concluding this Section of the Memoir, to emphasise the points that were made immediately above and in earlier sections relating to the quality of his scholarship in all the (intersecting) fields in which he worked and the enduring value of the contribution he made, not only to the phonetics and phonology of prosody and metre, but also, in 'Transitivity and possession', to the typological study of such grammatical categories as 'possession' (to use the arguably unsatisfactory traditional term), tense and aspect.

IX. His academic and scholarly 'legacy'

It now remains to bring together a few of the points that have been touched on in the preceding sections of this memoir and in so doing to make a brief assessment of Sidney Allen's contribution nationally and internationally to the advance of scholarship, in teaching, research and publication and otherwise, in the various positions that he occupied during his active career (and up to a point in retirement). I will pay particular attention to the role that he played in the establishment of linguistics as a more or less independent and autonomous academic discipline and to what may be referred to as its institutionalisation as such in Britain. Any such assessment is necessarily partial and personal, despite the assistance that the author may have had from friends and colleagues, and will be influenced by a variety of factors, including his own views on the current state of linguistics and also no doubt *pietas*.

Sidney did not, as has been said already, leave a 'school' behind him. Also, the fact that there were differences of kind and degree in which one might have been one of his 'students' makes it difficult to assess the effect that his teaching of linguistics and philology has had on the development of these subjects. This is something that I have emphasised in Section VI. But he was certainly an effective and charismatic teacher, and a significant number of those who attended his lectures or came into contact with him when they were students in Cambridge have made major contributions to

---

[12] 'Kalóyeros; an Atlantis in microcosm?' *Imago Mundi*, 29 (1978), 54–71. See also 'An addendum to Kalóyeros', *Imago Mundi*, 31 (1979), 94–6. He was made an Honorary Fellow of the Society for Cycladic Studies (Athens) in 1977.

the development of linguistics in the last thirty years or so. Some part of the credit for this can be attributed to the influence, directly or indirectly, of his teaching. But, as I have explained in Section VI, the principal contribution that he made to the promotion of linguistics in Cambridge was not as a teacher, but as someone who skilfully used his professorial authority and (in the early part of his tenure of his chair) his membership of the relevant university committees to get the Department of Linguistics established there and eventually a Chair of General Linguistics, separate from his own Chair of Comparative Philology. It should also be mentioned here that in the 1960s, when new departments of linguistics were being created in several British universities, his advice was regularly sought, and on several occasions he served on the appointing committee or acted as an assessor for lectureships and chairs.

The importance and enduring influence of his books and several of his articles has been noted in Section VII. Nothing further need be said here. But no assessment of Sidney's influence on the development of linguistics nationally and internationally could fail to mention his association with the monograph series 'Cambridge Studies in Linguistics', which was very much his 'brainchild'. It was founded by him and Michael Black of Cambridge University Press in 1969, and he served as chairman of the editorial board until 1982. In this role he was energetic and pro-active and assembled an international team of highly competent and committed co-editors representative of most branches of the subject. The series rapidly established itself as one of the major and most prestigious outlets for the publication of duly refereed, revised and edited Ph.D. dissertations and of other book-length works reporting the results of up-to-date research. By the time that Sidney retired from the editorial board, thirty-seven volumes had appeared (his own *Accent and Rhythm* being volume 12) and two further, equally successful, series (with the same editorial board) had been established: 'Cambridge Textbooks in Linguistics' and 'Cambridge Language Surveys'. The three series have played a major part in the development of linguistics, in Britain and abroad, and continue to do so. In many cases, apart from making accessible to students and teachers of linguistics reliable, up-to-date textbooks and works of reference, they have helped to establish their authors in their careers as university teachers and leaders of research groups in Britain and abroad. From 1963 until 1985, Sidney also served, with Anton Reichling and E. M. Uhlenbeck, as a co-editor of the international journal *Lingua* (based in Holland), which especially in the earlier period published a number of important articles written from a theoretical viewpoint which made them less readily publishable in some of the other major journals associated with national organisations or particular 'schools' and also published from time to time specially commissioned, *hors série*, volumes on particular topics.

Special attention must clearly be paid in the present context to the role that the British Academy has played in the establishment of linguistics as a recognised academic subject and to Sidney's involvement as a Fellow of the Academy, in this process.[13] This is the aspect of his academic 'legacy' with which I will bring this memoir to a conclusion.

Sidney was elected as a Fellow in 1973, as a member of Section 5, which at that time covered, 'Literature and Philology: Classical'. That this should have been his section of primary allegiance is natural enough, since his Chair of Comparative Philology was established in the Classical Faculty at Cambridge. There can be no doubt, however, that his election would have been strongly supported, not only by existing members of Section 5 with interests in historical and comparative linguistics, but also by many Indianists and anthropologists in Sections 4 ('Oriental and African Studies') and 12 ('Social and Political Studies') who were familiar with his work or were well disposed to linguistics. His supporters may also have included one or two members of Section 7 ('Philosophy').[14] Very soon thereafter, if not before, the process began which led eventually to the creation by Council, in May 1982, of Section 16 ('Linguistics'). This was part of a more general policy, the purpose of which was to give recognition to several subjects, including some of the social sciences, which, it was felt, were 'under-represented' in the Academy. As far as

[13] I am grateful to the Secretary of the Academy, Peter Brown, for having gone through the Archives and supplying me with much of the historical information that I have incorporated in this part of Section IX, especially in the footnotes.

[14] When I was elected as a Fellow in 1973 I was made a member of Sections 4, 5, 7 and 12. This clearly reflected the support that there was in all four sections for the promotion of linguistics, whether it was taken broadly to include philology or more narrowly (as was undoubtedly the case for some of its supporters) to refer to one or other of the contemporary schools of ('autonomous' synchronic) structural linguistics. My election took place under the special procedure of the then Bye-law 14(b), which empowered the Council 'to add to the list of candidates [put forward by the Sections] the names of persons whose qualifications do not come sufficiently within the purview of any particular Section'. By that time, by virtue of my responsibilities as Head of the Department of Linguistics (and Professor of General Linguistics) at Edinburgh, I had acquired an interest, not only in general, theoretical and descriptive linguistics, but also in psycholinguististics, sociolinguistics and anthropological (ethno-)linguistics, and I already had a background, and had taught and published, in classics and comparative linguistics and certain areas of the philosophy of language (see my 'Personal history' in Brown and Law, *Linguistics in Britain*). As will be clear from Sections VI and VII above, Sidney Allen's interests, and professorial responsibilities, were narrower.

linguistics is concerned, Sidney was involved from an early stage.[15] The inaugural meeting of Section 16 took place on 11 July 1984 and it held its first 'normal' meeting in January 1985. The Chairman was Frank Palmer (FBA 1975), at the time of his election a member of Section 4.[16] The first two Fellows to be elected as members of Section 16 were Anna Morpurgo Davies, Professor of Comparative Philology at Oxford, and Peter Matthews, Professor of General Linguistics at Cambridge. Their election can be seen as giving effect to the decision, that, under the rubric 'linguistics', the new Section would from the outset include 'philology', which had long been recognised in several sections of the Academy and which some Fellows including Sidney Allen (but neither Anna Davies nor Peter Matthews, nor I myself) would have seen as a different discipline from 'modern' linguistics (see Section VI above). The other twenty-three original members of Section 16 had exercised the option to join that they were given when it was set up, twenty of them also opting to maintain their existing sectional allegiance.[17]

In 2002, when Sidney Allen wrote (very briefly) of his election as a Fellow in 1973 and of the role that he himself had played in the setting up (eleven or twelve years later) of the Linguistics Section, he noted '[it] now numbers thirty-one members (plus seven "secondary" members from

---

[15] Others who should be mentioned specifically as having been especially supportive of linguistics (in the broadest sense) at that time were John Chadwick, Robin Matthews and Edward Ullendorff. I myself was involved from shortly after my election in 1973 and Frank Palmer from his election in 1975 (see the following footnote).

[16] Frank Palmer was Professor and Head of the Department of Linguistic Science at the University of Reading (and had previously held the Chair of Linguistics at Bangor, 1950–60). He had been a colleague of Sidney's at SOAS, where his research interests included Ethiopian languages (see Section VI above). He had been asked by Council in May 1982 to convene a specially appointed sub-committee 'to explore further the proposal . . . to create a new Section covering Linguistics in the broadest sense'. The other members of the sub-committee were Sidney Allen, Edward Ullendorff and myself. The sub-committee met on 1 July 1982 and reported to Council in October of the same year. (Sir Kenneth Dover, PBA 1978–81, was also a member, but did not attend the meeting.) The report was then sent to sections for comment (as were proposals for the division of some of the existing sections, including Section 12). Section 16 was set up by Council in May 1984.Without going further into the details, it may be said that when the new Section was established it operated, essentially, according to the recommendations of this sub-committee, as minuted and deposited in the Archives, and has continued to do so. In particular, it has as its members those 'who are primarily interested in language from a historical, descriptive, comparative, theoretical philosophical or psychological point of view'.

[17] More recently, the Academy has considerably restricted the possibility of multiple membership. But the 'hybrid' status of linguistics, straddling different areas of the 'humanities' and different social sciences, is officially recognised by granting to H4 a larger quota (25 per cent) of Fellows of 'secondary allegiance', in addition to its 'primary-allegiance' Fellows.

the sections of their "primary allegiance"'.[18] He was well aware, as were all of those who supported the setting up of the Linguistics Section, how important for the academic standing of the subject, nationally and internationally, had been its 'recognition' by the Academy, and he rightly took credit for the role that he himself had played in bringing this about.

SIR JOHN LYONS
Fellow of the Academy

Note. In preparing this memoir I have been greatly assisted by Anna Morpurgo Davies, Peter Matthews and Frank Palmer. I have had the benefit of conversations and correspondence with Mrs Diana Allen, who has answered some of my queries and shown me certain documents in her possession, of correspondence with Michèle Mittner, and, for Sidney Allen's time as a Fellow of Trinity, of conversations with Sir Andrew Huxley and Nicholas Denyer. George Hewitt has kindly checked certain sections of the memoir for me in draft. Since this is not only a formal memoir, but also a personal tribute, I wish to emphasise that the opinions and judgements expressed in it are mine alone (although they have been to some degree modulated and at times corrected after consultation with those named above who have helped me). I have drawn freely on the autobiographical materials that Sidney Allen deposited with the Academy, and incorporated some quotations from it in my text.

Select Bibliography of the writings of W. Sidney Allen

'Ancient ideas on the origin and development of language', *Transactions of the Philological Society*, 1948, 35–60.

'Some prosodic aspects of retroflexion and aspiration in Sanskrit', *Bulletin of the School of Oriental and African Studies*, 13 (1951), 939–46.

Phonetics in Ancient India (London Oriental Series, 1), (London, 1953). Reprinted 1961, 1965.

'Relationship in Comparative Linguistics', *Transactions of the Philological Society*, 1953, 52–108.

'Retroflexion in Sanskrit: prosodic technique and its relevance to comparative statement', *Bulletin of the School of Oriental and African Studies*, 16 (1954), 556–65.

'Structure and system in the Abaza verbal complex', *Transactions of the Philological Society*, 1956, 127–76.

---

[18] 'Personal history', 26. Sidney Allen did not have the benefit of the assistance that I have been given as far as the archival record is concerned and his account is not wholly accurate. Nothing that he says, however, seriously affects what I have recorded here. (The account that I have given in my own 'Personal history', in the same volume, also turns out to be inaccurate in one or two details, though once again not in any way that invalidates the substance of what is said above in the text or in the footnotes.

On the Linguistic Study of Languages (Inaugural Lecture), (Cambridge, 1957). Reprinted with foreword in P. Strevens (ed.), *Five Inaugural Lectures* (Oxford, 1966) and in J. P. Allen and S. P. Corder (eds.), *Edinburgh Course in Applied Linguistics*, I (Oxford, 1973).

'Some phonological characteristics of Rājasthānī', *Bulletin of the School of Oriental and African Studies*, 20 (1957) (In honour of Sir Ralph Turner), 5–12.

'Aspiration in the Hāṛautī nominal', in *Studies in Linguistic Analysis*, Special Volume of the Philological Society (Oxford, 1957), pp. 68–86.

Sandhi: the theoretical, phonetic, and historical bases of word-junction in Sanskrit (The Hague, 1962). Reprinted 1972.

'Transitivity and possession', *Language*, 40 (1964), 33–43.

Vox Latina: a guide to the pronunciation of classical Latin (Cambridge, 1965). 2nd edn. 1978.

'An Abaza text', *Bedi Kartlisa*, 19–20 (1965), 159–72.

'On one-vowel systems', *Lingua*, 13 (1965), 111–24.

'Prosody and prosodies in Greek' (Presidential address), *Transactions of the Philological Society*, 1966, 107–48.

Vox Graeca: a guide to the pronunciation of classical Greek (Cambridge, 1968). 2nd edn. 1974, 3rd edn. 1987.

Accent and Rhythm: Prosodic features of Latin and Greek: a study in theory and reconstruction (Cambridge Studies in Linguistics, 12), (Cambridge, 1973).

'The PIE aspirates: phonetics and typological factors in reconstruction', *Studia Linguistica et Philologica*, 4 (1978) (offered to Joseph Greenberg), Saratoga, 237–47.

'The PIE velar series: neogrammarian and other solutions in the light of attested parallels' (Commemorative volume: the Neogrammarians), *Transactions of the Philological Society*, 1978, 87–110.

'Kalóyeros: an Atlantis in microcosm?' *Imago Mundi*, 29 (1978), 54–71.

'An addendum to Kalóyeros', *Imago Mundi*, 31 (1979), 94–6.

'On "tenseness" in Modern Icelandic', *Transactions of the Philological Society*, 93 (1995), 1–16.

GEORGE ANDERSON

George Wishart Anderson
1913–2002

GEORGE WISHART ANDERSON WAS BORN ON 25 JANUARY 1913 at 25 Eliot Street, Arbroath. The date of his birth was appropriate for a Scot who was later to become a biblical scholar and a Methodist minister, for it is the day on which the conversion of St Paul is celebrated in the church, and also the day on whose evening the poet Robert Burns is commemorated. He was the elder son of George Anderson (1879–1957), who was a cabinetmaker, and Margaret Gordon, *née* Wishart (1880–1964). He was educated at Arbroath High School, and was awarded a Harkness scholarship to St Andrews University in 1931. There, he read Classics, and graduated with first-class honours in 1935. His studies continued at Cambridge, where he was trained for the Methodist ministry at Wesley House, and where he also read Theology at Fitzwilliam House (now Fitzwilliam College) in Cambridge University, and was placed in the first class in the Theological Tripos, Part IB in 1937. He spent another year reading for the more specialised Theological Tripos, Part II, in Old Testament studies, and was placed in the second class in 1938.

The next academic year was spent abroad in further biblical studies. Germany was, of course, not an appropriate place for such a study in the days of the Nazi regime, and Anderson went on a Finch scholarship to Sweden, a less common country for British scholars in which to pursue graduate studies. He went to Lund University without a knowledge of Swedish, but such was his linguistic ability that by the end of the first term he was able to submit a paper in that language. His special interest continued to be the Old Testament, and he was glad to be able to study under Professor Johannes Lindblom. Anderson made friends with a

Proceedings of the British Academy, **138**, 39–48. © The British Academy 2006.

number of Swedish students, and he acquired an interest in Scandinavian biblical scholarship that was to continue for the rest of his life.

After returning to the United Kingdom, Anderson served as assistant tutor at Richmond College, London, another Methodist theological college, from 1939 until 1941, and was ordained to the Methodist ministry in 1940. On 14 June 1941 he married Edith Joyce Marjorie (known as Joy) Walter (1912–1958), a tax officer with Inland Revenue, and the daughter of Edwin Harold Walter, and in due course they had a son and a daughter. In 1941 he also became a Methodist chaplain in the RAF, and he served until 1946 in Egypt, the Sudan, and Palestine, and was thus for the first time able to see the land that was the scene of most of the Old Testament story.

Anderson's next work was to teach Old Testament studies to candidates for the Methodist ministry at Handsworth College, Birmingham, from 1946 until 1956, and he was also a recognised lecturer at Birmingham University. Then, in 1956, he went back to Scotland and his own university as Lecturer in Old Testament Literature and Theology at St Andrews, but in 1958 he was appointed Professor of Old Testament Studies at Durham University. Two weeks before the move to Durham, his wife died. In addition to the feelings of loss, he had to care alone for their two children and to face the problems of moving house. Her death cast a shadow over all the time the family spent in Durham. However, on 27 July 1959 he married his late wife's cousin, Annie Phyllis Walter (1908–1999), a schoolteacher and the daughter of Alfred William Walter.

Anderson's final appointment was at Edinburgh University, where in 1962 he became Professor of Old Testament Literature and Theology. In 1968, after the retirement of N. W. Porteous as Professor of Hebrew and Semitic Languages, the title of Anderson's chair was changed to Professor of Hebrew and Old Testament Studies. He taught Hebrew to undergraduates in the Faculty of Arts, and lectured on the Old Testament to candidates for the ministry of the Church of Scotland and for the degree of BD. In addition, he taught graduate students, not only from the United Kingdom, but also from various countries, including several from South-East Asia. He was a lucid and thorough lecturer, and he took a personal interest in his pupils. He retired from his chair in 1982 and became emeritus professor.

The contribution made by Anderson to the study of the Old Testament was not confined to the universities and colleges in which he taught. He was an active member of the Society for Old Testament Study. From 1957 to 1966 he edited the Society's annual *Book List*, which contains brief reviews of books that had recently been published on the Old Testament and related subjects and is an invaluable bibliographical aid to those interested in biblical studies. The issues published during the years when Anderson was the editor were brought together into a single volume in 1967 as *A Decade of Bible Bibliography* (Oxford). It has also been the practice of the Society to publish from time to time, after intervals of some years, books containing a number of essays by various scholars surveying developments in scholarship in the preceding years. Anderson, who contributed to one such volume in 1951, was the editor of *Tradition and Interpretation*, which appeared in Oxford in 1979. He served as President in 1963 and as honorary Foreign Secretary from 1964 to 1974.

Anderson's interest in biblical scholarship outside the United Kingdom, which was seen already during his year at Lund, and which also appeared in his editing of the *Book List* and serving as Foreign Secretary, led him to play a part in the work of the International Organization for the Study of the Old Testament, which was founded in 1948. He was one of the group of scholars who founded the quarterly journal *Vetus Testamentum*, which was published under the auspices of the IOSOT, beginning in 1951. Anderson was a member of the editorial board from the beginning until 1975, and after that a member of the advisory committee for the rest of his life. He was the Secretary of the IOSOT between 1956 and 1971, and the President from 1971 to 1974, when its triennial congress was held in Edinburgh.

A contribution to the work of Bible translation was made by Anderson for three projects. First, he played a part in the preparation of an English translation of the Psalms (1993) that was intended to help those working for the British and Foreign Bible Society and others seeking to translate books of the Bible into a variety of languages throughout the world. It was intended that such an English rendering would bring the resources of modern scholarship to help translators to understand the meaning of the text which they were seeking to translate into their own languages. Secondly, he was responsible for the first draft of the rendering of one of the books of the Apocrypha for the *New English Bible* (1970). Thirdly, he was one of those who revised the *NEB*'s rendering of the books of the Old Testament for *the Revised English Bible* (1989).

Anderson received invitations to give special named lectures: the Charles Ryder Smith memorial lecture in 1964; the Fernley-Hartley lecture in 1969; the Henton Davies lecture in 1977; and the A. S. Peake memorial lecture in 1984. In addition, he was elected to the Speaker's Lectureship in Biblical Studies at Oxford University to give a series of lectures in 1976–9.

He was elected a Fellow of the British Academy in 1972, and was awarded the Academy's Burkitt Medal for Biblical Studies in 1982. The Royal Society of Edinburgh elected him to a Fellowship in 1977. The University of St Andrews conferred on him an honorary Doctorate of Divinity in 1959, and the University of Lund an honorary Doctorate of Theology in 1971.

Anderson's achievements as a scholar were honoured by the publication of two series of essays. The first was the January issue of *Vetus Testamentum*, 32 (1982), with articles by nine scholars, and a list of his publications. The second was a volume entitled *Understanding Poets and Prophets* (1993), which was edited by A. G. Auld, a former pupil, and contained twenty-eight articles and a list bringing Anderson's publications up to date. It is good that the latter publication was able to give a larger number of scholars an opportunity to honour Anderson than was possible in the 128 pages available in a single issue of a journal. It is a pity, however, that the preface to the latter volume (p. 11) said of the former that it 'was largely an "in house" affair', and that only three articles accompanied 'those by his journal collaborators'. In fact, only two articles were by members of the editorial board and two by former members, whereas five (not three) were by scholars without the same connection with the journal.

Two publications edited by Anderson have already been mentioned: *A Decade of Bible Bibliography*, and *Tradition and Interpretation* (for which he wrote an introduction about recent changes in Old Testament scholarship). His knowledge of Scandinavian languages enabled him to translate two books from the Norwegian. The first is *He that Cometh* (1956), by Sigmund Mowinckel, an important study of the origins of the messianic hope and its relation to ideas of kingship. The second, *The Ras Shamra Discoveries and the Old Testament* (1965), by A. S. Kapelrud, is an account of the clay tablets from the site of the ancient city of Ugarit in Syria on which were found texts in a hitherto unknown cuneiform alphabet and a hitherto unknown North-West Semitic language closely related to Hebrew. A further two books were entirely Anderson's own work. *A Critical Introduction to the Old Testament* (1959) was probably the best moderately sized work on the subject, and was widely used by students for many years. Unfortunately, it is in the nature of such works to become out of date in some respects unless they are regularly revised. A second edition in 1994 contained a revised bibliography and also a few pages summarising some recent developments in scholarship. Anderson told me, however, that he would have preferred if it had been possible to prepare a full revision. *The History and Religion of Israel* (1966), in the New Clarendon Bible series, is a text-book of a less advanced level, and a Chinese translation of it was published in 1990. Both books display good judgement and evidence of wide reading in the subjects discussed, and also Anderson's gift of concise and lucid writing.

Many of Anderson's publications took the form of articles in periodicals or other works. Some of them will not be considered here because they are examples of *haute vulgarisation*, such as the series of articles on books of the Old Testament in the *Preacher's Quarterly* between 1961 and 1964, rather than fresh contributions to scholarship. For the same reason there will be no discussion of such publications as essays in one-volume commentaries on the Bible or new bibliographies added to books by other writers. Sometimes, however, it is difficult to decide to which category to assign a particular publication. For example, a review article in the *Expository Times* for 1962 on T. C. Vriezen's *Outline of Old Testament Theology* was written with non-specialist readers in mind, but it is also worth studying by more advanced scholars. The following discussion of Anderson's work will focus attention on articles intended for them.

One of Anderson's earliest articles, which arose from his studies in Sweden, is 'Some aspects of the Uppsala School of Old Testament Study', in the *Harvard Theological Review*, 43 (1950), pp. 239–56. The article helped to inform readers about a group of Swedish and other Scandinavian scholars and their work on the Old Testament, who were challenging generally accepted views about Israelite religion and the composition and transmission of the books of the Old Testament. The background to the opinions of these Scandinavian scholars, who were far from agreeing with one another on every subject, may be seen in the work of earlier writers in Scandinavia between the two world wars. But the more recent scholars tended to go farther than their predecessors, and their approach took on a particularly aggressive form in the work of Ivan Engnell in Uppsala. The most striking aspects of the views of such scholars are summarised by Anderson as follows:

> In the fields of textual and literary criticism great emphasis is laid on the importance and reliability of oral tradition. In the study of religion the school is anti-evolutionist, and is concerned to stress the abiding positive influence of the cult, and the importance of the rôle both of king and prophet in the cult. These lines converge in a rigorous attack on the analysis of the literature and the reconstruction of the history of the religion which are associated with the name of [Julius] Wellhausen (pp. 239–40).

Anderson discusses in detail Scandinavian theories on these subjects, noting also dissenting opinions, such as G. Widengren's argument, which is based partly on a study of the Arabic evidence, that oral tradition was less influential than scholars like Engnell maintained. Anderson's primary aim in his article is to expound the views of the new school of scholars, rather than to assess their strength, but it is evident that he is far from accepting all the opinions that he describes. His disagreement becomes more plain in his later publications.

It was probably Anderson's next article that first drew attention to him as a promising Old Testament scholar. His essay on 'Hebrew Religion' in *The Old Testament and Modern Study* (1951), edited by H. H. Rowley, pp. 283–310, was one of the series of books prepared by the Society for Old Testament Study on recent developments in scholarly work, and Anderson had in mind primarily the preceding fifteen years. Not surprisingly, much space is devoted to Scandinavian work, but attention is also paid to other scholars such as the German Albrecht Alt and his writing on the God of the patriarchs, and the American W. F. Albright and his claim that it is justified to apply the term 'monotheism' to the religion of Moses, whereas the British scholar H. H. Rowley regards the expression 'implicit' or 'incipient monotheism' as more appropriate. Mention is made of the stress by some scholars on the importance of the cult, the status of the Israelite king and the theory of Engnell that the king 'in his cultic role' was 'identical both with the creator high god . . . and, as such,' played 'a decisive part, both as the suffering servant of Yahweh and as the victor over the powers of chaos' (p. 296). Anderson is sceptical about Engnell's ideas on the subject. Mowinckel's claim that the autumnal festival included a cultic enthronement of the God of Israel is criticised, and preference is expressed for Otto Eissfeldt's argument that 'proper names compounded with' the Hebrew word for 'king' are 'very rare until the end of the monarchy, which is hardly what one would expect if the Kingship of Yahweh were being annually celebrated in so popular a festival as that of Ingathering' (p. 297). Various other theories are considered, and Anderson comments in the final paragraph of his article that 'Hebrew religion cannot be described in terms of a smooth, orderly historical development' (p. 309).

A later article in the *Annual of the Swedish Theological Institute*, 6 (1967–8), pp. 4–19, discusses the career and publications of his teacher in Lund, Johannes Lindblom, whose views differed from those of the so-called Uppsala school. Lindblom wrote on various biblical subjects, among them the religion of ancient Israel, Job, and the prophets. His study of Isaiah 24–7 regarded it as a cantata composed for use in Jerusalem to celebrate the fall of Babylon to Xerxes in 485 BC. Lindblom also wrote on the Suffering Servant in Deutero-Isaiah, and more generally on prophecy in ancient Israel. Anderson writes appreciatively of Lindblom's work, and he was himself later to write on Isaiah 24–7.

In other articles, Anderson discusses particular passages of the Old Testament and also particular topics. His article on Isaiah 24–7 was read as a paper at an IOSOT congress and was published in *Congress Volume: Bonn 1962* (Leiden, 1963), pp. 118–26. He discusses various theories and argues (like Lindblom) that 'there is a substantial unity in these chapters', but it is 'the unity of a prophetic response to a particular situation', rather than 'the unity of a carefully articulated argumentative poem' (p. 122). These chapters 'are to be assigned to the earlier rather than to the later post-exilic period, a writing which is prophetic rather than apocalyptic in character' (p. 126). The reference in 26.19 to the swallowing up of death can be understood as a 'promise of national renewal', rather than an example of the later belief in individual resurrection (p. 126). Anderson notes affinities with Haggai and Zechariah (late sixth century), and presumably dates Isaiah 24–7 in the same period. Two shorter articles are a discussion of Psalm 1.1 in *Vetus Testamentum*, 24 (1974), pp. 221–3, in honour of Erling Hammershaimb, a Danish member of the editorial board; and of Micah 6.1–8 (especially of the last verse), in the *Scottish Journal of Theology*, 4 (1951), pp. 191–7.

An article that is concerned, not with a single passage, but with a subject that appears in a number of passages, is 'Enemies and Evildoers in the Book of Psalms', *Bulletin of the John Rylands Library*, 48 (1965–6), pp. 18–29. This is a subject that has attracted various theories, especially from German and also Scandinavian writers. Is the subject of the complaint to be understood as the nation as a whole, or an individual, and, if an individual, is he the king? Are the enemies foreign nations, or are they Israelite foes? Are they godless Jews in the post-exilic period, or do they belong to an earlier time? Is the reference to demonic enemies who threaten the king in the New Year festival? These and other questions have been asked, and corresponding theories have been advanced. Anderson states that there is 'no single solution which satisfactorily accounts for all the factors in the problem'. He also thinks that a number of the psalms have been altered and adapted to fit different situations. There 'is no single key to unlock all the doors', and 'In general, the prayers which they contain were not intended for use on one and only one occasion, but were used on many different occasions' (p. 28).

In an article in *Translating and Understanding the Old Testament: Essays in Honor of Herbert Gordon May* (Nashville and New York, 1970), pp. 135–51, Anderson shares in honouring another member of the editorial board of *Vetus Testamentum*. He discusses the vexed question of the nature of early Israel, with special reference to the theory of Martin Noth that it was a confederation of twelve tribes analogous to an ancient Greek amphictyony. Anderson does not find Noth's detailed theory convincing. 'The indications are', he thinks, 'not so much of centralization and unity as the fragments of a unity not yet realized, or rather of a lost unity surviving as an ideal. . . Further, the narratives about the rise of the monarchy presuppose an already existing consciousness of Israelite unity' (p. 149).

'Some Observations of the Old Testament Doctrine of the Remnant', in *Transactions of the Glasgow University Oriental Society*, 23 (1969–70 — but published in 1972), pp. 1–10, notes the various ways in which the Old Testament uses terms for a remnant, and he distinguishes between those that mean, for example, 'what is left over, without any further implication of good or evil', and those that have the connotation of a faithful few who hold a promise for the future. The latter type of passage is more appropriate to theories of a doctrine of the remnant. Anderson returns to the same subject in the *Annual of the Swedish Theological Institute*, 11 (1977–8), pp. 11–15, in an issue dedicated to Gillis Gerleman, who had been a fellow-student with Anderson and became a professor at Lund. The article is concerned with the doctrine of the remnant in the book of Zephaniah, and Anderson finds it in 2.3, and 9b; 3.11–13.

A substantial article on 'Canonical and non-canonical' in the first volume of *The Cambridge History of the Bible* (Cambridge, 1970), edited by P. R. Ackroyd and C. F. Evans, pp. 113–59, discusses 'The definition of Canonicity', 'Acts of canonisation', 'The enumeration and arrangement of the contents of the Canon', 'The Canon in different Jewish communities', and 'Canonical and non-canonical' (i.e. the apocrypha and pseudepigrapha).

A different type of subject is considered in 'Israel's Creed: Sung, not Signed', *Scottish Journal of Theology*, 16 (1963), pp. 277–85, which was Anderson's Presidential paper to the Society for Old Testament Study on 2 January 1963. He maintains that the Old Testament is a confessional document, though not one like the Westminster Confession. It is

> neither a consciously formulated propositional confession, nor simply the *disiecta membra* from which the story of Israel's religion may be recovered, but

a *corpus*, or, if you prefer, a collection of *corpora*, which both issued from and moulded the life of a religious community (p. 280).

The Psalter is the supremely representative theological document of the Old Testament precisely because in it you see most sharply not only the available material but also the problems which have to be faced in any attempt at a theological interpretation of the Old Testament (p. 283).

With this article may be compared Anderson's essay ' "Sicut cervus": evidence in the Psalter of private devotion in ancient Israel', *Vetus Testamentum*, 30 (1980), pp. 388–97, in which he discusses 'whether the Psalter reflects in any measure not only the liturgical worship of ancient Israel but also the inner devotional experience of individual Israelites' (p. 388). He advances arguments for believing that it does thus reflect such individual piety. Related to the conclusions of this article is the discussion of 'The Christian Use of the Psalms', in *Studia Evangelica*, 7 (1982), pp. 5–10, in which he examines ways in which Christians may legitimately use the psalms.

Finally, 'Two Scottish Semitists', *Congress Volume: Edinburgh 1974* (1975), pp. ix–xxix, is Anderson's Presidential address to the IOSOT at the congress over which he presided. He examines the question why, when William Robertson Smith was dismissed from his chair in Aberdeen, A. B. Davidson, who had been his teacher in Edinburgh, did not play an active part in his defence, although he did vote against his dismissal. Anderson accepts the explanation that, although Davidson accepted critical scholarship and agreed with much that Smith said, he thought that he was too aggressive and that his pugnacity was likely to harm the church. 'This may be a partial explanation'; Davidson's 'strategy was not revolutionary but Fabian' (p. xix).

It would be a mistake to look for radically new ideas and revolutionary theories in Anderson's scholarly writings. He was not that kind of scholar. His writings show thorough knowledge of the subjects discussed, a fair but critical evaluation of theories, a balanced judgement, and the presentation of conclusions reached by rational argument.

In character, Anderson was a modest, quiet and friendly person. As a teacher, his lectures were thorough and lucidly presented, as were the papers that he read at conferences. He took a personal and friendly interest in his pupils, and also in others whom he met. It was typical of him that, when I went to Birmingham University as a young and inexperienced temporary assistant lecturer, I found him welcoming, and a friendship began that was to last until his death half a century later. Nor was I the only young scholar to whom he offered friendship and encouragement. He had a quiet and gentle sense of humour and could enjoy a joke. He observed with humour the foibles of his colleagues in church as well as in the academic community, and had some amusing anecdotes to recount about them, but I never heard him say anything spiteful or malicious. While himself a loyal member and minister of the Methodist Church, he had a broad outlook and could associate happily with people of a different loyalty or faith, or absence of it.

Anderson's interests extended well beyond the limits of Hebraic, biblical, and theological studies. He was fond of literature and poetry, especially by Scottish writers, for he was proud of being a Scot. He was the chairman of both the Walter Scott Club and the Robert Louis Stevenson Club. He preferred these two writers to Robert Burns, though he read much of Burns's poetry in his latter years. He also taught himself Gaelic, and added that language to the many that he knew. Mention was made above of his knowledge of Swedish and his translation of two books from Norwegian into English. He also knew Danish and Icelandic. As well as knowing the language, he enjoyed reading Swedish literature and poetry. Such was his knowledge of Swedish that he was able to help someone who wished to find out about an ancient variety of Swedish turnip that was introduced into East Lothian, and who sent him an eighteenth-century document in Swedish about Swedish agriculture. Anderson was able to translate the document on sight, despite the fact that the Swedish of the eighteenth century differs from that of modern times.

His health was not good in his later years: he had several strokes and was bedridden for his last fifteen months at a time when he was saddened by the death of his second wife, which also brought home to him again the sadness of his first wife's death. Nevertheless, he remained remarkably cheerful and started reading a new edition of Scott's novels. He never lost the twinkle in his eye. He died on 17 March 2002 in his home at 51 Fountainhall Road, Edinburgh, and he was buried by his son and daughter on the twenty-fifth day of the same month in St Andrews in the western cemetery.

J. A. EMERTON
Fellow of the Academy

Note. I am grateful to Mrs Margaret Hewitson for her help in preparing this obituary of her father.

ALBINIA DE LA MARE

Giles de la Mare

Albinia Catherine de la Mare
1932–2001

ALBINIA DE LA MARE was one of the outstanding palaeographers of the twentieth century. Just as E. A. Lowe in his *Codices Latini Antiquiores* mapped the earliest surviving Latin manuscripts, and Bernhard Bischoff classified by date and origin the Carolingian manuscripts, she undertook the task of tracing the careers of the hundreds of scribes writing the newly introduced humanistic script in Italy in the fifteenth century. The tasks were different in many specific ways, but the methodological principles were largely the same. They consisted in training the memory to recognise the characteristics of script, what palaeographers call the *ductus*, and combining that expertise with a thorough knowledge of the texts which were being transcribed, of the patrons for whom the manuscripts were written, and of the broader cultural and historical context. Since the Italian scribes were more numerous, and since their works survive in greater number and are better documented, individual characteristics make the identification of a body of work by an individual scribe possible. These individual scribes have often left a considerable quantity of surviving identifiable manuscripts. It was de la Mare's achievement to demonstrate just how numerous these scribes were and how productive.

Tilly, as I shall call her from now on, since it was the name by which she was known, not only by family, close friends, and the wider circle of colleagues, but even by strangers who only knew her through her work, was born on 2 June 1932. Her father, Richard de la Mare (1901–86), was an influential publisher who joined the firm of Faber and Gwyer in 1925, and ended his career as Chairman of Faber and Faber, as it had become, from 1960 to 1971. The firm was known in particular for its poetry list. Under Berthold Wolpe's direction Faber books maintained a high standard of typography and design, and distinguished creative artists were employed on the book jackets and illustrations. Tilly was thus surrounded by beautifully produced books and introduced to the processes of their making from an early age. Her mother, Amy Catherine Donaldson (d. 1968), had trained and was active as an artist. Tilly's grandfather was the poet Walter de la Mare (1873–1956, OM, CH), who additionally wrote adult novels and stories, and verse and stories for children.[1] Tilly and the older two of her three younger brothers, Giles, Richard, and Benedick, were born in London where the family lived initially in Gower Street in Bloomsbury. Richard de la Mare later bought a large George I house in Much Hadham, Hertfordshire, in 1937, where he was able to display the Japanese porcelain of which he was a pioneer collector and create a beautiful garden.

Tilly was educated as a boarder at Queen's College, Harley Street (1947–51), and then went up to Lady Margaret Hall, Oxford, where she read Modern History. She was elected an Honorary Fellow of the College in 1989. She worked on her thesis from 1954 to 1961 at the Warburg Institute, London, being a Junior Research Fellow from 1957 to 1959, and completing her Ph.D. for London University in 1966. It was entitled 'Vespasiano da Bisticci, Historian and Bookseller'. The then Director of the Warburg Institute, Ernst Gombrich, suggested the subject and acted as her supervisor. Tilly took her dissertation in the direction of Vespasiano the *cartolaio*—who made an extremely successful business out of providing manuscripts, especially classical and humanistic manuscripts, for the libraries of the rich and famous—rather than of Vespasiano the historian, who wrote *Vite* of those same rich and famous. As a palaeographer she was largely self-taught, learning by looking, though B. L. Ullman's *The origin and development of humanistic script* appeared in 1960 while she was still writing her dissertation.

In 1962 she moved back to Oxford, where she had an initial appointment for two years to catalogue the bequest of manuscripts made by James P. R. Lyell (1871–1949) to the Bodleian Library. This is where we first overlapped. Tilly was appointed to the permanent staff as an Assistant in the Department of Western Manuscripts a year after me in 1964, and she remained in the library until 1988. We worked under Richard Hunt (1908–79), who was Keeper of Western Manuscripts from

---

[1] His poem 'A Lifetime. Epitaph for William Blake' was printed on the service sheet for her memorial service in the Chapel of King's College, 28 May 2002. It contains the line 'endless labour, shafts of bliss' which seems perfect for his granddaughter too.

1945 to 1975. Dr Hunt would appear each morning in Duke Humfrey's library and visit each member of the staff there to give advice, answer questions, and generally see what we were up to. The Lyell manuscripts were a miscellaneous collection, acquired by an intelligent but not exceptionally wealthy man between 1936 and 1944. He had been a London solicitor by profession, and lived at the end of his life in Abingdon near Oxford. The bequest consisted of a choice of one hundred manuscripts from a total collection of a little over two hundred and fifty medieval and postmedieval manuscripts.[2] The Bodleian acquired a further eleven manuscripts from the executors (classified as 'Lyell empt.'). These are also included in Tilly's catalogue. The residue of the estate was left to Oxford University for the foundation of the Lyell Readership in Bibliography. Lyell was able to buy with discrimination and for prices which now seem minuscule, manuscripts with historical importance because of their known provenance, or their textual interest, or because they were documented in some way. Lyell was also interested in their bindings. None of the manuscripts had extensive or high-quality illumination, few were Italian, and fewer still were in humanistic script. They were acquired from five London dealers, Quaritch, Maggs, Goldschmidt, Rosenthal, and Davis and Orioli, never at auction. In cataloguing them, therefore, Tilly had to start almost from scratch, both as regards her own knowledge and as regards any previous study of them other than what had been contained in the booksellers' catalogues.

It was a wonderful process of training on the job, supplemented by Richard Hunt's extraordinarily wide knowledge of all aspects of the medieval book. The Bodleian, and Duke Humfrey's Library in particular, was at that time a gathering place for a number of outstanding specialists in the university, who used it regularly. There was also a tradition of generous give-and-take between readers and staff at all times. If you wanted illegible script read, to decipher an erased monastic *ex libris* or to date an English hand, you asked Neil Ker or Malcolm Parkes. If it was a matter of the history of the university or a name in a pledge note you could apply to A. B. Emden. For bindings, collections, and the sale room there was Graham Pollard. For art-historical problems there were Otto Pächt and later Leon Delaissé. Other notable medieval scholars often in the library were Walter Oakeshott, Beryl Smalley, and Roger Mynors, the

---

[2] See N. R. Ker's first Lyell lecture printed as an Introduction to *Catalogue of the collection of medieval manuscripts bequeathed to the Bodleian Library, Oxford by James P. R. Lyell*, compiled by A. C. de la Mare (Oxford, 1971), pp. xv–xxix.

latter at that time engaged on his catalogue of the Balliol College manuscripts, which included the manuscripts purchased by William Gray,
bishop of Ely, from Vespasiano da Bisticci. The Reading Room, transferred for a time to the New Library while Duke Humfrey's Library was
restored from the ravages of the Death Watch beetle, could be a noisy
place, sometimes to the dismay of readers not involved in the loud conversations which took place there. Hunt, moreover, always encouraged his
staff to get to know the readers so that they could learn from them as well
as help them. Duke Humfrey's library was in short an academy such as its
humanist founder might have approved. Hunt himself was a scholar with
an encyclopedic knowledge and a prodigious memory.[3] He gave lectures
in the History School on palaeography, which he understood to be the
wider study of the manuscript book. It included not only the study of
script, but also codicology — such physical details of the manuscript as
parchment, collation, and ruling patterns. The study of texts and their
transmission was a central preoccupation, including such matters as
spelling, word division, punctuation, and *mise-en-page*. Hunt gave a series
of lectures specifically on the textual transmission of the Latin classics.
He himself could recognise particular types of handwriting, both generi-
cally, assigning date and origin, and also individually, identifying for
example marginal notes made by Petrarch in a fourteenth-century copy of
Suetonius in the library of Exeter College, Oxford.[4] He knew the handwriting of each of his predecessors in the library, and insisted we should
too. At one point the Oxford police even consulted him in the matter of
some anonymous threatening letters.

So much for the days before word processors and email. One techno-
logical innovation of enormous importance for palaeographers, however,
had already made its appearance, the photocopying machine. From then
on Tilly was able to amass the huge collection of photocopies of humanistic script, which provided a foundation for much of her later scholarship. The Music School, where the first photocopier was installed, was
presided over by W. O. Hassall, who, using almost entirely volunteer help,
pioneered the making of the Bodleian Library's colour film-strips of

---

[3] See the Introduction by D. G. Vaisey to A. C. de la Mare and B. Barker-Benfield (eds.),
Manuscripts at Oxford: an exhibition in memory of Richard William Hunt (1908–1979), Bodleian
Library (Oxford, 1980), pp. vii–ix. See also R. W. Southern in J. J. G. Alexander and M. T.
Gibson (eds.), *Medieval learning and literature: essays presented to Richard William Hunt*,
(Oxford, 1976), pp. v–vii; and R. W. Southern, 'Richard William Hunt, 1908–1979' in *PBA*, 67
(1981), 371–97.
[4] R. W. Hunt, 'The Exeter College Suetonius', in *Manuscripts at Oxford*, pp. 141–3. Reprinted
from *Times Literary Supplement*, 22 Sept. 1960, p. 619.

manuscripts. This was far in advance of anything achieved by any other manuscript library and remains even now unique. Tilly selected the folios to be reproduced and wrote descriptions, important for their original scholarship, for a number of film-strips of Italian humanistic manuscripts in the Bodleian and also in the College Libraries.

Since the nineteenth century there had been a debate in the Bodleian over methods of cataloguing manuscripts. On the one side was the scholar librarian E. W. B. Nicholson, who wanted a full description of all aspects of a manuscript. On the other was the pragmatist Falconer Madan, who in the end won the battle and wrote the early volumes of the *Summary Catalogue of Western Manuscripts*, published from 1895 onwards. Though the *Summary Catalogue* had been completed in 1937, Hunt was still engaged in writing volume 1, *Historical Introduction and conspectus of shelf-marks*. This and the index finally appeared in 1953, and Lyell had apparently been incensed by the delay in its appearance. It was therefore perhaps ironical that Tilly, who was definitely on the Nicholson side, should have been set to catalogue the Lyell manuscripts. Her catalogue eventually appeared in 1971. It remains a model of its kind not just for thoroughness but also for what I can only term its sympathetic insight. By that I mean a type of learning which leaves no stone unturned in order to contextualise a particular book in such a way that other scholars wishing to use it not only have all the guidance they need but also can find hints of further directions for research. An example is the description of Lyell MS 33, a genealogical Chronicle of the Kings of England written *c*.1469–70, which also includes material from Peter of Poitiers' thirteenth-century abbreviated sacred history, the *Compendium sacrae scripturae*. In under four pages she manages to compress all the information necessary to write a much longer scholarly article.

The Bodleian Assistants in the 1960s worked a thirty-five hour week, which included Saturday mornings when the library was open from 9 a.m. to 1 p.m. Evening duty once a week from 7 p.m. to 10 p.m. was obligatory and time sheets were filled in on an honour system. Tilly was able to do her own research in her 'own time', either after work or in one free afternoon a week. There was not then the almost insane degree of pressure to publish, which young scholars have to deal with nowadays. Nevertheless, the discovery of new material was an important task, and this inevitably meant an eagerness to make something known by quickly publishing it before someone else did. Tilly's early papers combined the subject matter of her dissertation with new discoveries concerning the manuscripts brought back from Italy by the early English humanists. Her first two papers dealt in this way with the bequests of William Gray and Robert Flemmying to Balliol and Lincoln Colleges.[5] It is important to stress that until she transferred to the University of London in 1989, Tilly did not have academic vacations or regular sabbatical leave (very occasionally short-term leave was granted in exceptional circumstances) to pursue her research. She was a night owl, and much of her research and writing was done after midnight, I suspect.

Tilly has left her own account of her career and her intellectual training and development.[6] In it she describes as a revelation the moment 'after a year or two of study' when she first realised that she could recognise the handwriting of a particular scribe in a manuscript now in the Fitzwilliam Museum, Cambridge. The manuscript's text was a Life of Charlemagne written by Donato Acciaiuoli. Vespasiano was 'almost certainly' the *cartolaio* responsible for the manuscript's production and binding. The scribe whose handwriting Tilly was able to recognise was Piero Strozzi, and the illuminator was Francesco d'Antonio del Chierico. The manuscript was presented as a gift of the Florentine Republic to Louis XI of France in 1461 by the Florentine ambassadors of whom Acciaiuoli was one.[7] Tilly published a study of Piero Strozzi in a Festschrift for the distinguished calligrapher Alfred Fairbank, which came out in 1965.[8] At that time she had identified thirty-six manuscripts in Piero's hand. By 1994 the total had risen to seventy-one.

Fairbank had collaborated with Richard Hunt on the Bodleian Picture Book on humanistic script first issued in 1960.[9] Fairbank continued to visit the Bodleian and his letters, instantly recognisable from his beautiful calligraphic hand on the envelopes, used to arrive regularly on Tilly's desk. His own publications on humanist script appeared in the

---

[5] A. C. de la Mare, 'Vespasiano da Bisticci and Gray', *Journal of the Warburg and Courtauld Institutes*, 20 (1957), 174–6. A. C. de la Mare, 'Vespasiano da Bisticci and the Florentine Manuscripts of Lincoln College', *Lincoln College Record* (1962–3), pp. 7–17.

[6] 'A palaeographer's odyssey', in J. Onians (ed.), *Sight and Insight. Essays on Art and Culture in honour of E. H. Gombrich at 85* (London, 1994), pp. 88–107.

[7] Cambridge, Fitzwilliam Museum, MS 180. Exhibited, *The Cambridge Illuminations*, P. Binski and S. Panayatova (eds.) (Cambridge, 2005), cat. 161.

[8] A. C. de la Mare, 'Messer Piero Strozzi, a Florentine priest and scribe', in A. S. Osley (ed.), *Calligraphy and Palaeography. Essays presented to Alfred Fairbank on his seventieth birthday* (London, 1965), pp. 55–68. Tilly's work was always of interest to practising scribes and *vice versa*. She was elected an Honorary Member of the Society of Scribes and Illuminators.

[9] *Humanistic script of the fifteenth and sixteenth centuries* (Bodleian Library Picture Book, no. 12). Introduction and notes by A. J. Fairbank and R. W. Hunt (Oxford, 1960; corrected reprint 1993).

Journal for Italic Handwriting, and in 1961 he had published a short note there on the Paduan scribe Bartolomeo Sanvito. James Wardrop's posthumous book based on lectures given in 1952, in which he identified Sanvito and provided a first list of his manuscripts, appeared in 1963.[10] Laura Nuvoloni has written a detailed account of Tilly's 'Sanvito adventure', as she calls the major project on which Tilly was working in the last ten years of her life.[11] As with Piero Strozzi, the list of Sanvito manuscripts was to grow and grow, as we shall see later.

The project to catalogue Major J. R. Abbey's Italian manuscripts originated at about the same time in the mid-1960s. Abbey had published as his Roxburghe Club volume in 1953 a catalogue by A. R. A. Hobson of a selection of his fine bindings. Anthony Hobson suggested that he follow this with a volume on his collection of illuminated manuscripts. Abbey's initial idea may have been to publish a selection of manuscripts from all periods and countries.[12] Richard Hunt was consulted and suggested instead that a catalogue of the Italian manuscripts would make a more coherent volume and that Tilly and I should be asked to write it. Most of the manuscripts written in humanistic script came from the library of St John Hornby, the founder of the Ashendene Press, who no doubt admired them as much for their calligraphy as for their illumination.[13] The resulting catalogue appeared in 1969.[14] It was the variety of Abbey's manuscripts which gave the collection its interest, since they came from all parts of Italy. Again it was a learning experience for both of us. Tilly's part of the Introduction still stands as an excellent overview of humanist script of the fifteenth century, in which she was able to point to

---

[10] J. Wardrop, *The Script of Humanism* (Oxford, 1963).

[11] L. Nuvoloni, 'The scribe and the scholar: Bartolomeo Sanvito and Prof. Albinia de la Mare', *Bulletin du bibliophile*, 2005/2, 247–70. She proposes to date the beginning of the 'adventure' specifically to 30 Dec. 1965, on the grounds that it was on that day that Tilly made notes on three Sanvito manuscripts bought for the Victoria and Albert Museum by James Wardrop. These must have been the first manuscripts written by Sanvito that she had seen in any library other than the Bodleian.

[12] My recollections differ somewhat from Tilly's in her 'Palaeographer's odyssey', p. 97. She says that Abbey met Hunt at the meetings of the Association Internationale de Bibliophilie in Oxford in 1965 and initially asked Hunt to catalogue his Italian manuscripts.

[13] Abbey acquired Hornby's manuscripts en bloc after his death through the offices of Sydney Cockerell, who was the executor. Cockerell had given him a couple of hours to make up his mind, and Abbey acknowledged it was the best investment he ever made. The manuscripts were kept in Abbey's flat in London, and we used to bring them down to Oxford, two or three at a time in a suitcase on the train!

[14] J. J. G. Alexander and A. C. de la Mare, *The Italian Manuscripts in the Library of Major J. R. Abbey* (London, 1969). The book was published by Faber and Faber.

characteristics of regional schools and make other important observations, such as the role of notaries in Italy in the development of humanistic cursive, especially in Florence. During the time we were writing the
catalogue Abbey was able to buy a manuscript of Petrarch's *Rime e Tri-
onfi* written, and perhaps also illuminated, by Sanvito, and in the relevant
entry the manuscripts attributed to Sanvito up to that time were
discussed.[15]

My own research for the second volume of Otto Pächt's catalogue of
illuminated manuscripts in the Bodleian Library, which contained the
Italian manuscripts, began in 1966. Owing above all to the purchase by
Oxford University of the library of the Venetian Jesuit, Matteo L.
Canonici, in 1817, the Italian manuscripts in the Bodleian are highly
important in both quantity and quality.[16] Richard Hunt and Tilly looked
at all the manuscripts which were included that were in humanistic script
and their comments contributed enormously to the value of the ensuing
catalogue published in 1970. Already by this time Tilly could confidently
attribute script to a particular region of Italy and give a date for it.

The opportunity to see and handle so many manuscripts at first hand
in the Bodleian, especially as the majority were not Florentine, was of
great value to Tilly in broadening her knowledge, and, since photographs
were taken for publication in the catalogue, she could photocopy them for
her own use. James Wardrop's collection of photographs had been given
to the Bodleian by his widow and photocopies were duly incorporated by
Tilly, who was also adding to her database photocopies from her own
purchases and from published sources. This material, and her own papers
which she bequeathed to the Bodleian, now form an invaluable source for
the study of humanistic script.[17]

Tilly's desk in Arts End and later in one of the Duke Humfrey cubi-
cles was famous among regular visitors to Duke Humfrey. It was, I think,

[15] J.A. 7368, acquired at Sotheby's, 11 July 1966, lot 265. Alexander and de la Mare, 1969, cat.
39, pp. 104–10.

[16] O. Pächt and J. J. G. Alexander, *Illuminated Manuscripts in the Bodleian Library, Oxford, 1,
German, Dutch, Flemish, French and Spanish Schools. 2, Italian School. 3. British, Irish, and Icelandic Schools*, 3 vols. (Oxford, 1966, 1970, 1973). I left the Bodleian for the University of Manchester, History of Art Department, in Autumn, 1971, and inevitably my contacts with Tilly were
less frequent after that time.

[17] The papers are being put in order and catalogued by Xavier van Binnebeke, who acted as
Tilly's assistant during her last illness. Tilly also bequeathed her small collection of manuscripts
and fragments, some of them gifts from Alfred Fairbank, to the Bodleian. Her reference books
and offprints were divided between the Warburg Institute in London, the Palaeography Room in
Senate House, London, and Lady Margaret Hall, Oxford.

a symbol of her scholarship and her way of working. Piled high upon it, beside it, and around it were books, files, articles, photographs and photocopies, index cards, letters, handwritten notes, and pieces of paper of every description. It was a dizzying and sometimes unstable conglomeration, untidy certainly, but not chaotic, for she could find there whatever she or anyone else was looking for. It symbolised a kind of scholarship, which is cumulative and also sedimented, for many of her projects went on for years and indeed were still in progress at her death. Her dedication to her profession of scholar librarian serving the public should also be emphasised. She created and maintained an index of new books in the fields covered by the open-shelf library in Selden End. The books themselves were exhibited before being returned to the book stacks. She annotated the catalogue of the library of Sir Thomas Phillipps to keep it up to date as manuscripts appeared in the auction and booksellers' catalogues or found permanent homes in public collections. And she answered enquiries about Bodleian manuscripts from scholars worldwide.

In 1970 an exhibition on the library's founder, Duke Humfrey of Gloucester, and on the early English humanists, was held at the Bodleian. This was another of Richard Hunt's interests and the catalogue of the exhibition was written by Tilly in collaboration with him.[18] The exhibition was organised as a tribute to Roger Mynors on his retirement from the chair of Latin at Oxford University. Here it was the scholarship of Roberto Weiss on humanism in England which was fundamental, but once again the exhibition made its original contribution by concentrating on the identification of script, both of the professional scribes like the anonymous 'Thomas S', later identified by Tilly as Thomas Candour, a friend of Poggio, and of the English humanists, men like Andrew Holes and Robert Flemmyng. They were identified whether they were scribes writing whole texts or owners and readers inserting short marginal notes. The result was to reveal how humanism as a movement was carried outside Italy not only by the patrons, but also by itinerant scribes. Humanism and humanistic script in particular could thus be seen in a different light, as an international movement and a two-way process with individuals both coming from and going to Italy. Many of the scribes working in Italy itself were born in the north.

---

[18] A. C. de la Mare and R. W. Hunt, *Duke Humfrey and English Humanism in the fifteenth century*, Bodleian Library (Oxford, 1970). See also A. C. de la Mare, 'Humanistic hands in England', *Manuscripts at Oxford* (see above, n. 3), pp. 93–101.

In 1973 the first volume of a projected series on the handwriting of Italian humanists was published.[19] This magisterial volume described as Volume 1, fascicule 1, was meant to be the first of a series, but unfortunately the project proved too ambitious and no further 'fascicules' were completed. It included the early humanists, Petrarch, Boccaccio, Salutati, Niccoli, Poggio, and the less well-known figures of Bartolomeo Aragazzi of Montepulciano, Sozomeno of Pistoia, and Giorgio Antonio Vespucci. It was subsidised by the Association internationale de bibliophilie through the good offices of Anthony Hobson and the volume was finely printed by the University Press, Oxford. As Tilly outlines the contents, 'each entry consists of a short biographical sketch, followed by notes on the handwriting and books of the humanist concerned and a bibliography'. The entries were accompanied by numerous fine-quality plates reproducing the script as nearly as possible in actual size, something which both she and Richard Hunt were very insistent on. All Bodleian photographs have an accompanying scale, a highly desirable practice followed by few other libraries. Tilly explained that the volume was intended to produce 'a body of generally accepted material which can be used for reference'. However, she also admitted that she had 'departed from my brief'. The entries on Sozomeno of Pistoia and on Vespucci were original contributions of great importance, especially the former, since Sozomeno is shown to have been an important pioneer of the new script. Her work on Niccoli's formal and cursive hands was also an original and pathbreaking contribution, especially the identification of his formal hand. The volume is a large folio and the index of manuscripts cited is in two columns and fills four and a half pages. One of Tilly's most spectacular discoveries came too late for the volume, when she later serendipitously found notes in Petrarch's hand in a fragmentary twelfth-century copy of St Ambrose's Letters. This discovery was published appropriately in the memorial exhibition catalogue for Richard Hunt of 1980.[20]

In the 1970s Tilly also published a series of important papers on the origins of Florentine humanist script, on the Florentine book trade, and on the libraries of particular collectors. She also wrote a detailed study of the earliest manuscripts connected with the humanist reform of script

---

[19] A. C. de la Mare, *The Handwriting of Italian Humanists*, Vol. I, fascicule 1, Oxford University Press for Association internationale de bibliophilie (Oxford, 1973).
[20] A. C. de la Mare, '"Sapiens ubique est civis": Petrarch's copy of Ambrose's Letters', *Manuscripts at Oxford* (see above, n. 3), pp. 144–6. The fragments are bound in Oxford, Bodleian Library, MSS Canon. Pat. Lat. 210, 229. See also 'Palaeographer's odyssey' (see above, n. 6), pp. 99–100.

and its three foundational figures, Coluccio Salutati, Niccolò Niccoli, and Poggio.[21] This was an area of study which had been handled already by Berthold Ullman in various articles, in his book of 1960 on humanistic script, and in his monograph on Coluccio Salutati of 1963. In these papers as in her book, she was building on his and other scholars' work, but also providing a new synthesis and adding much newly identified material.[22] Ullman, a student of the great palaeographer Ludwig Traube, had come to palaeography from his interests in the transmission of classical texts and in humanist culture, and he had relied primarily on the evidence of colophons and documented manuscripts, as opposed to the examination of the style of the script itself and the identification of unsigned manuscripts. In relation to Tilly's own broader interest in the actual physical production of manuscripts under the direction of the *cartolaii*, she discovered and published a document of great significance, the will in which the contents of a *cartolaio*'s shop were listed in fascinating detail.[23] She also discussed the libraries of two very important collectors and patrons, Francesco Sassetti and Cardinal Giovanni d'Aragona.[24] For both she contributed lists of manuscripts, many identified for the first time. The article on Cardinal Giovanni is typical in the richness of its footnotes, which are a mine of information not just on the patron but on the scribes for each of whom she provides long lists of manuscripts. She

[21] A. C. de la Mare, 'Humanist script: the first ten years', in F. Krafft and D. Wuttke (eds.), *Das Verhältnis der Humanisten zum Buch* (Deutsche Forschungsgemeinschaft, Kommission für Humanismusforschung, Mitteilung 4) (Boppard, 1977), pp. 89–110.

[22] B. L. Ullman, *The origin and development of humanistic script* (Rome, 1960). B. L. Ullman, *The humanism of Coluccio Salutati* (Padua, 1963). Other important scholars on whose work Tilly built include Augusto Campana, Giuseppe Billanovich, Armando Petrucci, Elisabeth Pellegrin, and Vittore Branca.

[23] A. C. de la Mare, 'The shop of a Florentine "cartolaio" in 1426', in B. Maracchi Biagiarelli and D. Rhodes (eds.), *Studi offerti a Roberto Ridolfi*, (Biblioteca di bibliografia italiana, LXXI) (Florence, 1973), pp. 237–48. See also A. M. Brown and A. C. de la Mare, 'Bartolomeo Scala's dealings with booksellers, scribes and illuminators 1459–63', *Journal of the Warburg and Courtauld Institutes*, 39 (1976), 237–45.

[24] A. C. de la Mare, 'The library of Francesco Sassetti (1421–90)', in C. Clough (ed.), *Cultural Aspects of the Italian Renaissance. Essays in honour of P. O. Kristeller* (Manchester, 1976), pp. 160–201. A. C. de la Mare, 'The Florentine Scribes of Cardinal Giovanni of Aragon', in C. Questa and R. Raffaelli (eds.), *Il Libro e il Testo* (Atti del Convegno Internazionale, Urbino, 20–23 settembre 1982) (Urbino, 1984), pp. 245–93. Tilly mentions the remarkable *Memoriale* of 1482 from the Cardinal listing the six principal scribes working for him in Florence. This together with two other letters written by the Cardinal to Antonio Sinibaldi was sold at Christie's in 1997. At the instance of Laura Nuvoloni and Christopher de Hamel they were bought by a group of Tilly's friends and given in her honour to the Bodleian Library, and are now Ms. Ital. d.31.

had identified the manuscripts in libraries all over Europe and in America, and careful first-hand examination of the originals showed that the cardinal's hat was sometimes overpainted with the crown of the King Ferdinand I of Naples, his father. In these and many of her other publications she also makes important observations on the illumination, for example on the origin and development of white-vine initials and borders, and the use of title pages.

In 1971 Tilly had written an article for a multi-author volume on Livy, which signalled another and increasingly important direction in her scholarship.[25] The later copies of classical texts had tended to be ignored by editors, except in the case of a few of the spectacular discoveries of the humanists. These later manuscripts are often lumped together in editions under the title *dett.* (the inferior manuscripts, *deteriores*). New interest in reception theory meant that greater attention was now being paid to the question of readership and the later annotation of texts. Tilly's paper listed known Florentine sets of Livy, dated them, identified their scribes and patrons, and in many cases reunited copies of the various Decades, which had got separated by time.

Other authors and texts in whose transmission she became especially interested were Eusebius's *Chronicon*, Horace, Petronius, Seneca, and Aulus Gellius. When a multi-author volume devoted to the problems of the textual transmission of Latin authors, appeared in 1983, Tilly's constant help and advice was acknowledged in the Preface.[26] A major contributor to the volume was Michael Reeve, now Kennedy Professor of Latin at Cambridge University. He and Tilly continued a fruitful interchange of mutual benefit to them both. These years were notable for an increasing interdisciplinary interest in the history of the book. Tilly was a founder member and zealous supporter of the Oxford Seminar in the History of the Book to 1500, which met quarterly and organised biennial conferences from 1985 to 2002 under the leadership of Linda Brownrigg

[25] A. C. de la Mare, 'Florentine manuscripts of Livy in the fifteenth century', in T. A. Dorey (ed.), *Livy* (London, 1971), pp. 177–99.
[26] L. D. Reynolds (ed.), *Texts and Transmission. A Survey of the Latin Classics* (Oxford, 1982). The contributors are listed as: P. K. Marshall, M. D. Reeve, L. D. Reynolds, R. H. Rouse, R. J. Tarant, M. Winterbottom and others. The volume was planned as an eightieth birthday tribute to Roger Mynors. Tilly had already collaborated with Richard Rouse on two publications of 1976 and 1977 on texts by Aulus Gellius and Seneca respectively. Another classical philologist who sought Tilly's advice on Renaissance manuscripts of classical texts is Stephen Oakley, Professor of Latin at Reading University.

and Margaret Smith.[27] The seminar held a two-day 'Tillyfest' in her honor in 1997, and a photograph shows her on the steps of the Law School in Oxford surrounded by a multitude of smiling colleagues.

In the early 1980s Professor Annarosa Garzelli had invited Tilly to contribute an account of Florentine scribes in the lengthy two-volume work on Florentine renaissance illuminated manuscripts she was preparing. The results of their collaboration appeared in 1985.[28] Professor Garzelli wrote a comprehensive and authoritative account of the illuminators active in Florence from 1440 to 1525 in Part 1 of the book, which is in Italian. Tilly wrote on the scribes in Part II, which is in English. Her text consists of a narrative account of the development of humanist script in this period, followed by lists of scribes with biographical information and *oeuvre* lists. In effect she was able to publish a large part of her thesis, though rewritten and greatly enlarged. Tilly continued to annotate her copy of this book to the end of her life, and so the plan by Professor Vincenzo Fera at the University of Messina to produce an Italian version of Tilly's text with these *addenda* incorporated and with a proper index is extremely welcome. Xavier van Binnebeke has been editing the revised text for the press.

In 1987 Tilly was elected a Fellow of the British Academy. She gave the E. A. Lowe Lectures in Palaeography at Corpus Christi College, Oxford in the same year. In 1990 she was elected a Fellow of the London Society of Antiquaries. By this point she had achieved an established international reputation leading to invitations to teach and to give papers at conferences in Europe and America. She had been invited to teach a course at Oxford University in Latin palaeography from 1100 to 1500 already in 1968–9. In 1974 she was a visiting lecturer in a Palaeography Summer Seminar at the Catholic University in Washington DC.[29] She later gave courses on Italian Humanistic Manuscripts at the Rare Book School in New York in 1986, 1987, and 1991. She was a Visiting Research Fellow at the J. Paul Getty Museum, Malibu, in 1992. She was elected a member of the Comité international de paléographie latine in 1986 and attended their conferences. She was also a visiting professor at the Istituto

---

[27] An important paper on Vespasiano given at the conference held in Leiden in 1993 was published in 1996. A. C. de la Mare, 'Vespasiano da Bisticci as Producer of Classical Manuscripts in Fifteenth-century Florence', in C. A. Chavannes Mazel, and M. M. Smith (eds.), *Medieval Manuscripts of the Latin Classics: Production and Use* (Los Altos Hills, 1996), pp. 166–207.

[28] A. Garzelli and A. C. de la Mare, *Miniatura fiorentina del rinascimento 1440–1525: un primo censimento* (Inventari e cataloghi toscani, 18, 19), 2 vols. (Florence, 1985).

[29] I am not sure if this was her first visit to the United States or not.

di Filologia Classica, University of Padua, 1987, at the University of Messina in 1991 and 1993 at the invitation of Vincenzo Fera, at the Scuola di Paleografia Musicale, Cremona (University of Pavia) in 1992, at the Scuola Normale in Pisa in 1998 and 1999, and at the University of Rome also in 1998 and 1999.[30]

In 1989 Tilly was invited to occupy the chair of Palaeography at King's College, London, following the death of Julian Brown.[31] It was a wrench for her to leave the Bodleian after nearly thirty years. Her father had moved to Cumnor outside Oxford where Tilly looked after him and continued to live after his death in 1986. The change meant a full-time commitment to teaching and the preparation of lectures and seminars.[32] As an academic she was much freer to travel, however, and an idea of the extent of the difficulties produced by understaffing and cuts in finance at the Bodleian at this period can be got from a paper she published in 1988.[33] There was also some danger that the chair would disappear in a time of financial cuts, and her friends urged her to accept for the sake of the discipline.

Her university classes were given in the Palaeography Room of the University of London Library in Senate House. This is a specialist library containing a fine open-shelf collection of catalogues, facsimiles and other publications devoted to the medieval and renaissance manuscript book, as well as to Diplomatic and Archives, and it formed a counterpart to the similarly focused open-shelf collections in the Arts End in Duke Humfrey. Tilly was a superb teacher and her enthusiasm and love of the subject together with her sense of humour proved irresistable to her students. Palaeography is not an easy subject to teach, but numbers in her classes increased and she began to have her own graduate students.[34]

---

[30] The latest *curriculum vitae* which I have had access to is dated 2000, and lists lectures given at Cesena, Cortona, Erice, Florence, Leiden, Madrid, Mainz, Milan, Montepulciano, Munich, Paris (École des Hautes Études), Pistoia, San Gimignano, Trieste, Urbino, Venice, and Verona in addition to those already mentioned.

[31] A typescript of her unpublished inaugural lecture, which was given on 18 June 1990 and entitled 'Close encounters of a manuscript kind', is among her papers.

[32] Her annual reports to the Wolfson Foundation, which supported her Chair, amply demonstrate how conscientious she was in performing her duties.

[33] A. C. de la Mare, 'Education, formation and conditions of work of manuscript librarians in England', *Bollettino dell'Istituto Centrale per la Patologia del Libro*, 42 (1988), 213–21.

[34] Laura Nuvoloni is now working in the Department of Manuscripts, the British Library. Cristina Dondi's London University doctoral dissertation has been published, *The Liturgy of the Canons Regular of the Holy Sepulchre of Jerusalem: a Study and a Catalogue of the Manuscript Sources* (Turnhout, 2004).

In the 1990s another major project began to take shape, a proposed book on Bartolomeo Sanvito, in which Tilly would collaborate with Dr Ellen Erdreich, who had completed her Ph.D. at Johns Hopkins University in 1993 on an illuminated manuscript of Petrarch written by Sanvito.[35] Tilly had a three-month fellowship at the Center for Advanced Study in the Visual Arts in 1998 during which she worked intensively with Dr Erdreich on the book, which, however, remained incomplete at her death on 19 December 2001. This project is being brought to fruition through the good offices of Anthony Hobson. Laura Nuvoloni is currently editing and completing her text, Ellen Erdreich will contribute a chapter on Sanvito as illuminator, and Scott Dickerson will compile the bibliography.

Since space does not permit and since Vincenzo Fera has included a fuller bibliography together with a very perceptive eulogy published in 2002, all Tilly's extensive publications cannot be mentioned here.[36] In the 1990s she continued to work in the various directions listed above. She had already extended her published studies of humanistic script into other regions of Italy, for example to Lombardy, with a paper of 1983 on Milanese humanistic script.[37] This was followed in 1985 by a paper on humanist script in the Veneto.[38] In 1995 she collaborated with other authors on a volume on the library formed by Malatesta Novello at Cesena, with its series of dated manuscripts written by scribes documented both from payments and in their colophons.[39] Here she was following in the footsteps of one of the great Italian philologists and palaeographers, Augusto Campana. She was also drawn into a number of exhibition catalogues and other publications, which originated in Italy.

---

[35] E. C. Erdreich, *'Qui hos cultus . . . pinxerit?': Illumination associated with Bartolomeo Sanvito (c.1435–c.1512)*, Ph.D. dissertation, Johns Hopkins University, Baltimore, 1993. The Petrarch is in the Walters Art Museum, Baltimore, W. 755.

[36] V. Fera, 'La trama interrotta. Per Albinia C. de la Mare', *Studi medievali e umanistici*, 1 (2003), 223–7. Other tributes are by D. E. Rhodes, 'Albinia de la Mare, maestra dei manoscritti. *In memoriam*', *La Bibliofilia*, 104/2 (2002), 209–18 (also includes a bibliography) and by M. Feo, *Il Ponte*, 58.1 (2002), 151–2. For a shorter notice see *Bodleian Library Record*, 17 (2002), 279. Obituaries appeared in *The Times*, 1 Jan. 2002 (by Christopher de Hamel), and *The Independent*, 3 Jan. 2002 (by Nicolas Barker).

[37] A. C. de la Mare, 'Script and manuscripts in Milan under the Sforza', in *Milano nell'età di Lodovico il Moro (Atti del Convegno internazionale, 1983)* (Milan, 1983), pp. 398–408.

[38] A. C. de la Mare, C. Griggio, 'Il copista Michele Salvatico collaboratore di Francesco Barbaro e Guarnerio d'Artegna', *Lettere italiane*, 37 (1985), 351–4.

[39] A. C. de la Mare, in *Libraria Domini. I manoscritti della Biblioteca Malatestiana: testi e decorazioni*, a cura di F. Lollini, P. Lucchi (Bologna, 1995), pp. 35–93.

For example she wrote entries on humanistic manuscripts in the
Biblioteca Classense Ravenna, in the series *Grandi Biblioteche d'Italia*.[40]
She contributed a paper setting out the chronology of Bartolomeo
Sanvito's manuscripts to the exhibition catalogue of a magnificent showing of Paduan illumination at Padua in 1999.[41] By this time the total of
manuscripts wholly or in part written by Sanvito known to her had risen
to one hundred and sixteen, and of those rubricated but not written by
him to sixty-four. It is now generally accepted that he was also active as
an illuminator, though the extent of his involvement remains under discussion. Tilly's last published article was also concerned with Sanvito. She
had observed that the manuscripts of Horace written by Sanvito form a
family. She concluded that he kept by him an exemplar, which he updated
with textual revisions and glosses. These were then incorporated in later
copies he made of the text. This shows that Sanvito was not only a scribe
but also a humanist who was actively involved in the editing and annotation of the manuscripts he copied. On the last occasion I saw her, in the
Radcliffe Infirmary in Oxford, she asked me to check the text of the
Horace written by Sanvito and now in the New York Public Library, for
a particular interpolation in the text. The resulting article, on which she
continued to work to the end, appeared posthumously in 2002.[42]

Ludwig Traube called his discipline a 'Hilfswissenschaft'. Tilly de la
Mare took the scholarly duty of helping others very seriously indeed.
Whilst she was at the Bodleian it was an established part of her duties and
as she writes in her paper on manuscript librarians in England: 'one can
sometimes spend days or even weeks on some queries'. The thoroughness
implied in the 'weeks' was of course one of the outstanding qualities of

[40] Entries by A. C. de la Mare in A. Dillon Bussi and C. Giuliani (eds.), *La Biblioteca Classense di Ravenna* (*Grandi Biblioteche d'Italia*) (Fiesole, 1996), pp. 66–7, 70, 88, 94, 110–11, 152.

[41] A. C. de la Mare, 'Bartolomeo Sanvito da Padova, copista e miniatore', in G. Baldassin Molli, G. Mariani Canova, *et al.* (eds.), exhibition catalogue, *La Miniatura a Padova dal medioevo al set-tecento* (Modena, 1999), pp. 495–511. While lecturing on Sanvito at the Scuola Normale at Pisa in 1998 she discovered an important early manuscript of Sanvito. It was made for John Tiptoft, Earl of Worcester. It thus combines her interest in Sanvito with her interest in early humanism in England. Tilly's entry for the manuscript is no. 97 in the catalogue.

[42] A. C. de la Mare, 'Marginalia and glosses in the Manuscripts of Bartolomeo Sanvito of Padua', in V. Fera, G. Ferraù and S. Rizzo (eds.), *Talking to the Text: Marginalia from Papyri to Print (Proceedings of a Conference held at Erice, 26 September–3 October 1998 as the 12th Course of International School for the Study of Written Records)* (Messina, 2002), pp. 459–555. An arti-cle in press 'The manuscripts of Braccio Martelli' will appear in G. Guest and S. L'Engle (eds.), *Illuminations: Medieval and Renaissance Studies for Jonathan J. G. Alexander*, to be published by Harvey Miller, Brepols.

her scholarship. It was also a duty, perhaps even a moral duty in her terms, to be thorough. So she continued with a demanding international correspondence after she had left Bodley, and even after she retired from her chair in 1997. The OBE which she was awarded in 1993 for 'Services to the study of Renaissance manuscripts' recognised not only her scholarship but also her sense of scholarly and civic obligation.[43] In summarising her achievement it might be said that, like Ciriaco d'Ancona the pioneer fifteenth-century collector of classical inscriptions, her aim was 'to awaken the dead'. The discovery of a map of Florence in which Vespasiano's house and garden were marked is a particularly vivid example of her success in bringing the past to life.[44] Her life's work went further than identifying and chronicling the careers of a multitude of scribes active in the Renaissance, enormous achievement though that was in itself. As Vincenzo Fera has observed, Tilly was able to demonstrate the central role of script and scribes in Renaissance culture. By so doing she showed that palaeography is more than just an aid to study, a 'Hilfswissenschaft'. It is a vital 'Wissenschaft' in its own right for a fuller understanding of the past.

In concluding this memoir I would like to stress what was perhaps the outstanding characteristic of this charismatic scholar, her *joie de vivre*. Those who knew her in Oxford in the 1960s recall her energetic Country Dancing, her ability to sing the lyrics of Gilbert and Sullivan, and her outstanding skill as a cook. As a girl she had been a keen horsewoman. She loved classical music and was an early devotee of the operas of Monteverdi. Her laughter was infectious and she gave a lift to any gathering of friends, whether at informal parties or learned conferences. She was a great traveller and eagerly accepted an invitation from Margaret Manion to visit Australia in 1999. A photo taken then shows her with Janet Backhouse and Lucy Freeman Sandler, all three wreathed in smiles and very evidently enjoying themselves. Those who crowded the Service of Thanksgiving for the Life of Professor Albinia Catherine de la Mare held in the Chapel of King's College, London, on 28 May 2002, and the

---

[43] Tilly was a member of the volunteer organisation for the protection of the citizenry in emergencies known as Civil Defence.
[44] The map is in a Ptolemy, Paris, Bibliothèque nationale de France, latin 4802. 'A palaeographer's odyssey' (see above, n. 6), p. 94, pl. 33.

many who could not be there on that day all mourned a greatly loved person of special importance in their lives.[45]

JONATHAN J. G. ALEXANDER

Fellow of the Academy

Note. Linda Brownrigg, Giles de la Mare, Martin Kauffmann, Laura Nuvoloni, Michael Reeve and Richard Rouse have kindly read this text and made numerous valuable additions, corrections and improvements, for which I am most grateful.

[45] The addresses given on that occasion showed the same deep affection. The speakers were Martin Kauffmann, Bodleian Library, Nicholas Mann, Warburg Institute, Jonathan Alexander, Laura Nuvoloni and David Ganz, Professor of Palaeography, King's College London. The address by her brother, the Reverend Benedick de la Mare, given at her funeral at St Michael and All Angels, Cumnor, where she is buried, stressed the more personal aspects of Tilly's life in a moving and eloquent way. He kindly provided me with a typescript of his text. Though I have concentrated here on her achievement as a scholar, her life was one, emphatically not two.

JOHN FLEMMING

John Stanton Flemming
1941–2003

1. The early years

JOHN FLEMMING WAS A FIRST-CLASS ECONOMIST in the field of macro-economics and fiscal policy. But his greatest contributions were, rather, in his general services to the profession and to British public life. He was public-spirited, upright and high-principled, deeply intelligent and strictly logical, quiet and reserved, kindly with a gentle humour, inter-ested in everyone and everything, widely read and a great listener. As such he made the perfect chairman, or committee member. Almost everyone enjoyed working with, or for, him; he had a wide and devoted circle of friends. Everyone sought to benefit from his advice and wisdom, and he gave that carefully and unstintingly.

As his surname suggests, the family may have emigrated from Flanders in the seventeenth century. By the mid-nineteenth century the Flemmings were established in North London as partners in a saddlery firm. John's grandfather, Percy, was an outstanding ophthalmologist and eye surgeon. In 1916 his son Gilbert joined up, as a volunteer, straight from Rugby School. After the war he went up to Trinity College, Oxford, and then entered the Civil Service in the Ministry of Education. He was living in the Trinity College Mission in Stratford, E15 when he married Virginia Coit. They set up home in a house nearby.

Gilbert and Virginia had four children, Nicholas (1936), Sara (1938), and twins John and Miranda born on 6 February 1941. When war came, they were evacuated to grandfather Percy Flemming's house in Pangbourne, Berkshire. It was here that John and Mandy were born, though the actual physical delivery was in a hospital in nearby Reading.

Proceedings of the British Academy, **138**, 71–95. © The British Academy 2006.

Gilbert was transferred during the war to the Cabinet Office, clearly a sign that his ability was recognised. At the end of the war he bought a sizeable house on Chiswick Mall, with a large garden facing the Thames, an astute purchase maintained for the next twenty-five years. Gilbert later returned to the Ministry of Education, and ultimately became Permanent Secretary. A KCB followed in 1953.

Having become a life-long socialist in the First World War, and a senior official at the Ministry of Education, Gilbert faced the typical British dilemma of what education to give his children. John and Mandy were sent for their first two years to the local primary school. But the results were not acceptable. John was then sent to Westminster Under School and on to Rugby. Initially John was not seen as particularly clever or intellectual. Westminster Under School has had good, and less good, academic spells. Perhaps John was there in one of the latter periods. Anyhow, he did *not* do notably well in his (Common) Entrance exam and entered Rugby in one of the lower forms. It was still the case then that public-school masters tended to direct the brighter boys into Classics and the less bright into science (including maths). Anyhow John was put in the scientific stream.

After starting in one of the lower forms, John worked his way up, gaining several distinctions along the way. Even so, he is not remembered as having been outstanding academically; bright, mature, very well read, widely knowledgeable about current affairs, but not academic as such.

The jump from being perceived as a bright, intelligent, mature, but *not academic*, boy in the mid-1950s to writing articles with a considerable mathematical content in some of the best economic journals in the mid-1960s is considerable. He must have had, and absorbed, good training in maths at Rugby. John naturally went on to Trinity College, Oxford, following family tradition, but he did not obtain a scholarship on entry into Trinity. Since he put Trinity down as his sole choice of college, Trinity might have felt that a scholarship would have been wasted on him.

Trinity is a small college. It did not have a reputation as one of the more academic colleges, being instead 'well-rounded'. Flemming did not, however, take advantage of the freer ways of Oxford undergraduate life to relax on his studies. Combining the maths he learnt at Rugby, his pervasive interest in current affairs and a willingness to work steadily and methodically, he first entered the academic scene by doing outstandingly well in the Prelims exams. This feat, and his continuing good performance at College Collections, marked him out as a potential first. He was clearly the best PPE student at Trinity, and most likely to get a first. Consequently his tutors would have paid more attention to him, notably J. F. Wright, the Trinity economist, with whom he subsequently wrote a joint paper. John confirmed the early promise he had shown in Prelims, and duly got his first.

Even more important, it was here that he met his wife, Jean (*née* Briggs). They met at a youth club where Jean came to demonstrate Scottish dancing, at the start of John's second year. They became inseparable, and were engaged in 1962. Despite his parents' concern at his youth, they married in 1963.

It was the best choice in his whole life. Jean possessed qualities of an extrovert gaiety for life, hospitality and social activities, that complemented her more austere and reserved husband. They had a happy and devoted family life, with four children, Rebecca (1966), Edward (1968), Thomas (1970) and William (1973). Apart from his year on a Harkness Fellowship (1968–9), at Harvard, the family never left Oxford.

2. Becoming a leading macro-economist

After he obtained his first, Wright recommended that John Flemming apply to Nuffield College. This he did with alacrity, despite having already passed the Civil Service exam and had a City job offer. He was elected to a Studentship from 1 October 1962, alongside, as fellow economic students, Martin Feldstein, John Helliwell, S. R. Merrett, Roger Van Noorden and J. S. Wabe, a select group. John did joint work with Van Noorden for a few years, became life-long friends with both the Feldsteins and the Helliwells, and collaborated with Feldstein all his life.

The economists at Nuffield included Philip Andrews, Hugh Clegg, Ian Little, David Munby and Terence Gorman. There was no formal supervision or training programme. John looked mainly to Ian Little for guidance. John Hicks also kept an eye on him. There were a number of Nuffield Student/Fellow seminars; John also attended the Oxford cost-benefit seminar, attended by such as David Henderson, Christopher Foster and Wright. The only formal course was by Gorman on econometrics. Gorman taught this extempore. Most, except Feldstein, found Gorman's exposition impenetrable, which may help to explain Flemming's subsequent reluctance to get involved in empirical work.

After just one year, he was elected to a teaching fellowship by Oriel College. It was a remarkably early appointment. He succeeded Eric

Hargreaves, in post from 1924 till 1963. Several of Flemming's better students during those years still remember the intellectual challenge of his tutorials, plus his sartorial inertia; he never changed out of the same brown jacket.

It was still then common in Oxford and Cambridge for the best young graduates to be appointed directly to the Faculty without having to progress through a graduate degree (Ph.D. or M.Phil.). Once so appointed, there was no further incentive to seek such a graduate degree; and John did not. Indeed, appointment to a Faculty position was seen as more prestigious than slogging through a US-style Ph.D.

Then during 1965, he was elected, jointly with Feldstein, to an Official Fellowship at Nuffield. There was supposed to be only one such economist appointment, but not only were they already working closely together, but also they were so young that, on the regular age/wage formula, they did not represent a financial burden.

His main companion, friend and professional colleague, with whom he was to remain close all his life, was Martin (Marty) Feldstein. They started joint work together soon after meeting, and published a joint paper (John's first publication) on 'The problem of time-stream evaluation: present value versus internal rate of return rules'.[1] Of the six papers Flemming published before 1972, four were joint with Feldstein, and several later sole-authored papers, notably his *Journal of Public Economics* papers (1976, 1977, 1978), drew on earlier work by, and/or discussions with, Feldstein.

His first solo article was on 'The utility of wealth and the utility of windfalls', in the *Review of Economic Studies*, 1969 (in a themed issue containing articles by many famous economists). This article showed many of John's traits. It was short and tightly argued. He used mathematical modelling, and liked diagrammatic exposition. The article develops one of his major research themes, that there may be discontinuities in otherwise continuous functions, with potentially important consequences. He took the same line, on the effect of imperfections in the capital market, in his next sole paper, on 'The consumption function when capital markets are imperfect'.

A second major research theme was the importance of expectations for macro-economic developments. He combined both themes, of jumps

---

[1] A longer version of this memoir is to be privately published by a publisher called Wilton 65. I hope that it will be forthcoming towards the end of 2006. It will contain a full, academic bibliography of his publications.

and expectations, in his justly applauded chapter 7 on 'The behaviour of price level and inflation expectations' in his book on *Inflation* (Oxford, 1976), and revisited the subject on several occasions. He was, however, dismissive of stronger versions of rational expectations, while supporting the weaker model-consistent expectations approach.

In the early 1970s John did several joint papers, including a technical, and mathematical paper with his previous tutor Wright. There was a more important final joint paper with Feldstein on 'Tax policy, corporate saving and investment behaviour in Britain'. This was a major exercise to explore, using a generalised neo-classical investment function, the effects on investment of accelerated depreciation allowances and various different forms of corporate tax. The empirical results suggested (almost implausibly) large effects. The paper was unusual for John in that it was not only quite lengthy, but also empirical and used econometric techniques. John made sparing use of empirical, or historical, evidence, and clearly preferred to avoid econometrics. This latter paper was largely completed while on a Harkness Fellowship at Harvard in 1968–9, where he worked again with Feldstein (who had left Nuffield in 1967); this was his, and his family's, only extended absence from Oxford from 1959 till his death in 2003.

The third of these joint works was his pamphlet with Ian Little, on 'Why we need a wealth tax'. The pamphlet was cogently argued, and included a number of themes that were to recur in his work, such as the disadvantages of taxes on income from capital and on transactions, and on the need for indexation during inflationary periods. They proposed that direct taxation should, ideally, be limited to two prongs, a tax on earned income combined with a tax on wealth, both appropriately indexed against inflation.

Around the same period, 1975–8, he was one of the more active and influential members, along with John Kay and Mervyn King, of the Meade Committee on 'The structure and reform of direct taxation'. This had been set up by the Institute for Fiscal Studies (IFS), and reported in 1978. Its main recommendation was to advocate the adoption of a 'new Beveridge scheme' which could help to mitigate the poverty trap with its excessively high marginal rates of implied tax. The committee felt that the British system of direct taxation was an unsystematic mixture of elements of tax on income and elements of tax on consumption expenditure, but were undecided whether to move towards a (more comprehensive) income or expenditure basis. They also reviewed potential reforms to corporation tax and taxes on capital.

After his joint work with Little, the bulk of his work became sole-authored. The decade of the 1970s was his most productive and successful as a pure academic, wherein he wrote some fifteen sole-authored articles in major journals and, of course, his one book on *Inflation*.

It would be otiose to go through these articles in any great detail. Amongst his continuing interests were 'the theory of the valuation and allocation of time', a topic which came back in another guise in his later work on environmental pollution. He did several general macro-economic studies, especially two contributions in *Oxford Economic Papers* (*OEP*). The first (*OEP*, 1973) examined how the consumption function might shift when persons were liquidity constrained and unable to borrow at reasonable rates because of imperfect capital markets. The second (1974) was a critique of A. Leijonhufvud's handling of wealth effects in his book *On Keynesian Economics and the Economics of Keynes*. John objected not only to the excessive aggregation (e.g. of real capital and bonds), but also to the argumentation that Leijonhufvud had adopted on the wealth effect of interest changes on consumption.

Another related field was the question of how, and why, real wages failed to adjust so as to eliminate unemployment. One of the concerns around then (1973–5) was how to bring about a reduction in real wages when money wages were indexed. He worked on that during his year on secondment in the Bank. Part of this work became public in his paper on 'Budgetary policy under indexation' (1975). Flemming proposed relating indexation to the GDP deflator rather than to the Consumer Price Index (CPI), and handling excessive real wages either by indirect tax cuts or by a direct payroll subsidy. He returned to this latter theme on several later occasions; it was probably the most heterodox measure he ever advocated.

John's other major field of interest, besides macro-policies, was in fiscal theory and policy. Following his wealth tax joint work, he submitted a model on the generation of inequalities in wealth, as a memorandum to the Royal Commission on Income and Wealth (1976), and followed that up with a paper in *Economica* (1979), modelling: 'The effects of earning inequality, imperfect capital markets and dynastic altruism on the distribution of wealth in life cycle models.'

Perhaps his most purely theoretical paper in the field was the first of his three consecutive papers in the *Journal of Public Economics* (1976, 1977, 1978). This discussed the advantages of different combinations of fiscal instruments, e.g. corporation tax, depreciation allowances and capital gains tax, for taxing away 'pure profits' with minimum distortion.

Given his interests in the issue of wage adjustment to reduce unemployment and in fiscal theory, it was always likely that he would combine the two; he did so in his 1978 paper on 'Aspects of optimal unemployment insurance'. This is, to my mind, one of his best papers. He argues that 'current levels of replacement (fifty to eighty per cent in the US and Western Europe) may rely on their rationalization on capital markets' imperfections'; if so, it might make sense to modify the benefit structure 'to introduce a loan element' with repayments related to subsequent earnings.

His middle paper in this series, 1977, is entitled 'Optimal payroll taxes and social security funding'. This title is somewhat misleading, since it is essentially about intergenerational taxation and redistribution via pensions, in an overlapping generations model. The paper emphasises the transitional problems of introducing a new tax with long-run beneficial effects, and the importance of expectations and announcement effects in such cases.

John was not essentially a monetary economist, though he attended Money Study Group conferences. It was, therefore, slightly surprising that he was to write his one book on *Inflation*, and, indeed, in that to espouse an eclectic form of monetarism, with sustained monetary expansion being a necessary and sufficient cause of inflation. Moreover, the book's style, literary and descriptive, rather than formal, mathematical and theoretical, is a-typical. Despite being 'written while I travelled on the train between my home in Oxford and a temporary job in the Bank of England' (Preface), it shows no signs of being influenced by his sojourn in the Bank. Instead his acknowledgements are mainly to his Oxford colleagues. But then the Bank had asked John to focus on issues relating to company behaviour rather than on monetary issues.

One advantage for John in adopting a broad monetarist approach to inflation was that it allowed him to criticise cost-push, especially trade union led cost-push, theories. Worker intransigence might push up the natural rate of unemployment, but could not lead to accelerating inflation unless the monetary authorities connived at that. He revisited this theme several times. Although he saw inflation as a monetary phenomenon, he was far from being an American-style neo-liberal monetarist. As is clear from his fiscal papers, he believed that government could, and should, intervene to improve economic outcomes by appropriate adjustments to taxes (and/or subsidies). On the other hand, he was not in favour of direct controls and constraints, for example over prices and wages. As was consistent with his usual good sense and balance, he mostly took middle-of-the-road, moderate positions on the ideological economic issues of the day.

He was therefore a natural to be one of the founder members of the Clare Group. This began in 1977, out of concern that political economy in Britain was becoming polarised between a left-wing, often interventionist Labour government and a right-wing, neo-liberal and monetarist Conservative opposition. The idea was to show that there remained a sensible, Keynesian middle ground. The key members were, perhaps, Robin Matthews, Master of Clare College, Cambridge (from whence the group's title came), Brian Reddaway and Dick Sargent (Economic Adviser to the Midland Bank, which explains where its papers were initially published). Other initial members, besides these and John, were Charles Feinstein, John Kay, Mervyn King (now Governor of the Bank of England), Peter Oppenheimer, Michael Posner, Alan Prest and Aubrey Silberston.

John wrote the third Clare Group paper, jointly with Tony Atkinson, who had joined subsequently, on 'Unemployment, social security and incentives'. This, like other Clare Group papers, was aimed at a wider range of informed and professional (Civil Service and City) readers than just professional economists. John found the policy positions, and the other members, of the Clare Group to his taste. He was a regular attender and also became chairman in its latter years, 1995–2003. The Group was eventually wound up in 2003, because it had served its purpose (no one any longer much disagreed with its main positions), and its founders had grown old. In the meantime, John contributed three more Clare Group papers, with Oppenheimer in 1996, on 'Are Government spending and taxes too high or too low?'; with Posner and Sargent in 1999 on 'Global stability: Risks and remedies'; and with Mike Artis, Matthews and Martin Weale in 2000 on 'Christopher Dow on Major Recessions'. By then not only had the *Midland Bank Review* been closed down, but the Midland Bank itself has been taken over by HSBC. So the Clare Group shifted its publication outlet to the National Institute of Economic and Social Research (NIESR) *Economic Review* (*NIER*).

His Clare Group membership was not the only indication that Flemming's status as one of Britain's best macro-economists was becoming recognised. At the remarkably young age of 34, he was asked in 1975 to take over from Reddaway and Champernowne as Managing Editor of the *Economic Journal*. With the *EJ* being generally seen as the leading British Journal (though probably behind the *Review of Economic Studies* in terms of technical merit), this was indeed a prestigious, though onerous, appointment (a role reviewed in Section 6 below).

Moreover, in the summer of 1979 it was suggested that he should apply for the Drummond Chair at Oxford, the most prestigious position in Economics there, to succeed Joe Stiglitz. Simultaneously, as will be shown in the next section, he was being pursued by the Governor, Gordon Richardson, and other senior economists there to return to the Bank as Senior Economist. He decided in September 1979 to take up the latter offer. It was a crucial decision since it shifted John from a pure academic track to a path as economist/administrator.

There were several reasons for this decision. John was irritated by the slow tempo of the professorial appointment board, who decided not to meet before the beginning of the Michaelmas Term. Moreover, as he had shown as early as his schooldays, John was fascinated by politico-economic processes, and keen to participate in policy issues, with the aim of improving general welfare. He wanted to play a role on a wider stage.

John rejoined the Bank, this time as a 'permanent' Bank official in January 1980.

3. At the Bank of England

John first joined the Bank of England on a temporary, one-year, second-ment at the start of 1975. In 1972 John and I had attended a Money Study Group meeting and the possibility of his coming to the Bank was raised; the Bank had offered such temporary positions to promising young macro/monetary economists for two decades by then. Lunch with the senior economist in the Economic Intelligence Department (EID), Leslie Dicks-Mireaux, was arranged; and both sides liked the idea. John, however, was Nuffield's joint Investment Bursar, with Uwe Kitzinger, who had gone to join Christopher Soames's cabinet in Brussels. By 1974, however, Kitzinger returned, and John could come to the Bank.

The plan was for him to work, in the Economic Section of EID, on the determinants of fixed investment and stockbuilding, and the links between financial markets and the real sector of the economy. At that time however, inflation in Britain had risen to its highest level (during peace time) of over twenty-five per cent. Its effects in distorting contracts and nominally fixed tax rates were becoming acute. So he began by attending an Institute for Fiscal Studies (IFS) conference on Indexing for Inflation, which included his paper on 'Budgetary policy under indexation'.

The same issues were also being considered within Whitehall. The Treasury was reviewing capital gains tax reform, and invited the Bank to comment. John became much involved. He also submitted a paper to a further IFS conference (1975), on 'Inflation, taxation, savings and investment'.

His skills as a macro/fiscal economist were much in demand, and he impressed top management in the Bank with his ability, common sense, broad wisdom and capacity to fit into the Bank's structure. As early as July 1975, Christopher Dow, chief economist and Executive Director, minuted Dicks-Mireaux, 'We spoke about trying to persuade Flemming to stay about which as you know the Governor [Gordon Richardson] has been very keen.'

John, however, felt that he should return to his academic career, but he agreed to continue on a one-day-a-week basis. The idea was that he would oversee research on company sector issues, particularly an exercise on company investment and profitability. This resulted in two papers in the *Bank of England Quarterly Bulletin*. John then became Managing Editor of the *Economic Journal*, and there were additional commitments in Oxford. So he stopped coming to the Bank in 1976, but it was indicated to him that he could return as a senior (Chief) economist, whenever he wanted.

He re-entered the Bank on 2 January 1980, but this time as one of the permanent staff. He entered with the rank of Adviser, but shortly was promoted to Chief Adviser. He became the Head of the Economics Division,[2] working to, and with, the Chief Economist of the Bank, Christopher Dow, one of the four Executive Directors of the Bank.

A crucial element in the work of the Economics Division was the forecasting round. Earlier in the 1970s the Bank had bought in an off-the-shelf medium-sized quarterly Keynesian model from the London Business School. The Economics Division was mainly organised around the model, with a Model Development Group, and a number of sectoral groups. The Treasury had its own model, which was structurally quite similar. All the main policy decisions, in both the fiscal and monetary fields, were taken by the Chancellor during these years. He, and his Treasury advisers, naturally used the Treasury's model. So the Bank's model was not directly used for policy purposes, except on occasions to support the Governor's private arguments with the Chancellor; nor could its forecasts be published, on the grounds that journalists would just focus on

---

[2] The Economic Intelligence Department (EID) had been split into two parts, the Economics Division (ED) and the Financial Statistics Division (FSD) in the meantime.

differences between the two models and use such differences as a stick to beat the government's policies/forecasts.

So the question naturally arose, What use was it? Arguments, which much involved Flemming, circled periodically around issues of either dropping forecasting altogether (but then how do you structure economic analysis?); or relying just on the Treasury's model; keeping the Bank model, but using fewer resources; or trying out different kinds of models; or sticking with the existing, unsatisfactory arrangements. It was frustrating and remained so until 1992–3 when Chancellor Lamont reversed prior constraints, and required the Bank to issue an independent Inflation Forecast in order to bolster the credibility of the newly adopted Inflation Targeting regime.

The early 1980s were a period when economic policy divisions in the country were sharp. The Bank was less plagued by such polarisation, with virtually no supporters either of Chicago-style monetarism or for a reversion to a command economy. Nevertheless, there were divisions, mainly over the question of how hard to press down on inflation through monetary and fiscal policies. The division between the economists dealing with the 'real' economy and those on the monetary side tended to mirror the split between those giving more weight to unemployment and growth and those putting more emphasis on controlling inflation. John was in the middle of the road on this, and always helped to reduce tensions by calm analysis and even-handed argument. Later in the 1980s, when monetary targetry had been abandoned, a quest arose for an alternative monetary anchor, and support for joining the Exchange Rate Mechanism (ERM) of the European Monetary System (EMS) developed in some areas of the Bank. John warmed to the notion of exchange rate targeting as a focus for monetary policy in an economy as open as that of the UK. Yet he continued to set out the pros and cons in a balanced way, and was not among those strongly pushing for ERM membership when this step was taken in 1990.

The core of life as an economist in the Bank lay in the assessment and forecasting of economic data. John was not, however, oriented towards empirical work. He was, on the other hand, much concerned with the proper specification of models. His main contributions on the modelling/forecasting side lay in the introduction of model-consistent (weak-form rational) expectations, wealth effects on consumption, and improved analysis of the transmission effects of monetary policy on expenditures.

Another reason for encouraging Flemming to come into the Bank was that the other senior economists there were not skilled in modern mathematical techniques, and John raised intellectual standards in the Economics Division. He established a Research Steering Committee, and kept a close eye on almost all research projects. All Economics Division members recall the quick, incisive, detailed and thought-provoking manner in which he handled the research exercises. He continued, and encouraged, the *Discussion Paper Series*. Seven such papers had been published before he arrived in 1980, and fifty-four were published by the time he left. He also initiated the *Technical Paper* series, some thirty-eight of which were published by March 1991, including his own with David Barr, on 'Modelling money market interest rates'.

The Economic Division remained under budgetary pressure throughout the 1980s. The Treasury was not persuaded that the Bank needed such a large model; moreover such models were coming under increasing criticism, notably that the so-called 'structural equations' were not based on micro-level optimising behaviour, and hence would be likely to alter in unpredictable ways whenever the policy regime was changed (i.e. the Lucas critique). Partly to make ends meet financially, the Economic Division increasingly resorted to hiring outside academic consultants. The technical and academic qualifications of the young staff economists in the Economic Division were raised by this infusion of outside academics, but it made management of work more difficult, since outsiders could not be directed in quite the same fashion. Moreover, John was perhaps too kind and polite, both as a chairman of committees and in his role as manager, to crack the whip. He was always willing to listen and to appreciate the arguments of others.

John became Dow's successor to the post of Chief Economist when Dow retired in 1984. Life as a top official in the Bank was quite different from being in a Division, however senior. Flemming became one of the small group of senior officials who formed a collegial cabal of advisers to the Governor, with a formal schedule all of their own, centering around a daily morning meeting called 'Books', when the important issues and market reports of the day were raised. At a lower, weekly, frequency there were meetings of the Bank's Court of Directors when the Chief Economist would be called upon to assess current developments. Beyond this, almost all the key briefing, policy decisions, and speech-writing were done in a collegial fashion, with inputs from some or all the Directors, more so from those with more direct involvement in the subject at hand.

A particular responsibility for the Chief Economist lay in preparing the economic assessment in the *Quarterly Bulletin* and in drafting letters which the Governor would send to the Chancellor on fiscal strategy.

John's background made him adept at this, and his counterparts at the Treasury were appreciative of his advice. Drafting the *Bulletin* assessment required a delicate balance between the Bank's view and the (political) imperatives of Whitehall.

All this involved a massive daily flow of paperwork, and a never-ending series of committee meetings. It was time-consuming and left little scope for Flemming to pursue his own research. Moreover as Senior (and then Chief) Economist his published words could be taken as representing the views of the Bank. So any publication needed to be seen in advance, and cleared, by his colleagues, and even shown in some cases to the Treasury, not a procedure encouraging outside publication. So he produced fewer papers while at the Bank than at any other time, until he became ill.

There were, however, a few facets of his own Bank work that did get published, notably his paper on 'Interest rates and macroeconomic policy', which sets out his view of how monetary policy should be run; i.e. that short interest rates would mainly affect nominal incomes via the exchange rate, and should be set so as to lead to sufficient appreciation (depreciation) to stabilise nominal income growth.

He was also one of the Bank's main strategic thinkers on the future direction for monetary policy. Issues where his input was important include: how to take account of the exchange rate; the costs and benefits of gradualism versus a step-change (an issue that resurfaced with a vengeance at the European Bank for Reconstruction and Development); money market operations and the resulting yield curve; fiscal issues, such as dismantling the National Insurance Contribution (NIC) surcharge, optimal debt policy and setting a framework for fiscal policy; and inflation targetry. He did take some strong stands against the prevailing wisdom, for example in favour of taxing commercial banks' 'excess' profits, against policy relaxation after the stock market crash of 1987, and against supposed restraint of monetary growth by 'overfunding'. He was also involved in making sure that deposit insurance in Britain would not be one hundred per cent, but would involve some co-insurance and be capped.

Nevertheless, as a good economist, he liked to weigh up the evidence in a dispassionate fashion, on the one hand and on the other hand. Whilst this provided 'balance', at the same time it led, quite often, to some frustration, both in the Bank and at the Treasury, at being unable to pin down exactly what he himself would propose, unless directly challenged. Whilst his balanced arguments taught his colleagues that issues were hardly ever black or white, such detachment was not always what a Governor, often in the midst of a policy fight, it might be with the Chancellor and/or the Treasury, wanted to hear; impassioned advocacy was not John's forte. The then Governor, Leigh-Pemberton, does not recall any occasions on which John 'crossed swords' with other officials over a policy issue. Perhaps as a result, Flemming sometimes had the impression that he was not taken to some of the key meetings.

Many who knew him felt that his comparative advantage was as an academic economist, not as an official adviser. In some respects it was not a sufficient challenge for his talents. So it was no great surprise when he announced in 1990 that he would be going; he left in February 1991. What was more of a surprise was that he left, not to return to an academic chair, but to become the Chief Economist at the newly established European Bank of Reconstruction and Development (EBRD).

4. At the EBRD

By 1990 Flemming had been in the Bank for ten years. Moreover, it seemed unlikely that he could rise higher there; his colleague, Eddie George, had a stronger relationship with Whitehall.

This was the time when communism had crumbled and the Berlin Wall had just fallen (1989). It was an exciting new beginning in Eastern Europe, and even required the development of an entirely new branch of economics, i.e. transition economics.

Jacques Attali persuaded President Mitterrand to sponsor a European Bank for Reconstruction and Development. It was established in May 1990, with Attali as first President, and sited in London. The EBRD needed a chief economist. Attali sought advice from a friendly economist, Jean-Pierre Fitoussi, who in turn asked Ken Arrow for his views. Arrow recommended Flemming. Fitoussi already knew and appreciated John. Attali was not only brilliantly clever but could also be devastatingly charming. He approached John in the summer of 1990, and even once whisked John off to Russia to see Gorbachev.

In such a new beginning there must have seemed to be great new opportunities to employ good economics to benefit mankind. Having been at the Bank, the EBRD's prospective mix of bankers, bureaucrats, lawyers and economists was familiar, and quite welcome to Flemming. Moreover he could do all this, and maintain his settled home life at Oxford. The combined pull-push factors were decisive. He agreed to join

EBRD as Chief Economist, and left the Bank in February 1991. Since it was a public sector body, he was able to join EBRD immediately.

As Chief Economist, Flemming was a member of the internal Executive Committee, consisting of Attali, the five Vice-Presidents, the Secretary General and General Counsel, together with John. This body took the key strategic decisions, and had collective decision-making responsibilities.

The Economics Department which Flemming took over was small, with never more than about six economists in the department during his stay, notably including his Deputy, Henryk Kierzkowski, a Polish economist, Philippe Aghion, a brilliant young French theoretician, and Steven Fries, an American economist, who arrived later in 1993. This was, perhaps, beneficial since John was not so much a manager, more an intellectual leader. Moreover his vision of the Chief Economist's office was as a small group to provide strategic advice to the President and to the Executive Committee.

Even with such a small group, a great deal was achieved. The earliest economics publications of the EBRD, the *Quarterly Economic Review* and the *Annual Economic Review* were primarily descriptive; Flemming participated, but did not have prime responsibility. By 1993, however, he designed the *Annual Economic Outlook*, which tried to assess progress in all transition economies. He had overall responsibility, and also wrote most of chapter 5, and parts of other chapters. This led directly on to the first *Transition Report*, again an analytical document, which was to become a regular, annual production. The first issue in October 1994 appeared after he had left for Wadham, but several of the chapters, chapter 1, the Summary, jointly with his successor Nick Stern, and chapter 3 on Institutional Strategy are his, and he had set the overall design.

In conjunction with Fitoussi, who had become a consultant, Flemming established an Advisory Committee of high-powered economists (including Arrow, Fitoussi, Lindbeck, Phelps, Solow, Spaventa and von Weizsacker from the West, and Aganbegyan and Kornai from the East). They met once or twice a year. Ed Phelps stayed a year at EBRD; and he and Olivier Blanchard were particularly active in support. With papers coming from this group, and those from the staff, there was sufficient to allow Philippe Aghion to suggest a new specialist journal. John undertook the administration necessary to start the *Economics of Transition*, with Aghion as editor. John also initiated their *Working Paper* series, and contributed a paper on a pet subject, the use of employment subsidies to deal with a temporary loss of competitiveness.

As at the Bank, Flemming did not then write many research articles, but drafted economic sections of speeches for Attali, and gave economic advice. Everyone, including hard-nosed practioners, soon came to recognise his wisdom and sought his advice. His reputation helped to underpin the EBRD's credibility in its early days. As usual, Flemming provided dispassionate, even-handed argument on both sides of the main issues, e.g. on the appropriate speed of reform, big-bang versus gradualism, and on the best approach to privatisation. Perhaps his main contribution was to emphasise the need to think how the EBRD could add value (relative to ordinary private sector capital flows), through its investments. He was keen that the EBRD should normally co-finance.

Flemming's influence on junior colleagues was inspirational, and they achieved much. He had a significant role in setting the EBRD's overall strategy. The mix of professions and nationalities in striving to make a success of a new regime was a heady and invigorating mixture. The first couple of years at the EBRD were enjoyable and successful.

Subsequently both the reputation of the EBRD, and John's work satisfaction, ran into a rough patch, in both cases largely due to difficulties with Attali. Jacques was more comfortable with some of his (French-speaking) colleagues than with those in the line of command, and on occasions would bypass John.

So, when an approach to become the Warden of Wadham came in the autumn of 1992, John was not that sorry to leave. That said, he was so well fitted to become head of an Oxford college that he might well have accepted under any circumstances, though the offer came perhaps a couple of years earlier than would have suited him best. His last, but important, contribution to the EBRD was to recommend Nick Stern as his successor.

Although John ceased being an EBRD adviser in 1994, he remained in contact with it and with transition economics. When he died, the majority of unpublished papers found on his desk were on this subject. It had become the field where he felt that he had most to contribute.

5.   Energy, the environment and the regulation of privatised utilities

The decade from the mid-1980s was turbulent for energy industries. The once dominating role of the coal industry, and its union, were broken. Nuclear power had promised much, but its drawbacks were becoming increasingly emphasised. There was a 'dash for [natural] gas'. In particular, the electricity and gas industries were privatised, with a somewhat ad hoc regulatory apparatus, whose constitutional structure and role was open to question. Against this background, there were calls for a review of longer term strategy.

The scientific community had a strong interest in energy policy, and the Royal Society wanted a proper scientific input into political decisions. There were also major economic, engineering and environmental considerations. So during 1992, in the context of the forthcoming (Heseltine) review of coal policy, discussion between the main academic societies resulted in setting up, in 1993, a study on Energy and the Environment in the twenty-first century, under the auspices of the National Academies Policy Advisory Group (NAPAG), consisting of the British Academy, the Conference of Medical Royal Colleges, the Royal Academy of Engineering and the Royal Society. There were even hopes that politicians would eagerly await independent, expert, academic advice on such technical issues!

Flemming was then moving from his full-time job at EBRD to be the Warden of Wadham, thereby enabling him to serve on such part-time committees. John had already, in 1991, become a Council member of the British Academy. His excellence on a committee would have come to the notice of leading officers of the Academy, notably the President, Sir Anthony Kenny, and Secretary, Peter Brown, both involved in the background discussions. Flemming was encouraged to participate. Both the Royal Society and British Academy wanted to avoid having the Working Party viewed just as a (natural) scientific study. At the October 1992 meeting to establish NAPAG, it was 'Agreed that the chairman for the group should have no professional commitment to any element of the energy business and should be sought from among the Fellows of the British Academy. Sir Anthony Kenny would propose a name.' So John also became chairman.

The majority of the committee nevertheless consisted of scientists and energy specialists. Several had strong prejudices that energy production should be allocated amongst primary sources on non-economic grounds, e.g. social, in the case of coal, and that a major role for nuclear power should be retained. To help provide balance, John recruited Helm, an Oxford economist, and Jon Stern, an energy expert from Chatham House.

Flemming's skills as chairman came into play, such as his willingness to entertain argument, his careful attention to detail and ability to draft, his essential decency and polite kindliness, his command of all aspects of the subject. He managed to obtain an agreed joint report in July 1995, though inevitably containing compromises, as on the future of nuclear power. Perhaps owing to such compromises, it did not have much impact on government policies, disappointing the academic societies. But even before the ink was dry, another similar exercise emerged.

Following each privatisation, an associated regulatory office was established, partly to encourage competition and competitive pricing in such essential but monopolistic industries. The NAPAG report had noted, however, that longer-term strategy should be adopted at the level of energy, or transport, or communications overall, but the regulators, who willy-nilly influenced policy, were established at the sub-industry level. Moreover, the appointment of individual Directors General had led to 'personalisation' of regulation.

Since its foundation in 1992, the European Policy Forum had been concerned about this. The Forum began a series of round tables looking at transferable lessons. David Butler and Richard Holme, having strong connections with both the Forum and the Hansard Society, felt that a combined effort could capture best practice. Butler suggested Flemming as chairman of an independent commission. The Commission on the Regulation of Privatised Utilities was set up in the autumn of 1995. Unlike NAPAG, there were no scientists, instead it consisted largely of economists (Bill Robinson, Margaret Sharp, John Vickers), persons directly concerned with public affairs, and Sir Bryan Carsberg, a former Director General (of Telecommunications).

Although the committee had more commonality than NAPAG, there were major sensitivities. The background was concern about the current regulatory regime, so the Directors General knew that the report might be critical, and likely to suggest changes to their existing roles. The Directors General were not required to give evidence to such a non-statutory body. Flemming's reputation, especially for fairness, however, persuaded them to give evidence.

On the difficult issue of whether to allocate responsibility to an individual, to an individual supported by a 'high-powered' advisory board, or to a three-person executive board, the committee would have preferred the latter, but was willing to wait until the regulatory structure could be consolidated to the overall industry, e.g. energy, transport, communications, rather than remaining at the sub-industry level, for instance, gas, electricity, rail, etc., but the problem of moving quickly to such a broader grouping was recognised. Perhaps the other main highlight of the report was the proposal to return responsibility for all *social policy* objectives, including taxes and subsidies, to the politicians, leaving the Directors General with duties of independent oversight on the utilities' market operations (chapter 3).

The report was completed in December 1996. Most of the work was done by the Secretary, Mark Thatcher, and by John. Mark recalls that they felt disappointed by the initial reception of the report. Nonetheless, the incoming Labour Government picked up many key points in its subsequent [Green] Paper, March 1998, on 'A fair deal for consumers'. As one member of that committee, a subsequent Chairman of the Office of Fair Trading, Sir John Vickers, noted, in 2001, 'a number of its recommendations are now actual or prospective policy'.

Following his role as chairman in both the NAPAG and European Policy Forum Hansard reports, Flemming was a natural choice to replace Aubrey Silberston, on the Royal Commission on Environmental Pollution in 1995. John joined the Commission while it was working on its nineteenth report, on *Sustainable Use of Soil*, February 1996, and played a full role in reports 20 to 24, on respectively *Transport and the Environment*; *Setting Environmental Standards*; *Energy—the changing climate*; *Environmental Planning*; and *Chemicals in Products*, plus the special *Report on Civil Aircraft in Flight*.

John's role was to remind the scientists, who, naturally, formed most of the membership, of economic verities, the need to balance benefits and costs, and the role of the price mechanism in relating resources to preferences in a socially optimal way, plus trickier issues such as the appropriate discount rate to apply to future, uncertain benefits and costs.

John maintained a balanced approach between the (laissez-faire/ decentralised) viewpoint that there was no need for environmental standards as such, only a need for ensuring the proper working of markets, price signals, internalisation of externalities, etc.; and, on the other hand, the (centralised/dirigiste) viewpoint that the government should direct people to use environmentally friendly goods/services, without employing market incentives (i.e. prices).

Flemming was honoured by a CBE in 2001, primarily for his role on the Royal Commission, but this represented only a small part of his contribution to his profession and country.

6. Services to the academic community

Flemming's academic promise was recognised early, and after only a year as a graduate student at Nuffield, he was made an Assistant Editor of the *Oxford Economic Papers* (1963–75). Later he also became Assistant Editor of the *Review of Economic Studies* (1973–5). The *Review* had established not only a reputation as a world-leading theoretical journal, but also that its Editorial Board should be a gathering-post for the foremost young British theoretical economists.

So Flemming was fully aware of the burdens that would be entailed by accepting the offer to become the (sole) Managing Editor of the *Economic Journal*, when that was made in May 1975. The *EJ* is, and remains, Britain's flagship economic journal, and the house journal of the Royal Economic Society. So this put John in a key role in guiding British economics during his tenure of office (January 1976 to June 1980).

Being Editor of the *EJ* is a massive task. The annual number of submissions then ran slightly above three hundred per year. The administrative task of keeping tabs on the refereeing process, and making sure nothing drops out of the system, replying to authors' (often angry) comments, is huge. The Managing Editor is also ultimately responsible for choosing which articles to accept. Indeed, John became the first *sole* Managing Editor since Keynes (Managing Editor 1912–45) got Edgeworth to collaborate in 1919. From 1919 until 1976 there were always two main Editors, and that practice was restored in 1980, when Charles Feinstein and John Hutton became joint Editors.

John looked to Associate Editors to help. On the reviews side, Donald Winch was appointed contemporaneously. But the other Editors were John's choice including, at differing times, John Black, John Kay, John Williamson, David Hendry, David Newbery and David Mayes. How did John manage this job? It must have taken an enormous amount of time and effort, especially since he was characteristically careful to keep the burden falling on his fellow Associate Editors as low as possible. He did not, however, change the balance, or structure of the *EJ* much. The balance of subject matter changed little, with perhaps a slight shift towards more analytical/theoretical papers, and away from statistical/institutional material. The location of authors remained constant. Subscriptions and Royal Economic Society membership drifted slowly down.

As already noted, John was appointed to the Bank as Chief Economist in 1980, so he had to wind up his role as Managing Editor as soon as possible. His successors (Feinstein and Hutton) were appointed early in 1980, and the June 1980 issue was the last for which John had primary responsibility. Thereafter for the next thirteen years at the Bank and EBRD, he had neither time nor, being in the official world, the ability to take on many outside non-academic roles.

He could, however, take on *pro bono publico* roles within the academic community. He had become an eminent figure in British economics. His personality and intelligence made him an excellent member, or chairman, of committees. So he was increasingly showered with invitations to serve on academic bodies. With his capacity for hard work and concentration, he took on many, perhaps too many, since he spread himself quite thinly.

Amongst these roles were:

- Member, Executive Committee, Royal Economic Society (1975–8), Treasurer (1992–8), Vice-President (1998–2003).
- Chairman, Economic Affairs Committee, Economic and Social Research Council (1981–4).
- Member, Advisory Board on Research Councils (1986–91).
- Fellow of the British Academy, elected 1991, Council Member (1992–5), Treasurer (1995–2003).
- Member, Policy Committee, Centre for Economic Performance at the London School of Economics (1993–2003).
- Chairman, Council of Management, National Institute of Economic and Social Research (1996–2003).
- Member, International Advisory Panel, OFCE, Paris (1991–4).
- Chairman, Clare Group (1995–2003).
- Chairman, Houblon-Norman Advisory Committee (1995–2003).

Flemming's positions as treasurer, both of the Royal Economic Society and the British Academy, involved a more specific function, than his other roles as chairman and committee member. In neither case, however, did any serious problem arise; indeed the Royal Economic Society made sufficiently large surpluses over these years to warrant the Charity Commission undertaking an investigation! John reorganised the way in which their investment portfolio was handled, and was beginning to do the same at the British Academy before his illness struck. But in both cases the job took only a few days a year, with meetings with accountants/auditors, signing off expenses, etc. As far as possible John did the work at a distance, from Oxford, and sought to avoid inessential meetings. His stature and probity were, however, such that when John told his fellow officers at the British Academy that it was all right to use the Academic Development Fund temporarily to help pay for refurbishing their new building, they all breathed a sigh of relief. If John said that some course of action was (ethically) acceptable, then it was so.

One of his roles in support of academia, which Flemming found particularly rewarding, was serving as an 'external' on the Council at Brunel University (1989–93) and then as Chairman of its Finance Committee (1994–2003). Martin Cave, the then Head of the Department of Economics at Brunel, and subsequently Vice-Principal, had, as a graduate student, known Flemming at Oxford, and first invited John to Brunel to participate, as an outside expert, on appointments committees for economists from the middle of the 1980s. Martin then recommended, and the university's Secretary, David Neave, supported, that he be appointed as an external member of the university's Council. The Council had some thirty-six members, of which the majority were externals, and usually met four times a year. At about the time when John joined the Council, Michael Sterling became Vice-Chancellor. Michael and John enjoyed each other's company; Michael managed to keep Council meetings relatively lively and entertaining; John was an assiduous attender.

Since his particular expertise lay in financial matters, he was asked to become Chairman of Brunel's Finance Committee in 1994, and also Chairman of the University Investment Committee. John was extremely helpful to the Director of Finance, John Clifford, in improving risk management techniques and analysing financial policy options. During this period from 1994 to 2002, Brunel was expanding fast, roughly quadrupling in size; while it did not face serious financial constraints, there was a need to adopt least-cost methods of funding the necessary extra buildings, such as student residences. John's commitment to Brunel involved a significant allocation of time and effort. He was happy to do this, partly because of his excellent personal relationships with all those closely involved, partly because he had worked all his life in relatively 'grand' institutions and felt some obligation to help with a less-favoured, and newly developing, academic institution.

Eventually the cancer that killed him forced him to give up these positions, though he made every effort to chair meetings even when seriously ill. He was awarded an Honorary Doctorate on 1 April 2003. The conclusion of the Public Orator's address reads:

> Chancellor, in recognition of all his contributions to Economics, Finance and Banking, and to Higher Education, and for the key role that he has played at Brunel University, it is my pleasure to present to you today John Flemming for the award of the degree of Doctor of Social Sciences, *honoris causa*.

7. Warden of Wadham College

In 1993, John was appointed Warden of Wadham College, when Claus Moser, his predecessor, retired. The previous Wardens were Maurice Bowra and Stuart Hampshire, so John became one of an illustrious succession.

Wadham was founded in 1610, and one of the many sadnesses of John's early death was that he missed the quater-centenary. Wadham is a beautiful, middle-sized and an academically successful college. In his printed Memoir of Flemming (*Wadham College Gazette*, January 2004), Dr Stephen Heyworth, the Senior Tutor, noted that,

> He could also contrast the forty-plus firsts achieved by Wadham in the 21st century with the one scored by Trinity in his Schools year (coyly acknowledging that that one was, of course, his own).

Coming back to Oxford to become Warden of a college was akin to coming home for Flemming, and he and Jean made the Lodgings into a family home that was to be shared with all.

Wadham was a well-run college, at peace with itself. The college had just undertaken a major building programme, with the completion of the Bowra building; apart from the usual creeping expansion in numbers, there was no major change required on that front. Flemming had no overt agenda for reform. Instead, like a good chairman (one of the main roles of a head of college is to act as chairman of college committees; most good heads have also been good chairmen; John was a brilliant chairman), he tried to make the manifold college committees see where their own consensus lay. Indeed far from having an agenda, an early and temporary concern was whether John might be too diffident in helping to steer the college and too shy for the social side of the job. But that concern soon evaporated. John spent much more time taking part in the life of the college than most Heads. His presence was much more than just a moment of companionship, it was also a symbol of his democratic conception of his role in Wadham, for he stimulated and enhanced conversation without ever dominating it, and thus became privy, in the most natural way, to how the opinions of his colleagues were shaping up in all sorts of areas, from college policy in its trivial and serious dimensions, to university and (inter)national politics.

Unlike the harmony within Wadham, the questions of the overall governance of Oxford and the distribution of decision-making power and responsibilities between the university's administrative centre and the individual colleges have become increasingly heated. Whereas Flemming threw himself whole-heartedly into college life, he was somewhat reluctant to get sucked into the swamp of university politics. Insofar as he did take sides, it was to uphold the independence and prerogatives of the individual colleges. He held the position of Chairman of the university's Conference of Colleges for some two years between 1995 and 1997, his main foray into the wider Oxford University scene. He also chaired the College Contributions Committee, charged with examining the rules whereby the wealthier colleges transferred funds to the poorer ones. This was a difficult and, sometimes bitter, matter, but John was able to apply his skills in fiscal policy to develop a more equitable system which received general approval.

So, Flemming was a 'hands-on' Warden, and this took up much of his time. In addition, he had the extremely wide range of outside commitments, such as the Royal Commission on Environmental Pollution, Brunel, NIESR, the Royal Economic Society, the Clare Group, etc., already noted in previous sections. So there was only a limited amount of time left to continue with reading and research in economics. But he continued that until he died

When he resigned as EBRD's Chief Economist, he was still working on numerous papers on transition countries in Eastern Europe, of which there were six (sole-authored) papers in 1993, and two in 1994, plus several other minor papers, and one more sole paper in 1998. He left some 74 unpublished notes when he died. Almost all of these relate to the period 1991–3, to his work at the EBRD, and to the transitional problems of Eastern Europe and the USSR.[3] Thereafter, academic output dropped, though balanced by his increasing contribution to the regulation of public utilities and environmental pollution, as already described. By 2000, however, he had already begun to suffer from cancer, and his publications cease. But that certainly did not stop his interest in the field, and he continued to participate in seminars and conferences until the end.

John was diagnosed with prostate cancer at the turn of the century. It was of the most malignant form. Initially he told only a very few, who had to know. Finally in May 2002, as the disease progressed, he felt obliged to inform the Fellows that he could only continue for a further year. He faced his terminal state with grace, endurance and bravery.

[3] My thanks are due to Joanna Coryndon, the Tutorial Office Administrator at Wadham, for copying and sending these on to me. In view of their contents, I have passed them on to the EBRD.

He died on 5 August 2003, five days after stepping down from being Warden, and having received an Honorary Fellowship from the College. The last word should go to his friend and earlier companion at Nuffield, John Helliwell, who wrote in Flemming's obituary in the *Daily Telegraph* (12 August 2003), that,

> If one could choose parts to assemble someone to epitomise the best of Oxford and British universities in general, the result would match Flemming. He was brilliant without being brassy, incisive in thought, precise in speech, encyclopaedic in knowledge, interested in everything he heard and saw, and a lively companion for all those lucky enough to share a journey, a job, or a dinner with him.

C. A. E. GOODHART
Fellow of the Academy

Note. In compiling this memoir my main debt of gratitude is to John's wife, Jean, who helped me throughout despite the pain that this caused her.

My thanks are also due to Felicity Russell, John's secretary; to Robin Matthews, who commented at length; to Mai Doan for research assistance; and to Vicky Baldwin, Amrit Bangard and Peter Marshall for help in transforming this into the British Academy format.

On the particular sections, I have been very grateful for help on:

1. *The early years*: Nicholas Flemming and Mandy O'Keefe, his siblings. Geoffrey Guinness, Tracey Broadhurst, Michael Hubner, Richard Butler and Clare Hopkins.

2. *Becoming a leading macro-economist*: Marty Feldstein, John Helliwell, Roger Van Noorden, David Butler, Derek Morris, Michael Steen, David Howell and Tony Atkinson.

3. *At the Bank of England*: Eddie George, Robin Leigh-Pemberton, George Blunden, Terry Burns, Chris Taylor, Gordon Midgley, John Townend and Ian Michael.

4. *At the EBRD*: Philippe Aghion, Steven Fries, Nick Stern, Robin Burgess, Willem Buiter and Jean-Pierre Fitoussi.

5. *Energy, the environment and the regulation of privatised utilities*: Mark Thatcher, Tony Leaney, Michael Banner, Dieter Helms, John Vickers, David Butler, Graham Mather, Peter Brown and Rosemary Ferguson.

6. *Services to the academic community*: Donald Winch, Peter Brown, Richard Portes, Penelope Rowlatt, David Neave, John Clifford, Martin Cave, Michael Sterling and Juliet Weale.

7. *Warden of Wadham College*: Ray Ockenden, Keith Dyke, Christina Howells and Alan Budd.

PATRICK GARDINER

Patrick Lancaster Gardiner
1922–1997

I

PATRICK LANCASTER GARDINER was born in London on 17 March 1922 to Alfred Clive Gardiner and Lilian Lancaster Gardiner, accomplished artists then living and working in Chelsea. Clive was a landscape and cityscape artist who later assumed the Principalship of Goldsmiths College; Lilian, who studied with Walter Sickert, became a successful portrait painter and was a considerable social presence in the London arts community. The Gardiners enjoyed an eclectic circle of friends who shared their attachment to the life of the mind and its aesthetic expression. The family home provided a lively domestic milieu for their two sons, Patrick and his younger brother Stephen, later distinguished equally as an architect and a writer on architecture and art. This circle was enhanced by the many political and literary associations of Clive's imposing father, the journalist and editor Alfred George Gardiner, better known simply as 'AGG'. AGG edited the *Daily News* from 1902 to 1919, when it was the major liberal daily in Britain (and the only prominent paper to declare its support for the Russian revolutionaries of 1917), wrote essays, commentaries and short stories, and took as much interest in cultural matters as political ones. Patrick Gardiner's childhood thus was spent in an environment that actively cultivated both the seriousness of purpose and the sensitivity to form that were to mark his work and character throughout his life.

Gardiner is best known and most widely esteemed for his work on the nature of historical explanation. This reputation as a specialist in the philosophy of history is certainly merited, but it is also incomplete and

Proceedings of the British Academy, **138**, 99–121. © The British Academy 2006.

somewhat misleading. It is incomplete because only one of Gardiner's three authored books and relatively few of his many articles and public lectures were concerned with the philosophy of history. It is misleading because it obscures the fact that historical explanation was only one arena in which Gardiner pursued the wider philosophical concern apparent in virtually all of his philosophical contributions, namely, the relation between 'personal' and 'impersonal' perspectives in various arenas of human activity. Philosophers sometimes refer to the 'limits of objectivity' in this or that subject area, and perhaps that phrase captures something of the problem informing and uniting Gardiner's work: how to delineate, in a given theoretical arena, the proper contributions of individual, first-personal or subjective points of view, as against those of more impersonal, objective or (sometimes) scientific ones.

That there exists a tension between first-personal and impersonal perspectives, and that it is important to achieve, where possible, some reconciliation between the two, are now familiar ideas in academic philosophy. Much of Gardiner's work, however, was ahead of its time in recognising the wider significance of this theme. By addressing the problem of the limits of objectivity in relation to a variety of philosophical issues, Gardiner presciently identified the source of a number of philosophical disputes well before they had properly developed. This was certainly the case in his treatment of historical explanation, and it is true too of his later treatment of the claims of the personal versus the impersonal in ethical life. The steadiness of this theme in Gardiner's writings will, however, be unobvious—even invisible—to anyone who does not actually read them. A catalogue of the titles or a glance through the abstracts of his published works does not reveal it. On the contrary, these easily suggest a philosopher of intellectually eclectic tastes contemplating a rather varied menu of theoretical issues—first occupied with Collingwood and Hempel on historical explanation (*The Nature of Historical Explanation*, 1952), then turning to the idealist and rather extravagant metaphysics of the German Idealists and especially Schopenhauer (*Nineteenth-Century Philosophy*, 1969, and *Schopenhauer*, 1964), and later being charmed by the literary and artful armchair psychologies of Kierkegaard and Sartre (*Kierkegaard*, 1989). In all the books he published, however, Gardiner's readers will find him repeatedly targeting the relation between the claims of first-personal, experience-based conceptions of some subject and those of more impersonal and objective ones. This target, pursued from the start of his philosophical life to its conclusion more than half a century later, was not unrelated to his love of the arts and his highly discriminating tastes in painting, poetry and music. After all, many of the best works of art—and particularly the best modernist works of visual and literary art which so intrigued Gardiner—maintain a precarious balance between two aims: on the one hand, the aim of portraying some subject faithfully and accurately and impersonally, and on the other hand, the aim of expressing the artist's (or some other subject's) highly specific, thoroughly personal and perhaps idiosyncratic manner of experiencing it. In any event, Gardiner's taste in philosophy more generally was not unlike his taste in works of art: he disliked sentimentality, ostentation and self-indulgence in all their forms, and yet admired works that bore the authentic stamp of the author's distinctive character and experiential point of view—so long as what they had to say could be held accountable to impersonal standards of intelligibility and truth.

Gardiner lived and was educated in his parents' Chelsea home until 1933, when he took up a place at Westminster School. Westminster proved to suit Gardiner perfectly as a second home, and the friends and interests he developed in his years there in some ways set the course for both his personal and intellectual future. Among Gardiner's contemporaries there were David Pears and Richard Wollheim, who in later years continued to count among his closest friends as well becoming valued philosophical colleagues. Another contemporary and associate at Westminster, if a less constant friend, was Hugh Lloyd-Jones, later to become Regius Professor of Greek at Oxford. These talented young pupils made the most of the freedom Westminster then offered to cultivate their particular passions and to plough their own furrows, encouraged by the eccentric housemaster, John Bowle, to pursue thought and enquiry—and especially historical thought and enquiry—with courage and conviction, wherever it might lead. Gardiner was a serious student whose passion for literature and history was so intense that many of his peers and teachers assumed that one or the other of these would be his lifelong vocation. They were mistaken.

Gardiner matriculated at Christ Church, Oxford, to read History in 1940, the same year in which Pears and Wollheim went up to Balliol. Just as they arrived, Oxford began offering shortened, two-year BA courses to conscriptable pupils, a category which included all three of the Westminster friends. Gardiner surprised his tutors by only taking a second in his Part I examinations at the end of his first year, but in his second and final year he won a first. Almost immediately after sitting their Final Honour Schools, Gardiner, Pears and Wollheim were called up, all into the Army. For the following three years Gardiner experienced a world for which Westminster and Christ Church perhaps had done little to prepare him. He saw action in both North Africa and Italy as an officer in an armoured car regiment—although he could not drive (and never learned to). His war experiences affected him profoundly by all accounts. While he valued all he learned from them, certain memories remained deeply unsettling, particularly those of the Battle of Anzio, south of Rome, where Gardiner had been among the survivors of a long and unrelenting enemy bombardment. They endured many long days huddled together in a small, ruined farmhouse, most of them—including Gardiner—eventually so deprived of sleep that mere rational fear gave way to terrifying hallucinations. Gardiner returned to Anzio some thirty years later with his family, and there he sought out, and found, the farmhouse ruin to which he owed his life.

The intensity of the feelings provoked by Gardiner's first-hand encounter with the realities of war may account in part for his somewhat surprising concern, later in life, with certain political and social events in the world. Both before and during the war, Gardiner followed carefully the rise of National Socialism, using his command of German to read Hitler's speeches and to explore in other ways the extraordinary political culture of Nazi Germany. Gardiner was, as Sir Peter Strawson once remarked, 'the least fanatical of men'; in both his work and wider life he maintained a deeply sceptical attitude towards fanaticism in any form. Indeed, part of the subtlety and intellectual depth of Gardiner's philosophical work derives from his aversion to extremes and dogmatic absolutes: philosophical analysis, in Gardiner's hands, seldom yielded up statements that were both universal (or even highly general) and true. Instead Gardiner felt that the task of philosophical reflection was in no small part to expose the disconnections, the distinctions, the anomalies and the exceptions which less cautious and patient disciplines may overlook in their enthusiasm for theoretical generalities. Fanaticism and dogmatism of one kind or another can infect any organised endeavour, and throughout Gardiner's several decades at Oxford they touched the philosophical community often enough, as certain of his peers embraced first one local philosophical fashion and then another: Ayer's logical positivism captivated Oxford philosophy in the late 1930s and was still setting the tone on Gardiner's arrival in 1940; this enthusiasm gave way, in the later 1940s and early 1950s, to an equally intense one for Rylean behaviourism and other Wittgenstein-inspired passions, on the heels of which followed an almost reverential preoccupation with Austinian linguistic analysis in the 1960s and into the early 1970s; finally, in the last years before

Gardiner's retirement in 1989, arrived Oxford's decade-long enchantment with the American philosopher Donald Davidson and everything to do with the truth-conditional semantics he had inspired—a phase with which Gardiner, by then long accustomed to Oxford's vulnerability to passing infatuations, was much amused. As these parades marched by, Gardiner always stood to one side as an interested, if often gently critical, observer. The pursuit of utopian fantasies, the demagogy of individual personalities and the discovery of final solutions were, he saw, as likely to mislead in philosophy as in politics and public life. Gardiner remained conspicuously aloof from the fads and fashions of academia and charted his own course throughout his philosophical career.

II

Gardiner, Pears and Wollheim all returned to Oxford after they were demobbed in 1945. Gardiner's reading during the war had turned increasingly to philosophy—most often German philosophy—and he took the opportunity offered to wartime servicemen to pursue a second honours course. This time, to the surprise of some of his friends, he set himself to reading PPE, taking a first in 1947. During his second round as an undergraduate in Oxford, he became more involved with the philosophical set at Balliol than with colleagues in his own college; he not only continued his friendships with Pears and Wollheim but developed new ones which were to prove strong and long-lasting with the philosophers Marcus Dick and Brian McGuinness, and the novelist Francis King, with all of whom he shared digs at one time or another. The most powerful intellectual influence on Gardiner at this time, however, was arguably that of Isaiah Berlin, whose historically imbued conception of philosophy and scepticism about the pursuit of generalities were naturally in sympathy with Gardiner's own dispositions. Gardiner's admiration for Berlin's philosophical judgement was reciprocated, and in retrospect it seems likely that their conversations mattered more to the direction of the work of both than either recognised at the time. In the event, it became clear to Gardiner even before sitting his examinations that philosophy, rather than history, was his proper vocation. But history was not just left behind: his particular interest in the nature of historical explanation and method was firmly in place and, on completing his second BA (and still just 25 years of age), he took up the research which would later become his B.Litt. thesis (1950) and his first book, *The Nature of Historical Explanation*, published in the Oxford Philosophical Monographs series in 1952.

The Nature of Historical Explanation effectively confirmed the speci-
ficity and legitimacy of a new subject area for philosophy—what in due
course came to be called the 'analytic philosophy of history'. Gardiner's
innovative project was organised around incisive and careful critiques of
two radically different accounts of what the historian is doing, or trying to
do, in offering explanations of historical events, and of what he *ought* to be
doing—what ought to be his standard-setting paradigm of explanation.
Along the way, Gardiner takes note of a number of his contemporaries and
predecessors from Wilhelm Dilthey to Karl Popper to Morton White, but
his two principal targets were the logician and philosopher of science, Carl
Hempel, and the former Wayneflete Professor of Metaphysics at Oxford,
the idealist Robin George Collingwood. The choice of these two thinkers,
representing versions of scientism and subjectivism respectively, showed
an appreciation of the insights of both with a desire to avoid the errors
of either. As Gardiner said of his subject,

> At one extreme lies the view that history is a branch of knowledge which is *sui
> generis*: at the other, there is the claim that it is, in some sense, a department of
> science or, at any rate, that it is capable of being transformed into such a depart-
> ment. Both of these views . . . lead to difficulties; yet both, I believe, are impor-
> tant. For the philosophers who say that history is *sui generis* are stressing those
> features of the methods, aims and subject-matter of the historian which lead us
> to discriminate between history and the natural sciences. And the philosophers
> who insist that history is 'really scientific' stress those features of the subject
> which lead us into regarding it as upon all fours with natural science.   (32)

Hempel's 'The Function of General Laws in History' (*Journal of
Philosophy*, 39 (1942) was published in the year Gardiner completed his
first degree in history. Its point of departure was the structure of explanation in the natural sciences. An event in the natural world, according
to Hempel's scheme, is explained if and only if the statement asserting
its occurrence can be deduced from premises consisting of, first, a well-
confirmed account of the instantial or determining conditions and, second,
a set of well-confirmed universal hypotheses or covering laws. Explanations
of this kind provide the paradigm, Hempel claimed, in terms of which
explanations in other arenas may be both interpreted and evaluated. His
article proceeded to assess historical explanations accordingly, insisting
that 'only the establishment of concrete laws can fill the general [historical]
thesis with scientific content, make it amenable to empirical tests, and confer upon it an explanatory function'. Unsurprisingly, history as it is actually practised comes off rather badly by Hempel's standards. The stuff of
which historical events are made—wars, class upheaval, plagues, the rise

of religions and value systems, the emergence of new foreign policies and so forth — are poor candidates for 'well confirmed' descriptive statements of the kind envisaged as premises of the first kind, and the general laws required for the second premise of the deduction would have to be so complex that they could scarcely be formulated. Moreover, even if a law or laws could be stated, it seems most unlikely that they could be 'well confirmed', for the historian, after all, is in a poor position to conduct the requisite vindicatory (or falsifying) experiments, and the number of past cases he might be able to cite in favour of some generalisation will always fall short of what would be needed to establish it as law. These and other worries led Hempel to conclude that historians seldom succeed in offering 'explanations' proper at all, but rather something 'that might be called an *explanation sketch*' consisting of 'a more or less vague indication of the laws and initial conditions' which needs 'filling out in order to turn into a full-fledged explanation'. Hempel went on to add insult to injury by noting that the method of producing 'explanation sketches' also features prominently in many so-called explanations in psychoanalysis. Both history and psychoanalysis fall short of the requirements of the paradigm of scientific explanation, and hence fail to count as offering *genuine* explanations altogether. It is, moreover, the very nature of their objects of enquiry that dooms them to failure. The aspirations of historical explanation, as Hempel conceived of it, can seldom if ever be satisfied; historical 'explanation sketches' will at best point in the direction in which 'concrete empirical research may tend to confirm or to infirm historical statements'.

Gardiner's masterful response to Hempel did not abandon the basic idea that something like general rules lie at the heart of explanation. He agreed that the *explicans* of an historical explanation must contain not only a set of instantial conditions but general statements linking those conditions in a coherent and theoretically satisfying way to the historical *explicandum*. But Gardiner emphatically denied that generalisations that fail to count as universal hypotheses need, for that reason to fail as acceptable premises in a genuine and fully legitimate explanation: the requisite generalisations need not be 'laws' in the sense that term carries in natural science. Of course, once the notion of a law is sufficiently diluted, we must also abandon the idea of 'deducing' a conclusion from it in conjunction with an account of instantial conditions. Rather than counting as laws, the historian's generalisations are 'judgments' or 'assessments' which serve to link in a rationally coherent manner the details of the initial, determining conditions and those of the target event to be explained. In scientific explanation, Gardiner observed,

there are prescribed tests in most sciences whereby it can be decided whether
or not a particular event satisfies a precisely formulated law. On the level of
common sense, although the margins are wider, the conditions under which a
generalization may be expected to hold are less explicitly stated; we are not usually in doubt about the possible effects of bricks striking windows or billiard-
balls colliding. Historical situations present a multitude of interrelated factors
whose relevance or irrelevance to the events we wish to explain is difficult to
determine. The more complex the events dealt with, the wider their spread in
time and space, the greater are the calls made upon the historian's judgment.
(98)

For Gardiner, the historian's judgements serve, as it were, as guiding
threads weaving together the multifarious details of the determining conditions and those of the event or events to be explained; like the 'general
or the statesman, [he] tends to assess rather than to conclude' (95). His
assessments, moreover, present all that is needed for a complete *historical*
explanation: they are not 'made or accepted, in default of something
"better"' (95–6). In short, historical explanations are not failed scientific
ones.

Gardiner was equally committed to denying, however, that historical
understanding is a matter of grasping some unique event, revealed by
personal insight or achieved by way of an intuitive, first-person act of
imaginative experience. He rejected the absolute uniqueness of historical
events: historians are not free to disregard general laws in their work of
reconstruction, and they very often find their answers by referring to
'general laws of human responses to specified types of situation'. While
it is a mistake to assimilate historical explanation to explanation in the
physical sciences, it is equally misguided to suppose that history is, as
Collingwood claimed, 'a self-contained world that must accordingly be
interpreted by methods bearing little or no relation to those used in
other branches of knowledge'. The 'methods' Collingwood (and his
Italian predecessor, Benedetto Croce) had in view appeared to follow
from the not-implausible view that human histories are concerned not
with sequences of physical events but with 'processess of actions',
which—in the idealist ontology—effectively consist in processes of *inner
thought* as opposed to 'outer bodies and their movements'. Hence
Collingwood's famous pronouncements that 'what the historian is looking for is these processes of thought' and that 'all History is the history of
thought'. This characterisation of the historian's proper subject-matter
can lead all too easily, as Gardiner observed, to the further idea that historians require some 'peculiar technique for looking at [the insides of historical events], analogous to the use by bacteriologists and astronomers

of microscopes and telescopes . . . . Thus a picture is presented which depicts the historian as a man who examines difficult, recalcitrant enti- ties—thoughts and intentions, plans and mental process—by means of intuition in a re-enactment of past experience . . .' (47–8). Collingwood believed that one could know someone else's activity of thinking only if that same activity could be re-enacted in one's own mind. Hence properly executed historical investigation itself, in his view, was principally a mat- ter of successfully executed imaginative re-enactments of the first-person experience of this or that historical agent.

Gardiner's systematic dissection of the various elisions and confla- tions comprising the Croce–Collingwood view of historical understand- ing was characteristically reasoned and judicious. He responded neither contemptuously nor dismissively to Collingwood's idealist convictions (as did so many of his colleagues), but gave as clear and fair a statement of them as he could muster before identifying the errors upon which they rested. In the course of dismantling the idealist structure Gardiner pre- sented arguments which constituted an early exercise in the philosophy of action, sketching an account of actions as a category of event susceptible to different kinds of explanation on different levels. This account has been described by some as influenced by Ryle's reductive accounts of human action, but I do not see Gardiner being tempted far in the direc- tion of logical behaviourism; he maintains throughout a sensible realism about psychological states such as motives, intentions and emotions. In fact, Gardiner's account of the relation between reasons and causes in the explanation of human actions has something in common with the theo- ries of action presented decades later (by Davidson and his protégés) that have found so much favour with Oxford philosophers in recent years. As Gardiner summarised his position,

> The conflict supposed to exist between materialistic and idealistic interpreta- tions of history is an illusory one. We are not confronted by two realms of causes intersecting or running across one another. What we are confronted by are various uses of the word 'explain'. To explain a person's action by giving the purpose it is designed to serve is not the same as to explain an action by refer- ring to a physical event or situation which caused it. And explanations in terms of reasons given, plans or policies adopted, principles followed, are likewise dis- tinct from causal explanations. . . . This is not, of course, to say that it is not possible to give a causal explanation of why it is that a person wants, intends, plans, or calculates something; such explanations, on the contrary, are fre- quently made. We can say that a boy wants to pass his examination because he has been promised a reward if he does so . . . and we can give explanations of a person's desires in physiological terms—his nervous or cerebral processes, for instance, or the behaviour of the ductless glands. . . . Such explanations are

> as important to the historian as to anyone else. All I have wished to stress is
> that to speak of a person's having, for example, a desire is not at all the same
> thing as to speak of his having a carbuncle on his toe or of his suffering from
> a disturbance of the nervous system, and that the interpretations or explana-
> tions containing the former kind of reference must make allowance for this
> distinction.   (136–7)

Gardiner made this case in part by showing how confused was the picture
of human action on which the idealist account rested—a picture that
seemed sharply to distinguish between the 'inner' and 'outer' dimensions
of a human action and that regarded the former (motives, intentions and
so forth) as invisible causal forces. Indeed, Gardiner found it ironic that
Collingwood should, after quite rightly insisting on a distinction between
thoughts and the ordinary, physical furniture of the world, go on to characterise the explanatory role of these 'inner entities' as if they were physical objects and events which just happened to stand outside of space and
time and could be neither seen nor touched nor heard.

Gardiner was to return some forty years later to Collingwood's idea of
history as 're-enactment' and respond to it very differently and far more
sympathetically. This was not because he had repudiated his substantive
views about the explanation of action—he did not do that—but because,
perhaps as a more seasoned and more charitable reader (and no longer
directly influenced by Ryle), he realised that his earlier interpretation had
failed to take into account Collingwood's rather metaphorical manner of
expression and had imposed too literal an interpretation on his central
claims. Gardiner's reconstruction of Collingwood forty years on por-
trayed his account of historical enquiry less as a piece of extravagant
metaphysics than as an attempt at somewhat poetically phrased phenomenology— an attempt to describe what it is like, from a first-person perspective, for the actual historian to reconstruct a sequence of past events
in a way that yields a meaningful narrative about human conduct. As
Gardiner put it in 'Collingwood and Historical Understanding', written
the year before his death,

> It seemed to some of [Collingwood's] early critics that . . . he was committed to
> a radical and ultimately unacceptable form of psycho-physical dualism. And to
> this was sometimes added the objection that awareness of the thought-side of
> an action which the re-enactment theory postulated required an intuitive cap-
> acity to apprehend the mind of an historical agent that transcended ordinary
> modes of cognition. I admit that I was amongst those who then held such a
> view. . . . [But] Collingwood need only be regarded as drawing attention to a
> type of understanding that is already familiar enough at the level of everyday
> experience. . . . If so, his conception of *Verstehen* as re-enactment could be seen

to entail no untoward consequences from an epistemological standpoint. On the contrary, he might be credited instead with giving it a more down-to-earth meaning and edge than ones favoured by some of its earlier idealist exponents. (112–13)

Gardiner charitably does not excuse his own earlier interpretation of Collingwood by citing, as he might, careless comments by the latter describing human motives and intentions as, for instance, 'hidden entities, lying within human actions as the kernel lies within a nut . . .'. It was entirely typical of Gardiner's personal character that he should have no hesitation in acknowledging some error on his own part, however justified, or that he would make a concerted effort to put that error to rights. As well as being 'the least fanatical of men', Gardiner was widely appreciated as being among the most driven by a concern for truth and the least driven by vanity or personal pride.

III

The decade or so following Gardiner's departure from Westminster was, in retrospect, one of extraordinary activity and changes for him: going up to Oxford and completing his first degree in history in just two years, in the following three years serving as a soldier at war, returning to Oxford to complete a further BA two years later, and finally moving on to write and submit what would be his first book—all the while maintaining an active correspondence and contact with family and friends, writing and publishing numerous poems (which he declined to have collected), drawing and painting and, in 1949, taking up his first academic post at Wadham College, Oxford. Brian McGuinness recalls that at the time of Gardiner's appointment at Wadham 'everyone wanted him around', not only because he was so nice and so intelligent but 'for general cultural reasons'. Maurice Bowra, the iconoclastic and exuberant Warden of Wadham, was particularly pleased with Gardiner's appointment, and a strong, if unlikely, friendship developed between him and the reserved young lecturer. At about this same time Gardiner's circles both of friends and philosophical colleagues began to widen beyond the Westminster 'Gang of Three' (Gardiner, Pears and Wollheim), and he began teaching undergraduates. One particularly quick young pupil, Bernard Williams, attended his class on the philosophy of history, marking the beginning of a life-long friendship. (Forty-seven years later, Williams would deliver the address at Gardiner's memorial service.)

The new graduate college of St Antony's was founded at this time principally for the study of recent and diplomatic history, and in 1952 Gardiner became a fellow there. With no undergraduate philosophers for him to tutor, his time at St Antony's was exceptionally unconstrained: one friend remarked that he had 'no idea at all what on earth Patrick did there'. It seems likely that Gardiner was amply occupied in a variety of ways, however. For a time he was engaged to the bright and beautiful Roxannne Boxer, a budding journalist and writer whom some felt certain would be Gardiner's life companion. But he broke off the engagement for reasons he kept to himself; soon after, Boxer married and moved to the Middle East. A subsequent friendship with Rachel Toulmin likewise failed to develop into a lasting attachment; she travelled to Italy on holiday with Frances Lloyd-Jones and there met and promptly married an Italian. It was also while Gardiner was at St Antony's that he first made the acquaintance of the young John Bayley and his striking fiancée, Iris Murdoch, both of whom became Gardiner's life-long—if not consistently close—friends. Gardiner's friendship with Isaiah Berlin likewise deepened during these years. Perhaps made more confident by his secure position within the university, Gardiner now began writing at a fairly furious rate and published a number of articles and reviews, having his say not only in professional journals within his subject, as a young tutor must do now, but in various popular and academic venues ranging from the *New Statesman* to the *English Historical Review* to *New Literary History*. Gardiner's years at St Antony's were certainly not wasted ones.

The most important personal event of this period was undoubtedly his introduction to Kathleen Susan Booth, known to all since her childhood as Susan. When they met in 1954, Susan, twelve years Gardiner's junior, was a talented pianist and somewhat reticent but brilliant undergraduate from Lancashire, then reading Ancient History at Manchester University. Her father, Herbert Booth, was an accounting clerk in the Railway Offices with little formal education, but he was a gifted pianist, possessed of an intellectual disposition, a passion for literature, and other talents which he cultivated by attending night school as an adult, where in due course he earned his A-levels. Susan Booth was her father's first child by his beloved first wife, who had died of cancer when Susan was fourteen and her brother, Richard, was just three. Her father was determined that his children would enjoy the academic opportunities he had himself been denied, and at no small sacrifice he ensured that Susan had piano lessons and was privately educated at St Anne's, a boarding school for girls near Windermere. Susan was just 20 when her university tutors offered her an opportunity to attend for a summer 'study period' at Cumberland Lodge, the hunting lodge at Windsor Great Park that the Queen Mother had transformed into an educational trust. That same summer Patrick Gardiner found himself accompanying some Oxford students to Cumberland Lodge for similar purposes, and it was in this romantic and high-minded setting that the two began their life together. They married a year later in 1955, after Susan completed her MA at Manchester.

Gardiner remained at St Antony's for three years after his marriage, setting up house with Susan just around the corner at Number 22, Winchester Road. These were both very happy and exceptionally challenging years for the young couple. Susan, who though possessed of great intelligence and taste, was exceedingly modest about her abilities, found Oxford's extraordinary culture both stimulating and intimidating. She never forgot her first introduction to certain of Gardiner's philosophical colleagues, including Stuart Hampshire, Freddie Ayer and Geoffrey and Mary Warnock, at a drinks party at 'Corpus' (Corpus Christi College). In conversation, the Warnocks assumed, or seemed to assume, that everyone present was some kind of philosopher, and they put various inquisitory questions to Gardiner's new young wife that, while not leaving her wholly speechless, did nothing to encourage her to return very soon to other gatherings of that kind. St Antony's College, by contrast, provided for both of the Gardiners an exceptionally informal and congenial environment that Susan greatly enjoyed. Women were welcome to dine on many occasions, and the lively presence at college events of John Bayley and Iris Murdoch (married about a year after the Gardiners) did much to encourage the idea that the life of the mind could be enjoyed, and shared, by men and women alike.

There were, however, pressures as well. Patrick was still establishing himself in the philosophical community at Oxford and was intensely occupied with the activities that so often follow the publication of a successful book. The Gardiners' first daughter, Josephine, was born in 1956; it was an event in which both parents delighted but for which neither was particularly well prepared. Susan, herself motherless and with no relatives nor even family friends at hand, found herself parenting, as she once put it, 'by luck and guesswork'. Her husband's natural inclination was to take a backseat (or even to step out of the carriage altogether) when it came to the practicalities of domestic life, which was not always the most helpful approach. Nevertheless, both remembered their early years of marriage as happy ones. In 1958 they moved to a delightful flat on the

first floor of Fairfield House, a spacious Victorian mansion with magnificent gardens on Pullen's Lane in Headington. (When they moved to
Wytham Village a few years later, they handed the Fairfield House flat on
to David Pears, who moved into it with his beautiful young bride, Anne
Drew.) Josephine's younger sister, Vanessa, was born in Fairfield House
in 1960. Gardiner and his wife both thought their accommodation
delightful and very suitable for a young family, but it had its eccentricities.
Immediately after Vanessa's birth, Gardiner's mother, Lilian, dispatched a
maternity nurse from London to Fairfield to 'help out'. On the nurse's
arrival, she announced that she would first deal with 'Cook' and put in her
orders for the kitchen, and then see to Susan and baby. Susan, still confined
to bed, gently broke the news that 'Cook' did not exist at Fairfield, and
that indeed she, Susan, would be doing the cooking—if any were done at
all. The next morning found the maternity nurse departing on the first train
to Paddington Station.

   In that same year Gardiner was offered the Fellowship in Philosophy at
Magdalen College, a post he was to occupy for the next thirty years. The
Magdalen fellowship was Gardiner's first experience as a full-time tutorial
fellow with all the responsibilities that then attached to that role, including
fifteen or more hours each week of undergraduate tutorials for students
reading either Greats or PPE or one of the various other philosophy joint
schools. Gardiner's colleagues heard few complaints: he was always interested not only in teaching, but in the pupils he taught, and they in turn
responded well to his sensitive and serious—but never humourless—tutorial manner. A number of former pupils recall Gardiner as more available
and sympathetic than many other Oxford dons, and there is no doubt that
he assigned great importance to his responsibilities as a tutor. Gardiner
would scarcely have understood the now-common notion that undergraduate tutorial teaching is a burden, unrelated to the 'higher' aims of
research and publication. On the contrary, he took his *raison d'être* as a
philosopher to be in part constituted by the difficult task of rendering his
subject both engaging and intelligible to young minds. He was intensely
(and unjustifiably) self-critical about his tutorial efforts as much as about
his other professional achievements, but this habit of imposing high standards on himself, seems not to have spoilt the fun of his tutorials nor to
have detracted from their value. The pupils who worked most closely with
him recall Gardiner's virtues as a tutor in terms that echo Bernard
Williams's account of his virtues as a friend: 'He did not talk up or talk
down to what one told him; he accepted that the unlikely would probably
have happened; and in considering someone else's situation, he had an

unusual ability not to be thinking, even covertly or by implication, about himself. His great charm, his sensitivity, and his capacity to find things funny, were there for others, not instruments of his will or his inclinations.' As one of Gardiner's former pupils myself, I would add that his evaluations of philosophical ideas and their expression were always thoughtful, insightful and carefully considered. Gardiner never spoke to impress or to intimidate or to fill a silence: he spoke when he had something to say that needed saying. For this and other reasons his opinions often commanded closer attention and greater respect than the pronouncements of certain of his more flamboyant (and self-satisfied) contemporaries.

As a senior member of college, Gardiner was loyal and willing, and served conscientiously in various administrative offices at Magdalen, including the office of Dean of Degrees and the Vice-Presidency. Administration and management were not, however, among his natural talents; while he commanded both affection and respect from his colleagues, few considered him suitable for any post carrying great responsibilities of that kind. On one occasion following the resignation of a college President, some well-meaning colleagues nominated Gardiner as an internal candidate to succeed to the post. A long discussion in the governing body ensued, from which Gardiner had of course to be excluded, concluding with the almost-inevitable decision to seek a candidate elsewhere. This was an unfortunate episode that caused Gardiner—never invulnerable to the emotion of embarrassment—some unhappiness. For the most part, however, his relations with his colleagues at Magdalen were exceptionally congenial: he was not an easy man to dislike.

Gardiner counted himself particularly fortunate in his philosophical colleagues at Magdalen throughout his many years as a fellow. When he was first appointed, Gilbert Ryle—Gardiner's sometime supervisor and friend—was Waynflete Professor. Geoffrey Warnock was the other tutorial fellow in philosophy, having replaced J. L. Austin in 1953 when the latter moved to the Professorship at Corpus Christi College. This too was a piece of luck for Gardiner, and not only because he liked Warnock. Austin's popularity and influence in Oxford had almost reached the status of a zealous and evangelical cult: Austin did not have students so much as disciples. He also conspicuously enjoyed the authority he wielded and did nothing to discourage the mixture of fear and envy with which he was regarded by many colleagues. Few personalities could have been less like Gardiner in disposition or less agreeable to him as a model of philosophical practice, and it was no loss to either man that they avoided becoming college colleagues. Instead Gardiner's first ten, very happy years at

Magdalen found him at table and in committee with two respected and familiar colleagues who were also, from a philosophical point of view, challenging without being cantankerous. In 1968, Peter Strawson succeeded Ryle to the Wayneflete Chair, and he and Gardiner soon became good friends as well as compatible colleagues. When Warnock retired in 1970 his fellowship went to a young philosopher, Ralph Walker, who shared Gardiner's interest in philosophical history and the history of ideas as well as his appreciation of the German rationalists. Walker's great personal integrity and intellectual seriousness, as much as his philosophical tastes, won Gardiner's respect and affection. Susan Gardiner, too, greatly liked her husband's new colleague. Magdalen, unlike St Antony's, did not often welcome women, let alone wives, into college; Susan generally shared rather less in her husband's day-to-day university activities after his move there, but both she and her husband counted Walker as much a personal friend as a professional colleague. Following his move to Magdalen, Gardiner was welcomed into 'Freddie's Group'—an invitation-only Tuesday-evening dinner/discussion group initiated by A. J. Ayer which counted among its members luminaries such as Stuart Hampshire, Peter Stawson and Ayer himself as well as certain of Gardiner's longstanding friends, including Isaiah Berlin, Bernard Williams, Brian McGuinness and David Pears. Freddie's Group was for many years a provocative source of new ideas and a venue in which to reconsider old ones, but on the whole it was a forum for pursuing the mainstream, contemporary concerns of Oxford philosophy—often topics in epistemology, metaphysics and the philosophy of language. The Group was perhaps particularly useful to Gardiner as a way of being regularly engaged with and keeping informed about such concerns while in his own work he was otherwise occupied with less fashionable ones. Among these, of course, was the philosophy of history: Gardiner put a great deal of energy and effort into editing *Theories of History* in 1959 as well as *The Philosophy of History* in 1974. Moreover, his specific and unusual expertise in two other, then-peripheral subject areas, philosophical aesthetics and post-Kantian German philosophy, meant that he was regularly responsible for the university's public lectures in both. Aesthetics and German philosophy both featured among the optional papers on the PPE syllabus; the demand for teaching in these areas was fairly limited, but they interested a sufficient number of undergraduates (and graduates) to make necessary a regular offering of related public lectures. For many years Gardiner was the only member of the sub-faculty capable of giving informed lectures of any kind in philosophical aesthetics, and he is credited with single-handedly keeping this topic alive in Oxford during three long decades when almost no one else was prepared to protect its place on the syllabus, let alone to teach it. (Iris Murdoch was the only other philosopher in Oxford at that time to take an active interest in aesthetics, and her interest was almost solely confined to the relations between art and morality; moreover, her approach was regarded by many of her colleagues as eccentric and 'insufficiently analytical'—which no one had reason to say of Gardiner.) Had Gardiner not offered to lecture on and tutor in aesthetics (both for Schools and for the B.Phil.) it is very likely that it would have not been taught at all. Only a few years before Gardiner retired from his tutorial fellowship in 1989, philosophical aesthetics began to enjoy a dramatic revival both within and outside Oxford; after many long years of delivering his university lectures to an audience of only four or five students (and sometimes fewer) Gardiner saw the numbers attending them double, and then triple and then quadruple. He was surprised and, while never given to even the most impersonal boast, he was very evidently pleased. Today, some sixty to seventy undergraduates each year sit the 'Philosophy of Art and Criticism' paper in Final Honour Schools, and nearly as many attend the related public lectures. But for Gardiner, however, that paper would probably have disappeared from the Oxford syllabus altogether.

Unfortunately, the importance of Gardiner's lectures was not matched by his enthusiasm for lecturing: although he fulfilled his remit capably and always very eloquently, he disliked—even dreaded—all kinds of public performance, and quietly suffered through the terms in which he was required for weekly appearances 'on stage' at the Examination Schools. Susan Gardiner, sharing her husband's aversion to any public spotlight, was sympathetic to his anxieties and did her best to bolster his spirits and confidence, but she recalled that the day or two preceding a lecture would invariably find Gardiner in a nervous gloom, writing and rewriting the material he was to deliver and often despairing of meeting his own, too demanding standards. The evening after the final lecture of the term had been dispatched, by contrast, was an occasion for celebration within the Gardiner household. As Susan remarked, 'The end of a term of lectures was like the beginning of a new life.' Gardiner's dislike for lecturing was shared by Isaiah Berlin, who advised him to 'never look anyone in the audience in the eye, but fix your gaze on the far left-hand corner where no-one's look will catch you either by chance or design'—a strategy they both relied upon throughout their lecturing careers. Berlin and Gardiner also collaborated to satisfy part of the lectures requirement by co-teaching several series of graduate seminars on topics in the history of ideas and the philosophy of history. By all reports, Berlin and Gardiner worked wonderfully as a duet when leading these seminars, as much because of as despite their very different styles, with Berlin's breathless and famously wordy soliloquies set off and punctuated by Gardiner's laconic but carefully targeted observations. Berlin appreciated the soundness of Gardiner's philosophical judgement in other contexts, too. He often consulted him about his work in progress and trusted Gardiner to deliver the right verdict on arguments or claims about which he himself felt uneasy or uncertain. Berlin eventually named Gardiner as one of his principal literary executors, a role which, following Gardiner's illness later in life, fell solely to Henry Hardy.

IV

Perhaps the greatest pleasure that philosophical activity afforded to Gardiner was to read and read again some text of complexity and depth that he felt he did not properly understand, and then patiently, and often very privately, to set about the task of making sense of it and to record what he took that sense to be. This pleasure led him (as it led Berlin) to attend to and learn from a number of thinkers whom others tended to ignore or dismiss as having little or nothing to offer to contemporary philosophy—figures such as Vico, Condorcet, Comte, Pascal, Schelling, Hegel and of course Collingwood, as well as two on whom Gardiner wrote full-length books: Schopenhauer and Kierkegaard. *Schopenhauer* appeared in 1963, just five years after Gardiner became a fellow of Magdalen and just three years after the unexpected death, at the age of 49, of J. L. Austin. It was not the best-timed of publications and it attracted little attention in the first instance, receiving only a handful of reviews. Two of the reviews questioned Gardiner's motives for writing the book at all: why would a respected analytical philosopher at Oxford devote so much time and effort to interpreting an obscure, long-dead German metaphysician, and particularly one known almost solely for his extravagantly gloomy portrayal of Reality as meaningless, chaotic and conflicted? The answer offered by the then-anonymous reviewer for the *Times Literary Supplement* was extraordinarily hostile, as was her review as a whole; she attacked Gardiner's personal integrity as much as his text, and did so in terms so contemptuous that any author, let alone one as diffident as Gardiner, would have found them distressing. Even Richard

Taylor's review in the *Journal of Philosophy*, while acknowledging the book's judiciousness and its author's admirable scholarship, suggested that Gardiner had set out simply to 'write a book about something or other that is presumed to have fairly widespread interest'. ('There are Pelican books on other great philosophers; why not one on Schopenhauer too?') Anyone acquainted with Gardiner knew that these suggestions were not merely unwarranted but absurd: no one was more certain to be guided in his work by personal conviction and purpose than Patrick Gardiner; his intellectual sincerity and natural integrity rendered him conspicuously oblivious to considerations of professional expediency or reputation. Despite its inauspicious first appearance, however, Gardiner's *Schopenhauer* is recognised by many today as still the best full-length study of *The World as Will and Idea* ever published in English: it is a text most tutors will recommend to students embarking on a study of Schopenhauer (and those who do not, should). Moreover, scholars still turn to Gardiner's book for illuminating and clear-headed suggestions about various of Schopenhauer's more obscure notions: it is particularly insightful about the problems associated, for instance, with Schopenhauer's determinism and his notion of a fixed, 'empirical character', with the 'Platonic Ideas' perceived through works of art and with the mysterious notion of 'Will' itself. The only competitor to *Schopenhauer* when it appeared was an able but very general and rather breathless survey text by Father Copleston. Gardiner's study was followed by two others: the first written by the philosopher D. W. Hamlyn and the second by the writer and journalist, Brian Magee. Hamlyn's effort was so unsympathetic to Schopenhauer as to appear deliberately obtuse, while some of Magee's commentary tended to err on the side of excessive charity. Gardiner's *Schopenhauer*, by contrast, was based on a patient mastery of the literature (in both English and German), was biased by neither contempt nor devotion, and was sensitively and lucidly expressed. More than that, it represents a real achievement in two other ways. First, without failing to be critical where appropriate, it makes the best possible sense of Schopenhauer's failed attempt to provide an 'objective metaphysics' of reality as it is in itself, independent of our experience of it; Gardiner acknowledges the intuitive attractions of Schopenhauer's vision of the libidinous 'Will' where deserved, brings out its non-accidental affinities with Spinoza's notion of Being as conceived *sub specie aeternitatis*, and draws attention to the influence it exercised on Freud. Second, and perhaps more importantly, Gardiner's book demonstrates the ways in which Schopenhauer's contributions as a phenomenologist—that is, his descriptions from the first-person, subjective point of view of different aspects of ethical, aesthetic and spiritual experience—are triumphs of armchair psychology on a philosophical par with the similar contributions of Hume, whom Schopenhauer greatly admired. Schopenhauer's 'Grand System' of German metaphysics—his attempt to explain the nature of human experience from an objective, mind-independent point of view— was clearly unsustainable. That notwithstanding, Gardiner makes it plain that as a phenomenologist of certain aspects of human experience Schopenhauer still has much to offer philosophers working in any tradition. In this respect Gardiner's book set the agenda for contemporary 'analytic' Schopenhauer scholars such as Julian Young, Christopher Janaway and John Atwell.

Gardiner's last book was a study of Søren Kierkegaard, the Danish existentialist—another philosopher whose contributions to the phenomenology of value had been largely neglected by the analytic tradition Although Gardiner's *Kierkegaard* did not appear until 1988, he had been preparing the way for it for over two decades, reading and writing about related issues of morality, authenticity and self-knowledge in both Kierkegaard and Sartre. This work appeared principally in lectures, including 'Sartre on Character and Self-Knowledge' (the August Comte Memorial Lecture at the London School of Economics in 1975) and, earlier, his masterful 'Error, Faith and Self-Deception' (delivered at a meeting of the Aristotelian Society in 1970). Gardiner first explicitly addressed Kierkegaard's moral phenomenology in his Dawes Hicks Lecture for the British Academy in 1968, titled 'Kierkegaard's Two Ways'. He there focused, as he did to some extent in his later book, on Kierkegaard's two volumes titled *Either/Or* (1842) which set out, through pseudonymous authors, two antithetical frameworks of value: the 'aesthetic' (ascribed to a young amoralist identified simply as 'A') and the 'ethical' (ascribed to an older man said to be a judge). As Gardiner himself summarised each:

> Aestheticism as exhibited in A's loosely related assortment of papers is seen to take on a lively variety of forms and guises; among other things, it is held to find expression in the characters of legendary figures like Don Juan and Faust, and it is also illustrated by an account in diary form of a step-by-step seduction. By contrast the position of the ethicist is set out in two somewhat prosaic letters which are addressed by the Judge to A and which include detailed critical analyses of the younger man's motives and psychological prospects. . . . Whereas the aestheticist typically allows himself to be swayed by what he conceives to be the unalterable constituents of his natural disposition, the ethically orientated individual is prone to look at himself in an altogether different light. Both his motivation and behaviour are responsive to a self-image 'in likeness to

which he has to form himself', his particular aptitudes and propensities being seen as subject to the control of his own will.

In Gardiner's British Academy lecture, as later in his book, he skilfully explores Kierkegaard's subtle analyses and insights into the value and dis-value of both positions and shows how they relate to certain alternatives presented in contemporary (analytic) moral philosophy. *Kierkegaard* also directly confronts the tension between the convictions born of personal, inward experience—including the convictions of spiritual faith—and those deriving from objective, impersonal investigation. In this context Gardiner deftly explores Kierkegaard's idea that questions of 'truth' may arise in two radically different ways, either by asking whether one's beliefs correctly target a 'genuine' object (whether they correspond to reality), or by asking whether one's attitude towards or conception of some object—genuine or otherwise—is 'truthful' (that is, authentic and ingenuous) or self-deluding. In Kierkegaard's words, 'When the question of truth is raised in an objective manner, reflection is directed to . . . an object to which the knower is related. . . . If only the object to which he is related is [true], the subject is accounted to be in the truth. When the question of truth is raised subjectively, reflection is directed subjectively to the nature of the individual's relationship [to the object].'

Reading Gardiner's study of Kierkegaard one discovers a thinker who, much like Gardiner, was preoccupied with the difficulty, both in theory and in life, of negotiating the competing claims of object and subject: on the one side, the claims of a mind-independent, objective reality—for instance, the reality represented in the descriptions of our best physical sciences—in which all phenomena, including human actions, are determined by causal laws and, on the other side, the reality of the experiencing subject, much of which eludes 'objective' representa-tion altogether, and within which each of us is a free, self-forming and morally accountable agent who acts on his own reasons and pursues his own ends. In this respect, Gardiner's *Kierkegaard* is a study of one thinker's attempt, at a very different time and place, to articulate the central philosophical and psychological concerns implicit in Gardiner's work throughout his life.

In 1985 Patrick Gardiner was appointed a Fellow of the British Academy. Four years later he retired from his tutorial fellowship and became an Emeritus Fellow of Magdalen. Gardiner did not, however, ever retire from philosophy: he continued working and writing, as he had for over thirty years, in his first-floor study overlooking the magnificent, rambling gardens surrounding the Dower House, the beautiful, gently derelict home in Wytham that he shared with his wife, Susan, and in which they raised their two children, Josephine and Vanessa. Gardiner never gave any sign of being particularly satisfied with his own accomplishments, but he was evidently very proud of those of his daughters. At the time of his death, Josephine was an accomplished journalist; she has now embarked on a second career as a developmental psychologist. Vanessa and her partner Alex Lowry are both painters who, showing great determination, have made successful lives for themselves, and for their daughter Jessie, as independent artists. Gardiner's marriage also brought him great happiness. He and Susan shared tastes in art, music, books and people; they both loved Italy, loathed ostentation and deceit, and were utterly indifferent to money and social ambition. Together they created, at the Dower House and in its enchanting gardens, a decorous, delicate and thoroughly unmodernised world in which one tended to feel oddly transported out of time, beyond reach of anything common or ugly or banal. Many guests, having visited the Dower House once, found themselves drawn to return time and again, with or without invitation, but never without good reason: for there they could reliably find unaffected human warmth, quiet English wit, good humour and conversation that was as intelligent as it was sincere. Although the Gardiners were in many ways intensely private, they had a great many friends— typically, friends they held in common—to whom they were deeply loyal and who reciprocated their commitment. There has never been a home, as one remarked, where the fires of friendship have burnt more fiercely.

The nature of this memoir has required that it tell the story of a single individual, rather than a couple. In some ways, however, this falsifies the life it records: Gardiner's philosophical achievements, as much as his personal happiness, were sustained, encouraged and occasionally rescued through his wife's deep love for him. The very intensity of this attachment, the closeness of their lives, created its own difficulties but their common generosity of spirit and capacity to delight in life's adventures and absurdities finally ensured that they passed their lives together not only as companions but as equals. The form of their alliance in some ways mirrored Gardiner's approach to philosophy: they lived in their own way and by their own time, according to their own standards, giving their all to whatever and whomever they loved and saw to be of value.

Patrick Gardiner died on 24 June 1997 after patiently enduring his doctors' various attempts to defeat a recurring illness. His wife followed him in 2006.

A. E. DENHAM
St Anne's College, Oxford

Note. I am grateful for the generous assistance of a number of Patrick Gardiner's friends, colleagues and family members. My greatest debt is to his late widow, Susan Gardiner. Josephine Gardiner also provided invaluable help. Professors David Pears and Ralph Walker and the late Professor Sir Peter Strawson all kindly submitted to interviews. Professor Brian McGuinness not only contributed to my research but helped me to avoid various errors and inaccuracies. I owe thanks to Patricia Williams for searching out the text of the memorial address written by her husband, Professor Bernard Williams. Henry Hardy and Francis King patiently answered a number of questions in correspondence, as did Dr Robin Darwall-Smith, Archivist of Magdalen College, and Judith Curthoys, Archivist of Christ Church. Peter Snow and Alan Bell of the Bodleian Library provided invaluable advice on research procedure. Professor Richard Dagger read the entire typescript and, with characteristic patience and tact, corrected several of its infelicities.

JAMES HARRIS

James William Harris
1940–2004

ENGLISH LAWYERS WHO VENTURE into the realms of ethics and philosophy find themselves open to attack on two flanks. On the one, equipped
with ancient Greek, modern German, and Polish symbolic logic, stands
a host of austere thinkers. On the other, fortified by the three certainties
of trust law, the rule against perpetuities, and the latest Miscellaneous
Provisions Act, is arrayed a band of practising attorneys. In the eyes of
the first group, many legal philosophers are mere dabblers, while the legal
practitioners suspect them of knowing no hard law.

Jim Harris, however, was proof against such attacks. He was most
unusual in combining the training, techniques and craft of a conveyancer
with the concerns and the learning of a philosopher. His abiding interest
in ethical theory was thus strengthened by his sound grasp of thorny and
frequently litigated legal problems. He used this experience, not only to
illustrate theses conceived in the abstract, but also as a means of explaining issues which, for the sake of justice, deserved patient consideration;
while his grasp of the practical problems thrown up by legislation, litiga-
tion, and modern medicine led him to reflect deeply on the many differing accounts of law and justice given by more cloistered minds. In
addition it was his lived experience of the routine of private law—the
contracts, conveyances, mortgages, testaments, statements of claim and
such like (the kind of work solicitors do all day)—which led to his fascination with the school of thinkers who attempt a general account of how
that unglamorous process all adds up: his thoughts and writings returned
to legal positivism again and again.

Jim Harris was born during a very bad air-raid on 17 March 1940 and
was always proud, not so much of the bombs or the date (St Patrick's

Proceedings of the British Academy, **138**, 125–143. © The British Academy 2006.

Day), as of the place: Southwark, but within the sound of Bow Bells and sight of Kennington Oval cricket-ground. His forebears on both sides were what used to be known as 'respectable working-class', his mother's family being Irish stevedores, his father's small tradesmen and skilled artisans, originally from Cornwall. At the time of his birth his father, in peacetime an engineer with the GPO, was serving in the Royal Engineers, and after Dunkirk Jim and his mother were evacuated to North Yorkshire where his younger brother and sister were born. At the age of four he lost his sight and, after the war, attended Linden Lodge in Wimbledon, a primary boarding school for blind and partially sighted children. There he flourished, winning a national children's poetry prize personally presented to him by T. S. Eliot, and starring as 'Sandra the Sea Princess' in a children's pantomime at St Pancras Town Hall. At home in the holidays he displayed a confident physical and intellectual independence, grappling with young bullies in Kennington Park, enjoying the thrills on the rides of Battersea Funfair, pedalling away at the back of a tandem, and beating all comers at chess. In all of this he was encouraged and supported by his own family who took his disability in their stride and encouraged him to enjoy the greatest possible freedom.

In 1951 he won a scholarship to the Royal Worcester College—also a specialist boarding-school for blind children which, like Linden Lodge, provided an educational environment designed to encourage pupils to the limits of their mental and physical abilities. The school excelled in the teaching of classics, history and mathematics so that he was soon able both to tutor his brother in Latin syntax and to astonish his father the engineer by resolving in his head quite complex problems of geometry. Outside the family home Jim's intellectual and scholastic prowess soon showed itself. His school reports were always glowing and he was a member of the Worcester College team that competed in the Top of the Form radio competition of the 1950s. He also pursued his acting career in such roles as Coriolanus and the prosecuting attorney in the Caine Mutiny Court Martial, attended dances at local girls' schools, and acquired his lifelong passion for cricket. Above all, from the moment he mastered Braille, he devoured books and, at home, unaffected by the maternal injunction 'stop reading boys, lights out', was able to send his fingers gliding over the pages under the bedclothes into the early hours. Rather than sampling superficially a wide range of topics, Jim liked to know things in detail. His particular interests included prehistory, 'popular' accounts of physics and astronomy, the history of ancient Rome and of the English civil war, the classic nineteenth-century English, French and Russian novels, and of course, again and again, the plays of Shakespeare, large stretches of which he knew by heart. He was also very fond of the music of Wagner and loved to sit through operatic performances reading the Braille libretto in the dark.

After leaving school he spent four months travelling on his own in different parts of France, and stayed with a variety of hospitable hosts: among them the Marquise de St Roc de Rocquentin in the Haute Savoie, Father Jean Remond in Bordeaux, and the Brignonan family in Finistère, from whom he learnt his excellent colloquial French and whom he revisited over many years. Acting was likewise a lifetime hobby, Jim's last theatrical performance coming forty years later as the corrupt proprietor of a tabloid newspaper empire in a north Oxford amateur production.

These interests, though always maintained, inevitably took second place to what became his main passion: the law, in both practice and theory. On going up to Wadham College, Oxford, in 1959 this was not perhaps his ideal choice of subject, but it did offer the prospect of secure employment. His tutor was Peter Carter, a man with a remarkable (and cultivated) talent for simultaneously terrifying and inspiring his pupils. Other undergraduates thought Jim unique in not being afraid of 'Magna Carter', though in truth Jim dreaded the verdict on his weekly essays: 'Oh no, not Harris's peculiar brand of mysticism again!' Of all the intellectual influences on Jim's development as a lawyer, Carter was certainly the most powerful: both positively, by insisting on the highest standards of accuracy and rigour, and negatively by inhibiting him for years from striking out with confidence in more speculative directions.

Outside the tortures of the tutorial, Jim immensely enjoyed his days as an undergraduate, riding on Port Meadow, rowing for his college in a Gentlemen's VIII, continuing his vacation travels in France and, during term, enjoying the company of the numerous young women who volunteered to read for him in those pre-electronic days (being rewarded with a meal every term), introduced him to their social circles, and helped him to his First in the Final Honour School. One of his many extra-curricular activities involved helping at a horse-riding school for disadvantaged children. It was through this that he met his future wife Jose, then a first-year undergraduate at Newnham College, Cambridge. At first slightly shocked by the apparent insouciance of this carefree socialite, she later realised that his life was built around an iron self-discipline, in which a regular and highly organised work routine was the *sine qua non*. In fact, beneath Jim's apparent and extraordinary self-confidence, lay a persistent sense of anxiety about letting himself and his family down by becoming dependent on them or on anyone else.

For a blind person aiming at a professional training in law, the solicitors' branch was more welcoming than the Bar. Several City firms were happy to offer Jim 'articles of clerkship' (nowadays called training contracts) but in those days they all expected the novice to pay them a premium of several hundred guineas and then work for nothing for three years. Fortunately, through the good offices of Professor Sir Rupert Cross (himself a blind Oxford lawyer and Fellow of the Academy), Jim found a firm in Hertfordshire which waived the premium, paid him six guineas a week, and, most importantly, provided an excellent working environment with no fuss over his disability. There he was soon given a good deal of responsibility and learned both the day-to-day routine of an office and the common legal problems of ordinary clients (most of whom were human beings, not big business corporations).

To increase his income, and because the topic appealed to him, he applied to the local Workers' Education Association which was recruiting tutors for adult evening classes in 'clear thinking'. Despite his outstanding qualifications, he was rejected on the explicit grounds that no blind person could do the job. This was a profound shock to him and was his first (though by no means his last) encounter with the prejudices of a supposedly educated quarter of the sighted world.

He returned to Wadham College, taking his BCL in 1966, and was then appointed a lecturer at the London School of Economics where he taught the technical subjects of property and commercial law. His interest in what his Wadham tutor had called 'mysticism', however, led him to a doctoral thesis (supervised by Lord Lloyd of Hampstead) in legal philosophy. This work, polished by his experience of then lecturing on the topic, formed the subject-matter of his first book, *Law and Legal Science*.[1]

On 26 October 1968—the LSE being closed because of student unrest—Jim and Jose were married at St Bride's Church in Fleet Street, where the Revd Dewi Morgan, with a due sense of the current mood, explained in his sermon that marriage was 'a revolutionary moment'. The bride was then just finishing her doctorate, and later, thanks to her rapid achievements as a social historian, became a Fellow of the Academy seven years before her husband. One of Jim's stipulations about married life was that they always live in a place where he could travel to work

---

[1] J. W. Harris, *Law and Legal Science* (Oxford, 1979).

under his own steam, so they bought an almost derelict house opposite
the Arsenal football ground, on the direct Piccadilly line to the LSE.
When his mother first saw it she burst into tears, but his father, who was
by then in charge of the GPO's apprenticeship scheme, soon found a
stream of young workmen to put matters right.

In 1973 Jim was elected a tutorial fellow at Keble College, Oxford,
(later his wife became fellow of St Catherine's College) and he threw himself into college life and the much closer relationship with his pupils than
had been common at LSE. His teaching style had none of his own tutor's
ferocity, and indeed the most common sign of a Harris tutorial was the
bursts of laughter of both him and his pupils. At the appropriate moment
in the afternoon he would advise them to put the lights on, leaving them
to wonder 'how did he know?' Yet behind the ease lay a certain rigour and
a knack for stretching the minds of his pupils—indeed one of them, now
a member of the South Africa Supreme Court of Appeals, remembers
his hours with Jim as 'austere but exhilarating', and 'dedicated to clear
productive thought'.

In college he played a crucial role in promoting the admission of
women and, both there and at home, was eloquent in defending the rights
of people he greatly disliked to do what they chose, provided they did not
interfere with him. A son, Hugh, was born in 1983 and developed early
an obsession with boats, graduating from models to a Freeman Mark
Two five-berth river cruiser, on board which his father took on a new life
as quarter-master, purser and second mate. Unlike the first London
home, their Oxford house met more readily with the approval of their
families: Belbroughton Road is bonny. At the end of a working day, Jim's
lean figure with its shock of white hair could be seen striding across the
road from his college and setting out along the quietest paths to his home.
Anyone who walked with him would be warned in advance of the pro-
truding branches of a hedgerow, or advised to cross the road to avoid the
places where, for Jim, the smell of canine urine was too pungent. A companion might also hear one of Jim's rare outbursts of irritation as he
encountered a motor-car parked selfishly on the pavement.

During these years at Keble, Jim read wisely, thought deeply, and
wrote lucidly. Looking back on his writings, his topics can be arranged
(more or less) into four categories: legal philosophy, the notion of precedent in common-law jurisdictions, property theory, and the jurisprudence
of human rights. It must be remembered, however, that he was frequently
working on more than one issue at a time and, inevitably, his reflections
in one area illuminated those in another.

Legal philosophy

Jim's book *Legal Philosophies*[2] was written for undergraduates, and gives
a straightforward account of certain basic thinkers and topics in the field
of legal theory. But his 1979 book on *Law and Legal Science: an enquiry
into the concepts 'legal rule' and 'legal system'*[3] goes much deeper, and seeks
to explain the logical status of statements made by those who describe,
or advise on, the current law of a given system—the legal profession,
whether practitioners or pedagogues. Harris makes it clear that he is
attempting no more than this; he is offering a positivist, not a political,
cultural, or historical, account. A somewhat similar approach was initiated in this country by Jeremy Bentham and John Austin, but Harris
adopts essentially the view put forward by the great Austrian jurist, Hans
Kelsen: that legal rules are entities identifiable neither with the events
which give rise to them nor with those which constitute their application
or enforcement.

Lawyers of all kinds have what Jim calls a 'caste' tendency towards
formal reasoning, that is an insistence that new legal problems be referred
not to 'extra-legal' policy considerations but to some feature of the
already given legal materials. (There is a mythical, but much admired,
Queen's Counsel who is said to have addressed the highest court saying
'Your Lordships will be pleased to hear that my argument has nothing
whatever to do with the merits of this lawsuit.') When lawyers advise their
client as to what 'the law' is on a given subject they assume that the following is the case: that legal duties (and hence, at the end of the day, the
possibility of official coercion) arise in this jurisdiction *only* if imposed by
rules originating in a certain limited number of sources or by rules sub-
sumable thereunder, and that relationships among these rules are governed by a certain ranking. Thus the lawyer may say that the money must
be paid because it is required by the tax demand of an official appointed
and empowered by regulations issued by the executive as required by an
Act of the Parliament; or, in this country, that the sum of money owing
is a debt recognised as due by a decided case of a court whose ruling other
courts are bound to apply and which no statute has impaired. In doing
so the lawyer is acting *as if* he or she is dealing with a non-contradictory
field of meaning underpinned by a basic norm excluding all sources of

---

[2] (London, 1980), 2nd edn., 1987.
[3] See above, n. 1.

coercion save those legitimated by or under the relevant constitution. This basic norm itself is *causa sui*, it is assumed just as causality is taken for granted by the mechanic who advises you that the rain will rust your bicycle.

If lawyers—insofar as they think about it—presuppose that the constitution was authorised and so their derivative advice is sound, what are they to make of political upheavals? Jim returned to this problem and to what he called 'Kelsen's pallid normativity' in a dozen or so articles published in this country and abroad and prompted by events ranging from the 1965 'Unilateral Declaration of Independence' in Southern Rhodesia to the birth of the Special Administrative Region of China in the once British colony of Hong Kong. He points out that if the UK were foolish enough to repeal the Hong Kong Act 1985 and purport to legislate for the territory, no Hong Kong official would enforce such legislation and no local lawyer would advise compliance. They would continue to behave as if the Basic Law, enacted by the National People's Congress of China, ought to be obeyed, and the legal positivist, neither approving nor disapproving, would describe this behaviour. Whether he or she was happy with it is a quite separate matter. Thus for some years and in many ways Jim—in opposition to his Oxford colleagues such as Joseph Raz and John Finnis—perceived the legal duty as being quite distinct from that of a moral order.

Precedent in the common-law world

By the 1980s, Jim's work was known world-wide and, with his family, he enjoyed visiting professorships in Sydney, Hong Kong and Princeton—and it was in the last of these that he discovered the facilities of scanning and digitalised voice-recording made available by the latest computers. The family travels fed his curiosity about the structure of legal systems and led him to consider a general and persistent feature of 'common-law' countries: the doctrine of precedent, whereby a single decision of a superior court is normally taken to indicate a general norm to be followed, where applicable, by lower courts and officials. He had first dealt with this in a chapter of his book on *Legal Philosophies*, written 'for the beginner', but a decade or so later returned to the topic in the wider context of conflicting decisions within the British Commonwealth. He also brought out, in 1991, a new edition of the masterly textbook on *Precedent in English Law* first written by the colleague who had arranged his articles of clerkship years before: Professor Sir Rupert Cross.[4] Thereafter he published notes on a number of English and Commonwealth cases which sought to solve emerging problems in the application of the hallowed doctrine.

Property theory

However, the area of interest which Jim maintained all his life and to which he made probably his most valuable contributions is one that has intrigued moralists, philosophers, economists and lawyers for many centuries: the institution of property. The topic has recently enjoyed a renewal of popularity among anglophone writers, and indeed an English translation of Pierre-Joseph Proudhon's 'What is Property' has been reprinted four times in the last decade.[5] The classical studies, however, tend to look only at landholding and to discuss it in elevated terms. By contrast Jim's earliest articles deal deftly with a number of intensely technical problems of entitlement to assets in general, including investment portfolios. The very first were written for a leading practitioner's journal and tackle the 280-word sentence of section 1 of the Variation of Trusts Act 1958 which had provoked wealthy families into making hundreds of applications to the Chancery Division. In 1969 Jim's two-part article in the *Conveyancer and Property Lawyer* provided the profession with a subtle and confident account of the effects of the statute, and six years later he followed this with a short but penetrating book on the subject.[6]

His second early paper addressed another very practical problem of property relations but went beyond a mere analysis of the relevant law to give a hint of the intellectual development Jim was undergoing. The issue arises where an owner of land allows another person to occupy it; the latter then claims to be a tenant, and so legally protected, while the former maintains that this was just a friendly arrangement. The courts state that their task is to decide what the parties intended but, as Jim drily pointed out, 'intention in this context cannot mean real intention, in the sense of an aim of which the parties could have been conscious, since what is posed as the content of the intention is a legal classification: and

[4] R. Cross and J. W. Harris, *Precedent in English Law*, 4th edn. (Oxford, 1991).
[5] Cambridge University Press, 1994, 1999, 2001, 2002.
[6] *Conveyancer and Property Lawyer*, 33 (1969), 113–34, 183–202. J. W. Harris, *Variation of Trusts* (London 1975).

achieving legal status (as distinct from achieving the consequences of such status) is not part of normal human motivation'. The courts' conceptual reasoning, he says, 'conceals a simple development in the law brought about by judicial revolution, namely that there are certain circumstances to which the courts will not apply the statutory and common law of landlord and tenant'. The most compelling such circumstance is the element of generosity on the part of the landowner.[7]

He then turned to the questions posed in the distribution of a fund where someone is given the power—or saddled with the duty—to select the recipients either at large or within a class designated by whomever established the fund—for instance, in a business context, a choice among employees, ex-employees, and their relatives or dependants.[8] In later years (assisted by an Academy research grant) he widened his range to address the views of Robert Nozick and other American 'libertarians' on the one hand, and the advocates of 'critical legal studies' on the other. He also took issue with the agile arguments of Ronald Dworkin, confronting Dworkin's superjudge Hercules[9] with Jim's own creation, a character whose name deliberately evokes the workaday world of the ordinary lawyer: Humdrum, a person who believes that it is possible to arrive at conclusions of law while remaining agnostic about the justice of his society. Jim uses actual—and difficult—reported cases about competing entitlements to a home to argue that Humdrum has, not only the ability to achieve some, if partial, alleviation of social distress, but also the prosaic merit that he can exist.[10]

It is clear, however, that Jim's finest and most sustained achievement is his book *Property and Justice*, first published in 1996, the year in which he was appointed to a professorship at Oxford.[11] Around that time a number of anglophone writers were producing works which examined anew the idea of, and the justifications for, the institution of property; and, as always, there were dozens of texts addressed to more technical, but not less troublesome, matters of practice. The two types of work were

---

[7] 'Licencies and Tenancies—the generosity factor', *Modern Law Review*, 32 (1969), 92–6.
[8] 'Trust, Power and Duty', *Law Quarterly Review*, 87 (1971), 31–65.
[9] Ronald Dworkin, *Taking Rights Seriously*, chap. 4 (London, 1978).
[10] 'Legal Doctrine and Interests in Land', in J. Eekelaar and J. Bell (eds.), *Oxford Essays in Jurisprudence, 3rd Series* (Oxford, 1987), pp. 168–97. 'Unger's Critique of Formalism', *Modern Law Review*, 52 (1989), 42–63. 'Is Property a Human Right' in I. McLean (ed.), *Property and the Constitution* (Oxford, 1999), pp. 64–87. 'Rights in Resources—Libertarians and the Right to Life', *Ratio Juris*, 15 (2002), 109–21.
[11] (Oxford, 1996), reprinted 2002. The work was supported by the British Academy, both through the award of a research readership and the allocation of a grant to meet costs.

written for different purposes and by differing authors. It is probably fair to say that you would be unlikely to hire anyone in the first category to draft a non-exclusive know-how licence, nor look to the second for a refutation of Hegel. As we have seen, however, Jim combined a critical understanding of the philosophers with an up-to-date interest—born of experience as solicitor and then tutor—in the day-to-day problems of the practitioner. Furthermore he was well aware that both of these groups have only words to work with, yet the second make their living by producing results in the real world, affecting the lives, liberty, and happiness of particular individuals.

So Jim resolves to take account of the real-life complexities overlooked by the philosophical accounts while avoiding being drowned in the morass of detail which is the practising lawyer's everyday concern. The task he set himself was twofold: to enquire into those reasons which allegedly justify property institutions and also to look at concrete problems of resource allocation; in a given case each may shed light on the other. On the way arise questions as to what kinds of things can we own—land and most tangible objects, yes, but what about our doodles, our fame, our contribution to a computer program, our detached body parts?

The book sets out to confront the fact that, not only is justice a greatly disputed topic, but so also is property. Both are legal and social institutions in which practical decisions have constantly to be taken, at macro- and micro-levels, about entitlements to things and about the powers to be exercised over them—and so, necessarily, over others. So, with an approach which is modest, lucid, and patient, Jim begins afresh with each. He doubts the merit of drawing deductions from some grand universal definition of property. The first half of the book addresses the question 'what is property', and the second considers whether it is just.

By using concrete examples Jim is able to show that there are certain features which are necessary but not sufficient conditions for property. The first is relative scarcity of the object in question—or, in the case of intellectual property, the artificial scarcity created by the very act of attributing property rights in the laws of copyright, patents and the like. It does not follow, of course, that all scarce resources should be allocated by property rules and transactions. For many reasons the welfare solution may be preferable—for instance education, health care, fire and police services are available without regard to property claims. The second essential is some kind of trespass rule imposing negative obligations (whether criminal or civil) on an indefinite number of people forbidding interference with what is allocated to someone else. But this again is not necessarily enough. For instance, in English law, the deserted wife may be entitled to stay in her husband's home and, if she registers this right so as to give notice to everyone, no one may interfere. But she cannot, by virtue of this protection, lease or give away her rights in the home. Her entitlement derives more from status and desert than from ownership. A further stage is reached when something that pertains to a person is, maybe within limits, theirs to use as they please and therefore to neglect it or to permit others to use it. And finally, full-blooded ownership occurs when the holder's relationship with the object is protected by trespass rules and also includes the power both to do as they please—to use, neglect, destroy it—or to transfer the thing (or a share in it) together with the same range of privileges over it plus the power, in turn, to transfer anew. That this last version is the default status for ownership is shown by our relationship with our most common possession: money. It works as money only by being transferred.

At this stage Jim has shown the necessity of trespass rules and of what he calls the ownership spectrum. Armed with this, he investigates actual modern property institutions. He does not limit his discussion to land but ranges from intellectual property through money, shares, goodwill, and the beneficial interests held behind a trust, showing that it is much more helpful to see ownership as a spectrum than as a single dominant and exclusive concept. Against this background one can see that property vested in public agencies or charities is held in 'quasi-ownership' because its holders may not destroy, or even neglect, it. But we describe such entitlements in terms of what the holder may not do—conceptions of private property are logically prior to those of non-private property. Similarly communitarian property (much beloved by some philosophers) can be described by its contrast with private property. Trespass rules protect the community against strangers, but, within the community, allocations and the powers of use and transmission are determined by internal regulations arising from the mutual sense of community.

Having, in the first part of the book, sketched what property institutions are like, Jim Harris then turns to examine the justice reasons for them. He stipulates a minimum for a just human association—while accepting that stipulations are never correct only more or less serviceable. His minima are: an acceptance of the natural equality of humans, so that like cases are to be treated alike; the assumption that autonomous choice over some range of actions is of value to all humans; and that prima facie all unauthorised invasions of bodily integrity are to be banned. But none of these leads readily to a justification of property. It is difficult to discern how, independent of social convention or law, a relationship between a person and a thing should be privileged and protected. Something linking the fact to a right must be found. Locke identified two arguments. The first, with which Jim strongly disagreed is the assertion of 'self-ownership' which runs: I am not a slave therefore I must own my body and my actions including those which create or improve resources, therefore I own the resources. The major unstated premiss here must be: what no one else owns I own; but this is manifestly false. Similarly Locke's and Mill's assertion that ownership arises from creation without wrong is flawed because it does not lead inexorably to the imposition of a negative obligation on others. Granted that the product would not have existed without my creation, it must be of potential use to others or legal protection against trespass would not be needed. So standing alone this argument fails. But it can be combined with others to give a justification for ownership.

If we accept that autonomous choice has a value it may follow that a person whose labour confers a benefit on others deserves to be rewarded—this forms a shell whose content may well vary: the reward may be determined by convention and be a knighthood (which is not a resource) or a Nobel Prize (a different resource) or simply the according of ownership rights and protections over the thing created (Blenheim Palace). This—together with an incentive argument—provides a basis for the recognition of intellectual property. (For instance the EU Council Directive of 14 May 1991 says: 'in respect of a computer program created by a group of natural persons jointly, the exclusive rights shall be owned jointly'.)[12]

Jim concludes his examination of justifying theories by arguing that there are no natural rights to full-blooded ownership, but that the notions of desert and of privacy provide the shells of claims which need to be filled in by other considerations. One is freedom: does the autonomous choice principle lead to the conclusion that property interests confer freedoms which otherwise would not exist? If so, this would go beyond the kinds of objects that might fall under a privacy principle since private ownership not only increases the freedom of individuals, it saves the costs of devising and policing a regime of communal use. The autonomous choice value also supports freedom to transfer the object. The choice to

---

[12] Council Directive 91/250/EEC article 2.2.

give away or sell the thing is prima facie as deserving of respect as the choice to keep or destroy it. This must, above all, be true of money.

So far Jim has shown that, to fulfil the basic justice requirements, everyone can insist that his or her society maintain a property institution of some kind. It must allow for the ownership of chattels and dwellings and money. But this discloses no good reason for intellectual property. So we turn to see if there are desirable social goals which cannot be achieved without a property institution. If incentives and markets increase social wealth then the costs of justice in the wider sense (defence, homeland security, public services) can be better met by taxation. Yet private ownership might be justified where it provides greater incentives than would public ownership and where its exploitation leads to greater overall wealth. Intellectual property is a clear example of the importance of incentives.

So, beginning with a minimalist conception of justice which did not include property Jim reaches the conclusion that its abolition would treat everyone unjustly. But is there any over-arching vision of justice which might determine what form the institution should take? Proudhon argues for equal division, but considers only land (as in fact do most of the modern 'libertarian' school). It is difficult to square this with the value of autonomous choice. Jim does accept that if a resource is a genuine windfall (with no desert or incentive considerations in play) then equal distribution is a just outcome. Thus an expired patent or copyright falls into the public domain. The wealth of a person who dies intestate without kin goes to the Treasury and is, presumably, used for the benefit of all. (Jim might also have pointed out that a similar principle ('general average') apportions equally the 'windfall' loss caused by a necessary jettison at sea.) Against this equality argument is that from existing social convention. This is no more a valid dominant principle than is equal distribution, but it may be relevant if a change to the current practice will involve costs and will, admittedly, produce no more benefit than the status quo: then the onus is on the proponents of change. This may be one reason why the gnarled conventions embedded in the technicalities of judicial precedent are so resistant to alteration.

Jim thus demonstrates that there are no natural rights which of themselves entail full-blooded ownership. He refutes the arguments from self-ownership and observes that speculations about prehistory have little to contribute. We are left with a mix of reasons which justify the variant forms of ownership: the need to fill basic needs, notions of desert, freedom, privacy, incentives, markets, and the moral independence which property may bring. Trespass rules underlie the institution as a whole: thou shalt not steal. The present state of property institutions in a given society deserves support if it is an honest attempt to meet the mix of property-specific justice reasons analysed in the book. But a just property institution alone and of itself is not a guarantee of a just society.

This major work does not address in any detail the insistence on, and persistence of, a stern documentary formality within the law of property. This is a feature with a long history and a bad reputation, as Hamlet notes when he finds a skull: 'a great buyer of land with his statutes, his recognisances, his fines, his double vouchers, his recoveries'.[13] It is still current, and most of the formality is imposed by legislation, so that for instance land contracts must be in writing and signed, a deed needs one witness to the signature, and a will requires two. In a number of perceptive articles, Jim comes to this question by examining those situations where people have intended to carry out some transaction but have failed to comply with the requisite formalities and have then fallen out. This is especially common where couples share a home whose formal paper title is vested in one of them ('Jack') but the other ('Jill') has been told, or led to believe, that she will have some right to the house. In a claim by Jill, we are not required to decide a challenge to Jack made by anyone else—i.e. it is not a question of an owner's rights against the world, but instead a matter of what Jim calls 'situated justice'. Jill's claim to the house—or a share in it—may arise from a number of grounds: Jack gave it her (he should have executed a deed of gift); Jack promised it her (he should have used a deed of covenant); she bought it by paying the previous owner or the mortgagee; she earned it by working on the house; Jack induced her to expect a share (in reliance on which she may have given up her own home); she deserves a share; she needs a home. Depending on the facts Jill may—as against Jack—win some interest in the dwelling on any of these grounds. But if Jill claims against Paul who has bought from Jack in good faith reliance on his paper title, the case is altered. She should win if, in compliance with the requisite formalities, she has been given or promised the house or a share, or if she paid for it. But other grounds such as desert or need will not suffice to deprive Paul of his ownership. In these articles Jim applies his general and well-argued perceptions of the difficult moral and ethical questions about reliance, labour, desert and the like to frequently litigated scenarios and offers a number of patiently rational and judicious arguments. He also seems to be moving away from his earlier

---

[13] *Hamlet*, V. 1. 114.

positivist insistence on the clear distinction between legal and moral duties.[14]

Even more difficult—and much more dramatic—are the problems posed by advances in the medical and biological sciences. Perhaps the law of property should not be called upon to answer them, but that is not how things have turned out: questions about entitlement to, or 'ownership' of, body parts are now constantly before the courts in many countries. In addressing such issues, Jim starts from an explicit—even vehement— refutation of the Lockean proposition that 'every man has property in his own person'. In a paper with the splendid title 'Who owns my body?' he contends that the 'self-ownership' tradition, whether in its libertarian or Marxist versions, is entirely spurious and its effects baleful.[15] From the proposition that I am not a slave, the conclusion that I own my body does not follow. With the abolition of slavery, human beings have been removed from the class of ownable assets. Only philosophers have sought to keep them there.

But our body parts, if severed with our consent, do seem to be physically capable of being the object of property relations and transactions. Presumably I could lawfully and effectively sell my hair-clippings if I could only find a buyer. In less trivial cases the problem is one of selecting the most appropriate regime to govern them. The common law refused to recognise the ownership of corpses, but we do not say that because no one owns a dead body anyone can take it. Instead we impose protection by conferring disposal powers and duties on certain persons (next-of-kin, religious functionaries, public authorities) but we deny them the full range of ownership powers. Similarly nowadays specific duties are laid upon public authorities in relation to human embryos and live gametes, and commerce in human organs is made a crime; but it is perfectly feasible to dictate what is to be done with such body parts without making anyone their owner.

In his novel *Virtual Light*, William Gibson's characters observe 15 November as 'a sort of Mardi Gras' to commemorate the birthday of J. D. Shapely, the promiscuous homosexual from whose viral strain was developed the vaccine that 'saved uncounted millions'. Shapely, we are told, 'had been very wealthy when he died'.[16] In real life, John Moore was not so fortunate. From his excised spleen the University of California

[14] 'Doctrine, Justice and Home-sharing', *Oxford Journal of Legal Studies*, 19 (1999), 421–52.
[15] *Oxford Journal of Legal Studies*, 16 (1996), 55–84.
[16] (London, 1994), p. 294.

(in whose medical centre the organ had been removed) developed and patented a cell-line which was said to be the basis of a three-billion dollar industry. Moore sued, arguing that in exercising dominion over the materials taken from his body the defendants had infringed his ownership thereof. The plaintiff did not claim the cell-line which became the subject of the patent, for that included inventive ideas contributed by the medical team. He claimed to own the materials from the moment they were removed, and his loss would have been measured by reference to their golden potential at that time. The California Court of Appeals found for Moore; the California Supreme Court, by a majority, found for the University.[17] Jim notes that, because of the way in which the action was framed, the courts were not free to construct a new category of entitlement to separated body parts: they were compelled, by the judicial role, to allocate to one side or the other full-blooded ownership carrying powers of transmission and thus of commercial exploitation. Given those constraints, Jim argues that Moore should have won: by the creation-without-wrong argument of Locke and Mill, it was Moore's consent which led to the appearance of a valuable resource. Any competent surgeon could have done the excision, but no other patient could have provided such a valuable cell-line. For Jim, however, it does not follow that this should mean full ownership over the separated body part. Since such entitlement does not apply before the operation, something more than mere excision is required to create it. The Supreme Court majority found this in the incentive to conduct important and beneficial medical research, and so awarded ownership to the Medical Centre. But Jim suggests an alternative attribution: to treat the discovery as a windfall and vest it in some appropriate agency mandated to exploit it for the public good. His general conclusion is that each person has a limited property interest in separate body parts; if he consents to their removal he creates them as a separate thing. But their potential as a commercial commodity should accrue to the community.

Jim's growing achievement as a theorist of justice who actually had a practical experience of its relations with property was recognised by the conferral of Oxford's Doctorate of Civil Law and his election to the British Academy in 2001. It also meant that he was much in demand as a supervisor of doctoral theses. He had a sense of humour, was genuinely interested in his pupils' ideas and—not surprising given his disability—

---

[17] *Moore* v. *Regents of the University of California*, 249 Cal. Rprtr. 494 (1988), 271 Cal. Rprtr. 146 (1990).

was a very good listener. In addition, developments in computer technology and the support of the RNIB and the Oxford University Recording Service made his work much easier, and his students were often amazed at how quickly he absorbed and responded to their drafts. He rarely questioned them about details, instead forcing them to think through the larger implications of any given argument or text. Several books published in the last decade or so began life as theses written under his supervision. His graduate seminar in property theory showed how this apparently worn out subject could be a key to urgent modern questions of moral and political theory, and it was common to have the class double in size as students of politics and philosophy came from all over Oxford to hear him.

Apart from his work in his study and the Oxford classrooms, Jim was an excellent, indeed a compelling, lecturer to a wider public. He was invited to China, Japan, and South Africa to debate Western conceptions of property, and in 2001 he delivered the Academy's Maccabaean Lecture in Jurisprudence entitled 'Reason or Mumbo-Jumbo: the common law's approach to property' in which, in an apparently effortless and lucid discourse, he investigated some of the underlying ethical justifications for the common lawyers' apparently hidebound and jargon-ridden approach.[18] Many of his admirers were hoping that he would now turn his attention to other developments in this area such as the partial exclusion of animals from, or the inclusion of one's image within, the domain of property law.

The jurisprudence of human rights

But Jim was growing more and more interested in the 'human rights' concepts that in many jurisdictions now shape legal thought and practice, and his disciplined curiosity remained unabated throughout his final illness. His projected work on Resources and Human Rights—based on an exploration of how far different jurisdictions treat scarce resources as 'human rights'—regrettably remained unfinished at the time of his death.[19] In September 2003, however, he rose from his hospital bed to lecture to the Society of Legal Scholars meeting in Oxford on how 'human rights' might avoid becoming noisy 'mythical beasts' signifying nothing (as claimed by rights-sceptics such as Hayek and MacIntyre). This was

---

[18] *Proceedings of the British Academy*, 117 (2002), 445–75.

[19] This project was supported by a major award from the Leverhulme Foundation.

achieved by a penetrating analysis of the differing ways in which the words are used in argument. The brilliance of that lecture transfixed his large audience and is marked by a rather drier tone of wit than is found in his earlier works. He observes that a humanist universal ethics has come to occupy the public space that official proclamations of religious allegiance once occupied and in some cultures still do: proclamations of human rights constitute supranational articles of faith. But—as with the older commitments—sincerity is not assured.[20]

With Jim himself, however, sincerity was palpable. He was eloquent in the defence of the rights of people he disliked, and whose practices he disliked very much, to do what they like provided they did not interfere with him. His students noted that he combined a strong personal sense of duty with a strong reluctance to argue for the imposition of duties on others. Although his family background was not particularly devout he acquired, from his schooling, a strong interest in religion both as an intellectual problem and as a way of life. As a child he had been baptised in Southwark Cathedral and, at the age of sixteen, he had, quite out of the blue, what he called a 'vision' of the immanent presence of God. He rarely referred to this but, when he did so it was obvious that it was a crucial moment in his life. He became a lifelong, if low-key, Anglican with a strong intellectual interest in all other kinds of religious belief. He had some unusual views about certain aspects of Christian doctrine—for instance, borrowing from J. L. Austin, he thought that Christ's crucifixion should be viewed as a 'performative statement' about God's eternal relation to man. He was an avid and critical reader of both modern and traditional theology and, just two weeks before his death on 22 March 2004, was working his way through a complete text of Aquinas's *Summa*, having become convinced that the select-extract editions he had previously read were inadequate. At about that time a number of his colleagues and former pupils had been planning a book of essays entitled *Properties of Justice*, stimulated by his writings and his teaching, and including a bibliography. It was to have been published in his honour and has now appeared in his memory.[21] He is buried in Wolvercote Cemetery, Oxford, under a large tree that also shelters two other lawyers and Fellows of the Academy: Herbert Hart and Barry Nicholas.

---

[20] 'Human Rights and Mythical Beasts', *Law Quarterly Review*, 120 (2004), 428–56.
[21] Timothy Endicott, Joshua Getzler, Edwin Peel (eds.), *Properties of Justice: essays in honour of Jim Harris* (Oxford, 2006).

A final and charming paradox for such a philosophical and practical property lawyer is Jim's attitude to his own belongings. Despite his intellectual obsession with 'ownership' as a legal and philosophical construct he was almost entirely uninterested in possessions, except as they made his life and work easier. He practised charity, both in looking after his family, students and friends, and in giving away his wordly goods, during his lifetime and by his will, to worthy (and in his wife's view often quite unworthy) causes.

BERNARD RUDDEN
Fellow of the Academy

Note. In writing this I have drawn on information kindly provided by Jim Harris's family, pupils, readers, and colleagues.

JOHN HURST

John Gilbert Hurst
1927–2003

JOHN HURST MADE AN IMPORTANT pioneering contribution in three separate but interrelated fields: medieval archaeology, post-medieval archaeology and ceramic studies. Before his lifetime's devotion to these three
disciplines they had not been taken seriously in Britain or Europe either
academically or professionally. Medieval archaeology was still the study
of major buildings seen through the records of historians and anti-
quarians, and of portable antiquities divorced from their context. Post-
medieval archaeology was principally the study of industrial relics.
Ceramic studies in the post-Roman period was the preserve of art collectors, anxious to understand the output of major factories and firms,
though a few people collected medieval pottery as examples of folk art. It
is a measure of Hurst's perceptiveness and persistence that all these three
fields are now studied more widely and practised seriously.[1]

[1] There have been a number of obituary notices and a limited biography:
P. Addyman, 'John Gilbert Hurst', *Medieval Archaeology*, 47 (2003), 195–7.
[M. Biddle], 'John Hurst: developing the new discipline of medieval archaeology, and supervising
the investigation of 3,000 deserted villages', *The Times*, 15 May 2003.
H. Blake and L. Butler, 'John Gilbert Hurst', *Post-Medieval Archaeology*, 38/2 (2004), 211–13.
C. Dyer, 'John Hurst: a founding father of British medieval archaeology, he realised the potential
of deserted villages', *The Guardian*, 13 May 2003.
C. Dyer, 'Obituary—John Hurst', *Medieval Settlement Research Group: Annual Report*, 17
(2002) [2003], 5–6.
J. Le Patourel, 'John G. Hurst—a potted biography' in D. Gaimster and M. Redknap (eds.),
Everday and Exotic Pottery from Europe c.650–1900: Studies in Honour of John Hurst (Oxford,
1992), pp. 1–15.
P. Rahtz, 'John Hurst', *The Antiquary*, 8 (Autumn 2003), 1.
A. Saunders, 'John Hurst: medieval archaeologist and inspector of ancient monuments', *The
Independent*, 9 May 2003.

Proceedings of the British Academy, **138**, 147–167. © The British Academy 2006.

From Cambridge to Cambridge

John was born in Cambridge on 15 August 1927 to parents with academic scientific training. His father, Charles Chamberlain Hurst, was a noted geneticist and his mother Rona (née Hurst) was a botanist specialising in plant genetics. His mother, who was Charles's cousin, was a teacher at Christ's Hospital in Horsham for over twenty years. Both parents valued the habit of keeping meticulous records based on accurate and sustained field and laboratory observations. These practices they encouraged in John when, early in his childhood, he declared that he intended to be an archaeologist. His imagination had been fired by the discoveries in Mesopotamia and Egypt, both much in the news during the interwar period. His interests were regarded seriously enough for him to be taken to visit ancient monuments in Leicestershire, around Burbage near Hinckley, to which his parents had moved after leaving Cambridge, and then to the many archaeological sites around Horsham in Sussex when his family lived there.

After local schooling he entered the upper school at Harrow (1943–5) but found little encouragement there for archaeology and, during wartime, little opportunity to make many local site visits. Two years of National Service were spent in the Army Intelligence Corps, reaching the rank of sergeant, during which time he was posted to the eastern Mediterranean, initially in Iraq, mainly in Palestine during the troubled period of the British Mandate, and finally in Greece. This enabled him to fulfil some of his early hopes and, in off-duty leave, to visit sites of all periods, thereby stimulating and satisfying his existing interest in antiquities.

John entered Trinity College, Cambridge (his father's old college), to study archaeology. If he had hopes of studying Egypt and Mesopotamia, he would have been sadly disappointed. If he had wished to become better acquainted with the classical civilisations, he would have had to transfer into the Classical tripos where archaeology, encompassing the study of ancient sites, sculpture and pottery, was a significant option. By pursuing archaeology he was committing himself to the prehistory of Britain and Europe with a minor excursion into the archaeology of Roman Britain. Furthermore, the academic content was factual and theoretical with no formal excavation requirement within the course. However, a number of the teaching staff conducted excavations during the summer and John chose to work for three seasons with Dr Grahame Clark at the water-logged mesolithic site of Star Carr near Pickering in north-east Yorkshire.

The year group was small: four graduated in archaeology, whilst another fourteen of his year took the anthropology option. John attained a II,1 in each year, graduating in 1951. Life at Cambridge had many compensations. Most of the leading prehistorians in the British Isles were invited to give occasional lectures. The Archaeology Museum was in the same courtyard as the teaching rooms. The student archaeology society had its own programme of talks and excavations, which included work on Roman and later sites within the county.

Medieval excavations

During the summer vacation of 1950 John and a fellow student Harry Norris started the excavation of a medieval manor house at Northolt 'to teach ourselves medieval archaeology'. This project continued with volunteer labour at weekends until 1970. The range of pottery from this site was considerable and John consulted the leading expert on excavated medieval pottery, Gerald Dunning, an inspector at the Ministry of Works. This contact had two unforeseen consequences of great significance for John's later career. The first was that he decided to undertake postgraduate study of the later Anglo-Saxon pottery of East Anglia, much of which was in the archaeological museum at Cambridge. The second was that, with his fellow graduate Jack Golson, he was invited by the Ministry of Works to direct a rescue excavation in Norwich. At St Benedict's Gates in advance of the city's inner ring road they excavated in 1951 and 1953 using the then approved method of a grid of box trenches supplemented by a few longer trenches (the Wheeler system). Although this approach was successful within the deep stratification in Norwich, it was proving to be less satisfactory at Northolt. Both Golson and Hurst wished to explore new techniques and at the Edinburgh meeting of the British Association for the Advancement of Science in autumn 1951 Professor Grahame Clark introduced them to Axel Steensberg of Copenhagen. Golson arranged to join Professor Steensberg for six months starting in May 1952 at Store Valby in Jutland where open area excavation on a village site was proving far more successful in retrieving transient features in soils of shallow depth.

Meanwhile in June that year John Hurst visited Wharram Percy amid the chalk wolds of east Yorkshire where the economic historian Maurice Beresford of Leeds University was exploring a deserted medieval village. Again Grahame Clark was the intermediary. He and Michael Postan, both fellows of Peterhouse, had convened a meeting in Cambridge in 1948 attended, among others, by A. Steensberg, W. G. Hoskins and M. W. Beresford to discuss the phenomenon of deserted medieval villages and to visit Leicestershire sites under the guidance of Hoskins. Beresford was then simultaneously recording and publishing Warwickshire village sites. At Wharram Percy, working from 1950 onwards, Beresford was hoping to establish the date of the village's desertion from the pottery and coin evidence. John immediately realised that trial holes and wall-hunting were unlikely to produce reliable results and he offered to direct the archaeological work, thereby allowing Maurice to concentrate on the social welfare of the digging team. With characteristic generosity of spirit, Maurice accepted this offer and there then began a most fruitful partnership of great significance for medieval village studies. As with Northolt, Wharram Percy was an excavation of long duration (1950–90) conducted in July each year with volunteer labour; the attendance of boys from Wetherby Approved School was not quite so voluntary. In the first season (1953) that Hurst directed, Jack Golson joined him and together they employed Steensberg's method of open area excavation, accompanied by the meticulous recording of every single find in three dimensions. From this work grew a research project that is still in progress. The initial meeting of Beresford and Hurst also led to the formation of the multidisciplinary Deserted Medieval Village Research Group in November 1952, opening the study to a wider range of participants than the private research interest of a few economic historians and historical geographers. These two initiatives launched Hurst firmly upon the archaeological path of medieval rural settlement studies.

The Ancient Monuments Inspectorate

After one year's postgraduate research at Cambridge supervised by Geoffrey Bushnell, the keeper of the archaeological museum, but with Dunning as his mentor, John joined the Ministry of Works as Gerald Dunning's research assistant, initially helping him to prepare reports on pottery submitted from soil clearance by workmen at historic monuments, mainly castles and abbeys, in Ministry guardianship. However John was soon in a position to influence the expansion of post-Roman archaeology at many types of site. In 1952 he gained a permanent appointment as an Assistant Inspector and was put in charge of all 'emergency', salvage or rescue excavation on medieval sites. This meant that he could formulate policy by adopting the practice of commissioning a large number of modest excavations (up to fifty per annum) rather than spend the budget allocation on a few big excavations led by senior academics, as his colleagues in charge of the prehistoric and Roman periods preferred to do. However, this strategy created the need for capable directors. John steadily assembled a cohort of excavation supervisors: some were amateurs wishing to undertake more paid work, others were university lecturers and students wishing to expand their field experience. The adult education tutors running their own field schools were another valuable recruiting ground, recommending promising students to him, whatever their age or youthfulness. Ex-servicemen were another reliable group with experience of field discipline, forward planning and adherence to strict timetables.

Conducting excavations in advance of destructive road or housing schemes was only part of John's remit. The other aspect was encouraging the excavators to write their full reports in their own time in the winter months whilst back in university or engaged in other employment; some permanent excavators were urged to complete their reports in the evening after a full day's work at a different site. This problem of unpaid post-excavation work was not solved for many years. The question of where to publish these reports also needed to be faced, especially when the discipline of medieval archaeology was still emerging and did not have a distinct learned society nor its own journal as the Prehistoric Society and the Society for the Promotion of Roman Studies provided. Furthermore, local county archaeological societies were often reluctant to accept lengthy and detailed excavation reports which might swamp the contributions of their own amateur members. The solution was to found a dedicated period society. From this dilemma arose the Society for Medieval Archaeology, though other factors and other scholars contributed to its foundation, as is detailed below.

John's success in formulating strategy and organising site excavation within the medieval period was recognised by the recently appointed Chief Inspector, Arnold Taylor, who promoted him to be Inspector in 1964. More significantly in 1973 Hurst was put in charge of all salvage work with the rank of Principal Inspector. Throughout the next seven years he ensured that there was a fair balance between the needs of the three main archaeological period divisions, and he also encouraged the examination of industrial and pottery-production sites of the post-medieval centuries. His ability to foster specific research programmes, as at medieval settlement sites, or to pioneer new lines of study, as at glass-making complexes, helped to create an awareness of the potential of such sites and to emphasise the need to consult the relevant documents as well as to appreciate the landscape setting through many centuries. On Taylor's retirement in 1972 John continued in a coordinating role in the Ancient Monuments Inspectorate in London although the parent ministry underwent a number of name changes signifying different political imperatives. Its latest version was, and still is, English Heritage in which John was appointed Assistant Chief Inspector in 1980—a post which he held until his own retirement seven years later. He took on new responsibility for the preservation of ancient monuments in direct care of English Heritage and for giving archaeological advice about their presentation to the public. The final phase was marked by a dispiriting downgrading in the value of scholarship and an undercurrent of hostility to the concept of protected ancient monuments, except as a medium for popularisation and as a source for raising revenue. This was a considerable disappointment to John, whose early career had flourished in an environment which had encouraged scholarship and scientific enquiry.

Another area in his professional life which brought both anxiety and challenge was the rise of the Rescue Movement in the early 1970s, whose members aimed to obtain from the Ancient Monuments Inspectorate in England and its parallel bodies in Wales, Scotland and Northern Ireland a far greater financial commitment to archaeological spending on excavation and survey ahead of massive capital expenditure on motorways, airports, industrial estates, urban renewal and new town development. Whatever his private sympathies may have been, and John was too consummate a civil servant to voice an opinion, when the political decision to increase government funding had been made, he and his fellow inspectors, especially Andrew Saunders as Chief Inspector, tried their best to create the most effective framework throughout the country with an archaeological presence in every local authority district. It was a period when long-standing friendships were under strain and when decisions on whether to support a city unit or a regional team could have long-term repercussions. It was also a period of uncertainty amid the 1974 local government and county reorganisation. Whatever the setbacks John never lost his sense of proportion and purpose; occasionally he would express himself to be 'very disturbed' at some outcome but this was the strongest expression of concern that he made. In the event the regional framework which the Inspectorate preferred was only adopted in Wales and environmental laboratories were only established in some major universities. Elsewhere local government units, whether city, county or metropolitan district, were the major employers as well as being the principal planning authorities. As a result of this devolution to local political units, John attempted to ensure that national research priorities, and not narrowly based political expediency, activated archaeological responses and that government money was well spent on archaeological reports and survey volumes of high academic quality. This policy was to be managed by a national Advisory Committee to decide on general principles and by Area Advisory Committees to assess local priorities for rescue archaeology. Although the broad principle was eroded by universities being unable to offer space to regional units and by most local authorities being too restricted to offer financial support to any staff other than those whom they were legally obliged to employ, the whole enterprise made archaeology of all periods more professional in its outlook, though with many unforeseen consequences.

Medieval archaeology

Although Rupert Bruce-Mitford had declared in 1948 that 'medieval and post-medieval archaeology may be said to have arrived' as a discipline, this was a rather over-optimistic assessment.[2] It needed John Hurst, David Wilson, then an assistant keeper at The British Museum, and Donald Harden, the Director of The London Museum, to harness the latent interest in medieval archaeology and found a society devoted to its study. This they did in a meeting at the Society of Antiquaries in April 1957, launching both a dedicated society and an annual journal of high quality. Bruce-Mitford was the first president, Wilson the secretary (1957–76), Hurst the treasurer (1957–76) and Harden the editor (1957–74). This long period in office by the founding trio ensured that the initial momentum and vision was sustained, although the president and the council members changed in triennial rotation. John's practice of conscientiously visiting every excavation that he had commissioned meant that he had direct contact with all the leading field archaeologists and was well able to recommend suitable members to serve on the Society's council. In similar fashion (Sir) David Wilson had close contact with the museum world. Together they ensured a well-balanced range of interests and periods. This variety and balance was also evident in the choice of locations for the annual

[2] R. L. S. Bruce-Mitford, 'Medieval archaeology', *The Archaeological News Letter*, 6 (1948), 1–4.

conference alternately in Britain and abroad and in the choice of subject matter in the valuable monograph series. Hurst subsequently served as vice-president (1977–9) and as president (1980–2). It was as president that he gave the final overview at the 1981 conference in Cambridge to celebrate the society's twenty-five years of development.[3] He then enjoyed the senior statesman role of honorary vice-president for the next twenty years.

This pattern of identifying an academic need for a society or a research group, of gathering a nucleus of committed individuals and then of founding a society with clearly defined research aims and a wide popular appeal was to be repeated a number of times in John's career. Two of the societies were broad period-based ones (medieval archaeology, post-medieval archaeology) and two were topic-based research groups (settlement, pottery). John's skill and originality lay in perceiving a need or an archaeological potential well in advance; he then created the necessary mechanism to achieve a satisfactory solution.

The study of pottery

The excavations at Northolt had produced a large and varied amount of well-stratified pottery, especially from the kitchen areas. The excavations at Wharram Percy were to produce far less pottery and to reveal a more localised supply chain. Both sites stimulated John in his ceramic studies and in Gerald Dunning he was able to share a common interest and to have as a colleague the one man who had specialised in medieval pottery for the previous twenty years and was ever generous with his time and knowledge. In many ways Gerald was omnivorous in medieval artefacts and would hoard information until an appropriate opportunity came to produce a national survey (e.g. of stone mortars, of wooden buckets or of ceramic chimney pots) stimulated by some find of exceptional interest. By contrast John was dedicated to pottery in all its post-Roman manifestations and ensured its prompt publication to help others working in the same field. Gerald had been his inspiration in the field of Saxo-Norman pottery in East Anglia, published in three linked articles (1955–7) and together they published symposium papers on Anglo-

---

[3] Hurst, 'Medieval archaeology twenty-five years on: summing up', in D. A. Hinton (ed.), *25 Years of Medieval Archaeology* (Sheffield, 1983), pp. 132–5.

Saxon pottery (1960).[4] However, a foretaste of John's later interests had been the publication, with Geoffrey Bushnell, of late medieval sgraffito ware from Cambridge (1953), his first significant article among more than 150 publications on ceramics.[5]

Pottery became Hurst's major research interest, perhaps even ahead of medieval settlement. He was aided by an encyclopaedic memory, powers of instant recall and a methodical approach to recording on large index cards in spiky handwriting, so compressed that only he could read it. At all the excavations that he visited, the pottery would be laid out for him to discuss and pronounce upon (never 'pontificate'); at museums he would ask to see recent acquisitions and problem pieces. On the Continent he was anxious to understand and unfold the backcloth of the locally produced wares against which to highlight the imports, initially those from Britain. However, as his confidence grew and his knowledge increased, he was examining all the pottery traded around the North Sea and then extended his range to the material imported from North Africa and the Levant. Although he was well aware that glass and metalwork provided other comparable containers moving along similar trade routes, he left their study to other specialists, such as Donald Harden on glass. Pottery was never for him an art object, but an entrée into the life of the potters, their methods of manufacture and production, their sources of ingredients and of artistic inspiration. It was a means of tracing trade routes and markets, of assessing its use in homes and craft workshops, and of understanding the mechanisms of its disposal. His early scientific parental influences meant that he was always willing to discuss pottery dating and characterisation with successive Ancient Monuments Laboratory directors, Leo Biek and John Musty. The possibility of dating kilns by archaeomagnetic variation and of distinguishing pottery by neutron activation or by heavy mineral analysis were stressed in John's writings and lectures. As early as 1958 he was participating in and promoting conferences on medieval pottery at such centres as Attingham Park, Preston Montford and Knuston Hall. A series of adult education evening classes

---

[4] Hurst, 'Saxo-Norman Pottery in East Anglia', *Proceedings of the Cambridge Antiquarian Society*, 49 (1955), 43–70; ibid., 50 (1956), 29–60; ibid., 51 (1957), 37–65; G. C. Dunning, J. G. Hurst, J. N. L. Myres and F. Tischler, 'Anglo-Saxon Pottery: a symposium', *Medieval Archaeology*, 3 (1959), 1–78.

[5] G. H. S. Bushnell and J. G. Hurst, 'Some further examples of Sgraffito ware from Cambridge', *Proceedings of the Cambridge Antiquarian Society*, 46 (1952), 21–6. For Hurst's later articles on ceramics up to 1992, see Le Patourel in note 1. More reports and articles will be brought posthumously to publication by his literary executor R. A. Croft.

at Goldsmiths College on the pottery of London and the south-east started in 1964 and attracted a large number of practising archaeologists, eager to widen their experience and contribute their own knowledge through pottery-handling sessions. John was initially a reluctant lecturer; he had developed a bad stammer as a child, caused when a naturally left-handed boy was forced to write with his right hand. He tried hard to overcome this defect whilst at Cambridge. Only with his wife Gill's help was he able to master this condition when speaking in public and gain the fluency which he later possessed. He proved to be a natural and sympathetic teacher, able to tailor his material to the skills and knowledge of his audiences.

All this time Hurst was widening his experience of pottery both in time span and in geographical range. This is marked by papers on stoneware jugs and Hispano-Moresque wares in Professor Barry Cunliffe's *Winchester Excavations 1949–60* (1965).[6] In the next decade he published on an extensive range of Continental wares: German stonewares, French maiolica, Spanish lustrewares, and Low Countries slipwares. Not content merely to give identifications, he increasingly stressed the trade patterns, as in papers on 'Near Eastern and Mediterranean Pottery in North-West Europe' (1968) and 'Trade in Pottery around the North Sea' (1983).[7] Often these papers were written in collaboration with Continental scholars who shared his enthusiasm and pooled their knowledge to promote research. The culmination of this study and fruitful partnership was his exemplary volume in the Rotterdam Papers series *Pottery produced and traded in North-West Europe 1350–1650* (1986) under a joint authorship with H. J. E. van Beuningen and D. S. Neal. This attractive volume did not mark the end of his interest in imported pottery, for John continued to write major articles, supply specialist reports, scour journals and visit sites and museums during his retirement. He was always aware of how the discipline was developing and in 2002 remarked slightly ruefully that the recent scientific evidence was 'playing havoc with many earlier identifications, so that the whole study is now in flux'.

[6] Hurst, 'Late Saxon and Early Medieval Coarse Wares from Winchester', in B. Cunliffe (ed.), *Winchester Excavations 1949–60*, I (1964) [1965], 123; 'Winchester Ware', ibid., 124–5; 'Firecovers (Curfews)', ibid., 126; 'Tudor-Green Ware', ibid., 140–2; 'Stoneware Jugs', ibid., 142–3; 'Hispano-Moresque Pottery', ibid., 144.
[7] Hurst, 'Near Eastern and Mediterranean Pottery in North-West Europe', *Archaeologia Lundensia*, 3 (1968), 195–204; Hurst, 'Trade in Pottery around the North Sea', in P. Davey and R. Hodges (eds.), *Ceramics and Trade. The Production and Distribution of Later Medieval Pottery in North-West Europe* (Sheffield, 1983), pp. 257–60.

Similarly the symposium on Anglo-Saxon pottery, held at Norwich in 1958, did not mark the end of his research on pre-Conquest pottery but it was followed by many specialist reports on excavated material and a substantial chapter in David Wilson's *The Archaeology of Anglo-Saxon England* (1976).[8] He was also in demand to provide overviews of the whole field of medieval (post-Conquest) pottery in England: the best survey was his new edition (1972) of Bernard Rackham's *Medieval English Pottery*.[9] However as his responsibilities at the Inspectorate grew and his opportunities for site visiting in England diminished, he realised that the informal handling sessions and the occasional adult education conferences on medieval pottery needed to be put on a more organised basis. He therefore galvanised a group of ceramics enthusiasts to establish the Medieval Pottery Research Group in 1975 and John was the obvious choice to be its first president (1977–80). He then served on its council for five years and was vice-president and chairman of its editorial committee from 1989 until his death. This Group has wrestled with problems of nomenclature of forms, descriptions of fabrics and minimum standards of publications. It has held conferences throughout the British Isles and, occasionally, abroad. It has also published in *Medieval Ceramics* other less usual domestic forms such as whistles, chafing dishes and fire-covers. When Michael McCarthy and Catherine Brooks published *Medieval Pottery in Britain and Ireland 900–1600* (1988) they paid a warm tribute to Hurst as one of the founders of their discipline, along with Dunning, Martin Jope and Jean le Patourel. Indeed the crucial role of Dunning in fostering medieval pottery studies had been marked by a festschrift on his retirement, of which Hurst was a joint editor (1974)[10] and by the creation of the Gerald Dunning Memorial Lecture, which Hurst inaugurated at Oxford in March 1982.[11] Throughout his decades of work on pottery John was always generous in assisting almost all the archaeologists of his generation and of the next in the identification of their excavated medieval pottery, often supplying them with specialist notes on unusual forms and on imported wares. This generosity of his time and the modest

[8] Hurst, 'The Pottery', in D. M. Wilson (ed.), *The Archaeology of Anglo-Saxon England* (London, 1976), pp. 283–348.

[9] Hurst (ed.), B. Rackham, *Medieval English Pottery* (London, 1972).

[10] Hurst, 'Sixteenth- and Seventeenth-century imported pottery from the Saintonge' in V. I. Evison, H. Hodges and J. G. Hurst (eds.), *Medieval Pottery from excavations: Studies presented to Gerald Clough Dunning* (London, 1974), pp. 221–62.

[11] Hurst, 'Gerald Dunning and his contribution to Medieval Archaeology', *Medieval Ceramics*, 6 (1982) [1983], 3–20.

way in which he offered his knowledge was often a source first of awe and then later of gratitude by the younger generation with whom he dealt on equal terms in the common quest for a greater understanding of their material and its wider significance.

Post-medieval archaeology

John's interest in pottery was not limited to the post-Roman and the medieval centuries. On many sites satisfactory attention was paid to the post-medieval deposits and the material evidence that they contained. It was soon realised that ceramics could become a useful source of information on household composition and food preparation alongside the seemingly closer dating given by clay tobacco pipes and base metal tradesmen's tokens. Hurst provided articles on post-medieval pottery from a bombed site in Exeter (1964) and on early eighteenth-century pottery from Flint Castle (1966).[12] At both sites he was concerned to understand the range of locally available products, which continued medieval potting traditions before the large commercial potteries of London, Bristol and Stoke-on-Trent dominated the market. To facilitate ceramic studies in this period Hurst and Ken Barton, curator of Portsmouth City Museums, brought together museum curators, art collectors and field archaeologists to form a Post-Medieval Ceramic Research Group in autumn 1963. This group held twice yearly meetings in different parts of the country to examine representative museum collections and to discuss new discoveries from excavations. The handling of the pottery was a regular feature and the willingness to share information was essential. After four years as a research group, an appeal was made to a wider audience studying other aspects of the material evidence from the post-medieval centuries before the onset of industrialisation. As with the foundation of the Society for Medieval Archaeology a decade previously, it was envisaged that the new society would be multidisciplinary attracting historians, historical geographers, economic historians, museum curators, art collectors, university archaeologists and field investigators. The Society for Post-Medieval Archaeology was founded in 1967 with Robert Charleston of the Victoria and Albert Museum as president and Ivor Noel Hume of

---

[12] Hurst, 'Post-medieval pottery', in E. Greenfield, 'Excavation of a bombed site in Chapel Street, Exeter', *Transactions of the Devonshire Association*, 96 (1964), 361–76; 'Early 18th-century pottery from Flint Castle', *Journal of the Flintshire Historical Society*, 22 (1965–6), 73–4.

Colonial Williamsburg as vice-president. This transatlantic link was an important feature of the society's membership growth and has continued to be one of its intellectual strengths. John served on the council or held the office of president (1970–3) or vice-president (1974–8) for most of the first twenty years of its existence. During his presidency he led a very successful conference to Rotterdam and Leeuwarden. He was always ready to give advice to the council, citing analogous situations from other societies on whose council he had served or indicating sources of funding which had been approached successfully in the past by comparable societies. John remained a staunch supporter of this society's research aims throughout his years of retirement.

Wharram Percy

With these two period societies and the Medieval Pottery Research Group, John had set the wheels in motion, had served faithfully for two decades and then bowed out secure in the knowledge that the organisation was strong enough to develop under its own impetus served by the next generation of committed officers. However with Wharram Percy and the research group on medieval villages there was a much closer identification between John and Maurice Beresford on the one hand and between the deserted village site and the national perspective on the other hand. Because these two scholars, once described as the prolix professor and the taciturn Man from the Ministry, had nurtured the discipline from the gamekeepers' cottages at Wharram, it drew them back each July both for the research excavation and for the furtherance of the aims of the Deserted Medieval Village Research Group. Both projects developed over time in directions that their founders certainly did not envisage in June 1952. Initially the question posed was when was the village deserted and what was the form and life span of the peasant house. When a stone-built manor house cellar was found under one flimsily built peasant house, this threw up new questions about village growth, tenurial history, street patterns and settlement blocks. The careful dissection of the roofless village church led to a better understanding of the central role of that structure in the history of the four settlements in the parish and of the diseases and causes of death of the population buried in the churchyard. The examination of the water mill introduced the excavation team to the problems of water supply and of sustaining an arable economy. Indeed as each new aspect of the village's physical evidence was tackled, so the mentality and the constraints of the inhabitants' lives were better appreciated. All this time the concentration was upon the field remains of a deserted medieval village and Hurst was fully supported by the documentary evidence supplied by Beresford. Articles on the research project and on the micro-topography of Wharram continued to bring the discoveries to a wider audience, as did features in popular magazines and on radio and television.[13]

During the first twenty years of the excavation Wharram Percy was a privately funded research project and no government resources were spent on Wharram. Only when it was given to the nation by Lord Middleton and became a Department of the Environment (later English Heritage) guardianship site in 1974 did the financial situation improve and the hand-to-mouth existence cease. In 1979 there began a formal partnership with Professor Philip Rahtz of York University. This made it possible to excavate at six different sites in each season, partly to assist in a more lucid presentation of the site to the public, but mainly to understand the village over a longer time span. Not only was the medieval village studied in greater depth, but also various strands of enquiry teased out the Saxon, Roman and Iron Age patterns of settlement and land use. As well as going further back in time, the project also went forward to the twentieth century by examining the more recent building and farming practices in the two settlements of Wharram Percy and Wharram-le-Street and their various dependent townships. At each new discovery or expansion of research, John reacted in mock horror at the increased complexity of the situation or at its implications for his previously published model. However he was too deeply committed a scholar to ignore such work; he made great efforts to assimilate the new research material though remaining sceptical of purely theoretical constructs. His paper 'The Wharram Research Project: Problem Orientation and Strategy 1950–1990' (1985)[14] showed how thoroughly he had absorbed the new thinking. This continuing expansion of horizons has been well recorded

---

[13] Hurst, 'Wharram Percy: a case study in microtopography', in P. H. Sawyer (ed.), *Medieval Settlement* (Leeds, 1976), pp. 117–44; Hurst 'The Topography of Wharram Percy Village' in B. K. Roberts and R. E. Glasscock (eds.), *Villages, Fields and Frontiers: Studies in European Rural Settlement in the Medieval and early Modern Periods*, British Archaeological Reports, International Series, 185 (1983), pp. 3–20.

[14] Hurst, 'The Wharram Research Project: Problem Orientation and Strategy 1950–1990', in Della Hooke (ed.), *Medieval Villages*, Oxford University Committee for Archaeology Monograph 5 (1985), pp. 200–4.

in Beresford and Hurst's popular book *Wharram Percy* (1990).[15] Meanwhile the scholarly reports on the various excavations have been prepared under Hurst's general editorship and six major monographs have already been published; four others are still in preparation.

The study of medieval settlements

Initially the focus within settlement studies targeted the anatomy of the deserted medieval village, its manor house, its church, the pattern of peasant houses, the green, the windmill mound or the water-mill pond with dam, surrounded by the patchwork of ridge and furrow arable cultivation, perhaps with quarries, woodland and permanent grazing. Articles and monographs described their appearance and distribution, their regional variation and historical evidence for patterns of desertion. Although the two most substantial works have been by Beresford, *The Lost Villages of England* (1954; 1983) and *Medieval England: an aerial survey* (1958; 1979) with J. K. S. St Joseph, John Hurst contributed to monographs on deserted villages in Oxfordshire and Northamptonshire.[16] Sometimes John would identify new phenomena or float fresh hypotheses, but he was always willing to modify his interpretations when faced with more convincing soundly based evidence. The work of collecting data was aided by a number of scholars in related fields, but the main task of recording and assimilating the data fell upon John Hurst and Maurice Beresford, aided at Wharram by members of a voluntary secretarial team. They were at the centre of the network, leading the research and coordinating information in the annual reports of the Deserted Medieval Village Research Group for thirty-four years. Additionally John was in a position to determine which threatened sites should be excavated and which surveyed. With the help of Professor St Joseph, air photographs were taken both as a record and as a means of interpreting the evidence in the field. John was also able to urge that a representative sample of fifty sites

[15] Maurice Beresford and John Hurst, *English Heritage Book of Wharram Percy Deserted Medieval Village* (London, 1990), 144 pp. The latest re-appraisal was Hurst, 'The Wharram Research Project', *Medieval Settlement Research Group, Annual Report*, 17 (2002), 8–10.
[16] K. J. Allison, M. W. Beresford and J. G. Hurst, *The Deserted Villages of Oxfordshire*, Leicester University Press: Department of English Local History, Occasional Papers, 17 (1965), 48 pp.; Allison, Beresford and Hurst, *The Deserted Villages of Northamptonshire*, Leicester ... Occasional Papers, 18 (1966), 48 pp.

throughout England should be scheduled for protection and that the six best preserved be taken into guardianship. In the event only three became monuments in state care. However as the study of villages extended into Wales, Scotland and Ireland, assembled in *Deserted Medieval Villages*, edited by Beresford and Hurst (1971; 1989), the wide variation in the evidence became clear—the product of different geology, climate and soils, the outcome of various social and tenurial patterns and affected by a diversity of pressures to relocate or abandon settlements. Dispersed settlement rather than the nucleated village needed a new range of survey and excavation strategies. Indeed just looking at the failures was bound to examine only a small part of rural agrarian and pastoral life. The canvas broadened and the Research Group dropped the restrictive 'Deserted' to encompass all types of settlement, not just the peasant house but all the phenomena pertinent to medieval rural life in Britain. Also site reports and book reviews publicised new research being undertaken in Europe. What had first been approached as a distinct study with a limited set of questions now became open-ended, embracing polyfocal village origins, field systems and soil quality, settlement boundaries, desertion and relocation, transport and land reclamation. A parallel study group, initiated by Alan Aberg and Jean le Patourel, concentrated on moated sites, first in England, then within the British Isles and finally throughout Europe (1971–86). These initiatives widened the orbit of the research group still further and the two parallel groups combined in 1986 to become the Medieval Settlement Research Group. John Hurst provided an assessment of the Medieval Village Research Group's aims and achievements (1987).[17] He had also contributed valuable survey articles 'The Changing Medieval Village in England' to J. Raftis, *Pathways to Medieval Peasants* (Toronto, 1981), 'The Medieval Countryside' to I. Longworth and J. Cherry, *Archaeology in Britain since 1945* (London, 1986) and 'Rural Building in England' to H. E. Hallam, *The Agrarian History of England and Wales II (1042–1350)* (Cambridge, 1988). These were his last major papers on rural settlement.

Within the new Medieval Settlement Research Group, Hurst and Beresford became the elder statesmen and the baton was passed on to the next generation who formulated new research strategies and tackled new types of terrain, such as Shapwick in the Somerset Levels or Whittlewood

[17] Hurst, 'The Work of the Medieval Village Research Group 1952–1986', *Medieval Settlement Research Group, Annual Report*, 1 (1986), 8–14.

in the forests of Northamptonshire. John was always encouraging, some-times startled by new insights with an amazed 'incredible', but always willing to evaluate them and study their implications. His approach remained alert and well informed, even after fifty years in this particular branch of study.

Learned societies

From the start of his career with the Inspectorate, John Hurst was assid-uous in extending his knowledge and his range of personal contacts. He was soon a familiar figure at lectures in London and at conferences throughout Britain. As his reputation grew he would be invited to inter-national conferences on rural settlement, especially the Ruralia series started in Prague, and on pottery and related artefacts, notably the gatherings in Rotterdam. In March 1958 he was elected a Fellow of the Society of Antiquaries of London, attending their Thursday meetings with great regularity as well as working in their unrivalled library throughout his career and his years of retirement. He served on its coun-cil and was appointed a vice-president (1969–71) when relatively young. He continued to serve the society on its research committee (1971–7), its executive committee (1979–84) and its finance committee from 1984. His attendance at and contributions to the other senior archaeological societies in London resulted in him being elected to the council of the British Archaeological Association (1960–5) and to that of the Royal Archaeological Institute (1965–70).

   The one society in which his membership owed more to parental example than to his official duties was the British Association for the Advancement of Science. Admittedly he also had encouragement from Grahame Clark at Cambridge, where the great majority of archaeology students took the anthropology route to their degree. He lectured on Wharram Percy and became a committee member of Section H: Anthropology at the 1953 meeting and was elected secretary of the sec-tion (1954–7), later serving as recorder (1958–62) and as section president in 1974. Additionally he served on the national council of the main Association between 1965 and 1970, an indication that his advocacy of field archaeology of the historic periods had received academic accept-ance among scientists. Wherever the Association held its annual meeting John would be in touch with local archaeologists to make sure that they contributed to the meeting handbook, led tours to the most significant

sites and gave lectures to set the local archaeology in a wider context. By
their collaboration with the area's geologists, soil scientists, historical
geographers, economic historians and museum curators, he hoped that
they would enrich their research. This concern for the wider context, both
his own and his parents, was also in evidence when John booked to join
a university-sponsored tour of the Galapagos Islands. He was bitterly
disappointed when illness prevented his participation.

Honours and festschriften

An even more treasured honour was his election as a Fellow of the British
Academy in 1987, an election which closely followed that of Maurice
Beresford. With characteristic modesty John regarded this not as a personal honour but as a collective recognition of all the team who had
worked together at Wharram Percy and in the research group on medieval
settlement.

John was also delighted by the bestowal of an honorary degree of
Doctor of the University of York in July 1995. The citation praised his
dedication to the study of deserted medieval villages and the encouragement of the discipline of medieval archaeology 'influencing an entire generation of medieval archaeologists and inspiring their research directions
for more than three decades. This was not a possessive role, because Hurst
was always approachable and always willing to share his expertise with
others.' It praised his leadership in founding societies and specialist working parties: 'Indeed between 1960 and 1990 it would have been unthink-
able to have launched a research group without his wise advice, his ready
co-operation and his extensive contacts.' Characteristically, he regarded
this honour as one to be shared by all those working with him in medieval
archaeology rather than his own personal reward.

A third well-deserved honour was the award of the Medal of the
Society of Antiquaries of London, presented to those who have provided
outstanding service to the Society or have significantly furthered the aims
of the Society. John was pleased to learn that he was to receive the medal
on 29 May 2003. Sadly he did not live to attend the ceremony and his
family accepted it on his behalf. However, he had privately expressed the
view that it was more a recognition of the growth of medieval archaeology and of the teamwork that it had generated in the past fifty years.
Professor Rosemary Cramp in her presidential address stressed that John
had shown leadership and inspiration at Wharram Percy, in rural settle-

ment studies and in medieval archaeology, and it was those particular personal qualities that were being honoured.[18]

All these three honours were a worthy acknowledgement of the high esteem in which the wider academic community held his scholarship. Two dedicatory volumes provide a more tangible indication of the warmth and affection with which he was regarded by his fellow workers in the two areas of research he had made particularly his own and in which his scholarship had been accompanied by a long commitment to the organisational needs of the research groups. He received a festschrift in July 1989 to mark his retirement two years previously and to record his outstanding contribution to the Medieval Village Research Group of which he had been the founder in 1952 and its secretary for thirty-four years until its transformation into the Medieval Settlement Research Group. This festschrift was jointly in honour of John Hurst and Maurice Beresford to recognise their exemplary partnership at Wharram Percy and in the study of medieval settlements. Most appropriately the volume was entitled *The Rural Settlements of Medieval England*, edited by M. Aston, D. A. Austin and C. Dyer and was presented to the recipients at Wharram Percy. This contained contributions embracing many different approaches from the younger generation of scholars, all disciples of Beresford and Hurst, and nearly all participants in the Wharram excavations

The second festschrift honoured the pioneering role that John had played in the study of pottery in Britain and Europe. *Everyday and exotic pottery from Europe c. 650–1900*, edited by D. Gaimster and M. Redknap, was presented at the opening of the Medieval Europe conference at York University in 1992 among a large gathering of British and Continental scholars. All the forty-four contributors felt that they had benefited to a greater or lesser extent from John's scholarship, practical expertise and personal guidance. They hoped that the choice of topics within the book reflected his wide-ranging knowledge and the breadth of his own research. In many cases reference was made to the unobtrusive help, the wide scholarship lightly carried and freely shared, and the inspiration which his research had been to them. Others have commented upon their prior expectations of an aloof omniscient scholar and the reality of an easy manner allied to a genuine interest in pottery studies that both ignored a generation gap and bridged a gulf in status between a high-ranking civil

[18] Rosemary Cramp, 'Anniversary Address 2003', *The Antiquaries Journal*, 83 (2003), 1–8, esp. 6–7.

servant and a junior museum officer. His enthusiasm and the lack of pre-tension made conversation and the exchange of knowledge fluent and mutually profitable.

What was seldom appreciated by all those whom John assisted in so many ways was that all this research and all these publications were pre-pared in the evenings and the holidays outside his official working hours. He did not have the luxury of a sabbatical year as university scholars might have. He seldom enjoyed subsidised research travel. Indeed the only help that he received was six weeks paid leave in May–June 1960 to work with Steensberg on the Borup Ris field survey, and a Leverhulme Travelling Grant in 1963–4 to examine post-medieval imported wares in Continental museums. All the published books, articles and reviews, as well as the voluminous correspondence arising from research and society business, were laboriously typed with one finger on an ancient and idio-syncratic machine. Only much later was his burden eased when book pub-lishers gave him some typing help and when he had official access to research assistants and draughts-persons. This makes his achievement all the more remarkable.

Family life

In many ways John kept his private life well separated from his public activities at work and research. It was at Cambridge he met Dorothy Gillian Duckett, an archaeology student at Newnham one academic year his junior. During his research year they collaborated in the Archaeology Society activities and later worked together at Wharram Percy. When he joined the inspectorate and was looking for suitable excavation supervi-sors, he chose Gill to direct medieval excavations at deserted villages (Hangleton, Wythemail) and later at moated sites (Ashwell, Milton). They married in 1955 and produced two daughters, Francesca and Tamara. The marriage was a successful partnership balancing Gill's extrovert mercurial temperament with John's taciturn and placid nature. When the family visited excavations in progress throughout England dur-ing school holidays John took the leading role, both as the commission-ing inspector and as the pottery expert. However, on their many visits to the Continent Gill's personality often broke the ice between experts who had communicated by letter but never previously met. The extensive sum-mer tours of European museums and excavations in an old Bedford van enabled John to build up his wide range of contacts and acquire an encyclopaedic knowledge of pottery and of excavation practices. Gill also collaborated with John in preparing the Medieval Britain annual survey in *Medieval Archaeology* for fourteen years and its counterpart in *Post-Medieval Archaeology* for four years.[19] Sadly Gill died in 1971, aged 39, leaving him to bring up his daughters with the support of his many friends and to care for a large house in Gloucester Crescent, London, overflowing with books, files of papers and card indices. After university, his daughters embarked on their careers, Francesca as a teacher and Tamara as a scientist. John was devoted to them and to his three grandchildren, Joseph, Charlotte and Megan, the product of Francesca's marriage to Bob Croft, the Somerset county archaeological officer.

He never remarried and never moved house until in his retirement he transferred to a former dairy with extensive outbuildings in a village near Stamford. These housed his library and his research materials (which will be deposited in the British Museum). John had a great interest in classical music, especially opera, and he had a collection of several thousand records amassed over fifty years. It was in the quiet village street that he suffered a vicious and senseless attack, unprovoked by one of the mildest of men and kindest of scholars. He died in hospital in Peterborough seven weeks later on 29 April 2003 from his severe injuries, prematurely ending the highly valued life of a friend still actively engaged in mature scholarship.

LAWRENCE BUTLER
formerly University of York

Note. I am grateful to Bob and Francesca Croft for generously assisting me with some personal and family details.

[19] J. G. Hurst, 'Medieval Britain in 1956: Post-Conquest', *Medieval Archaeology*, 1 (1957), 151–71; and in vols. 2–4 (1958–1960); D. G. Hurst, ditto, vols. 5–14 (1961–70); D. G. Hurst, 'Post-Medieval Britain in 1966: excavation and field-work', *Post-Medieval Archaeology*, 1 (1967), 107–21; and in vols 2–4 (1968–70).

CASIMIR LEWY

Casimir Lewy
1919–1991

CASIMIR LEWY WAS A MEMORABLE TEACHER of philosophy who left a deep imprint on the ways that subsequent generations of Cambridge philosophers (wherever they might work) thought, wrote, and taught. He was able to do so when the university still took its chief glory to be the way that it educated undergraduates. Dr Lewy, as he was always called by his charges, did not have students: he had pupils. He did not give graduate seminars: he lectured undergraduates about philosophical logic and analysis with a furious passion, an intimidating rigour and an unmatched body language. Yes, of course he had research students, many of whom had been his pupils, and some of whom now hold distinguished chairs of philosophy at Cambridge and elsewhere. But he better fitted the traditional model of the philosopher as teacher than the picture of the modern academic writing books, supervising graduate students, and attending committee meetings. But he was not a teacher in some timeless mould. He practised his art in the curious luxury of post-war Cambridge. He would meet each of his pupils for an hour a week, in order to discuss the written work that they had posted or delivered to him the night before. He had early acquired the conviction that one should publish only when one got something absolutely right, so he left very little in print. Many of his pupils have gone on to write a lot, but in hours of honesty they may still feel residual guilt at doing so. Even the most prolific of them have thrown completed book manuscripts in the dustbin as being not up to scratch.

Casimir Lewy was born in Warsaw on 26 February 1919, the son of Ludwig Lewy and Izabela Lewy, née Rybier. His father, who was a doctor, died when he was a boy, and so he grew up in his mother's family. The

Proceedings of the British Academy, **138**, 171–177. © The British Academy 2006.

city was cosmopolitan and for a time optimistic, a place where the middle classes could be proud of the intellectual and artistic activity in their midst. The Rybier family was itself involved in the musical life of the city. Casimir was sent to the Mikolaj Rej school at the age of eight. The school is named after the Renaissance poet and moralist, one of Poland's cultural icons. In 2005 the Polish parliament commemorated Rej's five-hundredth anniversary. In Lewy's day the school was owned by the Lutheran congregation, and it continues to be governed by the Mikolaj Rej school society, an organisation within the Evangelical Church. The school recently installed a plaque commemorating Casimir's attendance. In his youth it attracted a wide range of boys from the Warsaw middle classes, many of whom have gone on to pursue distinguished careers at home and abroad. He is remembered as being passionate about poetry, but at the age of fifteen he came across a philosophical article in a literary magazine that changed the course of his life.

The author was Tadeusz Kotarbiński (1886–1981), professor of philosophy and Dean of the Faculty of Human Sciences at the University of Warsaw. At that time Kotarbiński was an outstanding public figure, taking a vigorous stand against the combination of nationalist, clerical and anti-Semitic movements that were beginning to loom large in Polish public life. What Lewy found in Kotarbiński was a philosopher with deep metaphysical and epistemological concerns, whose research was conducted within the framework of the most rigorous logic. One of Kotarbiński's colleagues and closest friends was the leading logician Stanisław Leśniewski. Warsaw was briefly the most important centre in the world for formal logic. The Polish logical tradition, fully appreciative of the *Principia Mathematica* of Whitehead and Russell, developed its own distinctive approach, based as much on philosophical insights as mathematical techniques.

Lewy at once bought Kotarbiński's 1929 textbook on methodology, logic and the theory of knowledge, and decided to attend his lectures at the university. This he did, missing (with permission) his regular school classes whenever necessary. He graduated from Mikolaj Rej in 1936, and, at the age of seventeen, went to England, officially to learn English. But he needed philosophy, so he matriculated at Cambridge in October, intending only to spend the year. G. E. Moore and C. D. Broad were the Professors. They became his exemplars in philosophical method. He went from Fitzwilliam House to Trinity College. Supported by family and friends of the family in Poland and England, he stayed on to complete the Moral Sciences Tripos. He took a First in 1939, by which time—he was

20—he had already published short notes in *Analysis*, a journal that had recently been founded with the conviction that points in analytic philosophy could be rapidly resolved by brief statement and quick publication. (*Analysis* is still going strong, but lacks the messianic air of those early days.)

Lewy originally intended to return to Poland, where he in fact spent the Long Vacation of 1938 in the gloom of the Munich Crisis. But when he returned for his final year in Cambridge, it was, contrary to his plans, to be for ever. He began to work for his doctorate under G. E. Moore. The supervision was, however, more epistolary than in person, because Moore retired from his chair in 1939, the year that Lewy took his first degree. And in October 1940 Moore went to the United States to lecture at a number of American universities, not returning until 1944. Lewy's dissertation topic was, 'On Some Philosophical Considerations about the Survival of Death'. He proceeded to the Ph.D. degree in 1943, and in the same year presented the core ideas of his thesis to a meeting of the Aristotelian Society, and published them in its *Proceedings*.

Moore continued to edit *Mind*, the premier British philosophy journal, as he had done since 1921, and as he went on doing until 1944. In his absence overseas, the day-to-day chores of the job were assigned to Lewy. Editing an academic review was in some ways a more genteel affair then than it is today, but in other ways far more demanding of the editor. Moore read every submission, consulting other Cambridge philosophers only on technical issues in, for example, logic. He wrote copiously, in ink, to the authors. He proofread the galleys and the page proofs himself. Lewy of course assumed the latter duties and some of the others as well.

The way in which business was conducted may be suggested by a postcard. From Moore to Lewy, it is dated 'Sept. 25/43', bears a 3¢ stamp, and was posted in New York. It deals with getting twelve offprints of a Critical Notice (a long review) by Ernest Nagel to their author: 'We don't of course usually give off-prints of reviews; but whenever anybody has specially asked for them, I have always agreed to; and I think we can certainly afford it.' It begins with Nagel's address, discusses the issue in which the piece will appear, and ends by promising to send Lewy an article for the January number in a day or two. Despite the fact that such cards travelled by sea in the midst of the war in the Atlantic, things may have been arranged more expeditiously then, than in our instantaneous electronic village of today. After the war, and until the end of Moore's life in 1958, Lewy continued to have frequent discussions with his former teacher, and Moore chose him as his literary executor, as did C. D. Broad.

Wittgenstein was giving classes in Cambridge when Lewy arrived, and continued doing so—with breaks for example for his serving as a porter in Guy's Hospital during the war—until 1945. Lewy attended virtually all of these. The two men also went for walks together, as often as not discussing various nostrums for real or imaginary health problems, for both of them could be described as eccentric hypochondriacs. Unlike many other young men who attended those classes, Lewy never fell fully under the spell of Wittgenstein. I mentioned the three short pieces published in *Analysis* while Lewy was still an undergraduate. They are, respectively, on the very idea of (philosophical) analysis, on empirical propositions and the evidence for them, and on the (in quotation marks) 'justification' of induction. They are very much the work of a young man who has been attending Wittgenstein's classes, who has mastered the ideas but not imitated the style.

Wittgenstein appears to have fully respected Lewy's later persistent gnawing at logical difficulties in a way that he had learned from Moore. Moore and Wittgenstein shared a complete contempt for sloppy work, and each respected the other enormously, even though the ways they did philosophy, and their conclusions, were so at variance. Lewy learned from both the importance of being a *careful* philosopher, an adjective which was the highest praise in those circles.

He lectured in the Faculty of Moral Sciences from the time he took his doctoral degree until 1945, in which year he was appointed Lecturer in Philosophy at the University of Liverpool. In the same year he married Eleanor Ford, who was completing her studies at the London School of Economics which, during the war, was working out of Peterhouse, Cambridge. She too gained a Lectureship at Liverpool, in Economic History. There they continued until 1952, when Lewy took up a University Lectureship in Moral Sciences at Cambridge. As was too often the custom in those days, Eleanor Lewy gave up her promising career when they moved. Casimir seems to have regarded this as the natural order of things. They had three sons, Nicholas, Sebastian and John.

He became Sidgwick Lecturer at the University in 1955, and was elected to a fellowship at Trinity College in 1959. He became a Reader in Philosophy in 1972. He took early retirement in 1982. He was from time to time a Visiting Professor at American institutions—the University of Illinois in 1951–2, the University of Texas at Austin in 1967, and at Yale University in 1969. He was elected a Fellow of the British Academy in 1980.

Lewy in many ways identified with English life but retained a strong residual accent—one hesitates to say Polish, for the accent was all his

own. Perhaps because he was early troubled with a hearing problem associated with some ill-diagnosed neurological disorder, he lectured in a
strikingly loud voice, and often used that voice in private life as well. In
some sense he regarded himself as wholly British. On one occasion, walking alongside the pavement beside which a Volkswagen car was parked, he
exclaimed in a loud and very 'foreign' voice, possibly kicking the wheel of
the offending vehicle at the same time, that it was 'shameful that anyone
should buy such vehicles, when we make such good cars in England'. He
remained proud of his Polish origins when it was appropriate, being very
glad to be elected to an Honorary Fellowship of the Polish Society of
Arts and Sciences Abroad. And he took a wry pleasure when persons of
Polish descent attained eminence overseas—as when Zbigniew Brzezinski
became National Security Advisor to President Carter.

He was known to make use of his hearing aid, turning it down to
avoid boring public speeches. His pupils too sometimes had the impression that he would turn it down if one talked too long with the enthusiasm and misplaced conviction of an undergraduate. Oxbridge supervisors
in those days had varying mannerisms, some having the essay read to
them, others reading it in front of its author. Dr Lewy had always read
the work beforehand; he tended to ignore the worst bits of it, and conducted a challenging examination of the remaining weaknesses. During
his supervisions many topics were discussed in an open way, but his lectures were something else. In these public performances, he strode up and
down, immensely excited by each logical point, snapping his fingers when
he had demolished an error. Doubt was never an option. The effect was
not always desirable. In his first year logic course he would denounce certain conclusions urged in P. F. Strawson's *Introduction to Logical Theory*,
and in Strawson's influential 1950 paper, 'On Referring', which was a creative rebuttal of Bertrand Russell's 'On Denoting' of 1905. The latter in
certain ways was the inaugural statement of British analytic philosophy:
indeed in Cambridge it was called, in an odd mixture of joking irony and
iconic respect, the paradigm of philosophy. Whatever the merits of this
little debate, Lewy's dramatic put-down of Strawson had an unfortunate
consequence. It took a long time for many of his pupils to take Strawson's
later work seriously enough, and thus they may have missed some of the
most important philosophising of the second half of the twentieth
century.

His second year course on philosophical analysis did not practise
philosophical analysis at a primary level, but increasingly turned to questions arising from the very idea of analysis, and on to Moore's paradoxes

of analysis, to questions of propositional identity, and to the relation of entailment between propositions. An example of John Wisdom's, to the effect that a vixen is a female fox, might pass unnoticed elsewhere, but in Lewy's hands became a discourse on whether the statement was about words, about things, whether it was an identity, and how it could say anything. He published the definitive form of his way of doing philosophy in book form in his *Meaning and Modality* of 1976. Since conceptions of, and the practice of, philosophical analysis have changed so much in the subsequent three decades, and since the centre of gravity of this kind of work has shifted to the United States, many of the presuppositions of this book of lectures are no longer current.

The list of Lewy's publications occupies a mere page and a half at the end of a festschrift, *Exercises in Analysis by Students of Casimir Lewy* (edited by Ian Hacking, Cambridge, 1985). The published articles on philosophical problems simply stop. The results of the dissertation on life after death became the question of whether it was self-contradictory to suppose one could exist without a body. The same way of attacking a problem appears in a paper of 1944 printed in *Mind*. Moore himself encouraged the paper although he had qualms, expressed in five pages of comments written out in a small hand.

The question began with a version of traditional scepticism, expressed in a way then taken to be rigorous. Take the proposition that all my present and future evidence confirms that I am not now dreaming; conjoin this with the proposition that I am now dreaming. Is the result self-contradictory? (Already, in shortening the question slightly, I betray certain nuances that Lewy held to be important.) About half way through the essay the discussion turned to statements about material objects that I see plainly before me, and about which I have never had any problems. Take the proposition: 'I have all the evidence which I do have that there is a desk in my rooms, but there is no desk in my rooms.' Is that self-contradictory? After some argument Lewy urged,

> that it is *neither* right *nor* wrong to say that my evidential propositions do entail the 'desk proposition' and that it is *neither* right *nor* wrong to say that my evidential propositions do not entail the 'desk proposition'. In other words it is neither right nor wrong to say that the proposition ['I have all the evidence which I do have that there is a desk in my rooms, but there is no desk in my rooms'] is self-contradictory, and neither right nor wrong to say that it is not self-contradictory.

Yet even this did not satisfy him: 'I must confess I am still greatly puzzled, and I am probably very confused, about one of the things I have said in this paper . . .'—namely the 'neither right nor wrong' statement just set out. Many readers can only wonder what on earth is going on, but they should recall that less intricate reasoning had left philosophy bemused over the Cartesian doubt about dreaming, and troubled by scepticism about material objects, for many hundreds of years. There was a conviction that if only we took sufficient pains, we should either clear these matters up for ever, or better understand why we could not.

On the other hand, it was perhaps the feeling that the task was Sisyphean that led Lewy, then 25, to become less and less inclined to publish his work. He did present his results on entailment and propositional identity to the Aristotelian Society in 1964, but he became more content to work in the shadow of his masters. In the same year he delivered to the British Academy a masterly lecture on Moore's naturalistic fallacy, pronounced so long ago, in 1903, in *Principia Ethica*. He painstakingly edited Moore's *Lectures on Philosophy* and his *Commonplace Book*, and later Broad's lectures on Leibniz and on Kant.

Lewy died on 8 February 1991, in the days following an operation for cancer. His life as a philosopher was that of a teacher, perhaps the most honourable mode of all. He is commemorated at Cambridge by the Philosophy Faculty Library which is named after him, endowed in part by contributions from former students as a measure both of gratitude and as a token that such teaching should continue in that place.

IAN HACKING
Fellow of the Academy

DONALD MACDOUGALL   *Financial Times*

George Donald Alastair MacDougall
1912–2004

Donald MacDougall entitled his autobiography *Don and Mandarin*. In fact he spent two-thirds of his working life in 'Whitehall' and just one-third in academe, and he never regretted that. Sitting next to a young Research Fellow in Economics at a Nuffield College dinner, who had spent her career thus far at Oxford, and was planning her next move to an American university, he asked whether a spell in Whitehall would not be a good idea. She replied that it would be very bad for her career, as she would quickly become out of date with the literature. Donald's disapproval was evident when he told this story. What mattered most for him was economic policy. He was a great public servant, his most important work being as a young man during the war, but with a great many other significant contributions during his long life. He found economics intellectually fascinating, and, with his sharp mind, enjoyed the cut and thrust of argument, but it needed a practical bearing to engage him fully. He was unfailingly polite, never trying to use his authority or reputation to beat down an opponent, however junior. Instead, he took pains to be well briefed, and relied on his wonderful memory and immense knowledge of relevant facts and experience, and his ability to separate the important from the less important, to make his case. If he showed impatience, it was with those whose facts were wrong, and who were slow to recognise it. He had prejudices, described later, but accepted that others could reasonably differ on matters of judgement, so that discussion with him was always constructive. Away from economics he had a fund of amusing stories, and the gift of being interested in almost anything, and especially in the concerns of whoever was talking to him, so that they felt that both they and their opinions mattered. This

Proceedings of the British Academy, **138**, 181–205. © The British Academy 2006.

made conversation with him a rare pleasure, since most of us like to talk mainly of our own concerns.

Early life, 1912–39

Donald was born in Glasgow on 26 October 1912 and brought up there. His father helped to run the family china business, which failed to prosper, and died when Donald was seventeen. His mother's father had been a trader in West Africa, who had prospered, but, with nine siblings, she inherited enough for only her own needs. Fortunately, this grandfather had left sufficient in a trust for Donald to go to Balliol College, Oxford, in 1931. This followed his education at Kelvinside Academy, Glasgow, and then at Shrewsbury boarding school. There he specialised in mathematics, and was neither happy nor particularly distinguished.

Balliol was a complete contrast. He felt free to follow his interests, and started with a year of Honour Maths. Mods., at the end of which he got a Second, having expected a Third. Convinced that he was past his peak at mathematics, he switched to PPE (Philosophy, Politics and Economics) which he was allowed (unusually) to read for another three years. He enjoyed this enormously, his economics tutor being the brilliant Maurice Allen, who might nowadays be regarded as dead weight, since his research output was nearly nil. Encouraged by him, Donald won the George Webb Medley Junior Scholarship in 1934, thus becoming one of the two top economists entering their last year. His final Honours Schools examination in 1935 was, however, a disaster. The invigilator of the statistics paper (which should have been one of Donald's best) confiscated his slide-rule, never having seen one before, which drove him back to log tables which he had not used for some years, and resulted in a relatively poor mark. His two economics examiners were (Sir) Roy Harrod and C. R. Fay, who was Reader in Economic History at Cambridge. Much of Donald's viva (lasting over an hour) consisted of Roy and Donald trying to convince Fay that what Donald had written was correct. In the end, he was awarded a Second, although Roy argued strongly that he should get a First, and considered him the best economist that year. Some twenty years later, Fay suddenly sent Roy a postcard saying, in effect, that he thought they should have given Donald a First after all.

That Donald was the best economist of the year was confirmed by the award of the George Webb Medley Senior Scholarship, with enough money to finance two years of post-graduate work at Balliol, with Roy

Harrod as his supervisor. After a term floundering in attempts at mathematical economics, Roy advised him to state what he was trying to do in literary terms 'without ever using a so-called mathematical symbol of any kind'. Donald at first resented this, but on reflection concluded that it was one of the most important pieces of advice he ever had, and that his mathematics was inadequate. So he completely changed course to an empirical study of the iron and steel industry. As a by-product, he wrote a theoretical paper on 'The definition of prime and supplementary costs' which Roy said he must submit to Keynes, then editor of *The Economic Journal*. The latter wrote to Donald suggesting improvements, and it was published in the September 1936 issue. It helped to secure Donald his first academic appointment at Leeds University that autumn.

Having achieved financial independence, in July 1937 Donald married Chris Bartrum whom he had met on a family holiday in Austria two years before. There were two children of this marriage, John, academically inclined, who became Professor of Sociology at the Universty of Lowell in Massachusetts and has two children and two grandchildren, and Mary, who decided to live and work near the family home at Tayvallich, Argyll. The marriage proved not to be a happy one. He left her in 1975, asked her to divorce him, and in 1977 married Margaret Hall, a Fellow of Somerville College, Oxford, and the divorced wife of Lord Roberthall (referred to below). This marriage was entirely successful, ending with Margaret's death in 1995.

The 1930s were dominated by heavy unemployment and the growing threat of Germany, to both of which Donald reacted in an entirely practical way. He became President of the Balliol College boys' club, which brought him into contact with working class boys in the (then) slums of St Ebbe's in Oxford and at the annual camps. He also attended a camp for the unemployed in Durham in 1934, becoming medical officer there for ten days with a hundred men in his charge. He found TCP was a wonderful panacea. After two conferences in Germany while he was at Leeds, and a briefing by (Sir) Henry Hardman, then extra-mural tutor, he became better aware of what was happening there than many of his contemporaries. In 1938–9 he arranged for four German and Austrian students, some Jewish, to come to Leeds. As well, he and Chris took several refugees into their home as lodgers, and from one of these sprang a friendship which blossomed in Donald's last years (see below).

While at Leeds, Donald wrote the main chapter in *Britain in Recovery* (British Association, 1938) produced by a research committee of the British Association, of which Roy Harrod was a member. This involved piecing together statistics from many different sources to form a readable survey of the British economy from 1929 to 1937, a valuable education in itself. Donald's professor at Leeds, J. H. Jones, was chairman of the committee, and also a member of the Barlow Commission on the Geographical Distribution of the Industrial Population. Donald wrote two studies prepared for this Commission, one of which was published in the *Journal of the Royal Statistical Society,* 1940. All three of these studies were reprinted in Donald's *Studies in Political Economy vol 1* (London, 1975). They demonstrate not only his skill and care in handling economic statistics, but also his energy, when one realises how quickly they were produced at a time when he was preparing and delivering lectures, examining, getting married, and attending conferences in Germany.

War and the Prof, 1939–45

On 3 September 1939 France and Britain declared war on Germany, following its invasion of Poland. Not long afterwards, Donald was telephoned by Roy Harrod and asked to take the first train he could to Oxford for a possible job whose nature Roy could not reveal. Roy's colleague at Christ Church, Frederick Lindemann (later Lord Cherwell), Professor of Experimental Philosophy (i.e. physics) at Oxford, and known as the Prof, was a close friend of Churchill. With the advent of war, the latter had joined Chamberlain's Cabinet as First Lord of the Admiralty, and the Prof had accompanied him to an office in Whitehall, where he was expected to advise Churchill, not only on scientific matters, but on all aspects of the conduct of the war other than military strategy and appointments. Churchill did not confine himself to naval affairs, but wished to be independently briefed on all the papers coming to the Cabinet. The Prof had wide scientific knowledge, great intelligence, and supreme self-confidence; and could express himself clearly, forcefully and succinctly. In the years since the Nazi threat had started to grow, he had been associated closely with Churchill in his attempt to warn the country and galvanise the government, and he knew Churchill's methods. He had also developed a jaundiced view of the official mind. Now he needed an economic staff to help him, and had asked Roy to find him an economist to head it.

In his memoir *The Prof* (London, 1959), Roy listed the abilities he thought necessary for this post, to which he had given much thought. Naturally, the occupant must be 'of quite first-rate intellectual calibre', but any tendency to show off would be fatal. A young man would best accept the Prof's tendency to lay down the law about matters where he had no special qualifications, and yet the young man must be tough enough not to quail before Prof's overbearing manner. In the end, the Prof was open to reason. The man 'must not be too squeamish about figures, but willing to make a rough assessment on inadequate data'. Roy knew that a merely abstract argument meant nothing to the Prof—it had to be expressed in quantitative terms. This was the most important requirement. 'I regard my choice of man on that occasion as a stroke of genius, and my best contribution to the defeat of Hitler.'

Donald was introduced to the Prof in Christ Church common room, and from the start they clicked. Soon he was installed in the Admiralty and on the telephone to government departments seeking to extract data from them which, they realised, could be used to criticise them. Their immediate reaction therefore tended to be hostile. It required immense tact, but gradually, thanks to Donald, S Branch (as it was known) became accepted and respected in Whitehall, with additional clout and a wider role after Churchill became Prime Minister in May 1940. The staff consisted of some half a dozen economists, a scientific officer, an established civil servant, a few typists, clerks and computers (people, not machines) and some chartists, about twenty people in all. Donald was effectively the head of it from the beginning, and formally from mid-1942, when Roy left.

Their bread-and-butter work was to create and update charts on all aspects of the war effort. The Prime Minister pored over these, showed them to important visitors, and copies were sent (and updated) to President Roosevelt. The most interesting, exciting and difficult work was preparing minutes from the Prof to Churchill, on average about one a day. These arose sometimes through requests from Churchill, and sometimes on the initiative of the Prof or members of the Branch, mostly recommending action, since the Prof did not want to add to the pile of information which heaped up for the Prime Minister. They were kept very brief, but could take weeks to prepare. Nearly a third could be called scientific, for example, on the development of new weapons. Of the remainder, about thirty per cent were concerned with the armed forces, and it was here that the Branch was distinguished from the Economic Section of the War Cabinet secretariat, which was not concerned with the use of resources once allocated to military purposes. Two examples show how important it could be to cover that, both relating to shipping which was scarce for most of the war.

In early 1942 Donald discovered that vehicles destined for Egypt via the Cape were being loaded on to ships fully assembled, and that six to ten times as many could be carried per ship if they were crated completely knocked down (CKD). He worked out how much shipping this would save and the extra imports into Britain it would allow. The Prof told the Prime Minister, who was slow to react, so he sent him one of his very few minutes typed in red ink, and that turned the trick. After long arguments with the military, who objected to the inconvenience, Churchill directed that the vehicles were to be CKD to the greatest possible extent, with reports to him on progress (as was usual). Much shipping was thereby saved.

The Allies planned a major offensive late in 1942 in North Africa, with landings in Morocco and Algeria, and an advance westwards from Egypt, all imposing heavy demands on our shipping. Donald worked out that the ships left to bring imports into the UK were so few that there could be severe food shortages and factory closures for lack of materials. At that low ebb of the war, after a string of defeats, and with victorious German armies sprawled across Europe, including Russia, the danger to morale at home was serious. He kept warning the Prof who kept warning Churchill, but the latter was preoccupied with military strategy. Donald argued that the ships heading round the Cape to Egypt and the East should be cut from the previous 120 a month to sixty, and that military supplies in Egypt were adequate (some said for a hundred years war). The Prof accepted this but told Churchill that a cut back to forty or fifty a month was required, expecting to have it argued up by the military. At last Churchill listened and ordered a cut back to forty. The result was that the military campaign was successful, with no shortage of supplies, and that stocks of food and materials in Britain fell about as low as they could, but consumption was maintained. Donald described this as 'the most momentous macro-economic decision in which I have been involved'.

Towards the end of the war, the work in the Branch became more concerned with post-war economic policies. Much influenced by Donald, in early 1944 the Prof submitted a paper to the Cabinet which he thought could serve as a summary of the proposed White Paper on Employment Policy, subsequently published at the end of May 1944, and which anticipated much of it. Most of Donald's work on the post-war situation, however, related to our external economic problems. The most serious was that of paying for sufficient imports, given the collapse of our exports during the war, the heavy debts we were saddled with at the end of it, the sale of overseas assets and the worsening in our terms of trade. There was the related issue of post-war world trade and payments arrangements.

The Americans insisted, as a *quid pro quo* for Lend-Lease, that we should undertake to work towards multilateral non-discriminatory trade, including the elimination of Imperial Preference. There was a strong faction within the Conservative Party favouring, on the contrary, a strengthening of Imperial Preference, and the Prime Minister was constantly lobbied for this, for agricultural protection, and for exploiting our bargaining power as a large importer through bilateral agreements on Schactian lines. Both Donald and the Prof thought our bargaining power after the war would be weak, and that we would be best served by a world in which other countries in a stronger position were not allowed to restrict their imports from us, so that we needed internationally agreed rules to protect us.

The Prof attended the Potsdam Conference in July 1945, following the end of the war in Europe, and Donald joined him from Moscow, where he had been discussing German reparations. After the British general election and defeat of the Conservatives, he was recalled to London, the Branch was abolished, and he was awarded the CBE in Churchill's resignation honours. He returned to Berlin to work further on reparations as a member of the Economic Section of the Cabinet Offices, but left before the end of 1945 to take up a Fellowship at Wadham College, Oxford on the Prof's recommendation as a Professorial Fellow of the college.

Wadham College, 1946–8

The college imposed a heavy load of teaching on its fellows, having expanded its numbers to cope with the influx of ex-servicemen. I was one of these, and remember enjoying Donald's tutorials, both because I could follow his lucid arguments and because he made economics relevant to the post-war world. Besides tutorials, he lectured, examined, became Domestic Bursar, served on government-appointed committees, and published several articles. These grew out of work undertaken in the Branch on Britain's external economic problems, and three are reprinted in *Studies in Political Economy vol 1*. Easily the longest, on 'Britain's Foreign Trade Problem', took up about half the *Economic Journal* of March 1947 (the only other article being Austen Robinson's memoir of Keynes, who had died in 1946). I remember Donald lecturing to a crowded Wadham hall on this, the practical importance of the subject making a strong appeal to his largely ex-service audience.

A year later the same journal published a critique of Donald's article by Tommy Balogh (later Lord Balogh), who had beaten Donald to an

Economics Fellowship at Balliol in 1945, together with a reply by Donald (also reprinted in *Studies vol 1*). Balogh was an advocate of discriminatory trading blocs, bulk purchase, long-term contracts, planning and controls. He represented a widely held view that the success of the war-time economy, contrasted with the miseries of the 1930s, showed that planning and controls, both domestically and internationally, would secure a more stable, just and prosperous economic order. Against this Donald argued that non-discriminatory multilateral trading rules were in our long-term interests, given our weak bargaining power. In the shorter run, however, countries like ourselves in balance of payments difficulties, with inadequate foreign exchange reserves, should be allowed to impose discriminatory import and foreign exchange controls. It should be remembered that controls and shortages were widespread at that time as countries emerged from the war. Few thought that they should be quickly swept away, and Donald, like others, favoured a more gradual approach. He was well aware of the virtues of competition and market mechanisms (I remember writing him essays on this), but he argued pragmatically, and by appeal to the facts rather than to more abstract generalisations.

Paris, 1948–9

In the summer of 1947, Donald had rejected the opportunity to join Lord Franks's team in Paris which, with representatives of other European countries, responded to General Marshall's offer of US aid to help recovery from the war. A year later, however, Robert Marjolin, Secretary-General of the new Organisation for European Economic Cooperation (OEEC) in Paris, which resulted from this offer, invited him to be its first Economics Director, and he wanted to go. But he needed to get leave from Wadham, which meant, in effect, from the Warden, Maurice Bowra. The latter liked to decide things quickly, and Donald exploited this by marching into his room and asking 'Is there any reason why I shouldn't go to Paris for a year and work in the OEEC?' Since Bowra could think of no reason on the spur of the moment, but felt he must answer at once, he said 'No'. 'Thank you very much', said Donald, and went off to Paris that autumn. In 1949 he was pressed to stay for another year, but both he and the college rejected this. Then in July he received a letter from Bowra which began: 'I am in a quandary. Severe pressure is being put on me to say that you can stay away for another year. First a blackmailing Swede [Per

Jacobsen, future Managing Director of the International Monetary Fund (IMF)] and his wife came to see me and said "Haf you no lof for your country?" and threatened me with a hideous fate; now Sir Cripps writes in red ink to much the same effect. What am I to do?' A compromise was reached to let him stay until the end of 1949.

Donald was the most important writer and editor of the OEEC's *Interim Report on the European Recovery Programme,* as well as of the succeeding *Second Report* (which, however, was completed after he left). Both were needed in Washington to keep the aid flowing. He played a crucial role at the start of the OEEC's effort to free intra-European trade from the network of quantitative import restrictions that hampered it. He also recruited the first members of its Economics Directorate.

Wadham and Nuffield Colleges, 1950–1

In 1950 Donald was elected (the first) Reader in International Economics at Oxford, attached to Nuffield College, and so had to move there at the end of the year, although he continued some undergraduate teaching for Wadham. He published two of his best-known articles in the *Economic Journal* (December 1951 and September 1952) on 'British and American Exports: a Study suggested by the Theory of Comparative Costs' (reprinted in *Studies vol 2)*. This was a major piece of research for which he had a team of nine statistical assistants. The most quoted result was the direct relation between US:UK relative labour productivities and US:UK relative export quantities for different manufactures in 1937. He had used this, for a few products, when teaching the theory of comparative costs, but then found that it applied to many more when he examined it systematically. He followed this with the idea of a cross-section, as opposed to the more usual time-series, approach to the estimation of elasticities of demand (the extent to which quantities demanded respond to changes in prices) in international trade, by examining the relation between relative US:UK export prices and quantities for about a hundred manufactures in each of about twenty (mainly inter-war) years. He concluded that the elasticities were much higher than current time-series estimates had suggested, and which had resulted in wide-spread elasticity pessimism. In the early 1960s he published further estimates based on post-second world war data of productivity and exports for which the main important difference was in respect of US tariffs. Whereas in 1937 these had been 'made-to-measure', and so tended to be higher the greater the UK's comparative advantage, thus shutting our exports out of the US market, after the war this was no longer so.

The Prof again, 1951–3

In October 1951, the Conservatives defeated Labour and Churchill became Prime Minister once more with the Prof in the Cabinet as Paymaster General. Somewhat reluctantly, Donald got leave to work for him, and set up a smaller version of the Branch with two members of the wartime one and just three economists (the writer being one). There was a severe balance of payments crisis at the time, mainly due to the Korean War, which had caused a surge in commodity prices followed by a relapse. During the surge, the rest of the sterling area (RSA) had accumulated foreign exchange surpluses which showed up as large increases in the central gold and dollar reserves held in London. After a lag, these countries started to spend their wealth, and this coincided with the relapse in prices. On top of this, the UK Labour Government had launched a rearmament programme which led to a steel shortage, hampered exports of engineering goods, and with stockpiling and the worsening in our terms of trade resulted in a large deficit in our current account. So the reserves started to roar down even faster than they had roared up. Imports were already restricted by consumer rationing and import controls, and one of the first actions of the new government was to tighten these. A Commonwealth Finance Ministers' Conference was assembled in January 1952 at which the RSA countries undertook to restore equilibrium in their accounts later in the year by various economies, and the UK restricted imports still further and planned various deflationary measures including a tough budget in March. The Prime Minister, the Prof and Donald sailed to America to negotiate successfully for a million tons of steel. The fall in the reserves was thus intended to be ended by these measures.

It was then with astonishment that the Prof and Donald learned in late February that emergency action of a most radical kind was proposed by the Chancellor, R. A. Butler, involving blocking of ninety per cent of sterling balances held by non-sterling non-dollar countries, eighty per cent of those of the RSA countries, convertibility into dollars of the remainder and of further accruals, and a floating exchange rate for the pound. The plan was called ROBOT, possibly because the original authors were Sir Leslie ROwan (Treasury), Sir George Bolton (Bank of England), and

OTto Clark (Treasury). Butler admitted that these measures, unilaterally taken, would antagonise the governments of Commonwealth countries (whose reserves would largely be frozen and whose finance ministers had so recently agreed to a quite different set of measures), and those of Continental European countries, since the recently formed European Payments Union and the programme to free intra-European trade would be disrupted, and even that of the USA, since the floating rate was contrary to the provisions of the IMF and because of the effects on European recovery. He also admitted that convertibility of the pound into dollars would, in a world of dollar shortage, tend to make other countries restrict imports from the UK more severely in order to earn dollars, and that, on the domestic front, 'the basic idea of internal stability of prices and employment will not be maintainable. . . . It will not be possible to avoid unemployment. . . . The pressure will fall particularly on the cost of living.' Butler is even said to have admitted that the plan could mean the end of the Conservative Party for twenty years. Despite that, it appealed strongly to two instincts of senior ministers: it was represented as a patriotic necessity, and the more painful the measures the more effective they must surely be. The Prime Minister gave it his initial backing, and at the first meeting of a restricted group of ministers to be informed of it on Friday, 22 February the Prof's was a lone voice raised in opposition.

Over the weekend in Oxford, the Prof and Donald prepared a paper to go to ministers criticising ROBOT. This, first, pointed out that nothing substantial had happened since the Finance Ministers' Conference to justify emergency action now. The measures taken then needed time to take effect. (In fact, the fall in the reserves was $300 million in January, $221 million in February, $114 million in March, after which they remained steady until the last quarter of 1952, when they rose strongly.) Secondly, however, even if the reserves were going to plunge dangerously low (as the Treasury now warned), ROBOT would harm rather than help. The exchange rate would fall and this would worsen our terms of trade, thus increasing our current account deficit. Little alleviation could be expected from lower import quantities (already severely restricted), nor from greater export quantities (given the overloaded economy and the effects of convertibility admitted by Butler). The strain on our reserves would thus be greater, not less. Apart from that, there were all the external and domestic effects mentioned in the Chancellor's paper. A better alternative was to keep the rate fixed, and defend it with a tough budget, more import restrictions, and borrowing from the IMF and elsewhere.

In the end, after further meetings of ministers and the Cabinet, and much lobbying, ROBOT was rejected at least for the time being at a Cabinet meeting on 29 February. The budget, which had been postponed from 4 to 11 March, saw bank rate raised from $2\frac{1}{2}$ per cent to 4 per cent, a cut in food subsidies, and other tough measures. There had been rumours about a floating rate, but, with no announcement in the budget, it seems that speculation against the pound was ended. Although the need for emergency action was over, and the cycle proceeded on its way, the Treasury and the Bank of England tried in the summer once more to argue that disaster was round the corner and that ROBOT must be adopted. However, this time they did not get very far.

The episode was described by Donald as 'some of the most interesting and exciting periods of my life which I would not have missed for anything'. The Prof resigned in the summer of 1953 (and died rather suddenly in 1957, leaving a large void in Donald's life). He made sure that Donald became a Knight Bachelor in the Coronation Honours at the young age of forty. There is no doubt that both the Prof and Donald were correct in their view that the reserves crisis was temporary, and the alarmist forecasts of the Treasury and the Bank were proved wrong. There was no justification for the attempt to stampede the Cabinet into radical measures without proper consultation. While some historians of the period (e.g. Alec Cairncross, *Years of Recovery,* London, 1985) have taken the view that ROBOT would have been disastrous, both politically and economically, and that much, perhaps most, of the credit for stopping it is due to the Prof (with Donald's advice), others have demurred. Some have held that Eden's opposition was crucial, although he arrived a bit late on the scene. Others have stressed the long-term benefits of convertibility and a floating rate, both of which seem quite normal now (see, in particular, John Fforde, *The Bank of England and Public Policy, 1941–1958*, Oxford, 1992). A former Chancellor, Lord Lawson, has argued that, had ROBOT been adopted, the corporatist and interventionist tenor of policy, with wage and price controls, would have ended much sooner than 1979 (*Times Literary Supplement*, January 2004). But 'there is a time for everything', and the events in the years leading up to it prepared the country for 1979 and the ensuing radical measures. One needs to set out carefully the counterfactual of what would have happened in 1952 had ROBOT been adopted, not forgetting the unilateral blocking of sterling balances, if one is to make the case for it. An unappealing scenario can easily be constructed.

Nuffield College, 1953–61

Donald returned to Nuffield College in 1953 for his last stint as an academic economist, no longer as Reader in International Economics, but as
an Official Fellow, which gave him more freedom for research. With
Rosemary Hutt's assistance, he produced the first thorough study of
Imperial Preference (*Economic Journal*, June 1954), which showed how
unimportant it had become despite the fuss made over it on both sides of
the Atlantic. This was a typical Donald devastating appeal to laborious
facts, which everyone else blithely assumed they knew and were not prepared to take the trouble to check. Most of his time, however, was spent
on lectures, and then a massive book, on the world dollar problem. Well-
known economists had asserted that the USA would, for many years,
worsen the rest of the world's balance of payments by being super-
competitive, and as well would cause great instability through fluctuations
in demand. Donald's book (*The World Dollar Problem,* London 1957)
compels admiration for the quantity of relevant facts so carefully and
clearly marshalled. There are 200 pages of appendices, a third of the book,
and a wealth of sources cited, both of statistics and economic arguments.
The book was perhaps the first to discount the myth, then strongly
believed, that productivity in the USA must inevitably grow faster than in
the rest of the world. Its underlying methodology was a partial equilibrium analysis of trade in which exports or imports were determined by
trend rates of growth of demand and supply together with movements
along demand and supply curves due to changes in relative prices.
Different commodity groups were considered, and attention was also
given to services and capital movements. A 'dollar problem' was defined as
a tendency for the rest of the world to move into deficit at 'full employment', which required either unwanted and costly deflationary measures,
or devaluations, or trade restrictions. The tendency could be due to 'structural' reasons (shifts in demand or supply curves), or to a faster increase in
the general level of prices in the rest of the world. In the book, he took the
view that both structural and price level factors would be adverse for the
rest of the world. In a 1954 lecture he had been agnostic, and he was so
again in 1960, when he published a reappraisal of the problem, but in the
book he came down (cautiously) on the gloomy side. While most reviews
of the book were very favourable, and the short-term behaviour of the US
balance seemed to confirm its pessimism, two critics whom he respected
(Roy Harrod and Robert Triffin) expressed doubts about the whole
approach and the wisdom of making *any* predictions. The subsequent

course of events has borne them out, and it is sad that Donald's one big book, to which he devoted so much effort, and which contains a mass of interesting material, faded into oblivion in a few years.

Donald's chief research assistant for this book was Monica Dowley, who had also worked for him earlier on his study of elasticities in international trade. She remembers how pleasant it was. He never chided one for taking longer than expected, nor badgered one unnecessarily when one was doing one's best. Donald's secretary, throughout his years at Nuffield and later, was Audrey Carruthers, who was one of the few people able to read his handwriting. She produced meticulous typescripts of the book and his journal articles, with their numerous statistical tables, all before the days of word processors. He persuaded her to go with him to London when he went back to work in Whitehall, and she left only when she married Keith Skeats in 1968 and returned to Nuffield. She remembers how appreciative he was of long hours of work in London, and how he always remained calm then, despite being shouted at by George Brown, or being told to see the Prime Minister immediatedly.

Around this time Donald published two articles which exposed his views on exchange rates and inflation, both highly relevant to the problems on which he was to advise future British governments. In 1954 he criticised an article by W. Scammel which favoured floating exchange rates. His main counter-argument was that fixed exchange rates formed a bulwark against inflation, partly because trade union negotiators would then fear that large wage increases might price their members out of their jobs. However, he still wanted governments to adjust the rate in 'fundamental disequilibrium'. In fact, he favoured the adjustable peg system of Bretton Woods and the IMF. The importance he attached to trade union behaviour was also evident in his article on 'Inflation in the United Kingdom' (1959, reprinted in *Studies vol II*). He recognised that increases in unemployment would tend to slow down wage increases, but thought there was an independent element of 'trade union pushfulness' which needed attention, perhaps by some kind of incomes policy. Nevertheless, he saw that that 'bristled with difficulties', and, while 'not entirely unhopeful', feared that the outcome could well be more inflation or less employment and growth than the economy was capable of, or perhaps both. His realism on these matters put some of his academic colleagues to shame.

Donald made numerous visits overseas during these years, including six months in 1959 at the Australian National University, which led to one of his best-known articles on 'The benefits and costs of private investment from abroad: a theoretical approach' (republished in *Studies vol II*). This started with a beautifully simple partial equilibrium static analysis, which was then elaborated by successively dropping assumptions. Although a 'theoretical approach', it was informed throughout by the probable sizes of various effects. It is a model of how to use simple economics to attack a subtle problem, and stimulated work by many others.

Nuffield College obtained full control over its endowment in 1958, with Donald and Ian Little as its first Investment Bursars. They shifted the portfolio heavily into equities at the right moment when the 'cult of the equity' was taking hold. They went considerably better by outperforming the market by a wide margin from 1958 to 1961, when Donald left.

Neddy, 1962–4

By 1961 the UK economy had been growing more slowly than many Continental countries for a decade or more. Dissatisfaction with this had provoked debate about the role of (indicative) planning, which some thought explained, for example, France's success. A related explanation was thought to be the 'stop and go' policies followed in Britain, and in the middle of 1961 there was yet another stop resulting, as usual, from pressure on the gold and dollar reserves. To counter this, the Chancellor, Selwyn Lloyd, raised bank rate from five to seven per cent, and took other deflationary action, but he also proposed a move towards French-style planning. Eventually, a tripartite National Economic Development Council (Neddy) was set up, chaired by the Chancellor, with business and trade union representatives, which started a series of regular meetings in March 1962. It was supported by a National Economic Development Office whose Director-General was Sir Robert Shone and whose first Economics Director was Donald. Just as in the Prof's office in Whitehall, and in the OEEC in Paris, he had both to set up and run an economics staff to undertake a new task. It was a role he relished, and was to undertake again in the DEA and, to a degree, in the CBI.

He played an active part in two important parts of Neddy's work. The first was to promote faster economic growth, both by setting out what this would involve, quantitatively, given a target of four per cent per annum from 1961 to 1966, and also by detailing the supply- and demand-side policies required on such matters as education, training, research and development, labour mobility, regional development, the balance of payments, taxation, the level of demand, and prices and incomes. Two booklets, on the projections of national output etc. and on the policies, were published in 1963 after discussion in the Council, the hope being that, by convincing everyone that faster growth was feasible, and implementing the policies, it could be achieved. However, no mention of the exchange rate was allowed, and instead attention was given in the Council to the second part of Neddy's work, namely, obtaining a consensus on the need for slower growth in *nominal* incomes in order to obtain faster growth in *real* ones. Donald believed that his work on this, and the good relations achieved between the three sides of the Council, prepared the ground for more formal agreements between them after the change of government in 1964.

The DEA, 1964–8

By 1964, Donald had become convinced that devaluation had become a necessary precursor to faster economic growth. The situation was very different from that in 1952, when he had opposed devaluation. Exports were no longer hampered by a big rearmament programme nor threatened by a move to convertibility, imports were no longer restricted by tight controls, and our costs and prices had risen by much more than those of our competitors. But he still believed in the adjustable peg as a bulwark against inflation, and in the need for some form of incomes policy, and he was opposed to letting unemployment rise from its then low level. These beliefs fitted well with many of those held by George Brown, the minister given charge of the new Department of Economic Affairs (DEA) in the incoming Wilson administration. This, and his role in Neddy, made him an obvious choice as Director General.

On the key question of devaluation, Donald attended a meeting consisting otherwise of the Chancellor, Jim Callaghan, George Brown, and two top civil servants, William Armstrong and Eric Roll (both subsequently life peers), on the Saturday evening following the election. It was short, and indeed all the big decisions then were absurdly rushed. They went round the table asking whether anyone thought the pound ought to be devalued, and Donald was the only one to say that it should, giving brief reasons. Callaghan and Brown then saw Wilson and decided not to devalue, thus missing the best opportunity of fastening the blame on the

Conservative Government which had, in 1964, set off a boom which strained the balance of payments.

Little was done to restrain the boom, the government having been elected on a commitment to faster growth. Much of Donald's time was devoted to preparing a National Plan to achieve 3.8 per cent per annum growth from 1964 to 1970, a thankless task once the decision not to devalue was taken. Indeed one might criticise him for continuing with this work which absorbed skilled manpower, including himself, for little result other than to induce scepticism about the value of any planning at all. He could have taken a leaf out of George Brown's book by threatening to resign. There were successive runs on the gold and dollar reserves, which were met mainly by borrowing from abroad and imposing an import surcharge. Rapid growth in public expenditure and low unemployment were maintained. In the summer of 1965 a joint memorandum by Donald and three other leading economic advisers to the government—Neild, Kaldor and Balogh (the last having changed his view on the matter)—to Wilson, Callaghan and Brown seems at last to have convinced Brown of the need to devalue, but not the others.

After a traumatic meeting with the employers' side of Neddy, Brown obtained their approval of the National Plan, and then secured the backing of Neddy in August 1965, and it was published in September. But this was a hollow victory. Donald had to go round trying to convince everyone that the projections in the Plan could be met, although he realised how improbable this was. In July 1966, with yet another foreign exchange crisis, and foreign banks and governments becoming more reluctant to support the pound, severe deflationary measures were taken which extinguished what life remained in the Plan. George Brown threatened resignation several times, and eventually changed places in August 1966 with Michael Stewart at the Foreign Office. Donald found Stewart a model minister, and a marked contrast to Brown. The latter's erratic behaviour, his bullying and rudeness, as well as flashes of brilliance, resulted in many anecdotes recounted in *Don and Mandarin*.

Brown's most notable achievement was in the second main sphere of the DEA's activities, incomes policy. He had the background, experience and force of character to persuade trade union leaders to accept a succession of agreements to restrain wage increases. In this he was effectively supported by Donald, whose experience at Neddy has already been noted, and who formed good personal relations with successive General Secretaries of the TUC (George Woodcock, Vic Feather and Lionel Murray).

In November 1967 the pound was at last devalued, and Callaghan honourably resigned, succeeded by Roy Jenkins, who reversed the climb in public expenditure so as to make room for an improvement in the balance of payments. But the severe measures took time to have effect, and in 1968 there were further heavy losses of reserves and more foreign borrowing.

The Treasury, 1969–73

At the end of 1968 Alec Cairncross resigned from his post as Chief Economic Adviser in the Treasury to become Master of St Peter's Hall in Oxford. Donald had originally hoped for the Treasury post in 1961, when Cairncross succeeded Robert Hall. Now he secured it at Roy Jenkins's request. One of his main concerns at the Treasury was the organisation of the Government Economic Service (GES). He was the first Chief Economic Adviser to be given the title of the Head of the GES, but more than a title was involved. It grew rapidly: staff numbers increased from about 20 in 1964 to about 180 in 1969 and 280 in 1973, and needed better organisation. He appointed Peter Davies, an old hand in the Treasury, to do the job, and with him instituted reforms in selection procedures, career advice, the rationalisation of grades, and the reform of pensions. Donald was immensely popular with his young economists, being no great respecter of rank, and taking the trouble to point out why bad ideas were bad while welcoming good ideas from anyone. He is remembered with great affection.

Apart from that he was much concerned with budgetary policy, but less so with the balance of payments or the exchange rate or incomes policy for several reasons. By the summer of 1969 the current balance of payments had clearly moved into surplus at last. There were crises in August 1969 (when the French franc was devalued) and after August 1971, when Nixon suspended convertibility of the dollar into gold and floating rates became widespread, but it was other Treasury officials who were most involved here. In January 1969 Barbara Castle had issued *In Place of Strife,* setting out proposals to reform collective bargaining, with Wilson's backing, but there was insufficient Cabinet support to push these through. The result was, in effect, a collapse of serious attempts to restrain wages and an acceleration of their rate of increase.

For Donald's first eighteen months, the Chancellor was Roy Jenkins, whom he admired, and who was in sole command of economic policy to a much greater extent than the next Chancellor, Barber. For Roy, as an aid to forming his budget judgement, Donald devised a series of graphic ellipses showing the trade-offs between growth, unemployment and the balance of payments, as well as the uncertainties of the forecasts. These became known as MacDougall's flying saucers. One wonders whether other Chancellors could have coped with these.

The Conservatives won the June 1970 election, and initially eschewed incomes policies and tried to deal with wage-push inflation with an Industrial Relations Act and by referring particular wage demands to tribunals. Donald and Douglas Allen (Permanent Secretary to the Treasury, later Lord Croham) had to present the government's case at a court of inquiry presided over by Lord Wilberforce, to settle a pay demand by electricity workers which had led to power cuts. Despite their best efforts to put the case for wage moderation, the court awarded the electricians a large increase, and Wilberforce repeated the performance a year later for the coal miners.

Donald repeatedly warned Heath (the Prime Minister) and Barber (the Chancellor) that unemployment was likely to increase to a million with current policies, but they seemed unconcerned until November 1971, when a U-turn was begun, with more intervention in industry, more public expenditure, large tax reductions in the 1972 budget, and a target fall in unemployment from the million it had reached in January 1972 to 400,000 a year later—this despite Donald's warnings that such a rapid fall had inflationary dangers. The dangers were increased by the Bank of England's measures (which preceded the U-turn) to strengthen competition in the financial sector, freeing bank advances from quantitative restrictions and greatly increasing the money supply. The rate of increase of retail prices accelerated in 1972, and the government now attempted to negotiate an incomes policy with the TUC, but with little success, one obstacle being the Industrial Relations Act. Starting in November 1972 a ninety-day statutory freeze on pay, prices, rents and dividends was imposed, succeeded by other measures. Meanwhile the earlier expansionary measures led to a very rapid growth of output, which started to bump against the ceiling of capacity in 1973. Domestic pressures on prices were added to rapidly rising import prices, since world commodity prices boomed, and oil prices rocketed at the end of 1973. A state of emergency was declared, as coal miners and electricity power workers seemed intent on making the most of their opportunity. There was a general election in February 1974 which returned a minority Labour Government.

Donald left the Treasury in October 1973, having been asked to stay on a year beyond the normal retiring age of sixty. In retrospect, his stint there did not end happily. His advice seems to have been often ignored, but it was even worse than that. The situation had become as he had feared: it seemed that economic growth, low unemployment and low inflation, which the country had enjoyed for a quarter of a century after the war, were no longer even approximately compatible. Radical measures were required, and were finally taken by the Thatcher government. These involved the shock treatment of heavy unemployment and confrontation with some of the unions. Donald's memories of the 1930s, and his non-confrontational character, meant that he could not have supported them. It was therefore fortunate that his next career move was out of work for the government and into the Confederation of British Industry (CBI).

The CBI, 1973–84

While at the Treasury, Donald had become worried by the decline in profitability of UK industry, and had initiated work on this. The acceleration of inflation bore heavily on profits. There was no proper system of inflation accounting, so that both taxes and price controls, and perhaps even some companies' price-setting procedures, squeezed *real* profits and company liquidity. As the CBI's Chief Economic Adviser, which he had now become, Donald's task was to convince the government and trade union leaders of the seriousness of the situation and to persuade them to remedy it. His efforts began immediately after the first budget of the new Chancellor (Denis Healey) in March 1974 which had increased taxes on company profits as well as tightening price controls. After many meetings Healey was convinced, introduced a stock relief scheme in his autumn budget, and eased price controls, thus saving many businesses from disaster. Healey, in his memoirs, blames the Treasury for a bad forecast of company liquidity.

By May 1975 both pay and prices were increasing at frightening rates. The CBI Council then reversed its rejection of incomes policy of six months earlier and approved a three-year programme aimed at reducing inflation in stages. They were invited by the TUC to a meeting to discuss pay in mid-June. The CBI President was dissuaded by Donald from proposing a five per cent cut in real wages and instead, at the meeting, Donald explained the need for pay to increase much more slowly than prices had done in the previous year, and how this would result in slower price increases, and would benefit *real* wages. The immediate trade union reaction was that they could not possibly agree to wage increases smaller than previous price increases, but after further meetings the proposition was accepted, greatly helped by the Chancellor's warning of what would happen if inflation was *not* brought down. The outcome was a halving of the rate of increase of both pay and prices over the next year. All was not well, however, as the £6 pay formula squeezed differentials, and this squeeze continued in the following year, creating tensions. The large depreciation of the pound in the crisis of 1976 once again led to faster price inflation, and in 1977–8 pay accelerated. The Callaghan Government's attempts to rein it back resulted in strikes and the 'winter of discontent' of 1978–9, and the first Thatcher Government in 1979.

Donald worked hard to educate businessmen on the need for pay increases to come down if high inflation and rising unemployment were to be avoided—and found that they were surprisingly ignorant but keen to learn. Conferences with slide presentations were widely held, and leaflets and booklets distributed. From July 1979 the CBI pay campaigns became annual events which, he believed, gradually bore fruit, with the rate of pay increases decelerating and the country's international competitiveness at last improving. While the harsh economic climate was in good measure responsible, better understanding by business and labour leaders helped.

From 1976 on, with the advent of (Sir) John Methven as Director General and Harold (Lord) Watkinson as President, the CBI adopted a much higher public profile with the publication of major documents and a series of national conferences, in both of which Donald was much involved. In the first major document, *The Road to Recovery*, October 1976, there was the typical Donald economic arithmetic showing how taxes could be cut consistently with a reduction in government borrowing if the growth of output matched the government's own extrapolation of past trends. This was the first of a series of medium term economic projections published by the CBI, not as predictions, but to show what was practically achievable given the right policies.

One important projection, at a time of rapidly rising unemployment, concerned the growth of employment. The service industries were of key importance, and the CBI later set up, with *The Financial Times*, a regular Distributive Trades Trends Survey which complemented the well-established Industrial Trends Survey. Donald's new wife, Margaret, was an expert on the distributive trades, and took a great interest in this. He successfully converted Methven to the belief that services were just as 'productive' as manufacturing.

While achieving a higher public profile, the CBI continued to maintain relations with ministers and officials. Donald, with his great experience, had an important role. He got on well with both Healey and Howe, but found discussions with the latter sometimes frustrating. Donald thought that 'Putting an argument to him was sometimes like poking one's finger into a sponge and then, when you took it out again, finding the sponge exactly the same shape as before.' The incoming Conservative Government had quickly done much of what the CBI had asked for on the abolition of price, dividend and exchange controls. They had also shifted the burden of taxation from income to expenditure by lowering the absurdly high rates of income tax and substituting a higher rate of VAT. The CBI (and Donald) welcomed the former, but not the latter, and also had severe misgivings about monetary and fiscal policies over the next few years, which remained restrictive despite a deepening recession and a growing number of bankruptcies.

Early in 1979 Donald had been asked to prepare a 'child's guide' to the now fashionable monetary policy. He believed that the single-minded pursuit of targets for Sterling M3 and the Public Sector Borrowing Requirement (PSBR) was simplistic, and could depress output, employment and profitability far more than intended. While his paper was not circulated outside CBI headquarters, the arguments in it were repeatedly used in representations to Conservative ministers.

CBI representations generally included demands for cuts in government spending plans and less waste and inefficiency. After the 1981 budget, which Donald called a 'real shocker', and which CBI leaders condemned, they set up a working party to document the case for reducing the cost of public services, which was submitted to the Treasury, and welcomed by ministers, though not by all their officials. Donald's work on this reminded him of his wartime role with the Prof.

Two other topics which concerned Donald in the CBI were the exchange rate and the National Insurance Surcharge (NIS) which Healey had introduced, widely described as a 'tax on jobs'. These were linked inasmuch as both affected international competitiveness. In Donald's judgement, the pound had fallen far too low in the 1976 crisis, but subsequently recovered (partly thanks to North Sea oil) and by late 1977 was getting too high. He organised two inquiries of CBI members to gauge their attitude to a lower exchange rate, in early 1978 and in late 1979, but these showed that only about a half favoured it, despite some further rise. A year later, however, with still further rises, the mood changed strongly in favour of getting the rate down, representations were made to the government, and Donald argued strongly for depreciation in evidence to the House of Commons Treasury and Civil Service Committee in July 1982. The rate did come down, and eventually Donald's other long battle to remove the NIS was also won.

Coming from the Treasury and a long experience of official statistics, Donald was more aware than most of their weaknesses. He consequently paid more attention than was then customary to the CBI's direct information from businesses, and led the way in giving it proper emphasis in analysing the state of the economy. He also gave time to discussions of this with his staff, and successfully recruited a remarkable team to work for him (Roger Bootle, Charles Burton, Bernard Connelly, Giles Keating, Ian MacCafferty, Douglas McWilliams and Bridget Rosewell).

In a working life of nearly fifty years, with nine principal appointments, Donald's ten years with the CBI was easily the longest. It concluded with dinners, lunches and a huge reception, which he thoroughly enjoyed. He was a tremendous man for parties, giving well thought out speeches, amusing as well as interesting. This party was attended by the top brass of the CBI, past and present, by its staff, and by many friends in Whitehall, the City, the TUC, academia and the media.

Final years

Donald continued to be mentally very alert and interested in economic affairs until the end. His first self-imposed task was to write his memoirs (*Don and Mandarin*, John Murray, 1987). Besides describing a career with enough activity for several more ordinary lives, the book displays the expected accuracy and painstaking collection of facts about the events and people involved. Little is made of the many distinctions he gained: his knighthood (1953), CBE (1945), OBE (1942), Fellowship of the British Academy (1966), Honorary Fellowships of Wadham (1964), Nuffield (1967), and Balliol (1992) colleges, Oxford, Honorary Doctorates of Strathclyde (1968), Leeds (1971) and Aston (1979) universities, President of the Royal Economic Society (1972–4).

The economic issue that most concerned him latterly was the question of Britain merging its currency with the euro. He had long been interested in this topic, culminating in the MacDougall Report on *The Role of*

Fiscal Policy in European Integration, to the European Commission (May 1977). This consisted of a general report of some seventy pages, backed by seventeen papers, over 500 pages, by members of the group of seven economists responsible for the report and some others, and representing a tremendous research effort. It analysed the role of fiscal systems in eight existing economic and monetary unions, and in three unitary states. It showed the importance of public finance in reducing inequalities between regions and in cushioning fluctuations in incomes and employment. In the light of this, he was a firm opponent of a common currency for Europe, unless and until it became a federation with federal expenditure of at least $7\frac{1}{2}$ to 10 per cent of GDP. While aware that relative changes in price levels could take the place of changes in exchange rates, he did not believe the former could generally be brought about except at great cost in output and employment. Even after the Thatcher years he remained pessimistic about the possibility of flexibility of wage rates. He therefore played an active part in the campaign to keep the pound.

Soon after joining the CBI, he had become Chairman of the Executive Committee of the National Institute of Economic and Social Research, retiring in 1987. This kept him in touch with work on the current state of the economy, which always interested him, as well as making use of his contacts to obtain much needed funds for the Institute. He maintained contacts with Whitehall, and gave advice to Ed Balls, Chancellor Brown's adviser, on how to develop a stable macroeconomic framework, and on the best model for an independent Bank of England. He would go through some of the fine print of economic statistics and mildly berate sinners in the Central Statistical Office. To the very end he attended the Political Economy Club, and could cut through a diffuse discussion to the heart of the matter.

He had always been a great traveller. This memoir has omitted missions to or conferences in numerous places (e.g. Ethiopia, India, Jamaica, Japan, the UN in New York, and Venezuela). He continued to travel after his retirement, often visiting the West Indies, and going on fishing trips to Scotland or Ireland with Margaret. His sight had never been good, but began to give serious trouble in 1979. In 1980 he had a successful cataract operation, followed by another. In his last years, however, he became nearly blind. With typical practical determination he used modern enlargement devices to enable him to read letters, and listened to talking books. Despite his blindness he flew out to, for example, the West Indies accompanied, after Margaret's death in 1995, by Anne Patrick or one or other of his supportive family. He also spent many weekends in Essex with his step-daughter Anthea and her husband Max Wilkinson, and had a succession of devoted carers.

Further support was given by David Schmitz, the son of one of the refugees from the Nazis that Donald and Chris had taken as lodgers in Leeds so many years before. David had come to Britain to work, his parents having settled in the USA, and had looked Donald up, forming a friendship which lasted for thirty years until Donald's death on 22 March 2004. Because of his failing eyesight, Donald needed help in going through his papers, and this David enjoyed providing. David remarked 'To those of us who had the privilege to know him, he showed a kindness which was always sincere, never intrusive and always accompanied by his sense of fun.'

'Cast thy bread upon the waters: for thou shalt find it after many days.'

M. FG. SCOTT
Fellow of the Academy

Note. My main debt is to *Don and Mandarin*. I must also thank the following for suggestions, amendments to an earlier draft and encouragement: Sir Tony Atkinson, Christopher Bliss, Sir Samuel Brittan, Lord Croham, Monica Dowley, Just Faaland, Lord Healey, Sir Bryan Hopkin, Lord Howe, Lord Lawson, Ian Little, Douglas McWilliams, Robert Neild, Jack Parkinson, David Schmitz, Audrey Skeats, Sir Douglas Wass, Max Wilkinson, and Donald's children John and Mary. They are not responsible for errors that may remain.

COLIN MATTHEW   *Judith Aronson*

Henry Colin Gray Matthew
1941–1999

HENRY COLIN GRAY MATTHEW, historian and editor, was born on 15 January 1941 at 31 Island Bank Road, Inverness, the eldest son of Henry Johnston Scott Matthew, a consultant physician of note, and Joyce Mary McKendrick. The pursuit of medicine had been a strong family tradition; Matthew's great-grandfather, John Gray McKendrick, was a distinguished physiologist at Glasgow University and his grandfather, Anderson Gray McKendrick, was a medical statistician and epidemiologist based in India. With his father away in the war, Matthew received his mother's undivided attention during his early childhood in Edinburgh, and maintained with her a level of proximity never attained with his emotionally remote father. He later disappointed his father in choosing a non-medical vocation and it was left to his younger brother, Duncan, to keep the medical succession alive. Matthew was known to all by his second name Colin, a device that—for someone who later became so proficient at indexing and cataloguing—helped to distinguish him from his father, but his scholarly work always appeared under his initials H. C. G., mainly in deference to his mother's family line. Those were outward signs of early tensions that had a lasting effect both on Colin's personality and on his career trajectory. Notwithstanding, Colin remained in contact with his father, particularly in the latter's old age. Significantly, he later expressed admiration for the manner in which W. E. Gladstone, whose diaries he was to edit, had treated his own father.

Colin was brought up in an intense Scottish Tory Protestant milieu. It was a comfortable upper middle-class environment, but emotionally austere and occasionally severe, and it was a testimony to his independence of thought and to his temperament that he eventually shrugged off the

constricting impact of those initial experiences, and did not seek to repli-
cate them with others. His gentleness, loyalty, delight in his family,
integrity, and rock-solid support for friends and colleagues were among
his most remarkable features and cannot be separated from his scholarly
persona. Fortunately for him, for Oxford, and for historical scholarship,
a relatively slow start to his professional academic life was mitigated by
perseverance, serendipity and the confidence of his mentors and supporters, superimposed on a meditative intellect and a gift for thoroughness
that matured into profundity. The very distance he increasingly maintained from the world of everyday constraining convention sustained a
safe haven of originality. Colin's name will forever be associated with two
of the most grandiose and ambitious publishing projects to be conceived
and executed in the United Kingdom in the twentieth century: *The
Gladstone Diaries* and the *Oxford Dictionary of National Biography*. Rarely
had the University of Oxford witnessed such a sense of shock and grief
upon his untimely and sudden death on 29 October 1999 at the height of
his career, aged 58. In his funeral address, Sir Keith Thomas described
Colin as 'one of the few wholly irreplaceable people in this university'.[1] The
outpourings of praise and expressions of loss were a measure of a man,
loved and respected, who combined the finest scholarship with the most
generous of characters.

Colin's schooling began at the Edinburgh Academy, whose harsh,
almost militaristic, climate and mistreatment of those entrusted to its
care bequeathed to him a contempt for iniquitous authority and injustice,
if nothing else. Those years reinforced his own shyness and sense of
insignificance, and his suspicion of others' intentions, which he gradually
overcame in later life. Wisely, his parents removed him in 1954 to
Sedbergh, a public school in North Yorkshire, in which he was much hap-
pier and where he was partly coaxed out of his shell. The first among a
number of significant mentors was the sixth-form history master Andrew
Morgan, who exercised an inspiring influence over young minds and who
had caught glimpses of Colin's character and ability. Morgan cultivated
Colin's interest in history, while in parallel Colin developed an enthusiasm
for literature, including Scott, Dickens, Ruskin and Trollope, as well as
Balzac, discovered in the extensive school library collection; in one
instance even writing home to his mother with a request for books that
Morgan had asked to read. Morgan tapped into Colin's intellectual

---

[1] Sir Keith Thomas, Address at the Funeral of Colin Matthew, 4 Nov. 1999.

strengths, though he did not quite succeed in opening up the young pupil or in entirely augmenting his self-confidence. Some of Colin's internal energy was ploughed into sports, especially cross-country running— activities that, revealingly, he did not keep up once his intellectual vitality began to flourish in mid-life, with the exception of long walks with his children and the rather sedentary pursuit of angling. Colin also addressed the school debating society in which he played a major role; from being a tongue-tied outsider at Sedbergh he rose to become a prefect and head boy. He was, curiously, something of a disciplinarian himself, coming down rather heavily on his younger brother's 'slackness' when the latter joined the school in 1958. That training in outward self-possession may account for the later imperturbability of the otherwise retiring man, even when addressing an audience of 2,000 students on the occasion of receiving an honorary doctorate at McMaster University, Canada, in 1999.

Following Colin's good performance at A level examinations, he went on in 1960 to read modern history at Christ Church, Oxford, at the time yet another of the establishment institutions through which he seemed destined to progress, and with all of which he had a somewhat ambivalent relationship. At a future date, Colin referred to 'the extraordinary constitution of Christ Church—its balance between Church and State',[2] but he retrospectively mixed respect with a distance befitting his increasing egalitarianism and mistrust of hierarchy. At Christ Church Colin found another mentor in the person of the senior history tutor, C. H. Stuart, for whom he harboured a lifelong esteem, as he did for Morgan. Stuart focused on a Tory understanding of high party politics and on a narrow view of history as 'a body of material essentially known'.[3] Still carrying the marks of a politically staid upbringing, Colin at first joined the student Conservative Association. Stuart instilled in him the importance of historical accuracy and the imperative of analytical sharpness. Through his tutor Colin retained a deep appreciation of institutions and traditions and a focus on political history. However, differences of approach to history between Stuart and Colin became evident and Colin began to pursue his own, broader and less party-political, line. That those growing differences did not in any way allay the unremitting combination of public obligation and private loyalty that Colin was to display towards

---

[2] Colin Matthew, Address at Charles H. Stuart's Funeral, Christ Church, 16 Nov. 1991, in *Christ Church Report*, 1991, pp. 37–41.
[3] Ibid.

those who served him well is evident in his warm and personal memorial address for Stuart upon the latter's death in 1991.

Colin did reasonably well in his studies but had apparently decided not to go for a First, graduating with second class honours—at the time still undivided—in 1963. But he may have been as yet inadequately equipped for the assertive Oxford style. As a close colleague observed: 'His ruminative intellectual processes, the careful thought, were unsuited to the snappy demands of the three-hour examination.'[4] Colin also wanted to get the best out of Oxford, frequently attending Oxford Union debates; among others, his abiding literary interests were channelled into stage-managing undergraduate plays, including a thespian visit to Germany on one occasion. With his usual meticulous eye for detail and curiosity about minutiae, to be employed so brilliantly in his later editorship of the Gladstone diaries, he expressed particular interest in the logistics of props. His enjoyment of the theatre became a lasting pastime, although I recall us both falling asleep during a marathon eight hour production of The Greeks at the National Theatre. Colin's undergraduate and, later, postgraduate days were also graced by a number of friendships he forged with future distinguished historians such as Boyd Hilton and Ross McKibbin.

Following his undergraduate studies, Colin made a decision that was to change his life in more ways than one. He enrolled at Makerere University College at Kampala, Uganda, obtaining a Diploma in Education, where he met his future wife, Sue Ann Curry, an American studying for the same diploma under the auspices of the Teachers for East Africa programme. They were then both posted to northern Tanzania, as part of a package agreement to teach British history for two years as education officers in the Tanzanian civil service, Colin at Old Moshi school and Sue at Machame school. That fortunate encounter, facilitated by Colin's Land Rover and finally cemented by their marriage in Indianapolis—Sue's home town—in 1966, produced an extraordinarily cohesive and supportive partnership and provided the very tonic he needed. It was Sue above all who transformed his gaucheness into affability, his introversion into hospitability, and his public stiffness into a capacity to relax and enjoy the company of family, friends and even strangers. The aptitude had always been there, but it needed a magic key to unlock it. Colin's African sojourn also added a new dimension to his Scottish unionist heritage. Alongside

---

[4] Ross McKibbin, 'Matthew, (Henry) Colin Gray (1941–1999)', *Oxford Dictionary of National Biography*, Oxford University Press, 2004.

a sense of Britain's importance and a realisation of the outreach of empire he now developed a lasting empathy with the underdog and with the economic plight of the developing African nations. It profoundly opened him up to human chords and tinctures previously unknown. His embeddedness in the physicality of the Scottish terrain—to which he would later return regularly—was paralleled by an arduous climb up Mount Kilimanjaro, a feat that retained a hold on family lore.

Back in Oxford, the Matthews moved into a house on the Woodstock Road before finally settling at 107 Southmoor Road, interspersed by a short stay in Elsfield, a village just outside the city. Colin first studied for a diploma in economics and politics before commencing on a D.Phil. thesis under the supervision of A. F. Thompson (and the short-term guidance of Maurice Shock when Thompson was on leave). It was no accident that Colin chose the Liberal Imperialists (published as a book in 1973) as his topic. The subject partly appealed to him as an instance of the high politics and the preoccupation with Britain's mission in the world that he had imbibed from Stuart, but also as a dying, and ultimately abortive, moment in the life of a progressive and radical tradition. How good men could endorse imperialism on principle was an intriguing issue for a scholar caught between the call of duty, an understanding of politics as the domain of the respectable, and a personal, though not always conscious, urge to be different. He believed the central challenge of the 'Limps' to be 'What part should the idea of the "national interest" play in progressive ideology',[5] a question that unsurprisingly tied in his academic interest with his cultural hinterland. Tellingly, Colin described that dissenting yet patriotic Liberal interlude as 'unhappy'; in his first letter to me when still completing his thesis I was greeted as 'another moth drawn to the dying flame of liberalism'. But while abandoning hope of a resurrected Liberal party and anchoring his political allegiances resolutely with Labour, Colin regarded both on a broader time-scale as the British party of progress and social reform, to whose ideological mast he became firmly attached. *The Liberal Imperialists* was a substantively innovative but cautiously written study, attracting complimentary but few outstanding reviews, and in intellectual terms it was still a halfway house on the gradual road to self-discovery. It signalled Colin's longstanding interest in ideas as well as in the élites that bestrode the field of politics, though he was to express his dissatisfaction—echoed by some reviewers—that he had not linked them more closely together at the time. That interest

[5] H. C. G. Matthew, *The Liberal Imperialists* (Oxford, 1973), p. x.

always remained an undercurrent, resurfacing in an article on J. A. Hobson, Richard Cobden and John Ruskin, but never replacing Colin's fascination with the broad sweep of national history and with the mechanics of politics. Indeed, one project conceived in the early 1980s but never followed up was a proposed book to be entitled *The British Political Nation, 1832–1972*.

While completing his thesis, Colin secured a post at Christ Church that proved to be another turning point and a second stroke of luck when, now with a young family, he was casting around for employment in an academic world that was not enthused by the class of his undergraduate degree, nor overexcited by the subject of his yet unpublished thesis, meticulous though its scholarship had been. He was appointed in 1970 as lecturer in Gladstone Studies—designed as an underwhelming research post to assist Professor M. R. D. Foot in the massive task of editing Gladstone's diaries. Not the least of its attractions was its location in Gladstone's old undergraduate College rooms, which Colin—through Christ Church's generosity—took great pleasure in occupying for twenty-four years. Colin swiftly burst through the shackles of factotum and become the driving force behind the project, and in 1972 he replaced Foot, whose scholarly interests were now directed elsewhere, as editor. Volumes 1 and 2 had been edited solely by Foot, and although volumes 3 and 4 appeared under their joint names, it was Colin alone who contributed the first of his famous introductions to the diaries. Subsequently, the remaining ten volumes and the index were Colin's sole responsibility. In 1976 some alleviation of his academic prospects and joint role as breadwinner (Sue had embarked on her vocation as primary school-teacher, later head teacher, that was to make her an Oxford legend in her own lifetime) was afforded through his appointment as a Research Student (equivalent to a senior research fellow) at Christ Church. But a 'proper' tenured position was only secured at St Hugh's in 1978, when Colin was 37. Even then, it had been preceded by the gnawing doubts he had entertained as to whether he could compete with the rising stars of his discipline and by a rarely publicised anxiety about his future prospects, masked by the stoicism inculcated through his public schooling. In one case he withdrew his candidature when he became aware that a brilliant (and since then eminent) historian was applying for the same post.

Colin's election to a Tutorial Fellowship at St Hugh's as one of its first male Fellows, though not uncontested in the college's Governing Body, was to bear rich fruits for its history students. Colin's reserved and often quizzical manner, and his apparent want of ostentatious enthusiasm, apart from the odd glint in his eye, were soon transformed into assets as the depth of his commitment to teaching and to the well-being of his students shone through. He was superbly conscientious as tutor, but he was far more than that. The warmth and kindness he had quietly begun to display towards others was reflected in a non-patronising and supererogatory pastoral role, in the care he lavished and the time he found for undergraduates and graduates alike. One would frequently find one of them, temporarily rendered homeless, as guest in the Matthew household—probably the most open in the city—sitting in the living room while Colin was nonchalantly engrossed in a newspaper as if that arrangement had been in place for years. His concern for his undergraduates, and his involvement with graduates and their career prospects, forged open-ended and enduring relationships. While he rarely mentioned his work at home—unless requested, when he would happily hold forth—he did convey his worries about this or that student's personal difficulties, or applaud their achievements, and would go out of his way to help them overtly or surreptitiously. The protégé had become mentor and was matching, indeed exceeding, the assiduousness of his much-admired role-models.

As had been the case at Sedbergh, Colin gravitated, almost unaware and certainly never graspingly, towards the core of college life. He occupied the post of Senior Tutor from 1983 to 1987 and Fellow Librarian from 1991 to 1997, and he was closely involved in the group which supervised the construction of the Rachel Trickett Building on St Margaret's Road. In the early 1990s Colin stood unsuccessfully as an internal candidate for the Principalship of the college, attracted by the administrative and reforming possibilities of the office. He persisted with characteristic stubbornness despite attempts by friends to dissuade him from considering a position to which his contemplative and often withdrawn nature, and aversion to small talk, made him temperamentally unsuited, to say nothing about the intrusion on his research time. In strange contrast with his superior organisational skills, Colin's spacious room at St Hugh's was cluttered with books and papers that filled every available space from floor to ceiling, requiring careful navigation from door to desk. It was another symptom of his imperviousness to external trimmings but also a symbol of the opulence of his intellectual world. Needless to say, he knew his way around exactly.

In parallel, Colin was drawn into the activities of the modern history faculty. Although in later life he became more adept at public speaking, he hardly ever gave faculty lectures, preferring seminars and classes instead. He played a key role in the design of two new papers close to his heart, one on church and state in Victorian Britain, the other on late Victorian and Edwardian social policy but, as the topics indicated, always seeing those as conduits to the heart of his view of nineteenth-century Britain. He would chide those who, prey to their own secular interests, downplayed the role of religion in recent British history. While not himself religious or overly involved in the belief dimension of his historical subjects, he accepted the inevitability, possibly necessity, of the church as a cultural, political and social institution. The editing of the Gladstone diaries had brought out to the full his self-discipline, industry and capacity to conceive and carry out a complex intellectual and organisational project with vision and aplomb, while engaged in a host of other activities. Often writing early each morning before going to college, Colin was equipped with a disposition to work entirely without fuss, a trait all the more impressive when other responsibilities began to build up. He never shirked all those additional tasks, but took them in his stride as if no other course of action were imaginable. In particular, the lifelong thread of significance Colin accorded to libraries and to reading, not merely as instruments of individual research but as depositories of a national culture, was reflected in an accumulation of relevant offices. On a deeper level it may well have been homage to Gladstone's own extraordinary devotion to the written word, incarnated in the magnificent library of some 20,000 volumes at Gladstone's country residence, Hawarden. Colin was the literary director and vice-president of the Royal Historical Society; a curator of the Bodleian Library, Oxford, and chairman of the Friends of the Bodleian. In those roles and in his membership of the London Library he saw himself as proselytiser and recruiter, channelling a quasi-religious fervour into the safeguarding of those secular temples, the real treasure houses of the land. He also chaired the publications committee of the Oxford Historical Monographs, was a member of the Royal Historical Manuscripts Commission, and served on the advisory editorial board of the Bertrand Russell collected papers, edited at McMaster University.

Belatedly, Colin's academic achievement and ability moved out of the still waters of normality to the rapids of exceptionality. The craft on which he found himself steering that course were the Gladstone diaries, whose editing and analysis have become one of the crowning accomplishments of recent British historical research. Through the diaries Colin discovered skills and disseminated insights that transformed the appreciation of the most important British political figure of the nineteenth century. In so doing, he fine-tuned the writing of political biography as a complex interweaving of Gladstone's public and private persona; and he re-established biography as a form of national history, but one now based on immaculate and microscopic research of the highest order. Colin's virtuosity would transform a terse and staccato diary into a wholly human picture of the intellectual, moral and political cores of an unusually motivated, often single-minded, statesman, while reconceptualising historical biography as a means on which to hang the reconstruction of an entire era. To argue that Colin was fortunate in the individual he had been allocated to chronicle, a man already embedded in British historical mythology and blessed with the political longevity that ensured his dominance over the Victorian age, and in the source material at his disposal—an almost uninterrupted record with about 25,200 entries—would be seriously to undervalue the rereading in which Colin engaged and the profundity of his fusion of detail and grand narrative.

It took Colin a while to make his name through the diaries. To his bemusement, his first flash of fame was as decipherer of Gladstone's sign, at the margins of some diary entries, for flagellation, which the Victorian self-anointed moralist had inflicted on himself after his numerous clandestine 'rescue' meetings with prostitutes he apparently desired to reform. That news made headlines across the world, temporarily and wholly unexpectedly associating the rather decorous scholar with the cognoscenti of the *demi-monde*. Upon the publication of that section of the diaries, Oxford University Press had to design a special font for the whip sign. When stunning and formerly unpredictable success did eventually come relatively late in life, replacing the professional frustration and underachievement that Colin had to swallow in the initial years as the diaries' editor, it did not change him in the least. Remaining utterly devoid of airs, his modest disposition and matter-of-factness rose to the occasion, though in an uncharacteristic outburst Boyd Hilton recalls that upon Colin's election to a personal Oxford professorship in 1992 he thumped Hilton's bookshelves, declaring 'It'll show them!'[6] Appearances to the contrary, there always remained a sensitivity to outside views.

The process of editing the diaries culminated in a truly magisterial biography that was not originally intended as such but that emerged out of the series of commentaries-cum-introductions that Colin wrote during

---

[6] Boyd Hilton, 'Colin Matthew (1941–1999)', in P. Ghosh and L. Goldman (eds.), *Politics and Culture in Victorian Britain: Essays in Memory of Colin Matthew* (Oxford, 2006), p. 18.

218

most of his working life. To that monumental undertaking he brought
self-discipline, a relentless yet balanced work rhythm, and the consummate care with which he handled his scholarly responsibilities. Looking
back, Colin recalled: 'The introductions to the volumes were a challenge,
being written rather quickly every four years or so whenever the text of
each volume was nearly ready. This meant there were nearly 25 years
between my first and last effort, while the interpretation they offered had
to be consistent.'[7] Consistent maybe, but Colin's touch became more
assured and his voice more confident as the project unfolded. He exhibited a terrier's tenacity in pursuing any relevant aspect. The result was an
intense and imaginative lesson in history and its methodology not only
for Colin's readers but, in the course of preparing it, for Colin himself. If
other historians quarrelled with this or that interpretation or slant, and
they occasionally did, the volumes, separately and as a whole, were
accorded a chorus of acclaim. In 1991 Colin was elected to a Fellowship
of the British Academy, and later became its vice-president. Once
reassembled in two-volume book form, with two new chapters on the
period originally covered by Foot, the biography unsurprisingly won the
Wolfson Prize for History in 1995. There could have been few similar
'dead certs'. That said, it was also a work so dense in detail that all but
the most dedicated Gladstonians and professional historians would have
dipped into rather than perused it. Uncompromisingly directed at the
highest peaks of academic interest it was not, even when paperbacked, a
biography to be picked up at an airport for light reading. Yet, for those
who made the effort, the book was one of high drama, peppered with the
occasional wit and ironic sensibilities of its author.

Colin, like all previous biographers of Gladstone, addressed the
Grand Old Man's mutation from Tory to enlightened Liberal. However,
he did so in a wholly original manner, by uncovering the crises and agon-
ised introspection that not only accompanied, but preceded, the many
moves in that direction, as if primordial psychological forces had gripped
Gladstone and from which he had to seek relief in decisive political
action. From Colin's *Gladstone* there emerges a stunning, and occasionally startling, portrait of that rare British phenomenon—an intellectual
in the highest realms of politics and a moralist in a sea of expediency,
grappling both with a visceral personal religiosity and a tormented sexu-
ality. Colin was absorbed with Gladstone's riveting combination of a
deeply moral and cerebral nature and his shrewd command of detail as a

---

[7] Colin Matthew, 'Liberal with the Ink', *The Times Higher*, 12 May 1995.

practising politician, and he was particularly intrigued not just by the sep-
aration of Gladstone's private from his public life, but by the electrifying
points of contact between personal fragility and public determination.
That, at any rate, was the abiding image that Colin presented to the world
of scholarship and beyond. It dispensed with facile generalisations that
viewed Gladstone as quirky or insincere, translating through clear and
elegant prose a subject of great, almost heroic, complexity into a very
human and understanding depiction. Through Colin's own humanism, a
distant and austere icon had been demystified.

Colin's Gladstone was also a harbinger of political modernisation. He
was a populist in an enlightened sense, wise to the impact of direct
appeals to the rising political classes, and to the role of the media. He was
a politician of supreme professionalism, who had mastered financial and
fiscal policy in all its particulars and at one superhuman point was simultaneously Prime Minister and Chancellor of the Exchequer. His bold
attempt to change the British constitution on Ireland opened the constitution to further reform in the twentieth century. He was an impassioned
forerunner of what is now known as 'ethical foreign policy' and he anticipated, albeit embryonically, the morality of the diminution of empire. He
was a tireless campaigner and a fine orator, whose rhetoric both acknowledged and reflected the mixture of rational argument, passion and vision
that was to characterise the new mass politics. His embrace of liberalism
gradually took on the acceptance of a more tolerant religious and class
diversity, although at some cost. In Colin's words, Gladstone 'recognised
that Christianity had, by its assertion of individualism, dethroned the
Aristotelian ideal of an organic civil society'.[8] All of those Colin identified as crucial themes in the ascent of progressivism. Yet even as
Gladstone's conversion to Home Rule was a quasi-devolutionary move
ahead of its time, he turned in his final years obdurately away from the
innovative political strategy of party programmes and was incapable of
comprehending the more radical steps liberals were taking towards social
reform. And he was impervious to the new social organicism beginning to
emerge from the fringes of liberal political thinking or to the way in which
his faith in free trade could incorporate those new ideas. Gladstone's was
an organicism of tradition and adaptation, of thinking and acting, of the
civic and communal integration of interests, but not of social inter-
dependence promoted by a benevolent state. Here Colin may have been
too generous about the case for the continuity that Gladstone bequeathed

---

[8] H. C. G. Matthew, *Gladstone 1875–1898* (Oxford, 1995), p. 319.

the party he was so instrumental in shaping. But it was central to Colin's Weltanschauung that although—as a historian friend noted—his 'Whiggish (and Scottish enlightenment) sense of the continuity between past and present was in many ways unfashionable, [it] was one of the characteristics that gave his work its originality'.[9]

Out of a seemingly mundane set of lists of daily events and short comments that constitute the diaries—they were in effect an aide-mémoire—Colin constructed an elaborate, incisive and lucid account and interpretation, an exercise in applied erudition. As of volume 7 the text was amplified by an ingenious apparatus, adding to Colin's own notations and commentary on the memoranda Gladstone kept alongside his diaries, some of Gladstone's additional correspondence to which the diaries referred, and the Cabinet Minutes of meetings chaired by Gladstone. All those helped to bridge the gap between contemplation, discussion and execution. That feat of magnification while still heightening the resolution of the picture was no legerdemain, but the result of painstaking research, utter conscientiousness and integrity in linking measured assessment to miniscule fact, and the ability to penetrate the mind of his subject while paying due regard to the larger picture of national history that had always commanded Colin's allegiance. The index alone runs to almost 900 pages and, apart from thorough name and subject indexes (the latter a wonderfully entertaining and amusing read in its own right, with undertones of Pickwickian prose) it itemises the astounding record—entered daily by Gladstone himself—of his reading over 17,500 books. It justifiably secured the Wheatley Medal of the Society of Indexers in 1994.

Gladstone, unsurprisingly, became entwined both with Colin's private as well as public life. The Victorian statesman followed him home in the form of innumerable mementoes: plates, portraits, busts, jugs, puppets, clay pipes, and silk embroidery; and abroad, in the form of dwelling places, hotels, and vistas the Grand Old Man had occupied or enjoyed. Colin never saw that as an obsession; rather, Gladstone had become another close mentor and member of an extended family, whom one visited when passing through the neighbourhood, even warranting a special trip, and whose communications were preserved both out of fondness and respect.

If Colin was uncharacteristically in tears when writing up Gladstone's death and funeral, there was no parallel draining of his intellectual vigour.

[9] Hilton, 'Colin Matthew (1941–1999)', in Ghosh and Goldman (eds.), *Politics and Culture*, p. 24.

Through the diaries his interest had turned to political rhetoric, on which he wrote a fine article and to which he had planned to return. The triumph of the Gladstone diaries, however, paved the way for another opportunity bathed in even more luminous national prestige. Some time before all the ink on the former project had been spilled, let alone dried, Colin was approached in 1992 by Sir Keith Thomas, then President of Corpus Christi College, Oxford, and Ivon Asquith, Academic Director of Oxford University Press, to consider taking on a joint project of the British Academy and OUP, underpinned by a governmental grant made over to the University of Oxford: a complete revision of the *Dictionary of National Biography*. Colin consulted family and friends, seeking reassurance in his inclination to accept the offer. The advice he received was split, but those who encouraged him in that inclination had in mind his newly demonstrated organisational capabilities, his respect for a national ethos that the *Dictionary* encapsulated, and the formidable reputation he had established as an editor. Indeed, the extenders of the invitation regarded the immense task of seeing through a *New Dictionary of National Biography* contingent on Colin's agreement, there being no other obvious candidate in sight.

Colin accepted and immediately embarked on the task with extraordinary verve and boldness. The diaries had instilled in him a sense of historical purpose that he now brought to this new enterprise and he was attracted by the prospect of another grand panorama constructed out of discriminating detail. Told that the anticipated time to completion was twenty five years, his astonishing response was 'I'll do it in twelve'. Colin brought not only a natural leadership to the *NDNB* (ultimately published as the *Oxford Dictionary of National Biography* or *ODNB*) but a fresh vision of its contents, its scope and its contributors. He chose 'to be wary, as well as curatorial, about the old' *DNB*,[10] originally the brainchild of the publisher, George Smith, and Leslie Stephen. He praised Stephen for his 'absence of bombast', a trait Colin fully reproduced. But in an era of greater openness, and tolerance of private peccadillos, many memoirs needed to be rewritten or at least heavily revised. Moreover, Colin decided from the start on a far more expansive tapestry of national life than even Stephen's inclusive design had envisaged. True to Colin's 'organic' view of history and to his consideration for past scholarship, it was agreed that no existing name was to be dropped. But some entries of disproportionate

---

[10] H. C. G. Matthew, *Leslie Stephen and the* New Dictionary of National Biography (Cambridge, 1997), p. 1.

length were trimmed (Queen Victoria, Gladstone's nemesis, was appropriately cut down to size) and the balance had to be tipped against the
DNB's elitism and its cultural preferences, to say nothing of the contingency of the then available contributors. To that end, Colin also invited,
by means of a broadly circulated questionnaire, suggestions from far and
wide on individuals worthy of inclusion. A thorough search for women of
note, whose achievements had been overlooked in earlier *DNB* volumes,
was undertaken. Business people too required greater representation.
There was also a place for non-existing figures of mythical or legendary
significance that were enshrined in national culture—the very invention
of history, Colin knew, also made history. In addition, Colin conceived a
new class of group biographies, aimed at shedding light both on their
members and on their common activity.

Importantly, it was decided to publish the *NDNB* in one go—it
appeared on time, in 2004, in sixty volumes containing almost 55,000
entries, though sadly after Colin's death two-thirds of the way towards
completion. The *ODNB*, as it had become, was steered deftly to its conclusion by his successor, Brian Harrison. It was a readable, stylish,
unstuffy and often entertaining panoply of national life, intended by
Colin as a great and easily accessible depository for the elucidation of the
general public. Colin himself wrote or revised 778 memoirs, of which 141
were original replacements or new entries. Among those latter categories
were all the monarchs who had died in the twentieth century (he had a
sneaking admiration for the institution, if not for all its incumbents),
many Victorian clergymen and theologians, diplomats, newspaper editors
and journalists, civil servants, nineteenth-century historians, a fair sprink-
ling of Scots, and—in addition to Gladstone (and four other members of
his family)—major post-Gladstonian and twentieth-century politicians
such as Balfour, Asquith, Haldane, and Macmillan, as well as three individuals whose characterising description was heroine (Grace Darling),
impostor (Thomas Geeran), and arsonist (Jonathan Martin). Colin's own
predilections, but also his wide-ranging curiosity, were clearly reflected in
those choices. One side-effect of Colin's work on the diaries had been an
essay on Millais' portraits of Gladstone. He was consequently delighted
to be appointed as trustee of the National Portrait Gallery, a highly
useful link in the light of the innovative decision to illustrate the *ODNB*
prolifically.

Colin's insistence on high professional standards transformed the
ODNB mainly from the in-house generalist creation of its predecessor to
a well-oiled machine that drafted in a far larger number of national and

international specialists, under the direction of consulting editors to whom were assigned specific periods or topics and, one level beneath them, associate editors in charge of smaller thematic blocks. There was always room, however, for trusted friends and, in one case, for Colin's knowledgeable and judicious aunt, Jean Gilliland, who had volunteered to assist on the Gladstone diaries for many years and, now in her eighties, was assigned to revise or write 87 articles. Colin was quaintly scrupulous about introducing a rule of secrecy on who was writing on whom in order, as he saw it, to forestall interferences in the work of contributors. The technical challenge was immense, yet it was produced with a minimum of hitches. To that end, Colin and the project director, Robert Faber, set in motion a massive computerisation programme, both to facilitate the editing process and as the data base for a future on-line version. Colin was aware of the ephemerality of historical judgement and an electronic version would allow for the requisite suppleness of which the paper edition was devoid; yet for that reason precisely, contributors were encouraged to include current assessments of their assigned biographees; their entries, too, would become part of the changing stream of historical understanding. Colin's conversion to computer literacy was no less than miraculous in view of his previous record. Annotations and comments on the Gladstone diaries had been stored in shoeboxes on 5″ by 4″ cards. As late as the mid-1980s, when literary director of the Royal Historical Society, he had expressed great disquiet—while one commissioned volume was being prepared—at the absence of the printed word, fearful that the text would be wiped out in an electric storm or, perhaps, just trickle off the disk. To the incredulity of his friends, that inveterate scribbler of little notes now re-emerged—guided by the experts of OUP—as an aficionado and prophet of new information technology.

The quasi-military efficiency with which the *ODNB* was conceived, structured and executed was in stark contrast to Colin's often shambolic appearance. He gained a certain reputation for wearing odd socks, battered hats and crumpled summer jackets in winter. Usually open-necked, an unfashionable tie was stuffed into his pocket for moments of sartorial emergency. For those approaching Colin from the back when still in his twenties, the expectation of encountering an elderly man was abruptly shattered by the youthful, smooth face under the untimely white hair. Even in his fifties the face had not caught up with the elapsing years and his phenomenal energy seemed boundless. But the atmosphere at 37A St Giles, where a dedicated team of some forty people—though often above that number—was located under Colin's supervision, was as far from military as could be. Conversation at the morning coffee gathering could revolve around work or the latest cricket scores. Colin took care to treat staff as colleagues and friends—no doubt unconsciously under Sue's quietly radiant influence, but by now also under his own momentum. An annual summer party at home as well as regular staff field trips and picnics—the Rollright Stones, Warwick castle and William Morris's Kelmscott were among the destinations—punctuated the tight schedule. He always took his project secretary and personal assistant, Katherine Manville, out for lunch on her birthday. Nor did he ever fail to send each contributor a personal note of thanks for their memoir. Research institute, hothouse for budding talents, locus of a remarkable *esprit de corps*, 37A St Giles became one of the most unusual of Oxford's many dispersed centres. The very transience of the printed project and of some of its personnel—once their particular task had been completed they would move on—lent it an ambience that had to be savoured while it lasted. Colin's was an inspiring presence, leading not ostentatiously or forcefully, but by example, empathy and accessibility. He was first in his office in the morning and the last to leave. He was loyal and elicited loyalty. Despite the kudos that would have gone to the head of a less unassuming man, his natural humility in public and in private laudably continued to accompany his professional success. But while he never blew his own trumpet, he did so on every occasion for the *ODNB*. He toured extensively in the UK, in North America and in Australia, lecturing on its behalf. It was fitting, if tragic, that Colin's memoir was included in his own great editorial venture.

There was another side to Colin and it was a side that many people encountered first. He could be brusque and curt, which some saw as standoffish arrogance or dourness, when it was no more than a slight wariness and his habitual shyness. At other times aloofness merely covered an abstracted or otherwise engaged mind. One indication of that mulling-over process was a delay in responding to a comment or query, rather like the time-gap that used to characterise a transatlantic call. While others had moved on to another subject, Colin would suddenly break in with a measured observation relating to the previous conversation. Likewise, during the long weekends abroad taken regularly once or twice a year, he would without warning separate himself from wife and friends and meander down a side-alley, deep in thought or wrapped up in exploring a site of potential historical curiosity, to return rather surprised at the concern about his sudden disappearance. Colin's detachment is wonderfully captured by John Goto in a computerised artistic photograph of the trustees of the National Portrait Gallery. All the trustees are standing, looking at the paintings or conversing. Colin is the only seated figure in their midst, buried in a book, completely oblivious to those around him. But he had his pet dislikes and private contempt for certain individuals, mainly for those who had behaved shabbily or who were pretentious. When his patience with others ran thin, it could elicit a master-class in minimalist exasperation—a raised eyebrow, a quick roll of the eyes, a single damning sentence. When bored with them, he would simply walk away. He was also disdainfully unforgiving of the many contemporary politicians, mainly on the right of the political spectrum, who displayed lapses of integrity and honesty. Charitable as he was, he could also be greatly irritated by other scholars who free-rode on his meticulous Gladstone scholarship. On occasions such as those, flashes of contained anger would appear. But although Colin was neither gregarious nor light-hearted, and very serious about his principles, he could enjoy himself in company. True, at the annual Matthew household Christmas Eve party he remained in the kitchen, churning out large amounts of exceedingly potent eggnog, but he was always surrounded by groups of guests, especially the younger ones. His conversation over dinner was reflective and, when in the right mood, witty, cultured and entertainingly informative. He was not always averse to gossip, which he recounted with great amusement, or entirely above waspishness, for which his friends were thankful.

A generous amount of Colin's time was taken up with additional voluntary activities of a very diverse nature. He co-initiated a weekly Saturday morning meeting at the King's Arms, opposite the Bodleian. What began as a coffee break of young historians became a set that exchanged research ideas, discussed recent historical writing, or raised more general intellectual problems. Before it began to tail off, it embraced half a dozen of Oxford's nineteenth- and twentieth-century historians. Conversations with Colin's historian friends were crucial testing grounds and honing sites for his own work, and he always recognised that the diaries could not have been completed without their help. There was a passion about his non-academic as well as scholarly concerns. With a schoolteacher for a wife, Colin was always willing to address schools, local historical associations, or lay audiences on historical matters, as well as produce occasional pieces for more popular publications, and it was entirely apposite that the Colin Matthew lecture for the public understanding of history, sponsored by Gresham College and the Royal Historical Society, was established in his memory. He was also a dedicated bagpipes player, whether as an undergraduate having 'good fun', a performer at Sue's school, or accompanying her on New Year's Eve visits to the homes of schoolchildren, who listened in amazement at the doleful sounds emitted by that weird and often unfamiliar musical instrument (his deeply moving funeral aptly concluded with a solitary piper preceding the hearse around Christ Church's Tom Quad). Second-hand bookshops had a magnetic effect on him; he would often stagger out with a pile to be added to the tiny space still available on his study floor. In the last decade of his life he rediscovered photography, developing black and white negatives in the basement of his house with the usual dedication and perfectionism he brought to all his activities. His interest in memorial plaques and tombstones, his love of nature and of architectural curios, were buoyed up through that new passion.

Colin's political sympathies were focused on the local Oxford Labour Party, and he served for a while as chair of its North Ward branch. He was a staunch opponent of the fruits of Thatcherism, warning that the Conservatives were creating a state 'far less pluralist, more centralized, more draconian, more coarse, and more vindictive than that which they inherited'.[11] There could be a touch of rigidity about his politics, reflecting his perennial fidelity to institutions and his conservative ambivalence about change, and he remained a steadfast supporter of the Labour party even while colleagues left it during the tumultuous 1980s. A revealing window into Colin's public concerns may be found in his thrice yearly 'In Vacuo' contributions to the *Oxford Magazine* beginning in 1987. Most revolved around current education policy at national or university level, seeped in the lessons that constitutional history could impart. Colin carefully weighed various plans for university reform and advanced his own proposals. He also aired the concerns of the Bodleian. But the first Gulf War, the British taxation system, changes in Eastern Europe, mad cow disease, the death of Diana, Princess of Wales, and New Labour were also grist to his mill. Initially a strong opponent of what is now the European Union, voting against British membership of the EEC in the 1975 referendum, Colin's traditionalism was slow to dissipate. Whether this was a side-effect of his unease with strangers is difficult to say, but he was eventually weaned off that guardedness. That volte-face was caused in part through Sue's pro-European enthusiasm, in part through Gladstone's own example as frequent visitor to the Continent—eventually emulated by Colin himself. More importantly, referring to Gladstone's abandonment of a unitary state, Colin wrote that 'the

[11] Colin Matthew, 'In Vacuo', *Oxford Magazine*, Noughth Week, Hilary Term, 1988, p. 8.

European Union was based on just the sort of flexible and evolving constitutional arrangements which the Home Rule bills were intended to introduce'.[12] And following a visit to Andalusia in 1994, from which he returned greatly impressed by the revival of Spanish civic culture and by the EU funded motorway system, Colin observed: 'My generation—at school in the 1950s and at university in the early 1960s—thought almost without exception that Europe had much to learn from Britain: now one must draw the conclusion that, while Europe has something to learn from Britain, the reverse is equally or even more the case.'[13]

Colin's academic work notwithstanding, his family was his sanctuary and the core of his life. His constancy, tranquillity and equanimity were both nourished and felt at home. The strong complementarity of opposites with Sue gradually evolved into a profound and mutually enhancing bond, a powerful convergence of love, understanding and empathy. His children, David, Lucy and Oliver, were the focus of his deep affection and care. He was an admirable, if endearingly eccentric, father, quietly involved in every stage of his children's life, organising their birthday parties, reassuring in their teenage years, attending all parents' evenings at their schools, supportive in mundane ways of their activities and, surprisingly from their point of view, au fait with contemporary youth culture. He loved talking to young people and children, was interested in their lives, and treated them as his equals. They in turn were both fascinated and awed by the earnest yet unaffected imparter of curious facts that appeared unpredictably out of the blue. A non-interfering parent, he readily gave advice, but almost only when asked; encouraging his children to challenge received wisdom—as he did his students—and serving as lifeline in case anything was about to go badly wrong. Colin undertook the weekly shopping, helped by a bevy of forgiving shop-assistants who refreshed his spatial memory for where the goods were located, though he was notorious for entering a shop for one item and emerging with another instead. Treats for the children were often brought back in unconsumably large quantities. The annual holiday in Scotland, spent with immediate family, including his mother, and increasingly with hordes of his children's friends—necessitating the hiring of a minibus—was a time of resuscitation and pleasure. There Colin returned to the area of his early childhood, where his fondest memories of Scotland lay, for long walks in the hills, to which end he acquired—not without difficulty—navigational

[12] Matthew, *Gladstone 1875–1898*, p. 390.
[13] Colin Matthew, 'In Vacuo', *Oxford Magazine*, Noughth Week, Trinity Term, 1994, p. 3.

and map-reading skills. It would not be hyperbole to observe that Colin secured the prize of a double first in life that very few attain: the heights of professional achievement and of family happiness. The famous lines from Goethe's *Faust* that Colin chose to dedicate to his family in the preface to *The Liberal Imperialists* sum up where his ultimate contentment lay:

'Grau, teurer Freund, ist alle Theorie,
Und grün des Lebens goldner Baum'.

MICHAEL FREEDEN
Mansfield College, Oxford

Note: I have been greatly helped in the preparation of this memoir by Sue Matthew, in conversation and through the provision of numerous letters and papers. In addition, I am most grateful for the assistance of Ivon Asquith, George Garnett, Jean Gilliland, Ross McKibbin, Katherine Manville, David Matthew, Lucy Matthew, and John Robertson. Some of Colin Matthew's papers have been deposited in the Bodleian Library, Oxford.

EDWARD MILLER   *Peter Lofts*

Edward Miller
1915–2000

I

EDWARD MILLER, the eldest of the four children (three sons and one daughter) of Edward Miller and his wife, Mary Lee Miller, née Fowler, was born at Acklington, in Northumberland, on 16 July 1915. Within the family, he was always known as Eddie but to friends and colleagues he signed himself as Edward and later Ted. Mary Lee Miller's father was a builder, who had walked from Yorkshire to Northumberland and settled there. Edward Miller was a farm-manager—the subject of this memoir was to describe his own healthy appetite as that of a farmer's son[1]—and he and his family lived in a variety of places, mostly in Northumberland and always in the north of England. He was a keen local historian and anti-quary and had many short pieces published in *The Proceedings of the Society of Antiquaries of Newcastle-upon-Tyne*.[2] His occupation explains how it was that Ted Miller, as his pupils later noticed, possessed an under-standing of agriculture such as no books could impart. From his father, who, before his marriage, was for a time in charge of the bird colonies on the Farne Islands, he also inherited a lively interest in birds and wild flowers. Ted Miller always regarded himself as a Northumbrian, and when, in 1959, he delivered the St John's College, Cambridge, Lecture in the University of Hull, on the character and consequences for the northern

---

[1] Miller to Helen Cam, 21 Oct. 1945, after an excellent meal in a pub in the Vale of Clwyd: G[irton] C[ollege,] P[ersonal] P[apers], Cam 2/5/33.
[2] e.g. Edward Miller, 'Early Remains on Bolton and Titlington Moors', *Proceedings of the Society of Antiquaries of Newcastle-upon-Tyne*, 5th ser., 1 (1951–5), 78–86; 'Shilmoor', ibid., 333–5; 'Redesdale', ibid., 365–75.

Proceedings of the British Academy, **138**, 231–256. © The British Academy 2006.

counties of the long wars between Scotland and England (a lecture with a note of passion that still resonates) he declared himself to be one.[3] Family circumstances were somewhat straitened, and it was at first uncertain whether they would permit him to take up the place that he won at the King Edward VI Grammar School at Morpeth, Morpeth being too distant for daily travel. The local vicar, a wealthy bachelor, offered to pay for his education at grammar school and university, if he would later be ordained. But although his parents were devout church-goers, their eldest son was not. He was enabled to take up the place at Morpeth by the possibility of living during the week with his aunt, Margaret Miller, at Warkworth, the home to which he seems regularly to have returned during his undergraduate long vacations.[4]

In 1934 Miller entered St John's College, Cambridge, as an exhibitioner and in due course took starred Firsts in both parts of the Historical Tripos (1936 and 1937). His undergraduate career therefore coincided with a period in which the perennial dissatisfaction of the guardians of the tripos was temporarily relieved by their tinkering with the regulations regarding those aspects of it to which, as it happened, the young Miller was most strongly attracted. Hitherto, the constitutional history of England had been examined in two papers, with the year 1485 marking the break, and its economic history separately in a single paper covering the whole of time. Moreover, whereas those offering the constitutional papers had been required to display 'adequate knowledge of the general course of English History', in the case of economic history it was merely 'correct general knowledge ... rather than minute acquaintance with details' that counted.[5] Then, at the beginning of Miller's second year, the two elements were brought together.[6] And even if (because it was not a marriage of equals)[7] the liaison was to prove short-lived, nevertheless the questions now being asked did reveal a qualitative change in respect both of approach and of expectation. The shift from the invitation to reflect on the 'essence of Manorialism' to a requirement to describe the

---

[3] E. Miller, *War in the North: The Anglo-Scottish Wars of the Middle Ages* (St John's College, Cambridge, Lecture, 1959–60; University of Hull Publications, 1960), 22 pp., at p. 3.

[4] All his letters to Helen Cam and J. H. Plumb in the summers of 1936 and 1937 (cited below) were from this address.

[5] *Ordinances of the University of Cambridge to 10 October 1933* (Cambridge, 1933), p. 211.

[6] Ibid., pp. 709–13.

[7] In the first two years of the combined paper twice as many constitutional as economic questions were set: *Cambridge University Examination Papers, 1935–6* (Cambridge, 1936), pp. 740–2; *1936–7* (Cambridge, 1937), pp. 843–5.

social structure of *either* East Anglia, *or* the Danelaw, *or* the Vale of York was a shift in the direction of detail and the particular.[8]

No doubt that development was not unconnected with the arrival in Cambridge of M. M. Postan, whose lectures on 'English Economic History to 1688' were delivered for the first time in 1935–6.[9] For the study of the subject the coincidence of Postan's advent with Miller's entry into his second undergraduate year was altogether fortunate. It established a relationship between two scholars who, though lightly harnessed rather than being closely yoked together, were thereafter associated in giving their subject a profile it had not previously enjoyed. Also lecturing, on the constitutional side, was Helen Cam, the scholar for whom the young Miller's admiration and affection were abiding and unqualified. Other medieval lecturers listed included Gaillard Lapsley, Steven Runciman and three more, all Fellows of St John's: G. G. Coulton, C. W. Previté-Orton, and (from 1936) Geoffrey Barraclough. Then there was Hugo Gatty. Though not a medievalist, in St John's Gatty supervised the Middle Ages. A connoisseur of fine bindings, his medieval supervisions 'might be unorthodox', his obituarist was to report, and the volumes of Scarlatti, the Chinese figurines and the incense burners strewn around his gracious rooms[10] would have been correspondingly unfamiliar to the scholarship boy from Northumberland. Yet it was to Gatty, as one of 'two historians who taught me to see the history of the college as something which had a significance in English history and who, besides that, showed me many personal kindnesses', that in 1961 Miller's short history of St John's would be half dedicated.[11]

The co-dedicatee of that affectionate tribute was E. A. Benians, Master of the college from 1933 until 1952 and historian of the Colonies, whose relationship with Miller cannot have been strictly pedagogic since, even in the reformed tripos, there was no place in Cambridge for American and colonial history. But Benians was a Master of genius,

---

[8] Ibid., *1934–5*, p. 769; *1936–7*, p. 837. Cf. G. Kitson Clark, 'A Hundred Years of the Teaching of History at Cambridge, 1873–1973', *Historical Journal*, 16 (1973), 535–53, at 548.

[9] *Cambridge University Reporter, 1935–6*, p. 90. The chronological restriction (or challenge) was dropped from Postan's title in the following year: ibid., *1936–7*, p. 91. This course replaced that of J. Saltmarsh on 'English Institutions in the 11th and 12th Centuries', which in Miller's first year was all that had been available on the subject.

[10] M. P. Charlesworth, in *The Eagle* (St John's College, Cambridge), 53[234](1948), 126–9. Gatty had died in March 1948, aged 41.

[11] *Portrait of a College: A History of the College of Saint John the Evangelist, Cambridge* (Cambridge, 1961), p. xii.

whose custody of the college ensured that able men of limited means, such as he himself had been, were never lost sight of.[12]

In Miller's case, an indication of that ability, or at least of the reputation he enjoyed by the time he took Part I, was provided by his recruitment as the author of the medieval section of a projected Marxist history of England. And although it was, as he complained, 'of course impossible to write any kind of history of the Middle Ages in 20,000 words, and above all to write a satisfactory Marxist history', while accommodating all the simplifications that that necessitated,[13] he nevertheless declared himself 'fairly satisfied' at least with his coverage of the period 1250–1471. 'It goes against many of the conclusions held by modern scholars,' the second-year undergraduate assured Dr J. H. Plumb in one of a group of letters belonging to the summers of 1936 and 1937.[14]

For this period Miller's college record is meagre. In 1937, according to the Secretary of the College History Society (H. J. Habakkuk, Miller's senior by a year and evidently regarded by him as something of a bugbear), he 'read a very erudite paper on "The House of Percy and the Lancastrian Revolution"',[15] which, despite its erudition, cannot have gone down too badly, since in the following year he was Secretary of the Society himself. In this capacity he asked Plumb to read a paper,[16] and when Plumb failed to oblige, the Society was regaled by Christopher Morris, the tenor of whose talk on 'Gentlemen and Players, a Neglected Aspect of Social History' may not have been quite what Miller had hoped for, though it did combine two themes of central concern to him. With

---

[12] *Portrait of a College*, pp. 113–14; Peter Linehan, 'Piam in Memoriam: Group III 1894–1986', *Cambridge*, 35 (1994–5), 70–8, at 74.

[13] Uncatalogued papers of J. H. Plumb, Cambridge University Library. Miller to Plumb, 17 Sept. 1936: 'For purposes of simplification. I have permitted myself to repeat an exaggeration that I think both Marx and Engels were guilty of, no doubt from unconscious analogy with the simpler relations of the capitalist period—i.e. an exaggeration of the opposition of *two* classes in the Middle Ages.'

[14] Letters of 15 June and 29 July 1936, both addressed 'Dear Jack'. For an extract from the second of these, proposing a Marxist interpretation of the Wars of the Roses, '(broadly—Yorkist=bourgeoisie; Lancastrian=feudality)', but omitting Miller's crucial qualification 'tho it is not as simple as that, for there are divisions within the bourgeoisie as well as within feudality', see Michael Bentley, *Modernizing England's Past. English Historiography in the Age of Modernism, 1870–1970* (Cambridge, 2005), p. 179 (misdated 17 Sept. 1936). In the event the venture came to nothing ('Michael and I had a long talk with Roy just before I left; there seems every likelihood that the History is off': Miller to Plumb, 2 July 1937).

[15] *The Eagle*, 50[219](1937), 43.

[16] Letter dated 2 July 1937: 'I want a don to start off the season, and I think you would probably be more stimulating than most. Incidentally, Habbakuk will be there to ask questions, and it will amuse me to find someone who can deal with him on his own ground.'

memories fresh of the lordly Jardine's recent Ashes victory and with the defeat of the Spanish Republic already imminent, the development of the game, he reported, had been interpreted by the speaker

> as a movement of the proletariat perverted by the aristocracy and rescued by class collaboration (which reached its final triumph in the invention of leg theory bowling). At the same time, like Chekov, he [saw] in sport a certain guarantee against working-class revolution.[17]

But there was more to Miller's undergraduate years than high academic achievement and sport.[18] It was in this period of his life and through his friend, Leo Salingar, then an undergraduate at Emmanuel and later a Fellow in English at Trinity, that he met Fanny Zara Salingar, Leo's sister. Their marriage, in 1941, was to be a source of great happiness to both for nearly sixty years.

The Tripos concluded, Miller was elected by St John's to the Strathcona Research Studentship, and in May 1939 to a Research Fellowship. His dissertation for the fellowship competition, on 'The lands and liberties of the abbey and bishopric of Ely in the Middle Ages', was judged by the two referees, Postan and Cam, to be work of outstanding quality and even greater promise. The text, Cam noticed, escaped 'that heaviness which often haunts the beginner's presentation of such matters'; and Postan, while critical of occasional generalisations unsupported by 'either evidence or arguments', was confident that, 'properly nursed, Miller will rise to great eminence in medieval studies'.[19]

Miller had been working for only a year on the Ely material, while remaining registered in the University as studying for a thesis entitled 'Cambridgeshire landowners in the age of the Barons' Wars ($c.$1250 to 1320)'—a subject which reflected very clearly the influence of his supervisor, Helen Cam. As late as 19 March 1939, after 'six hectic weeks' writing the St John's dissertation, he reported to her his decision to adopt the break up of the knight's fee in Cambridgeshire between 1279 and 1346 as the point of departure of this work, 'and to begin by an attempt to discover what exactly this meant in social and economic terms.'[20] He worked for the dissertation mainly in London. His love of Italian food, encouraged

---

[17] *The Eagle*, 50[221](1938), 281.
[18] 'I have done a little work and have read a considerable amount of Flaubert, Céline's "Voyage au bout de la nuit" (I agree with Leo about it) and some Beaudelaire [*sic*] (rotten) etc.' (letter from Rouen dated 22 Aug. 1937). Eleven days earlier he had reported difficulty in getting the local chemist to understand his pronunciation of 'savon'.
[19] St John's College, Cambridge, Archives, D93. 62.
[20] GCPP, Cam 2/5/18.

by visits to Bertorelli's in Charlotte Street, conveniently near the British Museum, dated from this time. So too, his friendship with Rodney Hilton, then in the early stages of his work on the estates of the abbey of Leicester and other landowners in Leicestershire. They had in common, not only historical interests, but also, until a change in Miller's beliefs after the War, the strength of their commitment to Marxism. For a time they shared accommodation in London. Of their correspondence, it is now letters from Miller that survive. Towards the end of 1938, Hilton, then in Oxford, evidently consulted him about the overall plan and detailed contents of his thesis. Miller, still little more than a year into his own research, replied with authority.[21]

> ... about general approach. I don't think the two courses open are mutually exclusive. I think, in view of the nature of the town evidence, I should play for safety and start from the country. Do the Honour of Leicester estate and perhaps the ecclesiastical estates for which you have evidence. I don't think it is taking on too much at all. And make that the basis for your work. Any fragments from other sources you can fit into the general scheme will emerge from this study. My own view is that a possible method of approach is this:
>
> 1. Social position of owner of estate.
>
> i. Composition of revenue: Agricultural: wool, corn;
> Non-agricultural: rents, farms, proportion of labour services sold.
> Account rolls plus a little from rentals.
>
> ii. Demesne area and comparison with:
> Area of villeinage;
> Area of freehold;
> Area of leasehold
> Surveys, inquisitions post mortem when extents are given, Hundred Rolls, account rolls.
>
> 2. The tenants: development of capitalist peasantry and prosperous rural middle class.
> Extents and surveys, inquisitions post mortem, rentals, account rolls.

In London, at the Institute of Historical Research, Miller attended the famous seminar of Eileen Power and Postan on medieval economic and social history. Power was then Professor of Economic History at the London School of Economics, and Postan, University Lecturer, and from

---

[21] Letter dated 13 Nov. 1938, and written from an address in Hampstead. In this letter and in that from Miller to Hilton cited below (pp. 239, 247–8), punctuation and the numbering of items have been supplied or corrected where this seemed necessary for consistency or clarity.

1938 Professor, of Economic History at Cambridge. It was at this time, and at the Public Record Office, that Miller first met Marjorie Morgan (later Marjorie Chibnall).[22] Postan's return to Cambridge in 1939 coincided with the removal there of the London School of Economics, and the formation of a new seminar, presided over by Power, until her untimely death the following year, and by Postan, when his wartime duties at the Ministry of Economic Warfare, London, permitted. In a membership that as well as Marjorie Morgan, included Elizabeth Crittall, Dorothea Oschinsky, and R. A. L. Smith, Miller was not the only participant of whom more would later be heard in medieval studies. But he was unusual in being the pupil of Helen Cam, with whom he was now working for the M.Litt., and whose ideas on constitutional history and on the influence of constitutional developments on economic and social history were powerful and enduring influences on his own perception of these subjects.

The members of the new seminar were waiting to be swept into various kinds of war service. In 1940, Miller was conscripted into the Suffolk Regiment, but in the following year commissioned in the Durham Light Infantry. His early experiences as a soldier included a winter in Kendal, where, though joined by Fanny, he acquired a life-long distaste for the Lake District. However, he never forgot and often recounted with keen pleasure how, on one occasion in this period of his war service, on leading his platoon into a clearing, he came upon other soldiers sitting in a circle and eating eggs (legitimately purchased from the local populace) and listening spellbound to a story told by their leader: this was Lieutenant Southern, also of the DLI. 'One piece of really good luck'—he reported to Helen Cam at the beginning of 1942—'is that I have a fellow subaltern in this unit by name R. W. Southern—one time fellow of Balliol and expert on the 12th century. Naturally we get together a good deal and historical gossip gets a chance. Its rather nice to have a kindred spirit on tap.'[23]

His passage through Staff College at Camberley was to him the supreme experience of his war. The after-effects of a severe attack of bronchitis limited the forms of active service open to him in 1944–5

---

[22] 'Many thanks for the introduction to Miss Morgan, whom I duly met at the PRO, and who has much wisdom to impart': Miller to Cam, 19 March 1939 (GCPP, Cam 2/5/18).
[23] Miller to Cam, 23 Jan. 1942: GCPP Cam, 2/5/23.

during the push of the British and American forces into Germany and towards Berlin, but, now with the rank of major, he was in Germany by the end of May 1945. Prepared to some extent for the work by a crash course in German, he served on the Food-Agricultural Branch, Economic Division, of the Control Commission for Germany. From Berlin on 21 October 1945, he wrote to Miss Cam:

> My present role here is somewhat amusing. In view of the fact that I am rela-
> tively literate and able to write minutes, they have made me British Secretary of
> the Quadripartite Food-Agriculture Committee of the Control Council. In that
> capacity I have had to play quite a major part in writing some of the basic
> policy documents governing German agriculture and food production—all of
> which is [so] completely fantastic that I cant believe its true. So you see what a
> medieval historian is capable of! The interesting thing is working with the other
> nations—with the Russians who know and say what they mean, and we don't
> like it; with the Americans who don't say what they mean; with the French who
> don't know what they mean. Heaven preserve me from too long a sojourn in a
> world of diplomats and politicians. I feel too much like one who has fallen
> amongst thieves.[24]

He also took part in the interrogation of some leading Nazis. Later, he remembered Albert Speer as the only one among them who expressed no remorse.

II

In 1946, Miller was one of the young dons released expeditiously from the services at the request of their colleges and that of the university MPs.[25] He was already a research fellow of St John's. But since his election in 1939 the situation there had changed. Then, with Geoffrey Barraclough recently arrived, Miller can scarcely have hoped for a St John's anchorage after the end of that Fellowship. Now, however, with Barraclough gone to Liverpool and Coulton and Previté-Orton both carried off by the winter of 1946–7, his future there was assured. Director of Studies in his college,

---

[24] GCPP Cam, 2/5/33.

[25] On 11 Jan. 1946 the Council of St John's, on learning that Miller's war service would terminate on 15 Jan. 1946 'agreed to permit him to resume his Fellowship under Title A from that date
for a period equal to the unexpired period, i.e. until 6th October 1947': St John's College,
Cambridge, C.M. 1815/4. The calculation implies that Miller had already enjoyed four of the
nine terms of his fellowship, i.e. until June or September 1940.

in 1946 he was appointed Assistant Lecturer in History and, in 1950, succeeded to the Lectureship in Constitutional History vacated by Helen Cam on her recent departure for Harvard. Following the accepted convention for one who held prestigious college and university appointments, Miller abandoned all thought of completing a Ph.D. He remained a fellow of St John's and a university lecturer until 1965, and from 1961 combined these offices with that of Warden of Madingley Hall, a spacious establishment outside Cambridge which doubled as the University's 'House of Residence' for graduate students and academic visitors and a venue for courses mounted by the Board of Extra-mural Studies.

His return to Cambridge after the War coincided with a waning of his Marxist conviction, as is hinted at in a letter to Hilton of about this time:

> Re the January assembly—I will come if I possibly can: my political rest is partly enforced, but also a need to decide some political problems. But on theoretical points, my views remain and my interests are not dead. The difficulty, however, is that I am examining for the Open Schols which begin on Jan. 8: before term begins there will therefore be one mad rush. However, its early to say yet. Keep me posted.[26]

In fact, an episode occurring while he was still in the army had fatally undermined his enthusiasm for Marxism. This was the sudden disappearance, never explained, of a Russian with whom he had formed a friendship while both were attached to the Food-Agriculture Committee in Berlin.

No one reading *Portrait of a College*, written by Miller to mark the four hundred and fiftieth anniversary of St John's, or the sparkling account of the foundation that he had published in the *Victoria County History* two years earlier, could doubt the author's great affection for the college of which by then he had been a member for twenty-five years or more.[27] He looked back on his years at St John's as a golden age, his widow would later recall. He was very much the good college man— or rather, the good college chap: a favourite word of his— and a model lecturer and supervisor blessed with a rare capacity for clarifying material without simplifying it. As Tam Dalyell, who heard him lecture at the beginning of his career, has said of him:

> For a first-year undergraduate, ... Edward Miller's lectures on medieval English history were a godsend. Clear, obviously deeply well-prepared, devoid

---

[26] Letter dated 23 Oct. 1946, and written from St John's College, Cambridge.
[27] 'St John's College', *V[ictoria] C[ounty] H[istory]*, *Cambridgeshire*, 3, pp. 437–50.

of pomposity, ... with a twinkle in his eye, he would explain the medieval
decrees and laws, why ostensibly they were promulgated, and then give the
actual reason that motivated the king and the barons.[28]

It is not difficult to understand why he was so much in demand by the
WEA. Puckishly revelling in the quirkiness of human behaviour, whether
in the 1260s or the 1960s, he is remembered by the present writer (PAL)
as an early critic of Elton's *Tudor Revolution in Government* but on only
one occasion as expressing exasperation at the work of his medieval colleagues, namely the onslaught on Stubbs mounted by H. G. Richardson
and G. O. Sayles in *The Governance of Medieval England*, almost, so it
seemed, because Cam and Maitland (another hero) were not there to
defend the citadel.[29] As tutor (1951–7) he was often to be found, unusually for a don in those days, puffing his pipe over 'a quick half' with a
pupil in the Blue Boar or the college buttery before setting off across the
Backs to be driven home to Madingley by Fanny. Small in stature and a
bustling presence, he radiated merriment and good humour, with a
throaty chuckle his most distinctive characteristic. Cheerfulness was
always breaking in. Field sports were a passion. A guileful bowler and
energetic out-fielder in his youth, by the mid-1960s he was regularly to be
found on the boundary or touch-line, duffle-coated in season in the role
of spectator, or more profitably engaged indoors at a game of room
cricket with his colleague, R. E. Robinson, the historian of Africa, and
sundry undergraduates. College legend had it that sometime in the freez-
ing and glass-rationed winter of 1947 Miller had gone to a neighbouring
room to quell a contest involving the then-undergraduate Robinson, a
hockey stick and a squash ball—and had joined in: he came to scold and
stayed to score. His record 227 not out has never been bettered. While not
for this reason perhaps, in 1969 there were those who wanted him as
Master. Yet though Miller was impossible to dislike, he was also difficult
to know. He spoke sincerely when he said that he liked to be 'invisible'.

---

[28] *The Independent*, 6 Jan. 2001. At the time of writing, Mr Dalyell was the Father of the House
of Commons. The exceptional quality of Miller's lectures is exemplified in the notes taken by,
and still in the possession of, Dr Ronald Hyam, Emeritus Reader in British Imperial History and
Fellow of Magdalene College, who as a St John's undergraduate attended his course in 1956–7.
[29] For Maitland on Stubbs, see his 'William Stubbs, Bishop of Oxford', in S*elected Historical
Essays of F. W. Maitland*, ed. H. M. Cam (Cambridge, in association with the Selden Society,
1957), pp. 266–76; and for Cam on Stubbs, see her 'Stubbs Seventy Years After', *Cambridge
Historical Journal*, 9 (1947–9), 129–47.

III

If Miller had any regrets about his professional life during his years at St John's, it was that although he had presided with Postan at the graduate seminar in Economic History, few of the research students whom he had been invited to supervise worked in his own principal field of research: by a natural process, Postan, as Professor, had the prior claim here. *Progress and Problems in Medieval England* (1996), the Festschrift marking Miller's eightieth birthday in the previous year, reflects this state of affairs. All the contributors to this outstanding volume wished to honour one who had been for so long, in the words of the preface, 'in the creative forefront of their field of study',[30] yet only three, George Holmes, Anthony Tuck, and Jenny Kermode, had been his research students, and only Holmes and Tuck had been so at Cambridge. When, in 1965, he accepted the Chair of Medieval History at the University of Sheffield (one of several that he was offered about this time), it was rumoured that he was disappointed not to have been offered the Chair in Economic History from which Postan was about to retire. But the only Cambridge chair which he had ever hoped for was the Chair of Medieval History, filled in 1955 by the election of Christopher Cheney. The considerations which prompted his decision in 1965 were very different from the one attributed to him. In both term and vacation, Madingley Hall imposed a heavy burden of hospitality for a warden and his wife as conscientious and naturally hospitable as Ted and Fanny Miller. And with supreme tact both wished to leave Cambridge before their son, John, entered Jesus College to read History. By the time they returned to Cambridge in 1971, John Miller, later Professor of History at Queen Mary College, London, was a research fellow of Caius College.

In 1965, with eleven full-time academic staff and between twenty and twenty-five students taking Final Honours every year, the History Department at Sheffield was relatively small; and despite inevitable growth in the post-Robbins years, it always offered scope for Miller's genius for collegial life. In his Inaugural Lecture, he argued vigorously for the ways in which a knowledge of medieval history may contribute to a critical understanding of the present, including the making of modern states, and drew attention to the duty of history teachers in universities to

---

[30] Richard Britnell and John Hatcher (eds.), *Progress and Problems in Medieval England: Essays in Honour of Edward Miller* (Cambridge, 1996), p. xiv.

teach 'those general audiences which a developing democratic system of education is bringing into our universities'.[31]

To the disappointment of his younger colleagues, Miller attempted no significant changes in the syllabus, dominated by British History, that he found at Sheffield. To have done so would have been to incur the risk of a protracted disagreement with Professor Kenneth Haley, co-head of the department, who was deeply attached to the existing syllabus,[32] and for this Miller was unwilling. But his introduction of tutorials as a regular feature of teaching arrangements, hitherto characterised by lectures with a small admixture of seminars, was a notable innovation. He himself took pupils in this way (and indeed lectured) in modern as well as medieval periods, and in Sheffield as in Cambridge became renowned as a teacher. Michael Bentley, now Professor of Modern History at St Andrews, has described the life-enhancing effects for him of Miller's tutorials when he was a student at Sheffield.

> Essays were submitted in advance, and he was waiting with his list of points and questions to discuss. (. . .) Three images stay in the mind. First, he treated us as though we were important people. Second, he made us feel that spending an hour talking about history was a very exciting and worthwhile thing to be doing. Third, we emerged, or I did, anxious to read everything, absolutely everything, that he had talked about. He said nothing flashy or particularly remarkable. But the manner of his teaching was quite remarkable in its effects and he communicated the idea of 'love for one's subject' without effort or contrivance.[33]

To young members of the staff at Sheffield with careers to build, he gave encouragement and support; and he and Fanny were renowned for their hospitality. His readiness to listen to the students on any topic, in the bar and elsewhere, did much to ensure that the department had a relatively easy passage through the student troubles of the late 1960s. But he was not forgotten in Cambridge. In 1969, he delivered the Ellen McArthur Lectures there, for which he chose the title 'Economic Change in Medieval England', and in 1971 he received and accepted the prestigious invitation to become Master of Fitzwilliam College. On leaving Sheffield, he received a remarkable tribute from *Darts*, the student newspaper, printed

---

[31] *The Relevance of Medieval History* (Inaugural Lecture, University of Sheffield, 10 Nov. 1965), 14 pp., at p. 13.

[32] For Haley's view, see Mark Greengrass, 'Kenneth Harold Dobson Haley, 1920–1997', *Proceedings of the British Academy*, 101 (1998), 407–15, at 413.

[33] Professor Bentley to the authors, 1 Nov. 2005.

under the heading *Edward Miller: The Conservative as Progressive*: 'It is doubtful if there is anyone in the university held in such wide regard, right through the university (. . .) and he must be held largely responsible for running a department in which harmony and friendliness have been more conspicuous than friction and alienation.' In the following year, the University of Sheffield conferred on him the honorary degree of D.Litt.

IV

As a reviewer (a role in which he had few equals) Miller moved confidently in worlds as remote from each other in time and place as those of Robert Latouche and Lawrence Stone.[34] His capacity to do so reflects a deep understanding of the history of a Europe that did not stop at the Channel ports. The same quality, together with meticulous scholarship and an equable temperament, made him an ideal editor of wide-ranging works with many different contributors to keep on the rails.[35] His interests as a scholar centred, however, on the social and economic history of medieval England. As discussion of these themes gathered momentum in the 1950s and 1960s, and social history acquired the quantitative dimension that economic history already possessed, they tended increasingly to receive separate treatment. Miller always regarded them as inseparable and believed that neither could be understood apart from a legal and constitutional context.[36] History with so few frontiers could easily have been rather baffling to those who attempted to engage with it, but on paper Miller had the unfailing clarity that was also admired in his lectures. He was averse to model-making, as tending to remove variables from the total environment in which they existed, and on one occasion quoted Postan with approval on this point: '. . . if it is the theoretician's job to remove from his argument the considerations which do not happen to be

---

[34] *English Historical Review*, 72 (1957), 486–8; *Historical Journal*, 9 (1960), 133–6.

[35] M. M. Postan and E. Miller (eds.), *Cambridge Economic History of Europe*, 2: *Trade and Industry in the Middle Ages*, 2nd edn. (Cambridge, 1987); M. M. Postan, E. E. Rich and E. Miller (eds.), ibid., 3: *Economic Organization and Policies in the Middle Ages* (Cambridge, 1963); E. Miller (ed.), *Agrarian History of England and Wales*, 3: *1348–1500* (Cambridge, 1991).

[36] 'The revulsion on my part from the purely economic is even stronger than it used to be', he wrote in a two-page *tour d'horizon* of the Cambridge historical scene and other academic matters addressed to 'Dear Helen' on 18 March 1949: 'I don't know how the Board envisage the future, but next year at least I do the whole course [of English constitutional history to 1485]': GCPP, Cam 2/2/12.

"strictly" economic, it is the historian's function to bring them back'.[37] Never much attracted as a historian by economic theory, he became even less so, and in his later years claimed, somewhat unconvincingly, to be wholly ignorant of it. On more than one occasion he pointed out that in the Middle Ages the explanation of economic developments often lay outside the economic system: this was, indeed, one of his core beliefs as a historian.

Within each area of concern, he liked to tackle large problems. But however large or small the problem, he brought all the relevant variables to the surface—a capacity demonstrated to perfection in his discussion of the fortunes of the urban and rural cloth industries in England in the thirteenth and early fourteenth centuries. If readers begin this essay (as some, following the lead given many years previously by Professor Eleanora Carus-Wilson, may still do)[38] believing that the principal factor at work was the proliferation of water-driven fulling-mills situated in the countryside, they know by the end that the complicated story also involved the fortunes of the Flemish cloth industry, industrial strife in the urban industry at home, the development of English fairs as centres of distribution for English and foreign cloth, and the fiscal policies of Edward III.[39] In discussion, he moved easily from the general to the particular and seemed always to have a remarkable store of particulars to hand. This feature of his work reflected the wide reading and extensive note-taking, often in local record offices, that preceded and accompanied every new research project. At his death, some thirty large card indexes of extraordinary range and detail, written in his neat and unvarying hand, witnessed to the time and energy that he spent in the search for primary sources and the collation of printed material, from his time as a research student to the Fitzwilliam years and beyond. Willing as he was to speculate, he always made it clear when he was doing so, and a reluctance to rest any argument on such a foundation helps to explain why some of his most important publications had exceptionally long periods of gestation —though the delays that are a hazard of contributing to multi-author volumes, as Miller did on many occasions, also played their part.

---

[37] E. Miller, 'The Farming of Manors and Direct Management', *Economic History Review*, 2nd ser., 26 (1973), 138–40, at 140; M. M. Postan, *Fact and Relevance: Essays on Historical Method* (Cambridge, 1971), p. 121.

[38] E. M. Carus-Wilson, 'An Industrial Revolution of the Thirteenth Century', first published in *Economic History Review*, 11 (1941), 39–60.

[39] E. Miller, 'The Fortunes of the English Textile Industry during the Thirteenth Century', ibid., 2nd ser., 18 (1965), 64–82.

However, slowness to publish, for whatever reason, sometimes makes it difficult to follow the development of his ideas or shifts of interest over time. He often wrote on controversial topics, but never with the killer instinct: he was moderate in advancing his own views and valued moderation in others. He was also modest about his own work and generous in acknowledging the influence of others on his ideas—traits that made it easy for readers to undervalue his originality.

The Abbey and Bishopric of Ely, published in 1951 but dating as an enterprise from the late 1930s, is still the classic account of the formation of a great ecclesiastical estate in the late Old English period and its fortunes during the immensely complicated period of the Norman Conquest.[40] Moreover, in tracing the effects of the bishop's lordship on local societies in East Anglia over a much longer period, when such an estate provided the inescapable nexus of relationships for all its tenants, free and unfree, Miller discussed issues that were to be at the centre of debate about agrarian society in this period for many years to come.

Concurrently with the writing of *Ely*, Miller pursued his wider interest in medieval landowners and landownership and in the manor, the basic territorial unit of the latter down to the fourteenth century. In particular, he wished to discover how manors differing in size and form from each other adjusted to the developing cash economy, and what influenced the choice of villein or wage labour on manorial demesnes.[41] He was also interested in the reasons why from an early date many large landowners had leased their manors for fixed renders in cash or kind, known as 'farms', but had taken them in hand again in the years around 1200 and begun to exploit them directly for market profits.[42] He felt challenged by the views of the Marxist historian, E. A. Kosminsky, who concluded from the evidence of the Hundred Rolls of 1279 that the form taken by feudal rent in the thirteenth century, in the swathe of Midland England covered

[40] E. Miller, *The Abbey and Bishopric of Ely: The Social History of an Ecclesiastical Estate from the Tenth Century to the early Fourteenth Century* (Cambridge, 1951).
[41] Ibid., 80–112; E. Miller, 'La société rurale en Angleterre (X^e–XIIe siècles)', in *Settimane di Studio del Centro Italiano di Studi sull'Alto Medioevo, 13: Agricoltura e mondo rurale in Occidente nell'Alto Medioevo (Spoleto, 22–28 Aprile 1965)*, 111–34, at 129–31. For Miller's first published remarks on demesne labour supplies, see 'The Estates of the Abbey of St Albans' [a review article on A. E. Levett, *Studies in Manorial History* (Oxford, 1938)], in *St Albans and Hertfordshire Architectural and Archaeological Society Transactions*, NS, 5 (1936–8), 285–300, at 289. In style, this article is indebted to Maitland. Miller did not repeat the experiment.
[42] E. Miller, 'England in the Twelfth and Thirteenth Centuries: An Economic Contrast?', *Economic History Review*, 2nd ser., 24 (1971), 1–14, at 7–14; E. Miller, 'Farming of Manors and Direct Management', 138–40; cf. Edward Miller and John Hatcher, *Medieval England: Rural Society and Economic Change, 1086–1348* (London, 1978), pp. 204–13.

by this source, varied directly with the size of manors and of the estates to which they belonged.[43]

These concerns Miller shared with a number of scholars, including Postan, whose essay, published in 1937, on the chronology of labour services had become the take-off point for much of the debate, and Rodney Hilton and Marjorie Morgan. Postan had shown that many obligations to perform labour services that had been commuted into money rents in the twelfth century were reimposed, and in some cases augmented, in the thirteenth century.[44] Here and elsewhere,[45] he implied, or stated explicitly, that the practice of leasing manorial demesnes in the twelfth century reflected contraction in the economy as a whole, to be contrasted with the expansion to come in the thirteenth-century. In important monographs published within a year of each other (1946/7), Morgan and Hilton demonstrated that the labour service obligations of villeins, even if completely enforced, were inadequate for demesne needs on a wide variety of manors, involving many different kinds of lords: much hired labour would always have been needed to fill the gaps.[46]

Miller's views on these problems were distinctive. He pointed to the limitations of the Hundred Rolls and all sources recording the obligations of villeins but not the extent to which these were used from year to year: for information of the latter kind, different sources are needed.[47] Into the discussion of the leasing or farming of manors in the early Middle Ages and the virtual end of this system in the years around 1200, he introduced a new factor: an attitude on the part of landowners to their estates that for the greater part of the twelfth century was only distantly related to the underlying economic trend and should not be used as a kind of barometer to ascertain that trend.[48] Large landowners were for a long time

---

[43] E. A. Kosminsky, 'Services and Money Rents in the Thirteenth Century', *Economic History Review*, 5 (1935), 24–45, at 40–3; E. A. Kosminsky, *Studies in the Agrarian History of England in the Thirteenth Century*, ed. R. H. Hilton, trans. Ruth Kisch (Oxford, 1956), chaps. 3 and 5.

[44] 'The Chronology of Labour Services', *Transactions of the Royal Historical Society*, 4th ser., 20 (1937), 169–93; revised in M. M. Postan, *Essays on Medieval Agriculture and General Problems of the Medieval Economy* (Cambridge, 1973), pp. 89–106.

[45] 'Glastonbury Estates in the Twelfth Century', ibid., pp. 249–77, at pp. 276–7.

[46] R. H. Hilton, *The Economic Development of some Leicestershire Estates in the Fourteenth and Fifteenth Centuries* (Oxford, 1947), pp. 76–7; M. Morgan, *The English Lands of the Abbey of Bec* (Oxford, 1946), pp. 87–96.

[47] See, e.g., his review of Kosminsky, *Studies*, in *Economic History Review*, 2nd ser., 9 (1956–7), 499–501, and the postscript to his postcard of 17 Oct. 1958 inviting Helen Cam to supper before her talk to the St John's History Society: 'I still remember with awe your devastation of poor old Kosminsky' (GCPP, Cam 2/7/9).

[48] 'La société rurale en Angleterre', 118–23; 'England in the Twelfth and Thirteenth Centuries', 8–12.

well served as consumers by taking food farms, or renders in kind, from a selection of their manors. It was not until the years around 1200, when their consumption needs were growing, but the cash incomes drawn from their remaining manors were squeezed by the effects of prodigal subinfeudation on the part of their predecessors earlier in the century, that they were tempted to take their demesnes in hand and enhance their incomes by producing for the market. It mattered, too, that by this date the necessary bureaucracy of literate servants was available to manage manors used in this way. Very tentatively, he suggested that small landowners, having small and administratively flexible manors, probably adapted more quickly to market incentives.

Miller did not publish these views in their entirety until the 1970s. Remarkably, however, a letter to Hilton, who had apparently sent Miller a copy of the proofs of his own forthcoming book for comment, suggests that his views were already well developed in 1946, within a very short time of his return to academic life after war service. A cautious reference by Hilton to the possibility that labour services were less efficient than wage-labour elicited another remarkably authoritative, not to say penetrating, response from Miller, including brief critiques of the ideas of Kosminsky and Postan.[49]

> This raises a very big problem, where I feel that you have rather begged the question (as to some extent Kosminsky does, though he does raise it, if I remember rightly—I'm speaking without my copy by me). The following points occur to me:—
>
> 1. What is the evidence for the efficiency or inefficiency of the labour service system as compared with the wage labour system under medieval conditions? (NB— modern efficiency of labour depends partly upon provision of economic incentives, which demanded in first place a long process of psychological habituation; and as we have seen recently these can easily break down if the circumstances for which they were devised are not present: e.g. if [the] purchasing power of wage[s] is diminished or avenues of expenditure closed etc.). Moreover, [the] lord had in [the] manor court formidable machinery for increasing efficiency, and it is applied indifferently to villeins and hired labour.
>
> 2. What is the evidence for the fact that there was a large scale transference from serf to wage labour on the smaller estates? Most of it I have seen merely suggests that there *never* were large scale labour services on many of the small estates.
>
> 3. Evidence based upon surveys (Hundred Rolls, Inquisitions post mortem, terriers etc.) conceal[s] one vitally important fact about the organisation of the thirteenth-century great estate: that there was a very great deal of wage labour

[49] Letter dated 23 Oct. 1946, and written from St John's College, Cambridge.

employed. Indeed, my impression is that serf labour *in general* tends rather to be the reserve for periods of heavy demand for labour. The day to day tasks (shepherds, carting, even ploughing, etc.) [were] done mainly by *famuli*.

In fact, I am more and more coming to the view that the factors of differentiation between the large and small estates, and the classes who owned them must be sought along quite different lines:—

(i) An original difference determined by the scale of ownership as a factor of *demand*: the large household (monastic, baronial, episcopal) demands a steady flow of commodities from a wide area, which naturally finds expression in stereotyped quotas (e.g. food farm system) and stereotyped labour organisation (villein services). The small estate, on the other hand, is more flexible because more individual—both in reflecting individual requirements and probably more detailed individual management. There was thus from the beginning a tendency for far less stereotyped arrangements, both in cultivation and labour, than on the larger estates.

(ii) The reaction of these two types of estates to the twelfth-/thirteenth-century boom is a logical corollary of their different scale and their differing organisation.

   (a) It was easier to change the production pattern and the flow of commodities in the small than on the large estate—it was generally more compact (therefore market pull can be canalised into one direction) and its organisation was in any case more flexible.

   (b) Postan's thesis tends to conceal another basic characteristic of the thirteenth-century movement. By concentration on the demesne/villeinage relation, he makes it appear that the issue of the thirteenth century is one of money rents v. labour services. Now, all I have seen of the records of the period goes to show that this is not true. Rents increase as well as services, even more than services, on the great estate (and in the process reflect the changing valuation of land as a source of subsistence plus labour—the former a dead loss more or less to the landowner—to a source of profit). For this, on the large estate, there was an ample reserve, since subsistence requirements were met by a relatively small portion of the estate, and management problems restricted to some extent the profitable exploitation of the rest. On the small estate, on the other hand, the advantages of commercial exploitation were probably enhanced by the fact that it was a more manageable unit—and from that point of view the easiest source of working capital was probably partly found in such villeinage as there was. Therefore the primary tendency for the smaller estates to depend largely on wage labour was probably enhanced.

After arguing briefly that the most important difference between large and small or medium-sized estates was not their contrasting modes of production but their social function in supplying the needs of very different kinds of consumers, he concluded:

> I'm sorry about this dethroning of Kosminsky: but I do feel that he is quite wrong. However, perhaps I am just at sea. I have merely tried to rationalise on *facts* which he simply seems to ignore.

In these decades, the wider understanding of economic change in the Middle Ages was profoundly influenced, first, by Postan's belief in the alternation of ebb and flow, of contraction and expansion, and in due course by his analogy between the agrarian economy of medieval England and the (then so-called) under-developed economies of the twentieth century. Miller was sympathetic to both these ideas, and, at an early date in the discussion stimulated by the analogy of under-developed economies, argued persuasively that even when expansion occurred, it was accompanied by too little qualitative change for long-term gains to be secure.[50] It was generally agreed that, within these limits, the thirteenth century was a period of expansion; but the underlying trend in the twelfth century, a period of many violent fluctuations, was harder to identify. Miller argued convincingly, and was the first to do so, that this, too, was an expansive century and continuous in this respect with the thirteenth: the growth of population, of overseas trade, of towns and internal markets, pointed to this conclusion.[51]

In the later Middle Ages, when, on a modest estimate, the population of England probably fell to about one half what it had been in 1300, and structural changes were conspicuous features of the towns and countryside inhabited by the residue, the underlying economic trend has proved even harder to identify. Miller hesitated to accept Postan's diagnosis of economic contraction and himself pointed out that 'economic growth' would not do either.[52] As a pragmatist, however, he wrote authoritatively on many of the changes making up the puzzling whole. *The Agrarian History of England and Wales, 3: 1348–1500*, for which the contributions had been first commissioned some twenty years previously under a different editor, and which was finally published under Miller's editorship in 1991, is a major contribution to the history of the diverse local and regional economies and societies which assumed new forms in this period. Miller wrote a masterly Introduction, in which he traced the attainment of a new, if fragile, balance between land and people, favourable to small and middling farmers though less so to large ones. Although only a minority of peasants enjoyed social promotion, many had 'more to eat

---

[50] E. Miller, 'The English Economy in the Thirteenth Century: Implications of Recent Research', *Past and Present*, 28 (1964), 21–40.

[51] E. Miller, 'England in the Twelfth and Thirteenth Centuries: An Economic Contrast?', 5–7; and for expansion in the North, E. Miller, 'Farming in Northern England during the Twelfth and Thirteenth Centuries', *Northern History*, 11 (1976 for 1975), 1–16, at 6–7.

[52] Review of M. M. Postan, *Essays on Medieval Agriculture*, in *Economic History Review*, 2nd ser., 27 (1974), 681–2; Miller, 'The English Economy in the Thirteenth Century', 38–40.

for more of the time' than in the past.[53] But he also contributed the sections on Yorkshire and Lancashire, and, on the withdrawal of another contributor,[54] those on the southern counties.

War in the North, the St John's College, Cambridge, Lecture delivered at Hull in 1959 and published in the following year, retains all its authority as an account of the effects of the long wars between Scotland and England on the northern English counties;[55] and in an essay contributed to the memorial volume for David Joslin, in 1975, Miller suggested that the economic consequences of the taxation needed to pay for the king's wars in the years around 1300 may have been as significant as the consequences for constitutional development.[56] He also foreshadowed later work in this field by pointing out that the peasant contributed more than his lord to these taxes.[57]

As urban history moved in these decades from the study of gilds and other institutions, and liberties, to the more humane study of urban populations (how they were recruited, stratified, earned their wealth, if any, and spent it) Miller, in embracing the new concerns, never lost sight of the institutions and liberties. His article on the city of York in the Middle Ages, for the *Victoria County History*, still one of the best histories of a medieval town or city in print, treated both in depth and gave him an appetite for more.[58] When this was published in 1961, however, he had acquired an interest in the interaction between urban and rural populations. Indeed, his correspondence with Hilton in 1938, previously referred to, already reflects this interest, for it urges Hilton to scan his sources for rural landowners holding land or burgages in the town of Leicester.[59] Principally, however, this interaction was reflected in migration (in both directions) and in the investment of wealth made in towns in rural as well as urban property; the latter process he described as 'a constant haemor-

---

[53] *Agrarian History of England and Wales*, 3, pp. 1–33, at pp. 15, 32.

[54] I take this opportunity of expressing regret for a withdrawal that was my own and accepted with the utmost courtesy by Edward Miller (BFH).

[55] See above, n. 3.

[56] E. Miller, 'War, Taxation and the English Economy in the Late Thirteenth and Early Fourteenth Centuries' in J. M. Winter (ed.), *War and Economic Development: Essays in Memory of David Joslin* (Cambridge, 1975), pp. 11–31, at p. 27.

[57] Ibid., pp. 17–18.

[58] Miller to Cam, 8 Aug. 1958: 'I have enjoyed doing [*VCH, Yorkshire: The City of York* (1961), 25–116]. Indeed, I have decided that urban history contains so many unsolved problems that I ought to do more of it. But I have no plans for that at present: the next assignment is some vulgarisation for Longmans' (GCPP, Cam 2/7/9).

[59] See above, n. 21.

rhage' of capital from industry and trade into real property.[60] From this
interest flowed a more specific one in the identity of the ruling oligarchies
in towns, or, as they are often called in modern historiography, the patri-
cian class. Eventually, Miller's investigation of these, the dominant
burgesses, comprised a geographically dispersed sample, extending from
Newcastle-upon-Tyne in the north, to Southampton in the south. The oligarchies, he found, were indeed oligarchies, but open to recruitment from
below, relatively short-lived, and, given their investments in rural property,
separated by no very clear line from the local gentry.[61]

    In *Historical Studies of the English Parliament*, Miller and E. B. Fryde,
his co-editor, set out to provide a 'convenient compendium' of some of the
essays which, beginning with Maitland's on the Lenten Parliament of 1305,
had 'shaped the way in which historians of the present day regard the
beginnings of English parliamentary history'.[62] The two volumes are dedicated to Helen Cam, as 'one of those who enlarged the horizons of English
parliamentary studies'. They represent a major contribution to the historiography of the English parliament, and Miller's Introduction to the first
volume, covering the period down to 1399, provides a critical review of
developments in that period, in an essay of great and confident learning.
Inevitably, much of this volume is devoted to the beginnings of representation and later growth in the powers of the commons in parliament. In a later
essay, he pointed to the consequences for parliament of the lack of a firm
distinction in England between the gentry and leading burgesses: this made
it natural that both should eventually come together in political life as the
commons in parliament. Thus to some extent, parliament was moulded
by social developments in town and countryside.[63] Yet it was, in words of
G. O. Sayles which he quoted with approval, 'the child of the monarchy',[64]
and its rise reflected the 'state-building' on the part of the monarch that
provided a persistent thread in Miller's understanding of English history.

---

[60] 'The English Economy in the Thirteenth Century', 37.

[61] E. Miller, in *VCH Yorks: The City of York*, pp. 40–1; E. Miller, 'Rulers of Thirteenth Century
Towns: The Cases of York and Newcastle upon Tyne', in P. R. Coss and S. D. Lloyd (eds.),
Thirteenth Century England, I, *Proceedings of the Newcastle upon Tyne Conference, 1985*
(Woodbridge, 1986), 128–41; E. Miller, 'English Town Patricians, *c.*1200–1350', in A. Guarducci
(ed.), *Gerarchie economiche e gerarchie sociali, secoli XII–XVIII: Atti della «Dodicesima
Settimana di Studi», 18–23 Aprile 1980* (Florence, 1990), pp. 217–40.

[62] *Historical Studies of the English Parliament*, 1: *Origins to 1399*; 2: *1399–1603* (Cambridge,
1970), 1, p. ix. See also E. Miller, *The Origins of Parliament* (Historical Association pamphlet,
General Ser. 44; London, 1960).

[63] 'Rulers of Thirteenth Century Towns', pp. 141–2.

[64] *Historical Studies of the English Parliament*, 1, p. 6.

State-building, however, was under way long before there were parliaments.[65] From the tenth and eleventh centuries, Miller argued, it provided
a context for economic change, for it was in these centuries that government in England first extended its activity to this sphere of life. But its
greatest effects on society were felt in the twelfth and thirteenth centuries.
In an ambitious paper delivered to the Royal Historical Society in 1952,
he compared the policies of the French and English monarchies towards
feudal fiefs and in particular the desire of feudal tenants to establish the
right to alienate these when family or other needs made this desirable.[66]
On this occasion he anticipated a conclusion to which he subsequently
returned many times, namely that in England at this time, government so
shaped private law that feudal tenants became landowners, and land, no
longer the basis of feudal obligation, became an economic asset for all
those fortunate enough to own it.[67] Political involvement followed naturally for many who did. But there was a two-way traffic in these matters,
and at times in the later Middle Ages the economy led and government
could only follow. In a virtuoso comparison of economic policies in
France and England, in *The Cambridge Economic History of Europe*, 3,
Miller pointed to the dominance of, first, wool and later cloth in
England's overseas trade to an extent affecting the very structure of economic life here. In ways having no parallel in France, it facilitated the
development of a doctrine akin to economic nationalism and this in turn
brought financial and diplomatic advantage to the Crown. For this, parliament provided a forum, and England's precocious centralisation the
necessary administrative base. Mercantilism lay ahead.

On moving from Sheffield to Cambridge in 1971, and leaving the
work-load of a professor and head of department in the one place to

---

[65] For this paragraph, see E. Miller, 'The State and Landed Interests in Thirteenth Century
France and England', *Transactions of the Royal Historical Society*, 5th ser., 2 (1952), 109–29;
E. Miller, 'The Background of Magna Carta' (review article on J. C. Holt, *The Northerners: A
Study in the Reign of King John*, 1961), *Past and Present*, 23 (1962), 78–83; E. Miller, 'France and
England', in *The Cambridge Economic History of Europe*, 3, chap. 6, pp. 290–338; E. Miller,
Government Economic Policies and Public Finance, 900–1500 (C. M. Cipolla (ed.), The Fontana
Economic History of Europe, 1: The Middle Ages, chap. 8; London, 1970).

[66] Miller to Cam, 4 Feb. 1952: 'I've been getting completely out of my depth over French and
English economic policies in the Middle Ages—for Camb. Econ. Hist. vol. III (. . .). I tried to
compare Anglo-French attempts to tackle the problems of the land-law in the 13th cent. for the
Royal Historical Society this autumn—a frightening experience which I don't think quite came
off' (GCPP, Cam 2/2/12).

[67] Cf. Miller and Hatcher, *Medieval England: Rural Society and Economic Change, 1086–1348*,
pp. 176–8.

assume that of a head of house in the other, Miller abandoned the intention to write the book on the medieval nobility for which he had been committed to a publisher for some four or five years. Given his new circumstances, the decision is understandable. On a smaller scale, however, and taking in his stride many reviews, he published prolifically during the Fitzwilliam years, not least on peasant society, with which he had first engaged when he embarked on a study of the see of Ely and its estates in the late 1930s. In *Medieval England: Rural Society and Economic Change, 1086–1348*, written jointly with John Hatcher and published in 1978 (presumably the 'vulgarisation for Longmans' to which he had referred in 1958), nothing that had earlier seemed important to Miller in this wide area of concern is neglected, and standards of living and problems of poverty receive a more extended treatment than had been possible in his other recent works.[68] (The vivid treatment of poverty in his lectures is still remembered.) His willingness to lecture for the Faculty, after his return to Cambridge in 1971, on industry, commerce, and economic policy in the Middle Ages underlines his interest in topics which, as he had always believed, were not only intrinsically important but also had implications for the agrarian life of the period. *Rural Society and Economic Change* and a second volume, *Medieval England: Towns, Commerce and Crafts, 1086–1348*, published by the same authors in 1995, set a new standard for textbooks in all these fields.

V

Although founded a century earlier, Fitzwilliam House (its title since 1924) did not secure collegiate status in the University of Cambridge until 1966, and Miller was the first Master to be elected by the Fellows. When he assumed office, the college lacked endowments, and being, in consequence, dependent on fee income, had a very large number of Junior Members, of whom it could accommodate, at most, only half. Ten years later, when he retired, the endowments, though augmented by contributions from the university which his high profile on central university bodies had, without doubt, helped to secure, were inevitably still inadequate, and the buildings were no more extensive. In 1971, however, there were needs of a more intangible kind as compelling as the needs for money and buildings. For several reasons, the campaign for collegiate status, beginning in the 1950s,

[68] Ibid., pp. 128–33, 147–61.

had opened divisions that were not quickly healed after its success. Among the greatest needs in this period were the attainment of a true collegiality among the Fellows and more widely in the college, and the integration of the college in the life of the university. It was also vital to restore harmonious relations with the Fitzwilliam Society (comprising Old Members). Miller, possessing as he did an outgoing personality, an infectious sense of humour, and long experience of Cambridge, was the man the hour required. He was, moreover, a good administrator, and it was felt as a further advantage that he had been at a northern grammar school.

The new Master was also a good listener, and as a chairman he sought consensus: he presided but did not lead. Nevertheless, the admission of women in 1979, a controversial matter among the Fellows, reflected his own common-sense view that a more balanced society would result from the change. When, near the beginning of his Mastership, a minor revolution among the Junior Members set aside the existing claim of the Amalgamated Clubs, dominated by the Sports Clubs, to speak for the whole student body, he greatly eased the transition by his active cooperation with the new and much more representative Junior Members' Association. If sportsmen lost some ground in this change, sport itself enjoyed a novel degree of encouragement from a Master who was frequently to be seen on the touch-line and towpath. But he was interested in all aspects of undergraduate life and involved himself enthusiastically in others beside sport. He also supervised undergraduates for the Historical Tripos. Reaching out to Old Members, he continued the strenuous efforts of his predecessor, Walter Grave, to heal the breach with the Fitzwilliam Society to such good effect that it twice elected him as its President. As for meetings of the Governing Body and its committees, they became notably more good-humoured and relaxed than previously.

Miller's return to Cambridge occurred in a difficult period for the Faculty of History, since, for the time being, the university could not afford to fill the vacant Lectureship in the Social and Economic History of the Middle Ages: this remained vacant until the appointment of Dr (later Professor) John Hatcher in 1976. On Miller's election in 1971, Postan, who, in these circumstances, continued to lecture and hold classes and seminars in retirement, invited him to share in this work, and Miller immediately did so.[69] His service on the central bodies of the university,

[69] Letter from Postan to Miller dated 2 June 1971 (Cambridge University Library, Add. 8961/I/55). On 16 Dec. 1971, Postan wrote to Professor F. H. Hinsley, Chairman of the History

including the Library Syndicate, which he chaired, was much less congenial to him than any form of teaching, but crucially important for the college, in integrating Fitzwilliam in the life of the university. He received an invitation to become Vice-Chancellor but, mindful of the likely financial burden to the college, felt unable to accept. In 1975, he told Postan that the General Board, the Council of the Senate, and their committees, had 'virtually destroyed' his freedom in afternoons and evenings.[70] However, a highly developed, perhaps over-developed, sense of duty prevented him from seeking to avoid any chores of this kind. Miller's ten years as Master form a distinct period of consolidation in the history of the college, and his own part in this was a large one. And there were evidently some chinks in his Cambridge timetable, for from 1972 until 1979 his expertise in both rural and urban history found a new outlet in his chairmanship of the Victoria County Histories Committee of the Institute of Historical Research; and his fifteen active years (1974–89) as Chairman of the Editorial Board of the *History of Parliament.* began in the same period. He was elected FBA in the year of his retirement.

VI

Since Fitzwilliam College had no Master's Lodge at this time, retirement, in 1981, involved no change of residence, and Ted and Fanny Miller continued to live at 36 Almoners Avenue, as they had done throughout his Mastership. He greatly enjoyed working with John Hatcher on *Towns, Commerce and Crafts, 1086–1348* (1995), and the publication of *The Agrarian History of England and Wales*, vol. 3, under his editorship four years earlier was a personal triumph. He took particular pleasure in seeing his two grandsons growing up, and they for their part were devoted to him. But in only his second year of retirement, while on holiday in Rouen, where he had summered as an undergraduate, he suffered a punctured lung after falling in a shower. His stamina and his ability to speak in public for any length of time were permanently affected. Later, failing eyesight and deafness added to his reluctance to move far from home, as on the Swan Hellenic cruises which he and Fanny enjoyed at an early stage

---

Faculty Board, to say that he and Miller would repeat their discussion class in English Social and Economic History in the Middle Ages in the next Michaelmas Term, and would offer a lecture course then if no lecturer had been appointed in the interval (ibid.).

[70] Letter from Miller to Postan dated 20 March 1975 (ibid.).

of retirement. Despite these afflictions, however, a visit to the Kirov Ballet not long before he died gave great pleasure, and only a very few days before the end members of his family heard him explaining the meaning of some entries in Domesday Book to his granddaughter-in-law, who had expressed an interest in the matter. He died in Addenbroke's Hospital, after a very short illness but a long period of debility, on 21 December 2000. In accordance with his wishes, his funeral was private and there was no memorial service.

BARBARA HARVEY
Fellow of the Academy

PETER LINEHAN
Fellow of the Academy

Note. Letters from Edward Miller to Rodney Hilton, now in the possession of Jean Birrell, are cited with her permission, and we owe to her our knowledge of their existence. Letters now in the Postan papers, and reports on Edward Miller's fellowship dissertation, submitted in 1939, are cited with the permission, respectively, of the Syndics of Cambridge University Library and the Council of St John's College, Cambridge. Extracts from the letters of Helen Cam are cited by permission of the Mistress and Fellows of Girton College, Cambridge. The obituary of Edward Miller published in *The Independent* of 6 January 2001 is cited with the permission of the Editor of *The Independent*. For a further account of his Cambridge and his Sheffield years, see Peter Linehan *et al.*, *The Eagle* (2001), 80–8.

We are also indebted to the following for direct or indirect help with the preparation of this Memoir: Mrs Fanny Miller, Professor John Miller; Professor Michael Bentley, Professor Richard Britnell, Dr Marjorie Chibnall, Professor John Crook, Professor Christopher Dyer, Professor Paul Harvey, Professor John Hatcher, Professor George Holmes, Professor Sir James Holt, Dr Philippa Hoskin, Dr Ronald Hyam, Professor Brian Johnson, Professor Edmund King, Professor R. I. Moore, Mr William Noblett (Cambridge University Library), the Archivist of Girton College, Cambridge (Ms Kate Perry), Lady Cynthia Postan, Professor Richard Smith, Dr Peter Southern, Dr Henry Summerson, Dr David Thompson, the Archivist of St John's College, Cambridge (Mr M. G. Underwood), and the Keeper of Manuscripts and University Archivist, University of Cambridge (Dr Patrick Zutshi).

MICHIO MORISHIMA   *Dorothy Hahn*

Michio Morishima
1923–2004

MICHIO MORISHIMA was one of the most distinguished economic theorists of his generation. He taught in Japan at Kyoto and Osaka
Universities and in the UK at the University of Essex and the London
School of Economics where he spent the last thirty-four years of his very
creative life. He was a Visiting Professor at the University of Essex 1968–9
and the Keynes Visiting Professor there 1969–70 and Professor of
Economics, later the John Hicks Professor of Economics at the LSE. He
was a Senior Visiting Fellow at All Souls College, Oxford, where his
friend and mentor Sir John Hicks, FBA was the Drummond Professor of
Political Economy. He also held a visiting position at the University of
Siena in Italy for nearly thirty years from 1970. He was elected Foreign
Honorary Member of the American Academy of Arts and Sciences
(1975) and of the American Economic Association (1979).

Michio Morishima was born in Osaka on 18 July 1923, the son of
Kameji and Tatsuo Morishima. He grew up in Kobe and during his teens
would visit his parents in Beijing where his father worked in the airline
sector. He joined Kyoto University where he read as an undergraduate, as
an act of defiance against the then prevailing anti-British hysteria in
Japan, Hicks's *Value and Capital*, the seminal book on economic theory
published in 1939. He was conscripted into the Imperial Navy in 1943 but
due to his shortsightedness was employed in wireless operations and code
breaking. He continued his study of mathematics while in the Imperial
Navy. He graduated from Kyoto in 1946, where he continued to teach and
had a grant to pursue research. His report for the research grant was an
innovative extension of some ideas in Hicks's classic work but did not
appear in an English translation until well after his reputation was

Proceedings of the British Academy, **138**, 259–281. © The British Academy 2006.

established as a leading economic theorist in the West as much as in Japan. He began to publish articles from his thesis in leading English language journals in the 1950s.

From Kyoto he moved as an Assistant Professor to Osaka, whence he had the opportunity to visit Oxford on a Rockefeller Foundation grant in 1956 and meet his mentor John Hicks. Michio and his wife Yoko, whom he married in 1954, travelled by boat, that being his preferred mode of travel and spent a year at All Souls College where Hicks was a Fellow and the Drummond Professor of Political Economy. He visited Oxford again in 1963–4. His impatience with the conservatism of his Japanese colleagues and his love of Britain brought him to the University of Essex in 1968 as the Keynes Visiting Professor. He moved to the London School of Economics in 1970 and taught there till 1984 as Professor of Economics and then as the Sir John Hicks Professor of Economics 1984–8. He was awarded the Order of Culture (Bunka Kunsho) of Japan by the Emperor in 1976, the Fellowship of the British Academy in 1981 and an Honorary Fellowship of the LSE upon his retirement in recognition of his many contributions to the School. He was awarded honorary doctorates from the universities of Paris, X (1988), Siena (1991) and London (1995).

Morishima remained engaged with matters Japanese throughout his life, writing prolifically in Japanese on current issues. He also wrote *Why Has Japan 'Succeeded'?* in 1982 and then *Japan at a Deadlock* in 2000. His textbook for undergraduate economics, *The Economic Theory of Modern Society* (1976), was unlike any other economics textbook since it took a broad sociological and political as well as economic approach to the subject. He made it the basis of a very successful first-year undergraduate course he taught for many years at the LSE. Despite his insistence on rigour even at that level and his own way with the English language, undergraduates took to him. At a student Rag Festival, Morishima received thunderous applause when he rendered 'What Shall we Do with the Drunken Sailor?' all dressed up in a sailor's shirt and torn trousers, a pirate's patch across one eye and cutlass in hand. In each year he taught the course the students specially asked him to join in, and he was happy to play along.

Morishima was not just a distinguished economic theorist but he was also a research entrepreneur at a time when such a label would have been laughed at in academia. His role in directing the Institute of Economic and Social Research at the University of Osaka made it a world-class institution. At the LSE he was the pivotal fund raiser and creative brain behind the Suntory Toyota International Centre for Economics and Related Disciplines (STICERD). The grant of £2 million to the LSE by the Japanese corporations Suntory and Toyota represented the first major donation any Japanese company had made abroad and it was at Morishima's behest that it came about. As a winner of the Emperor's Order of Culture, the highest civilian honour Japan confers on its citizens, he was able to seek an appointment with the Japanese Prime Minister while the latter was in London for a summit. Morishima argued that Japan's economic success had not been matched by a rise in international respect for the Japanese because the Japanese had not done what rich countries were meant to do—donate money abroad for charitable purposes. In the event, it was again Morishima who was able to persuade his school friend and the head of Toyota, Mr Saji, to make a contribution. He was willing, but did not want to be the sole donor. The cooperation of Suntory was soon forthcoming, and the result was the Suntory Toyota Centre. But it almost did not happen since the recipients at the LSE had their own suspicions of all this foreign business money invading British universities. Morishima had to be at his persuasive best in the LSE Academic Board to reassure his colleagues that there was no hidden agenda behind the donation. It was genuinely for research. That bit about 'related disciplines' was designed to placate the suspicions of his non-economics colleagues at the LSE that yet again the economists were going to aggrandise themselves. STICERD has proved an immensely useful resource for all social sciences at the LSE, and will remain the best memorial to Morishima's many talents as a researcher, persuader and a cultural ambassador for his home country.

Morishima was among the first generation of Japanese economists whose work became accepted in the international economics fraternity. Japan has a long tradition of economic thought which drew upon diverse Western sources such as the German Historical School, Marxism and classical political economy and neoclassical economics. But few Japanese economists wrote in English, and before the Second World War only Shigeto Tsuru, who had studied at Harvard, had gained international prominence. Post-war Japan saw well-trained Japanese economists ready and able to make a foray into the international arena. It was easier for these economists to communicate in the common language of mathematics with their fellow economists. An earlier era, when a lack of English language proficiency would have put the non-English-speaking economist at a disadvantage, was rapidly yielding to a phase where economic theorising had to be done in a mathematical idiom since rigorous arguments were difficult otherwise. It was Morishima's mentor Sir John Hicks along with Paul Samuleson who were the twin pioneers of this transformation in the mode of economic theorising. Hicks's *Value and Capital* (1939, 1945) and Samuelson's *Foundations of Economic Analysis* (1947) heralded this approach.

The Econometric Society had been established in 1931 as an international society for the statistical and mathematical study of economics and its international meetings around the world became a forum for young economists of various nationalities to display their wares in a polyglot environment where everyone spoke algebra. Ichimura, Nikaido, Inada, Uzawa, Negishi were soon names among the speakers at such assemblies. Morishima was far and away the most prominent among them and became the first Japanese to be the President of the Econometric Society in 1965.

After his retirement from the LSE in 1988 he continued to play an active part in the research life of STICERD and continued to publish. In 1992 he published *Capital and Credit* which is the capping stone of his life's work and then in 1996 he published an English translation of his 1950 Ph.D. work as *Dynamic Economic Theory*, thus bringing his life's work into a closed circle. He wrote his book *Japan in a Deadlock* in 2000 to account for the change in Japanese fortunes. He died, aged 80, on 13 July 2004, leaving behind his wife Yoko and two sons and a daughter.

Contributions to economic theory

Introduction

Morishima's contributions to economic theory were many. He contributed to the areas of value theory, in particular the existence of equilibrium and stability, both static and dynamic; macroeconomic theory of growth and the theory of money and capital. It is rare for any one person to have attempted research in all these diverse areas but in Morishima's work there was also an underlying architecture which put his seemingly diverse contributions into an overall framework. It was a very ambitious research programme that he undertook and he came close to achieving it completely. To put this in context, one needs to understand the circumstances in which theorising was being carried out in the post-war period.

During the inter-war period, economics had undergone two major revolutions. One was the Keynesian Revolution wherein Lord Keynes had offered a general theory of the determination of aggregate output and employment along with a policy toolkit to prevent the recurrence of mass unemployment. The other revolution was the systematisation and analytical proof of the theory of general equilibrium of Leon Walras. Walras had sketched the theory in his *Elements of Pure Economics*, published in 1874 (final and fourth edition in 1926), but a rigorous proof had been lacking. During the inter-war period, first the Swedish economist Gustav Cassel and then the German statistician Abraham Wald had offered rigorous proofs of the proposition that the markets for myriad commodities and services could be simultaneously in a market clearing equilibrium without the intervention of any outside agencies.

There were, however, many ruptures and fissures despite, and in some cases because of, these twin revolutions. A major rupture was the one between the classical—Adam Smith/David Ricardo—political economy which was founded on a Labour Theory of Value and whose orientation was economic growth and capital accumulation and the neoclassical theory of resource allocation in a static or steadily growing economy, inaugurated simultaneously by Carl Menger of Vienna, Stanley Jevons of Manchester and Leon Walras of Lausanne. The Labour Theory of Value had difficulty accommodating the influence of pure scarcity— non-reproducible commodities—on the value of a good, and, more seriously, of the contribution of durable capital to the formation of value. Capital, even when produced with previous labour inputs, could not be reduced to dated labour inputs in any simple fashion. There had to be a discounting/compounding role for the rate of interest. Thus the value of any commodity was determined not by the total labour embodied in it (as the simple classical model would have it) but also by the time pattern of the inputs and a rate of interest, which in its turn could not be explained by a Labour Theory of Value. This lacuna was important because it also raised the question of the relative contribution of labour and machinery (capital) in generating profits. Marx had attempted an explanation of profit based solely on the contribution of living labour and the surplus extraction process, which he claimed was unique to capitalism. But if dated labour was as important as living labour and the interest factor entered the determination of value crucially, profits could be as much due to machinery and its productivity as due to labour. There was also an unanswered question as to what explained the rate of interest. There was a technical as well as a moral/political issue here as to the origin and justification of profits.

Neoclassical theory proposed a marginalist calculus based on the utility of consumption and the opportunity cost of inputs expended to generate an explanation of value. It had no problem in explaining the value of rare objects. Its model of competitive equilibrium also eliminated profit as a separate category of income. In equilibrium there were zero profits. Capital inputs were just like labour inputs and their reward was determined by their marginal productivity. There was no surplus value and no exploitation. An elaborate explanation of interest rates was given by the Austrian economist Eugen von Bohm-Bawerk in terms of a theory of productivity based on the 'roundaboutness of the process of production'. Thus the longer the time between initial input and final ouput, the longer that is 'the period of production', the more productive the process. But such processes could only be sustained by voluntary savings which released the resources required for the investment over the period during which no output appeared. The abundance of savings assured a low interest rate. The willingness of people to forgo immediate consumption had to be rewarded by the payment of interest on their savings. Productivity and the willingness to wait thus explained the role of interest rates.

This happy picture was, however, abstracted from trade depressions and business cycles, from the problems created by credit booms and busts and by the periodic bouts of rising and falling prices. Price inflation and deflation were explained solely at the aggregate level by the quantity of money; there was no micro theory of money nor did money seem to play any role in production or consumption in the neoclassical theory. Attempts to link credit growth and cycles were made by the Swedish economist Knut Wicksell and the Austrian economist Joseph Schumpeter. Wicksell traced the cyclical processes to the divergence between the money rate of interest at which firms could borrow and banks lend and the natural rate of interest which determined the basic profitability of investment. (Friedrich Hayek noted that the natural rate of interest was a surrogate name for the rate of profit since Marxist polemics had given profitability a bad name.) Schumpeter posited long cycles caused by innovations which permanently changed conditions of production by the introduction of a new product or process, e.g. railroads, which in their turn brought in imitators and by-products which created a boom and bust cycle of around fifty years.

Neither Wicksell nor Schumpeter dealt with the problem of the durability of capital. Capital generated a stream of income by its productivity. It eventually depreciated and had to be scrapped. The value of capital is merely the discounted sum of its prospective income stream. Yet the valuation of capital as it aged during the process of production required some arbitrary assumption as to how its productivity declined. This was also the case if a new invention made a piece of capital obsolete during its physical life. Only in a static world with no uncertainty could one predict the life time of a capital asset, its income stream and hence its value. Away from this, the valuation of old second-hand capital caused problems.

Karl Menger, the mathematician son of the economist Carl Menger, ran a seminar at the University of Vienna in the 1930s. It was at this seminar that Abraham Wald gave the solution to the problem of the existence of equilibrium in the Walrasian model of multiple markets. He allowed for prices to be non-negative rather than strictly positive and then applied a fixed point theorem to prove existence. A more significant paper was by J. von Neumann in which he posed the problem of growth in a multiple good economy in terms of linear equations. He treated capital goods as time dated and so a one-year old machine could be different from a two-year old machine; indeed a two-year old machine is part of the output of a process in which the one-year old machine along with labour and raw materials produces some output. This notion of joint production completely solved the problem of valuing durable capital by replacing a durable capital good by its sequence of time dated activities. The dual to the quantitative input output equations were the price cost equations. Von Neumann proved that an equilibrium growth rate of the primal problem matched the equilibrium profit rate of its dual.

Von Neumann's paper was not translated into English till 1945 but it had a profound effect on theorists, especially on Morishima. Wald's paper was also revived only in the post-war period. Before that John Hicks had tried in his *Value and Capital* to introduce English-reading economists to the Walrasian model. Hicks synthesised the Marshallian partial equilibrium theory of consumers with the Walrasian theory of multiple markets and went on to speculate on dynamics as well. It was to be profoundly influential for the post-war generation of economists.

Morishima's economic writings

It is against this general background of developments in economic theory that we can look at Morishima's contribution. I shall refer below to Morishima's research programme in the Lakatos sense.[1] Unlike many other economists, Morishima's lifetime work is designed around an architectural blueprint which is clear from the early days of his published work (those in Japanese, as *Dogakuteki Keizai Riron* (*DKR*), later translated into English as *Dynamic Economic Theory* (*DET*), 1950/1996.[2] (I shall refer to *DET* as an early work although it is the last to be published in

[1] Lakatos' idea of a Scientific Research Programme is discussed in I. Lakatos and A. Musgrave (eds.), *Methodology of Scientific Research Programmes* (Cambridge, 1970).
[2] Morishima's writings will be referred to by date of publication alone. See the list of them at the end of this memoir.

English thus far. It is very formative in the Morishima Research Programme.) In a sense it is a work of breathtaking scope not attempted during this century by many other economists. The work encompasses general equilibrium theory (Hicks's *Value and Capital* style) with hetero-geneous capital, growth and money, much of it covered in the framework of a von Neumann linear technology. Along the way Morishima tried to include within his framework the economics of Ricardo, Marx, Walras and Keynes. These are not separate works; they are part of a coherent attempt to tackle one of the most intractable problems in economic the-ory, namely the construction of an adequate theory of a dynamic grow-ing economy with heterogeneous capital and money as well as credit or, to put it another way, a theory of how the capitalist economy works.

Few have attempted this task. Marx in the nineteenth century was the first such economist. Walras did not deal with dynamics, except in some pregnant but not fully worked out remarks in the concluding chapters of his classic work, or with heterogeneous capital. Hayek was the first among the twentieth-century economists to attempt this. Hicks, Morishima's hero, was another. In his own special way, Paul Samuelson has done this, though scattered across a large number of papers rather than in books. Robert Lucas is another contemporary economic theorist who can be said to have consciously tried to emulate Hayek, though he has stayed clear of heterogeneous capital.

In what follows I shall first outline Morishima's writings in their chronological order and then pick up the central lineaments of the under-lying architecture which in my view makes Morishima's work a research programme.

Morishima's first book was his thesis and this was published in Japanese in 1950 (*DKR*) and translated into English only in 1996 as *DET*. This is itself a bold and innovative piece of work, typical of a confident and talented 26 year-old. It is a project of 'the mathematization of *Value and Capital*'. It is concerned mainly with deriving the stability conditions for a tatonnement process with competition and no false trading (for the non-economist, tatonnement is the process of price fixing by higgling). Morishima does this for a linear and a non-linear case. He then goes on to discuss dynamic stability conditions. Along the way there is a running sub-ordinate theme of a theory of money and the comparison of the loanable funds and the liquidity preference theories of interest. In several places, Morishima corrects his hero Hicks and derives more rigorous results. Chronologically this book belongs to the same generation of books as *Value and Capital* (second edition of 1946) and Samuelson's *Foundations of*

Economic Analysis (1948). It is mathematically advanced and theoretically sophisticated. Had it appeared in English in the early 1950s, it would have saved a lot of work which replicated Morishima's results.

Some of the results of *DET* were published in *Econometrica* and in the *Review of Economic Studies* (1952; 1957). But it was the publication of *Equilibrium, Stablity and Growth* (*ESG*) in 1964 that brought Morishima's name to a much wider audience. By 1964, Morishima had added to his earlier heroes—Marx, Walras and Hicks, the name of J. von Neumann. Von Neumann's work on growth was to be the grammar of Morishima's work in the next two decades. All the major themes come together in this book. Linear production systems are treated in terms of stability of equilibrium and growth paths. Morishima is quite eclectic in covering Joan Robinson's *Accumulation of Capital* (1956) as well as the Turnpike theorems which were inspired by Hicks's work on growth in linear systems.

Morishima's next book was his first attempt at formulating his own growth theory. *The Theory of Economic Growth* (*TEG*), 1969. It is in many ways within the mainstream of the 1960s growth theory except that it innovates in a number of ways. In one sense, Schumpeter's theory of innovations and growth was always an alternative theory to that of Marx when it comes to rationalising surplus value under capitalism. If Marx searches for surplus value in the contribution of living labour, Schumpeter locates it in innovations which generate surplus monopoly profits which are eaten away by competition. Marx was aware of the constant revolutionising of the technology under capitalism but he did not connect it with the periodic upsurges in productivity and profitability. Morishima tried to tame Schumpeter's somewhat fuzzy ideas into a linear technology mould. But that was to come much later after *TEG*.

Then there is a long detour in Morishima's work. It may be that he was disappointed by the reception of *TEG*, or that he needed to reconnect with the themes of his thesis. But the next three books present a mathematical treatment of the ideas of three leading economists of the nineteenth century—Marx, Walras and Ricardo, in the order in which they were dealt with by Morishima. (Morishima wrote other books as well, in 1976 and 1984, but as they deal with general issues rather than economic research. I want to leave them out of this account.) In all three books, Morishima did the double task of reintegrating the work of these economists in the modern economic mainstream using the 'grammar' of *ESG* but at the same time using their ideas to extend the span of modern theory. Thus his treatment of joint production in Marx and of the cash balances in Walras, or the bold attempt to marry

Ricardo, Keynes and Walras in one model in the Ricardo book readily come to mind.

It is then in *Capital and Credit* (*CC*) that Morishima came out with his own generalisation of all the various strands which had been moving in parallel in his work thus far. *CC* is subtitled *A New Formulation of General Equilibrium Theory*. This is an ambitious title and it proclaims in one sense the closure of the Morishima Research Programme. As he said:

> In this volume, I complete this [i.e. escape from the narrow confines of General Equilibrium Theory] process and present the model which I finally reached and which I hope may serve as the analytical base for multi-disciplinary extensions of the general equilibrium theory on which economists must work in the future. This I consider may at least temporarily be regarded as the terminus of my long journey.   (*CC*, p. 2)

Here the Walrasian theory is updated to take into account capitalist production (rather than petty commodity production without an entrepreneur and no finance constraint, as is usual in the standard theory) along with money and finance, innovation, equilibrium as well as disequilibrium. This is the complete Morishima with his formulation integrating all his favourites—Marx, Walras, Keynes, von Neumann, Hicks and Schumpeter—in a theoretically rigorous and mathematically tight framework.

It is then to fill out the map of his theoretical odyssey that Morishima had his 1950 work translated along with related papers published since then. Thus *Dynamic Economic Theory* is a coda to the entire œuvre and has to be consulted at various places to unravel the trajectory of Morishima's thinking. It stands at the beginning and at the end of his work. So a simple schema would be as follows:

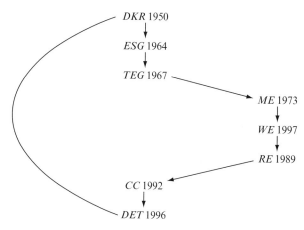

Now it is time to turn to a theoretical discussion of the content of the Morishima Research Programme (MRP).

Themes in the Morishima Research Programme

There are five themes in Morishima's Research Programme. In one sense, they are separate because on any one of them one could spend a lifetime of research, and some economists have done so. But in Morishima's work, there is an attempt to synthesise these in one overarching framework. It is my contention that he was always conscious of such a possible synthesis. In his *Capital and Credit* (1996) he gives his answer. The themes are:

- Tatonnement Exchange: Existence of Equilibrium and Stability
- Non-Tatonnement Exchange: Existence of Equilibrium and Stability
- Dynamic Stability: Correspondence with above
- Growth with heterogeneous capital, innovations and money
- Money and Credit in a theory of capitalist economy: Growth and Cycles

These five themes span the comparative static and dynamic areas of economic theory as they also cover microeconomic and macroeconomic issues. It is along this grid of five themes that Ricardo, Marx, Walras, von Neumann, Schumpeter, and Keynes are arrayed. Of course there are gaps. Keynes has nothing to say on the exchange stability problems, but the whole issue of non-tatonnement trading is very relevant to the microfoundations of Keynesian economics because of the persistence of false trading which the Walrasians deny. (False trading is explained further below.) Early on in his work, Morishima was aware that Walras himself did not subscribe to the 'no false trading' rule. As he says in the preface to *DET*:

> he [i.e., Walras] assumes that tatonnement is truncated so as to make effective transactions at a point in time when general equilibrium has not yet been realized. Then individuals' or firms' endowments change, which initiates a new tatonnement, thus contradicting the so-called Walrasians; the real Walras is a disequilibrium economist, at least in the field of dynamics. (*DET*, p. xiii)

This is the burden of the first of the eight articles added to the original thesis in *DET*. In the thesis itself, Morishima innovates in the theory of the firm by separating the production planning and supply planning periods in chapter 1. Then he surveys the stability conditions of tatonnement exchange as stated by Samuelson, Hicks and his teacher Sono. This was the real frontier of economic theory at the time Morishima was writing his dissertation and his confidence in pointing out where his seniors are wrong is remarkable. The essence of the problem is as follows.

For any commodity, let there be demand and supply functions which are well behaved. Now the tatonnement theory says that if the market starts out at a price away from the equilibrium given by the intersection of the demand and supply curves, then the price must change until the equilibrium point is reached. But how? Walrasians posit an auctioneer who would call out prices and register demands and supplies at each price. No trades are made until the auctioneer is satisfied that demands and supplies balance, that is there is no false trading. This is patently unrealistic and yet this has been the workhorse of stability of equilibrium theory. Further, of course there are n commodities and there is complementarity/substitution between them. While the conditions of equilibrium in the n commodity case with complementarity/substitutability were being established by Samuelson, Hicks, Arrow, MacKenzie and Sono, and led to an extensive use of matrices in economics, the corollary of no false trading equilibrium is, for example, that there can be never be involuntary unemployment. This cannot be and was not comfortable for many Keynesians who cared about the consistency of micro and macro theories with each other.

Morishima makes it clear that he prefers the case in which trading takes place at each price, but the price changes if at that price after transactions are closed there is excess supply or demand. Thus, after each price is called out and trades are done (taking the case of excess supply), demands and supplies are revised at the new price. Thus, some traders may buy/sell at a price higher/lower than the equilibrium price. This non-tatonnement process was much less thoroughly explored at the time when Morishima wrote his thesis and he makes a contribution towards that later in *DET*.

But, apart from the non-tatonnement problem, even the stability proofs are not all they seem to be. Are we exploring the path of convergence of the 'groping' prices, i.e. virtual prices at which no trades are carried out and hence within 'the market day', or are we talking of the path of equilibrium prices arrived at, at the end of the tatonnement in each market day from one day to the next? This distinction was not made at all clear in the pioneering literature, as Morishima points out in a critique of Samuelson (*DET*, pp. 37–9). Morishima takes up the later problem in his dynamics sections which occupy the third chapter of *DET*.

One of Morishima's incidental contributions to economics has been to bring to light much analytical work written in Japanese in the 1940s, but not known to an international audience due to the language barrier. Mathematics was the common language in these contributions. Morishima brings out the relevance of these articles and puts them into perspective. *DET* is full of references to such contributions by Professors Sono, Tanaka, Yasui and Yokoyama.

But stability of exchange equilibrium in either of the two forms was not enough. A further question arose of the sense in which one could talk about the stability of equilibrium. Within the Hicksian week, the groping process traces out a path of virtual prices which converge to equilibrium under certain well-known conditions. But what of the sequence over several weeks of the equilibrium price? What are the dynamics of the path itself? It is this question that Morishima picks up in *DET*, and pursues over his entire career. It is obviously connected to the stability of a growth path; each time period's income is solved out and we examine its stability. What for the microeconomist is a long week within which a price has to be arrived at is for the growth theorist just a point in time—a year or just 't'. So the path of income is analogous to the path of equilibrium, i.e. 'end of tatonnement' prices. Morishima's discussion of growth paths was therefore always concerned not only with the quantity variables such as income and the stock of capital but also with prices and interest rates.

In 1964 Morishima's first book in English, *Equilibrium, Stability and Growth* (*ESG*) was published. In some respects this is a drastic change of direction but only in terms of techniques rather than content or themes. Morishima adopted the mathematical techniques that von Neumann initiated by his classic article (1937/1945–6).[3] This meant that linear technology with or without joint production forms the bulk of the themes of this book. Since von Neumann paths are maximal growth paths, albeit under stringent assumptions of free disposal etc., but the technology also allows one to treat many commodities at once so the normally macroeconomic growth theory could be cast in microeconomic terms opening up possibilities of a micro-macro synthesis.

In *ESG*, Morishima tries to integrate Walras into the growth story, which had not hitherto been attempted, and he also gave prominence to Marx's work on accumulation at the same time. In 1964 it was still bold to broach Marx's name in American academia but it was the beginning of a trend that was to catch on. (At that time Samuelson was the only other

---

[3] J. Von Neumann, 'Uber ein okinomisches Gliechungssystem und sein Verallgemeinrung des Brouwer' schen Fixpunktsatzes', *Ergbinisse eines mathematischen Kolloquiums*, 73–83, translated into English as 'A Model of General Economic Equilibrium', *Review of Economic Studies*, 13 (1945–6), 1–9.

prominent mainstream economist who had discussed Marx.)[4] Thus were born Walras–Leontieff and Marx–von Neumann models which became workhorses in Morishima's Research Programme.

ESG is thus growth oriented with emphasis on linear technology and balanced maximal growth paths with fixed coefficients. But there is also a chapter on a spectrum of techniques. This is Morishima's response to the then ongoing capital controversy between Cambridge, England, and Cambridge, Massachusetts. Morishima is able to start with discrete technologies as he has his linear techniques at hand. He is able to generalise the effects on changing coefficients due to change in factor prices. The jump along different factor combinations available in discrete terms traces out a surrogate production function which is not the neoclassical production function of the smooth variety but a close analogue. He does not yet discuss reswitching. This issue was to arise two years later.

ESG is even then a tidying up, synthesising book. Various results are derived and neatly put in relation to each other. What others had done, Morishima does with much greater generality. But very soon after *ESG*, Morishima came out with his, as yet, most ambitious work. This was *Theory of Economic Growth* (*TEG*). Unlike *ESG*, *TEG* is both a new book setting out new results, and an advanced textbook, and was used as such by Morishima in his M.Sc. course on economic growth at the LSE. Here Morishima does more than most growth theorists of the day. He sets out in a rigorous multisectoral framework—the von Neumann model—and integrates Walras as well as Hicks and Malinvaud into this framework. Prices are solved out along with quantities throughout. Turnpikes are discussed under various assumptions. But he also deals with the issue of the optimality of the maximal growth paths. Now, while the Fundamental Theorem has been proved for timeless competitive economy or even its Arrow–Debreu version, Morishima was the first, I believe, perhaps the only theorist, to face up to the issue of Pareto Optimality of a variety of growth paths. Thus, consumption figures much more in *TEG* than in many other books on growth, and it is also modelled along class lines separately for workers and capitalists.

Yet *TEG* is also a major deviation from the high road of the Morishima Research Programme. It is much more mainstream than *ESG* or *DET*. It ignores money, Keynes, Marx and Schumpeter. It is the most non-monetary of all his books and issues of credit and capital are not

---

[4] 'Wages and Interest: A Modern Dissection of Marxian Economic Models', *American Economic Review*, 47 (1957), 884–912.

engaged. To a large extent the apparatus of General Equilibrium Theory (GET) is too confining. Morishima was to acknowledge this in *Capital and Credit*: 'It is no exaggeration to say that I confined myself throughout my life in the narrow realm of GET.'

In his long escape from GET, he regarded *TEG* retrospectively as an experimental work. Yet as he says again in the Introduction to *CC*:

> after 1964, I groped for a more satisfactory model of general equilibrium. At the same time I learned from great masters of the classical period, Ricardo, Marx and Walras, how to construct a dynamic model.

Morishima was not happy with the outcome of *TEG*. He says as much in his preface to *DET*. Thus started his long detour via Marx, Walras and Ricardo, until he could come back to his major concern. The Marx book came out at a time when the study of Marx as an economist was at its peak in academia. Samuelson had engaged in a debate with Baumol in the *Journal of Economic Literature* (1971), about the validity of the notion of exploitation. There was the background of Paris 1968, as well as the Prague Spring, the Vietnam War and the rise of a radical students' movement in the USA and Europe. Japanese economists had also been traditionally divided between Marxists and non-Marxist economists, as Morishima explains in the Preface to his book on Marx. While Marx's economics had been studied off and on since the first publication of *Volume III* of *Capital,* starting with Bohm-Bawerk, there had been no full treatment of all aspects of his economic work by economists. Joan Robinson's 1949 *Essay on Marxian Economics* is an introductory guide to Marx rather than an examination of his work using the tools of economics. Paul Sweezy's *Theory of Capitalist Development* (1942) was also introductory and omits many of the themes Morishima tackles. Morishima's book was the first book in English to introduce Marx to a new generation of economists using a language they would understand.

Yet in the context of the Research Programme, Marx is a distraction, or at least the Marx dealt with in the 1973 book. While Morishima deals with the statics and dynamics of Marx's growth and exploitation theory and tackles the joint production with innovative insights, there is no money and practically no technical progress in this book. This is partly because Marx's remarks on these two topics are much less systematic than his work on surplus value or accumulation. It was also these latter topics which were subjects of debate at that time. Yet given Morishima's interest in money and technical progress, it is surprising that he did not get into these aspects of Marx's economics. Marx's role in Morishima's Research

Programme is to set down the lines for multisectoral growth and propose a way in which heterogeneous capital can be consistently aggregated using labour values.

The crucial bridge in the escape from GET towards the completion of the Morishima Programme in *CC* is provided by Walras. This is obviously not the way Walras has been thought of in the literature. Walras is the fount of General Equilibrium, which is supposed to be neoclassical economics and is contrasted to Keynesian economics. Thus economists think that Walras provides consistent microfoundations for a full employment/all markets clearing theory of the macroeconomy. Morishima has a different Walras in his book which has the intriguing subtitle; the full title is *Walras' Economics: A pure theory of capital and money.* Now Walras is not associated with either of those two topics. But Morishima takes Walras beyond the conventional interpretation, both by reading the later chapters of the *Elements of Pure Economics* that others do not read, and by correcting and extending Walras where he is either incomplete or wrong.

The centre of attention is Say's Law. Morishima's purpose in the book is to see whether he can exploit Walras's work to provide the microfoundations of Keynesian macroeconomics. He focuses on the contrast between nominal demands (neoclassical) and effective demands (Keynes) as well as the doctrine that investments adjust to savings (neoclassical) and that investments are prior and savings adjust (Keynes). Walras had a four class model—landlords, workers, capitalists and entrepreneurs. But entrepreneurs have no income; they work on altruistic principles. Morishima thus adjusts the investment function as well as giving entrepreneurs an income (profits) which makes the model closer to real capitalism. But he also generates a lot of fruitful ideas on Walras's monetary theory especially as to why one needs a theory of accumulation and growth, i.e. a story with time and future in it in order to have a rationale for holding money in a Walrasian world. In a static general equilibrium, money can, and does, play no role. This simple and powerful result was ignored in much of the work on money in a general equilibrium model which was done in the 1960s and 1970s under the leadership of Frank Hahn but which never resolved the question of the essential role of money in a GET.[5]

Thus one has to have growth and accumulation to have money (Walras). But the world does not obey Say's Law and investment func-

---

[5] The best reference here is J. M. Grandmont, *Money and Value* (Cambridge, 1983).

tions are central to a capitalist economy (Keynes). Capital is heterogeneous (von Neumann), but can be aggregated in labour time if one so wishes (Marx). But capitalism may be unstable and have cycles (Marx, again). At this stage the scene was set for Schumpeter or a full scale treatment of Keynes. But then instead we have a book on Ricardo. Why Ricardo? As Morishima says, in the preface to the Ricardo book, having worked on Marx and Walras and found common congenial elements among their theories, attention had to be paid to 'their common guru Ricardo'.

But the real purpose is also to get back to the origins of Say's Law in Ricardo and trace the story right up to Keynes and his denial of Say's Law. To quote again from the preface:

> I have given up my original idea to conclude the trilogy with Keynes. I have instead been concerned, in this volume, with transition from Ricardo (who highly appraises Say's Law of markets as a 'very important principle') to Keynes (who rejects the law). Via this channel, a number of Keynesian problems, especially the problems of effective demand and unemployment, are introduced and discussed ... Also I try and identify the epoch of Ricardian economics and those of Walrasian and Keynesian economics, in parallel with this transition.   (*RE*, p. viii)

The heart of *Ricardo's Economics* (*RE*) is in the final section entitled 'Three Paradigms Compared'. Again, Say's Law is at issue. Indeed I would argue that it was Morishima's unhappiness about Say's Law, reflected as far back as his thesis (*DKR*) which finally tore him away from balanced growth paths and stability of exchange equilibria and Turnpikes, and led him to make the detour he did. He describes Ricardo, Marx and Walras as 'the first generation of scientific economics', i.e. general equilibrium theorists who did not confine themselves to static models. Of these three, Ricardo established Say's Law as a dominant mode of theorising about economics, Marx did not subscribe to Say's Law but failed to dent its influence, and Walras confirmed it in the earlier parts of *Elements* but in later parts, on growth and money, needed, according to Morishima, to depart from it. It was Keynes who remained his hero, though a flawed one, since he did not provide sufficient microfoundations for his theory. So Walras is harnessed to the task of filling this lacuna.

The usual departures from Say's Law involve a non-trivial role for money and/or a growth process via an active investment function. Ricardo has neither and so can subscribe to Say's Law. Marx had both but his investment function was very restrictive and made no use of money or credit. Walras had money towards the end of *Elements* but his growth theory lacked an investment function which led the way for savings to adjust to it. Keynes of course had money and investment functions, but he did not spell out why and how the general equilibrium properties of exchange equilibria and production equilibria are violated. Growth is not sufficient since von Neumann paths satisfy GE properties as *TEG* showed. Money is the real culprit or an investment function which has a role for entrepreneurs.

In *RE*, a model is set up in which excess demand and supply for labour and capital are modelled in a simple diagram (*RE*, fig. 6, p. 218). Here, around an equilibrium point, zones of excess supply and demand for the two factors are mapped out. The work is reminiscent of the almost exactly contemporary work of Malinvaud, *Theory of Unemployment Reconsidered* (1977), in which different concepts of unemployment— Keynesian, classical, etc.—were mapped out in a two quadrant diagram. But Morishima's axes are the real wage and the output capital ratio. (Morishima was later to discuss Malinvaud's work in *CC*). In figure 7, a Walras/Keynes version of the Ricardian diagram in figure 6 is produced. Within the same general model all the three paradigms are embedded. Again the investment function turns out to be the crucial relationship for the Anti-Say's Law result that Keynes established.

After *RE*, all the pieces were in place. The time had come for a new assault on the fundamental problem of economic theorising—a theory of how the modern capitalist economy works. But this had to be tackled with a modicum of realism, so the Arrow–Debreu story or even the von Neumann story were out. Money had to play an essential role, but not just in the consumer portfolio but in enabling investment. So it had to be credit with banks playing a crucial part, as they do in Schumpeter's model. For Morishima, Schumpeter's great contribution is not the notion of the entrepreneur, since that can be found in Walras, but the fact that bankers finance entrepreneurs and thus credit plays a crucial role in capitalism (*RE*, p. 202). Production was not the same as supply and production possibilities were not given; they were created by an entrepreneur. So entrepreneurs had to be given an active role. Above all equilibrium was not guaranteed at full employment since Say's Law did not always hold.

This is the background to *Capital and Credit: A new formulation of general equilibrium theory*. This is Morishima's escape from Hicks (*Value and Capital*) whom he continues to respect and admire. By now he is unhappy with GET since

> In the purifying process, however, they have lost various ingredients which played essential roles in the pre war theory. When I was taught the principles

of economics, a first year undergraduate course by Professor Takata in 1942, stars were E. von Bohm-Bawerk, K. Wicksell, and F. A. von Hayek. All these names are not frequently mentioned in post war general equilibrium theory. (*CC*, p. ix)

Hence

In this volume I will try and formulate the type of general equilibrium theory which such economists as Bohm-Bawerk, Wicksell and Hayek were concerned with. I shall also try and extend their type of capital theory so as to make it compatible with Schumpeter's theory of money and credit.   (*CC*, p. ix)

Then of course there is Keynes and Anti-Say's Law. Yet the old favourites are not ignored. Austrian capital theory with all its conundrums about time and the period of production is replaced by von Neumann's method. Hicks is there with his distinction between flexprice and fixprice. Then we come to the point early on:

in spite of the existence of involuntary unemployment, I describe the state obtained at the end of a period as an equilibrium, rather than a disequilibrium state. This is because conditions are realized in the economy at the end of a period, under which entrepreneurs have no incentive to change their scale of operations and workers do not propose an alteration of wages; hence there is no change in employment.   (*CC*, p. 19)

The major change in *CC* is that banks play a crucial role in financing production. Thus how much entrepreneurs undertake to do depends on the availability of credit. This is Schumpeter rather than Keynes. While in Keynes's scheme entrepreneurs may underinvest because of expectations or a low marginal efficiency of capital relative to the rate of interest, Schumpeter allows for overshooting of credit creation by bankers (as do Hayek and von Mises and Wicksell). Thus inflation as well as underemployment is possible. But Schumpeter has an inbuilt tendency for his economy to revert to a long-run stationary equilibrium, while Morishima wants to allow for motion which does not terminate in a stationary state or a long-run Walrasian General Equilibrium of the Hicks's *Value and Capital* type.

Thus the core of *CC*, the last two chapters in effect, is concerned with innovations and their financing and monetary disequilibrium. Of course, there is much along the way. Thus the *DKR* distinction between production and supply is reintroduced. Production technology is not given but chosen by the entrepreneur. To allow for a general model, the device used in *WE* and *RE* of splitting the economy into Say's Law and Anti-Say's Law activities is introduced again. There is a scope for Anti-Say's Law if production is financed by credit, and this of course requires that it is not instantaneous but has an input–output lag. With instantaneous production and investment adjusting to savings, Say's Law is confirmed. But in any realistic capitalist economy, it breaks down due to the presence of credit. The amount of credit determines activity in the Anti-Say's Law sector (manufacturing industry, in other words), and this, via the multiplier, determines the overall levels of activity and employment. This need not be full employment.

The classical and Walrasian dichotomy, of real economy, where relative prices equilibrate, and the nominal sector (quantity of money), where the absolute price level is fixed, is no longer valid.

> [N]either of the subsystems is self contained. The real system presumes that the rate of interest determined in the monetary sector prevails in the real sector, and conversely, the price level of the monetary system adjusts the rates of profits such that the rate of profits of banks corresponding to it is equal to the general rate of profits of the industry determined in the real system. Therefore the dichotomy of the whole system is impossible. (*CC*, p. 151)

It is only by omitting banks and the financial requirements for production that the dichotomy is sustained.

In the last chapter on Monetary Disequilibrium, Wicksell's cumulative process is examined from the point of view of von Neumann. The real system establishes the rate of profits (=rate of growth) but it leaves the price level indeterminate. We are in the Wicksell world here, not the Schumpeter/Keynes world. The credit creation by bankers determines the nominal level of interest with the natural rate given by the real system. Then the monetary side determines the price level by the intersection of the money demand function and the real growth rate. But it is not a stable equilibrium. It is a kind of IS–LM model, but with its axes as interest rate and price level rather than income. The Hicks/Walras world will be stable. You have to introduce the departures from the Wicksell/Hicks/Walras world to get the instability Wicksell wished to demonstrate. (Recall that Myrdal in his *Monetary Equilibrium* (1939) had shown that Wicksell's proof of his equilibrium proposition was flawed.)

> It is worth emphasising that the constancy of the natural rate of interest . . . is the most important premise of the Wicksellian theory of the cumulative process, otherwise the gap between [the natural rate] and the [money rate] would have reduced or expanded, rather than remained unchanged. This means that monetary equilibrium, where the [natural rate] is equal to the [money rate] and the price level is constant, may be stable or unstable rather than neutral. This conclusion however follows, even though the money rate of interest is kept constant, from the fact that the natural rate is revised due to the changes in the

real side of the economy. The Wicksellian thesis of monetary neutrality may not be the correct conclusion if the real economy is not assumed to be stationary. (*CC*, p. 180)

So we now enter a new development in monetary and growth theory. If the economy is growing and/or if the natural rate is a variable, then we need to extend Wicksell's analysis which assumed a constant natural rate. To model this Morishima goes back to the classic case of constant growth rate and that is the von Neumann path, which is of course the maximal growth path under certain assumptions. But the natural rate may be above or below the von Neumann rate, and, if the natural rate is also variable then the gap between the natural and the money rate is variable over the cycle. Thus if the natural rate is above the money rate and the von Neumann rate, then inflation follows but that may reduce the natural rate. If it then crosses over to being below the money rate, deflation follows and the natural rate may approach the von Neumann rate from above. Prices keep falling, and the economy may converge to the von Neumann rate.

In the converse case, the economy starts off with the natural rate below the money rate and below the von Neumann rate and then deflation comes first as the natural rate approaches the von Neumann rate from below. Once it crosses over the constant money rate then inflation follows and the economy approaches the von Neumann rate in an explosive inflationary situation (*CC*, fig. 3, p. 182).

This is the most sophisticated discussion of money and growth in the classical Wicksell framework that I know of. A variable natural rate is seldom modelled, and the deflation/inflation cycles enrich the Wicksell model greatly. But we are still in the world of Say's Law. What happens if we break away from it? The shortage of credit will restrict the economy below full employment as Keynes envisaged, and abundance of credit will start off an inflationary growth process as Schumpeter said. This then is the climax of the entire edifice of Morishima's work. He can now combine Anti-Say's Law with credit and disequilibrium. Credit creation determines the natural rate via the Anti-Say's Law sector which is often the most innovative and dynamic. To quote him again:

As I have sufficiently emphasized, the real sector and the monetary sector are bilaterally coupled under Anti Say's Law, and the bridging of these two is crucially important, in order for the economy to work smoothly and efficiently. The efficient use of money for the sake of development of the economy, nevertheless, has been almost entirely neglected by economic theorists, because the neoclassical general equilibrium theorists who support Say's Law have been

> accustomed to the traditional method of dichotomizing the economy into two separate sectors, real and monetary. The linkage has been left for a long time in a state of being unexamined.   (*CC*, p. 186)

No longer, after this book.

The final attack then is on the citadel of the classical and neoclassical monetary theory, and indeed the general equilibrium theory of Ricardo and Walras, we find in the textbooks. This is the Homogeneity Postulate by which nominal variables cannot have real effects and so money must be a veil. But of course the Homogeneity Postulate requires that a monetary shock be evenly spread across all agents (not only helicopter money, but each punter getting a proportionately equal amount to his/her initial, i.e. pre-shock, endowments). It also requires that the elasticity of demand with respect to money balances be identical across all agents. Morishima shows in the final pages of *CC* that neither of these assumptions is likely to be fulfilled in a monetary economy. Agents after all include households and firms and the Anti-Say's Law firms are much more credit sensitive than other firms for one thing. And if the Homogeneity Postulate falls, so does the Quantity Theory.

Conclusion

This has been an all too brief tour of the various theoretical writings of Michio Morishima. There is, as I argued at the outset, an architecture and there is progress towards a final vision set out early in his thesis. The challenge of integrating money and growth with general equilibrium but without Say's Law has been accomplished. There is much more to be gained from a careful study of these writings and one can only hope that future scholars will mine the rich source of theoretical insights in the decades to come.

MEGHNAD DESAI
London School of Economics

Michio Miroshima's Writings

Entries marked by * were published by Clarendon Press, Oxford. The rest were published by Cambridge University Press, Cambridge.

(1950) *Dogakuteki Keizai Riron* (Kobundo, Tokyo) (*DKR*)
(1964) *Equilibrium Stability and Growth** (*ESG*)
(1969) *Theory of Economic Growth** (*TEG*)
(1973) *Marx's Economics: A Dual Theory of Value and Growth* (*ME*)
(1976) *Economic Theory of Modern Society*
(1977) *Walras' Economics: A pure theory of Capital and Money* (*WE*)
(1986) *The Economics of Industrial Society*
(1989) *Ricardo's Economics: A general equilibrium theory of Distribution and Growth* (*RE*)
(1992) *Capital and Credit: A new formulation of general equilibrium theory* (*CC*)
(1996) *Dynamic Economic Theory*, an English translation of *DKR* above with additional articles (*DET*)

Books with co-authors not referred to in the essay above
M. Morishima *et al.*, *Theory of Demand: Real and Monetary* (New York, 1973)
M. Morishima and G. Catephores, *Value Exploitation and Growth* (London 1978)

BRIAN REDDAWAY

William Brian Reddaway
1913–2002

I

PROFESSOR W. B. REDDAWAY, invariably known to friends and colleagues
as Brian Reddaway, was an exceptional economist who had a huge influence on how economics in Cambridge has been taught and researched.
He held leadership positions in the Faculty of Economics and Politics
at Cambridge for twenty-five years, between 1955 and 1980. For nearly
the first fifteen years he was Director of the Department of Applied
Economics (DAE), succeeding Sir Richard Stone, the founding Director.
The DAE was established after the Second World War on the initiative
of J. M. Keynes. It was set up as the research arm of the Faculty of
Economics and Politics, providing facilities for teaching staff to carry out
applied economic and social investigations. In 1969, almost at the end of
his tenure as DAE Director, Reddaway was elected to succeed James
Meade in the Chair of Political Economy, the senior chair in economics
in Cambridge. Reddaway held this chair until 1980, when he formally
retired. He continued his association with the Faculty for many years
after this, doing occasional lecture courses, or one-off lectures: he positively loved lecturing on applied economic subjects and helping younger
colleagues with their research.

As is the custom in Cambridge's collegiate university structure, in addition to his successive university posts in the Faculty, which began in 1939
on his appointment as University Lecturer, he held a Fellowship at Clare
College for sixty-four years (1938 to 2002). He took a very active part in
college life, including college teaching and helping to manage the college's

Proceedings of the British Academy, **138**, 285–306. © The British Academy 2006.

investments. It was acknowledged that he accomplished all these tasks extraordinarily well.

This commentary on the professional life and work of Brian Reddaway is written by a close colleague who regarded him as one of his valued mentors. My main purpose is to reflect on and to appraise Reddaway's legacy in relation to economics, to policy-making and to general social welfare. Often, Reddaway's references for his students or colleagues included a statement to the effect that it was his practice to tell nothing but the truth. The present memoir aims to do the same in its historical assessment of his career and his contributions.

In carrying out this task, I intend to focus on some key analytical issues and paradoxes relating to Reddaway's professional life as a teacher, scholar and Cambridge academic. First, anyone who has closely examined his career is struck by the paradox that, although he had enormous influence on economics in Cambridge and, through policy-making and advice, on the world outside, his impact on the economics profession itself in the narrow academic sense of the term was much smaller, particularly outside the UK.[1] This is in sharp contrast to Stone, who, it is generally recognised, had very little impact on the Economics Faculty in Cambridge, but had a large following outside Cambridge and won the Nobel Memorial Prize for Economics in 1984.

A second paradox in Reddaway's career is that politically he was a liberal who believed in the market economy and advised the Confederation of British Industry. Yet he was invited by the Cambridge Political Economy Society, a group of Cambridge left-wing economists who in the late 1970s founded the *Cambridge Journal of Economics*, to become a patron of the journal. Reddaway not only accepted the invitation, but actively helped with the journal's work.

Thirdly, any discussion of Reddaway's professional career in Cambridge would be incomplete without recognising his exceptional commitment to teaching and examining students, and taking the democratic governance of the university seriously, devoting substantial time and effort to it. Reddaway's Socratic approach to teaching sprang from and contributed to the Cambridge oral tradition. It had a profound influence on generations of students who went on to shape the culture of economic debate in Britain, and in international organisations.[2]

---

[1] The 'narrow' economics profession may for practical purposes be regarded as being represented by academic economists working in universities and research institutions.
[2] Michael Posner, obituary of W. B. Reddaway, *The Guardian*, 5 Sept. 2002.

II

My professional and personal association with Brian Reddaway goes back more than forty years, to January 1963, when I came to Cambridge from the University of California, Berkeley, to work with Robin Marris at the DAE on managerial capitalism. I was still a graduate student in Berkeley and had worked as Marris's research assistant when he was a visiting professor there a year earlier. At the DAE Reddaway had just started a project on UK corporate finance and, because of the obvious synergy of this project with that of Marris's, it was decided that the two should be run jointly by Marris and Reddaway. Reddaway, at that time and for many years afterwards, wrote, under the nom de plume 'the Academic Investor', a highly regarded column for the *Investors' Chronicle* in which he regularly reported on the results of his college's portfolio, which he helped to organise. This led to his keen interest in corporate finance and behaviour and hence in these research projects.

There was a tempestuous start to my association with Reddaway when I started work on the project. One afternoon in the DAE common room we embarked on a serious and noisy disagreement about econometrics and time series analysis. Reddaway was scathing about the regression analysis of economic time series, as it led to spurious correlations, for reasons which are much better understood today than they were then. I provided what I thought was a spirited defence of the textbook model of doing such regressions, which at Berkeley I had been taught was an adequate approach to the problem.[3] Reddaway was not at all convinced, but never held my wrong-headedness against me, regarding it as an honest difference of opinion. What was remarkable about this exchange was that it took place between a graduate student and a highly distinguished economist for whom academic hierarchy seemed to have no relevance. Indeed one of Reddaway's characteristic traits throughout his professional life was that he was interested only in the validity or otherwise of the argument being made, rather than the formal status of the person making it. This did not always endear him to his senior colleagues, whose sometimes feeble arguments might be summarily rejected in public. Brian Reddaway

---

[3] See Ron Smith, 'The Development of Econometric Methods at the Department of Applied Economics' in I. Begg and B. Henry, *Applied Economics and Public Policy* (Department of Applied Economics Occasional Paper (Cambridge, 1998). Interestingly, as Smith notes, the textbook model referred to above came from the DAE itself during Stone's period as Director. It is associated with the work of Durbin, Watson, Cochrane and Orcutt, all of whom worked at the Department under Stone.

was a blunt person and habitually called a spade a spade, though neither with malice nor with any intention of point scoring.

Born on 8 January 1913, the son of W. F. Reddaway and Kate Waterland, née Sill, Brian Reddaway came from an academic Cambridge family with firm roots in the university. His father was a historian and a Fellow of King's and the first Censor (Head) of Fitzwilliam House, before that institution became a full-fledged college. He wrote extensively on countries around the Baltic, Russia, Poland and Scandinavia. This academic background gave the younger Reddaway total self-confidence, which later led him to become the scourge of the central bureaucracy in the university. He was extremely critical of administrative inefficiency and regarded administrators as the servants of the dons and students, rather than their masters. Many senior university administrators found themselves at the receiving end of his sharp comments.

Reddaway was educated at King's College School from 1920 to 1924, at Lydgate House (a boarding school at Hunstanton in Norfolk) from 1924 to 1926 and at Oundle from 1926 to 1931. He was a brilliant student and in 1931 won a scholarship to read Natural Sciences at King's College, Cambridge. In the event he was advised to do Mathematics in the first year and Natural Sciences in the last two years. However, after obtaining a First in Part 1 Mathematics, he opted for Economics instead, because of his strong concern with mass unemployment and widespread poverty in the 1930s. He had the great fortune of being personally supervised by Richard Kahn and John Maynard Keynes, neither of whom he disappointed. He visited Russia with his father soon after his graduation, and used this opportunity to do independent research on the Russian financial system (with the blessing of his prospective employer—the Bank of England). An essay based on this material won him the university's coveted Adam Smith prize, and on Keynes' recommendation was subsequently published in 1935 as *The Russian Financial System* by Macmillan. A book that I understand continued to be included in LSE reading lists for more than three decades.

III

After a short stint at the Bank of England, where the structure seemed to provide scant prospects for early promotion, Reddaway worked for two years in Australia, Keynes having recommended him to L. F. Giblin, Professor at the University of Melbourne and also a recently appointed non-executive Director of the Australian central bank. Reddaway apparently spent two happy and productive years as a tutor at the University of Melbourne while also assisting Giblin at the central bank.[4]

Reddaway quickly made his mark on the Australian scene. First, he published a review of Keynes's *The General Theory of Employment, Interest and Money* (London, 1936) that is regarded as a classic interpretation of the book.[5] Second, he took a prominent part in the ongoing debate on wage levels in Australia. The Australian government at that time favoured wage cuts in order to enhance the competitiveness of the country's mining and manufacturing industries. The trade unions were naturally opposed. Reddaway testified in the Commonwealth Arbitration Court in favour of the trade union position that real wages should be raised rather than cut. The Court accepted almost fully the 23-year-old Englishman's recommendations and the resulting wage award lasted fifteen years, and came to be called the Reddawage. In 1938 Reddaway returned to England to a Fellowship at Clare College. Nevertheless, throughout his career he maintained his early connection with Australia and visited the country many times.

Brian Reddaway and Barbara Bennet's marriage in 1939 generated an environment in which both blossomed and which was highly supportive of their offspring and younger generations. The Reddaways had four children, Peter, Lawrence, Stewart and Jacky. Since Brian's death (Barbara died earlier in 1996), they have provided us with their reflections (as well as those of others) on their parents and on their family life together which suggest that they were a happy, cohesive family in which both parents fully participated.[6] The Reddaways had a modest, almost abstemious lifestyle and it seems that their savings were spent on family holidays that were quite frequent. Stewart observed that 'Dad provided us with a loving and secure home background. This was based on what he did for us, on his relationships with us and on the very happy marriage between him and mum.' Daughter Jacky notes that their parents formed 'a remarkable partnership which provided great comfort and stimulation to their family . . .'. Peter writes:

---

[4] Lawrence Reddaway (ed.), *William Brian Reddaway, 8 January 1913–23 July 2002 and Barbara Augusta Reddaway, 15 August 1912–15 September 1996, Memories* (Cambridge, 2003).

[5] *The Economic Record*, 12 (1936), 28–36.

[6] The rest of this section is based on an excellent collection of *Memories* of Brian and Barbara Reddaway by their children, friends and associates from all over the world, put together and edited by Lawrence Reddaway (see above, n. 4). The quotations all come from this booklet.

Dad was an undemonstrative, but loyal family man. Although Mum initiated virtually all family and social events she always got his full support. He pulled the carrots, picked the gooseberries, tidied the flowerbeds, mowed the lawn, laid the table, poured the gin and tonic and carved the roast chicken. He then contributed in lively style to the conversation, throwing in, often with a theatrical flourish, stories from his repertoire of some twenty wellworn favourites.

Peter notes that in general he brought up his children more by example than instruction.

Lawrence says that Reddaway was 'thoroughly English by both birth and habit but thoroughly international in his outlook . . .', yet he lived all his life in Cambridge. The Reddaway family had lived in the city for one hundred and twenty years, ever since Reddaway's father entered the Leys School. From this base in Cambridge, Brian and Barbara travelled widely and spent time in several European and Third-World countries as well as the US and Australia. He was evidently a good linguist and, apart from German and French, he especially learnt Spanish before going to Argentina to advise the government.

In their middle age, the Reddaways devoted a great deal of their time and effort to their extended family. As well as their four children, Brian was survived by nine grandchildren and one great grandchild. Brian and Barbara had by their grandchildren's accounts extremely good relations with the second generation.

Reddaway's prodigious research output and contributions to the work of the Faculty, University and governments in the UK and abroad, owed a tremendous amount to Barbara. Her social skills were very helpful in softening his critical, and often abrupt, way of interacting with colleagues, students and friends. Friends and research students from around the world were always welcome at their Cambridge home. I have the most wonderful memories of Barbara's cheerfulness and gaiety and remember with pleasure her remarks congratulating me on my promotion to a personal Chair in Cambridge: 'The whole world will rejoice at the news of your Chair.'

IV

Turning to Reddaway's research contributions, he was certainly not an orthodox or a traditional economist. By this I mean that he was much less concerned with economic doctrine than with solving practical problems. The solutions to these problems inevitably required theoretical understanding, and, when the theory was not available, he had to craft it him-self, as we shall see in the case of his Foreign Direct Investment (FDI) study. Most importantly, for him quantification was essential to the exam-ination of economic phenomena, particularly if the aim was to draw policy conclusions. He had a distinct methodology and approach to eco-nomics. He himself suggests in his autobiographical entry in *Who's Who in Economics* (3rd edn., Cheltenham, 1999) that his most important schol-arly contributions included two large projects—one on the effects on the UK balance of payments of direct investment overseas by UK compa-nies, and the other on the then recently introduced selective employment tax—both of which he undertook at the DAE in the 1960s. These proj-ects involved large survey teams and raised important conceptual, statis-tical and data questions. In tackling these he combined great imagination with exemplary economic sense. The results were reported in 1967 and 1968 (FDI),[7] and 1970 and 1973 (Selective Employment Tax).[8]

In order to indicate the nature and qualities of Reddaway's research, two areas will be reviewed in some detail below: his work on foreign direct investment (FDI), and on Indian planning and economic development.[9] The commentary will focus not so much on the specific conclusions reached, but on the methods used and how the research was done. These studies also bring out Reddaway's attitude towards (a) the role of the gov-ernment and (b) the use of mathematics and econometrics. Both (a) and (b) in turn are helpful in clarifying his approach to economic research. He himself summed up his way of doing applied economics as follows:

> I have attempted to tackle *practical* problems, whether on full employment, growth, underdeveloped economies, inflation, the effects of direct investment overseas, the selective employment tax, or the investment of portfolios. To do so, I have sought to combine theory with realistic data and to look for the fac-tors which are quantitatively important, rather than those which are intellectu-ally stimulating. I have tried to be pragmatic in my choice of methods for tackling problems and to be clear about the alternative position with which comparisons are effectively being made (and to be sure that it is a meaningful and consistent one). Favourite slogan for pupils and research colleagues: 'It

[7] *Effects of UK Direct Investment Overseas—Interim Report* (Cambridge, 1967); *Final Report* (Cambridge, 1968).

[8] *Effects of Selective Employment Tax*, 2 vols. (Cambridge, 1970, 1973).

[9] Other notable areas of his research, which will not be covered here, include labour markets, structural change, demography, economic growth and contributions to economic history. See further W. B. Reddaway, 'Recollections of a Lucky Economist', *BNL Quarterly Review*, 192 (March 1995) and G. C. Harcourt, 'Reddaway, William, Brian 1913–2002', in Donald Rutherford (ed.), *The Biographical Dictionary of British Economists, 2, K–Z* (Bristol, 2004), pp. 998–1003.

> is better to be roughly right than to be precisely wrong (or irrelevant).'
> (Reddaway, *Who's Who in Economics*, 1999, p. 932, emphasis in the original)

In other words, in the real world, even though data are scarce, it is better to have rough orders of magnitude than none at all, in order not to operate entirely in the realm of abstraction. If data (or theory) did not exist, Reddaway's method was to use surveys to ask people for the information. If existing theory was inadequate, he would attempt to extend it to fill the gaps. However, the latter was not his prime aim. Colleagues recall him referring to theory as 'talky talk'.

V

These attributes of Reddaway's research methods are illustrated by the FDI study, which raises complex issues of applied economic analysis. Moreover, although the context today is very different, the subject itself is even more important now than it was then.[10] The terms of reference for the FDI exercise were 'to study the effects of direct outward private investment on the United Kingdom balance of payments and on the United Kingdom economy generally'.[11] There were very few published statistics available on the subject and Reddaway and his colleagues had to use extensive survey data to obtain the information at company level needed for this research. At the outset, Reddaway set out the issues as well as his basic methodology in non-technical and non-mathematical, but nonetheless rigorous, economic terms. He identified the gaps in information and indicated how they would be filled in the course of the research. He noted:

> We live nowadays in a managed economy. It follows that *any* question in macro-economics can be answered only on specified assumptions about the Government's policy (and powers) in managing the economy. Strictly speaking, there are as many answers as there are varieties of assumptions which one thinks it useful to make. . . . There is no single 'other things being equal' which it is *clearly* right to assume.[12]

---

[10] Today, it is not only the government and the CBI who are interested in such research, but even more so the workers who fear job losses from overseas investment by advanced country corporations (see further A. Singh, 'Globalisation and the Regulation of FDI: New Proposals from the European Community and Japan', *Contributions to Political Economy*, 24:1 (Aug. 2005), 99–121.

[11] *Effects of UK Direct Investment Overseas—Interim Report*, p. 15.

[12] Ibid., p. 167. Emphasis in original.

The simplifying, but plausible, assumptions he outlined about the government's role in relation to the basic analysis of the effects of a marginal increase in overseas investment (FDI) by British companies, included the following:

> a) The government's major objective is to secure a level of total demand for the output of British goods and services which gives 'full employment', and in the main it is successful.
>
> b) At times of balance of payments crisis this objective has to be (and is) subordinated to 'the defence of sterling'. . . ..
>
> c) In striving for (a) the Government operates on the internal components of demand . . . and leaves exports and imports free from direct manipulation; the exchange rate is held constant.[13]

Reddaway further suggests that the effects of FDI can be assessed only on the basis of comparisons between what actually happened and what might otherwise have happened. He argues that this raises three kinds of problem:

> a) What sort of assumptions should be made about the nature of the alternative position?
>
> b) How can those assumptions be translated into figures?
>
> c) How can these figures be used to answer the really important questions?[14]

Reddaway proposed that, on these assumptions, together with his carefully set out counter-factual (what would have happened otherwise), if an extra £100 million of overseas direct investment occurred in a particular year, the effects on the UK economy might be summarised as follows:

> i) There are x million pounds additional exports—and we hope to find x.
>
> ii) x million pounds *less* is spent on home investment in marginal developments.
>
> iii) The levels of employment, consumption, imports and national income are unaffected in that year.
>
> iv) $(100 - x)$ million pounds of additional overseas debt is incurred (or portfolio investment may be reduced, or reserves used).[15]

Much of the information needed for Reddaway's enquiry had to come from the British companies that normally undertook FDI. He noted that:

---

[13] Ibid., p. 168.
[14] Ibid., p. 86.
[15] Ibid., pp. 169–70.

we realized at an early stage that we were engaged in a difficult pioneering process. . . . The project would need to be an exercise in co-operation, with personal contact between the research team and company representatives playing a very important role.[16]

The survey indeed included difficult questions, some of a counter-factual and hypothetical kind, which company officials were not easily able to answer without help from the research team. Reddaway therefore placed responsibility for deciding on final figures for the research project on the researchers rather than on the companies, because the former were familiar with the logic of the problem and had also accumulated experience from interviewing a number of companies in the sample.

This detailed description of Reddaway's approach to the FDI research indicates important differences between his methods and those conventionally used in such analyses. The first is his use of plain English (instead of mathematical equations) to set out from first principles the basic methodology to be used. Second, though they were elementary, the statistical methods employed in the FDI study were in my judgement wholly appropriate to the nature of the economic problem and the available statistical data. A conventional study would have used multiple regression equations and employed statistical significance tests to draw inferences about the population. In Reddaway's view, these were often misleading, an issue that is discussed below. Third, he regarded assumptions made about the role of government to be critical in applied economic analysis of real world problems. (This issue is discussed further from a theoretical perspective in section VII.) Finally, contrary to the prejudice in the profession against interviewing business people (which basically still prevails today), Reddaway's basic analysis of the effects of FDI was based on survey data derived from business people's answers. He not only valued their answers but encouraged close cooperation between them and members of his research team. Reddaway's approach to the last point is now gaining ground, at least in business schools. In view of the dearth of appropriate official data in many fields, survey data have become increasingly important in economic research.[17]

---

[16] *Effects of UK Direct Investment Overseas—Interim Report*, p. 141.

[17] Professor John Toye has pointed out to me that Reddaway did not always maintain such high standards in his writings. In his *Economics of a Declining Population* (London, 1939), he took at face value the Enid Charles projections of a fast declining UK population. Reddaway's response to this lapse was that everybody at the time (Keynes, Meade, Joan Robinson) accepted these demographic projections. As Toye rightly notes, this study does not fit in with the Reddaway reputation 'for thinking things out from first principles and for seeking "to combine theory with realistic data", which characterises most of his work.' See also above, n. 8.

VI

Reddaway's book *The Development of the Indian Economy* (London 1962) is a highly unusual but a very important contribution to studies of planning and economic development. The book won high esteem from most (but not all) scholars in India and abroad. Despite very changed circumstances, its messages continue to be highly relevant for India and many other countries. The book arose from an Indian Planning Commission request to Reddaway to assess the consistency and viability of their recently formulated Third Five Year Plan.[18] From the start, he noted that although Indian plans did not have to be as comprehensive as Soviet five-year plans, the Third Plan nevertheless required more detailed elaboration to be useful as a practical planning instrument. Reddaway's approach was to examine the extent to which the plan was consistent with the available foreign exchange and the resources available for internal investment for each year, and the results were incorporated in the revised Third Plan. Apart from difficulties relating to the consistency of the Plan, Reddaway was also concerned that the Plan document should be drafted and presented in a way that made it credible, so that it could generate the necessary support and action.

The book drew a sharply critical article in *Oxford Economic Papers* (15:3 (Nov. 1963), 308–17) from a leading Indian economist, Professor Padma Desai. In response, in the same issue of the journal, the author vigorously defended his position. ('The Development of the Indian Economy. The Objects of the Exercise Restated', ibid., 318–32). Desai argued that the book did not set out a fully specified planning model so that it was difficult to judge whether the plan was efficient or not. She also thought that, from the information given in the book, the model was under-determined, i.e. the number of variables to be determined was greater than the number of equations. She further expressed irritation over the fact that Reddaway had not bothered to specify his model in terms of equations, which she regarded as essential to understanding the underlying economic and statistical analysis.

In response, Reddaway observed:

> I saw, and still see, no advantage in expressing the reasoning in the form of mathematical equations. Such equations are a useful device where there is a great deal of *mutual* dependence of variables, because a verbal description cannot then easily show the interactions and the process of mutual determination;

---

[18] Reddaway visited the Commission in 1959–60 on sabbatical leave from Cambridge.

moreover, it is then very laborious to arrive at the solutions which fit the conditions, except by some mathematical process analogous to the solution of simultaneous equations; and one might fall into the trap of not realizing that the system was under-determined, and arriving by trial and error at a set of figures which fulfilled the conditions but had no superiority over many other sets which would also do so.[19]

Reddaway went on to explain the limited focus of his exercise. The text of his book made it clear that he was not providing a model for the Third Plan, but only checking the viability of the plan formulated by the Commission. He also argued that his model was not underdetermined.

As is clear from the quotation above, Reddaway was fully aware of the advantages of the use of mathematics for expository purposes in certain situations, but also thought that a number of interactions between variables in the real world did not fit easily into formal equations. He was certainly no mathematical ignoramus, having obtained a first class in Mathematics Part I, as noted earlier. My own experience is that he was not hostile to the use of mathematics in empirical analysis provided it gave added clarity or substance to the argument. My book on takeovers included a chapter on the methodology of discriminant analysis and its relationship to other multi-variate methods. The discussion was in terms of matrix algebra.[20] Reddaway was extremely supportive and in fact helped me correct some errors that mathematical colleagues had missed. Also, it is not generally known that he played a key role in the appointment of Frank Hahn, a mathematical economist, to an economics chair in Cambridge.

VII

Reddaway's work on Indian planning naturally raises questions about his attitude towards planning in general, and more broadly his views on the role of government in advanced and developing countries. Although

[19] 'The Development of the Indian Economy. The Objects of the Exercise Restated', *Oxford Economic Papers*, 15:3 (Nov.), 326. Reddaway made a similar point in his 1936 review of Keynes's *General Theory*. He was critical of Keynes's exposition with respect to the mutual determination of savings, investment, income and rate of interest. Although he sympathised with Keynes's strictures about the spurious air of precision introduced by too much mathematics, he nevertheless felt that it was difficult to express in words the solution to a system of simultaneous equations. A shorthand equation system would have been much more useful.
[20] A. Singh, *Takeovers: Their Relevance to the Stock Market and the Theory of the Firm* (Cambridge, 1971).

politically a liberal, believing, as did Keynes, that resource allocation should by and large be left to the market, he thought that social welfare could often be improved by government action. During the Second World War Reddaway was seconded to the Board of Trade where he worked as Chief Statistician. In that capacity he helped to design the clothes rationing system and also among many other things, helped notably to improve the UK indices of industrial production and consumer prices.

Reddaway's attitude towards government intervention was greatly influenced by this wartime experience. At that time, among the government economists, Reddaway was regarded as being very much on the interventionist side. The statisticians at the Board of Trade were half-jokingly nick-named the 'Gosplanners' because of their interventionist outlook. In contrast, other government economists, notably James Meade and John Maynard Keynes, were called 'thermostaters', indicating that they believed in limiting government intervention, to macroeconomic policy to ensure full employment. In this view, microeconomics should entirely be the sphere of private households and firms. Reddaway was a pragmatic economist and a problem solver par excellence. These attributes, as well as his wartime experience, led him to regard the government as part of the solution rather than the problem. Indeed he took a very active part in government activity and policy making on various occasions. Reddaway served the UK and other national governments and the international community in a number of different ways, making notable contributions to the work of each.[21]

Reddaway's expertise was also used in a number of British colonies to construct indices of retail prices, which were often socially sensitive. Reddaway was evidently able to carry out these technical tasks well because he was aware of their social dimensions, and was willing to consult with the relevant groups and build a social consensus. He thereby avoided the social disruption which often followed the introduction of new price indices.[22] After the war Reddaway served on Royal Commissions and equivalent bodies and high-level government committees in the UK, Australia and a number of developing countries. He also acted as Director of the Research Division of the Organization for European Economic Cooperation (OEEC), the body implementing the Marshall Plan which subsequently became the Organization for Economic Cooperation and Development (OECD).

---

[21] I owe these points to Professor John Toye.
[22] Reddaway, 'Recollections of a Lucky Economist'; Obituary in *The Times*, 2 Aug. 2002.

In his role as member of the UK Prices and Incomes Board, and of the State of Victoria Liquor Board in Australia, Reddaway was perhaps ahead of his time, in that he took very serious account of the prevailing administrative and customary social arrangements, how their operation affected outcomes and how at the policy level such arrangements could be improved.

Similarly, in his review of Keynes's *General Theory*, mentioned earlier in a different context, Reddaway's critical remarks concerning the omission of the institutional factors which constrain economic agents, were also ahead of their time. In a notable passage, Reddaway wrote:

> The logic of the argument would be improved if the rate of interest were not so frequently used to represent the cost of raising capital; particularly in Australia the other elements, such as quantitative control of credit, are often far more important, and the rates applicable to different industries and borrowers may move differently for institutional reasons.   (p. 107)

An important theoretical contribution, for which he does not always receive due credit, is his explicit introduction of the role of government into Keynesian analysis. Reddaway, and others who had reviewed *The General Theory* when it was first published, were asked to revisit their reviews and comment on them in the light of subsequent events. He responded with a whole new article, which makes an important contribution to Keynesian theory. He confessed that in his 1936 review he had been insufficiently critical of the way the role of government had been presented in *The General Theory*. He considered that with the big increase in the 'size of government' in the post-Second World War period, in many industrial countries, the government's consumption and investment behaviour was increasingly central to the workings of the modern economy. However this was not necessarily subject to the same considerations as those that influence corporate and household behaviour. Reddaway therefore suggested that the government's savings and investment functions require separate treatment.[23]

This theoretical perspective on the government's role in the economy has serious implications for applied economic work. Reddaway argued that, unlike Keynes in *The General Theory,* who in effect assumed that fiscal policy was neutral, in the post-Second World War economy in which government expenditure was relatively high, it was not legitimate to assume that fiscal policy would necessarily be distributionally neutral.

[23] 'Keynesian Analysis and a Mixed Economy', in Robert Lekachman (ed.), *Keynes' General Theory, Reports of Three Decades* (London and New York, 1964), pp. 108–23.

Each government was likely to have an agenda of its own and to use changes in taxation and expenditure to achieve social goals such as full employment, price stability and enhanced social welfare. Hence, it was necessary to take into account the detailed macroeconomic assumptions associated with its monetary and fiscal policies.

These points were fully taken on board in Reddaway's own empirical work, as we saw in our discussion of his analysis of the effects of FDI.

VIII

I turn now to the question of Reddaway's legacy and the nature of his influence inside and beyond Cambridge, during his long period of leadership in the faculty. Reddaway exercised intellectual influence on the 'narrow' academic economics profession, as defined earlier, as well as on the broader public, through a number of different channels. First and foremost, he led by example and over time his own research, including that described above, became more widely known and increasingly influential. Secondly Reddaway's influence came from the work of the DAE, where he was a hands-on director. Thirdly, and very importantly, Cambridge students trained in 'Reddaway economics' spread his approach to the City, the government, the media and other places where they went to work. Posner noted that this led to an improvement in the level of economic comment in the UK.[24]

Reddaway's assumption of the directorship of the DAE in 1955, on Stone's appointment to his chair, led to a decisive change in the department's research agenda. Under Stone's leadership the DAE had built up an international reputation as an outstanding centre for research in econometric theory. Stone's was a hard act to follow, but Reddaway did so with great energy and total conviction. He changed the direction of the department's research towards applied economics and economic policy.

Under his leadership in the 1960s the DAE was a vibrant and exciting place, which was generally regarded as one of the world's leading institutions for applied economic research. Reddaway, as many observers have noted, was in his element as the director.[25] He was a liberal academic in the best sense of the term and let a hundred flowers bloom. The DAE hosted projects on a wide range of subjects, notably including economic

---

[24] Obituary in *The Guardian*, 5 Sept. 2002.
[25] See for example, G. Whittington, 'Professor W. B. Reddaway', unpublished MS, 2002.

history, corporate finance, labour markets, regional economies and economic sociology, to each of which he himself made significant contributions. Reddaway provided autonomy to the investigators, but they had to perform to his high intellectual and critical standards. He was unstinting in his help when a project, for whatever reason, got into difficulties or an investigator sought assistance.

In my view, one reason why the department was so successful at this time was that it had under the same roof economists with effectively two different approaches to applied economics—that of Reddaway himself, as outlined above, and that of Stone, who continued to have a large research group in the department even after he resigned the directorship. However, by then, Stone's interest had shifted from theoretical to applied econometrics, and his new group worked mainly on the latter issues.[26] The Cambridge Growth Project, which he and Alan Brown co-directed at the DAE, was concerned with a real world question of applied economics and policy analysis—to formulate a comprehensive indicative plan for the UK economy. However, its methods differed from those of Reddaway and his collaborators, in that it made extensive use of applied econometrics.

I believe it was the unexpected synergy between the economists working on the growth project and those working in the non-econometric Reddaway paradigm which made the department *the* place to do applied economic research. The diversity of its research output was widely appreciated. The institution had a vigorous research culture and enormous self-confidence. Instead of being the research wing of the faculty, it acquired its own intellectual autonomy and became as well if not better known than the faculty, which still included among its teaching officers legendary figures like Richard Kahn, Joan Robinson, Nicholas Kaldor, James Meade, David Champernowne and Richard Goodwin.

Reddaway's influence on the 'narrow' academic economic profession, at least in the UK, was probably also advanced by his high public profile in the 1960s, with memberships of Royal Commissions and important government committees, his Fellowship of the British Academy in 1967, and his Presidency of the Royal Economic Society. Between 1971 and 1976, Reddaway also edited the *Economic Journal* together with Cambridge colleagues David Champernowne and Phyllis Deane. In that capacity he and his colleagues did influence the academic economic profession, not only in the UK but also in the USA and elsewhere, in the sense that unneces-

---

[26] R. Smith, 'The Development of Econometric Methods at the Department of Applied Economics'.

sary mathematics in articles was discouraged and papers were selected on their economic merit rather than because of the sophistication of the techniques used. Authors were encouraged to present their critical assumptions and their main results in plain English. However, after he and his co-editors left the journal, the academic profession followed the more mathematical US pattern. Some of the reasons for this are indicated in the following account.

Despite the modus vivendi between Reddaway and Stone and their respective research groups at the DAE, in the 1960s, Reddaway's own attitude to econometrics did not move far from that of Keynes's critique of Tinbergen.[27] The Cambridge Keynesian economists continued in general to be sceptical about the subject, on the familiar grounds that there are far too many relevant variables as well as possible interactions between them in the real world for econometrics to be able to cope with. The problem is compounded by frequent structural changes in economic relationships. However, at a more elementary level Reddaway was highly critical of normal econometric practice for not distinguishing statistical from economic significance. This is a simple point and one might think that it would apply only to a small minority of poor practitioners and would disappear over time.

Subsequent research, however, suggests that this does not seem to be the case. McCloskey and Ziliak found that of the 182 full-length papers published in the 1980s in the *American Economic Review*, 70 per cent did not distinguish between economic and statistical significance.[28] Many people have suggested that, as a result of the publication of this article itself in a leading journal, the situation must have greatly improved, as this is an elementary point which everybody can understand. But not according to Ziliak and McCloskey (2004). They find that in the 1990s, of 137 papers using a test of statistical significance in the *American Economic Review*, a huge 82 per cent 'mistook a merely statistically significant finding for an economically significant finding'. Their survey indicated that a large majority (81 per cent) believed that looking at the sign of a coefficient rather than its magnitude was adequate from an economic perspective.[29] The authors attribute this sorry state of affairs partly to the race to get articles published in academic journals, and to the belief

---

[27] 'Professor Tinbergen's Method', *Economic Journal*, 41 (1939), 558–68.

[28] D. N. McCloskey and S. T. Ziliak, 'The Standard Error of Regressions', *Journal of Economic Literature*, 34:1 (Mar. 1996), 97–114.

[29] S. T. Ziliak and D. N. McCloskey, 'Size Matters: The Standard Error of Regressions, in the *American Economic Review*', *Journal of Socio-Economics*, 33 (2004) 527–46.

of most contributors that journal referees like to see statistically significant positive results.[30] Such considerations may also have been responsible for the roll-back of Reddaway's way of doing economics from the pages of the *Economic Journal* after he ceased to co-edit it.

IX

Whether or not Reddaway had significant lasting influence on academic economics outside Cambridge, he certainly had an enormous impact within it. As Professor of Political Economy, he took a full part in teaching, examining, Tripos reform and examination reform. He was Chairman of the Faculty Board of Economics and Politics for most of the 1970s, when there were frequent clashes with the university's General Board, i.e. the central administration. He was an outstandingly good lecturer and teacher. He also understood that in order to influence teaching, one had to take a full part in examining. This is because, in the Cambridge system, the examination questions this year usually become next year's teaching questions for the students' tutorials. Reddaway was successful in the early 1960s in introducing a compulsory paper in economics and social statistics for most second-year students. This was however rather different from statistical papers in other universities. It did not require much statistical technique, but emphasised empirical analysis of economic issues; particular attention was given to national income accounting and to the balance of payments identities and statistics. Effectively, it was a paper in applied economics which had seemingly simple questions, but which would even today test Ph.D. students in economics at most universities. Reddaway's questions were carefully crafted to test the student's ability to use real-world data to illuminate economic issues.

These questions, which came to be known as 'Reddaway-type' questions, were very important to the teaching of economics in Cambridge. Normally one might not want to reproduce an examination paper in a Fellow's memoir, but in this case it forms a significant part of Reddaway's

---

[30] McCloskey and Ziliak's papers have recently been criticised by K. D. Hoover and M. V. Siegler, 'Sound and Fury: McCloskey and significance testing in economics', unpublished MS (2005). Even if one were to accept Hoover and Siegler's main point (and many will not) that significant tests have the merit of providing an assessment of the strength or weakness of the signal, nevertheless, McCloskey and Ziliak have performed a signal service by insisting on the distinction between economic and statistical significance in all areas of applied econometrics.

impact on Cambridge economics, and so is important to his intellectual legacy. He set the following typical question in the 1964 examination for second year undergraduates.

> You are employed by a business tycoon of uncertain politics, who got a II.1 in economics, but did not take the statistics paper. You find that he has gone away for the afternoon leaving the following note:
>
> 'I spent yesterday evening between two old College friends, T. Ory and L. Abour. Ory was trying to convince me that the economic record for 1959–63 reflected great credit on the government, because there had been good rises in all the following real terms:
>
> (a) The total production of goods and services.
> (b) Output per head in manufacturing.
> (c) Foreign trade.
> (d) Capital formation.
> (e) Personal consumption, both in total and per head of population.
>
> Moreover he insisted that there were other favourable features, such as:
>
> (i) Unemployment has been negligible.
> (ii) The growth in the quantity of money had been no greater than was justified by the rise in production.
> (iii) The rise in prices had slowed down to an easily tolerable pace.
> (iv) The balance of payments had on the whole been favourable.
> (v) The international position of the pound had been strengthened.
>
> On the other hand Abour maintained that in a progressive economy it was natural to have rises in all the items in Ory's list, and the real feature of the period was their smallness. As for his other points, Abour's rejoinder was as follows:
>
> 1. Unemployment had been rising throughout the period.
> 2. The movements in the quantity of money were, as such, of no real importance.
> 3. The rise in prices had been far from negligible, and had been kept down largely by the stability of import prices, for which even a Tory government could hardly claim the credit.
> 4. By the relevant tests, the balance of payments had been unfavourable, and indeed the Government had used its bad state as an argument for keeping down wages.
> 5. We ended the period with less reserves than the start, and greater liabilities.'
>
> Please get out the statistics which you consider relevant for judging the truth of the above matters, prepare tables and/or graphs in such a way that I can draw conclusions from them, and *write notes on what your own conclusions are*, indicating any places where these are of a subjective character (emphasis in original).

The students were provided with the National Income Blue Book and another government source book, *Economic Trends*. This was virtually the whole examination, to be completed within three hours.[31]

---

[31] I have abbreviated the question slightly.

Reddaway's academic legacy includes his commitment to intellectual rigour, and to the teaching and welfare of the students. He also believed in extending to them the democratic governance of the university. In the 1970s as Faculty Board chairman, he sided with the students and the majority in the faculty, in conflict with the central authorities over students' demands for representation and for changed methods of assessment. He was in the forefront of these struggles with all his formidable debating skills. Thus student participation in the university governance was another important aspect of Reddaway's legacy as a Cambridge academic.

This is perhaps best represented by an example—an extract from Reddaway's 'fly-sheet' responding to the one from the conservative dons on the issue of declassing of the Part I exam. It is classic Reddaway and is also worth reproducing at some length to indicate the kind of energy and commitment he brought to this task.

DECLASSING IN PART I OF THE ECONOMICS TRIPOS

(Reply to the *non-placet* fly-sheet)

I am circulating this fly-sheet as the representative of the Faculty Board of Economics and Politics who was appointed to reply to points made in the *non-placet* fly-sheet.

Attempts to confuse the issue

The fly-sheet confuses the issue by exaggerating greatly the importance of a very modest proposal. Its conclusion, 'Declassing signposts the road to uniform mediocrity', is a pure assertion, supported by no evidence whatever, and reached only by a series of leaps in the argument.

Let me give two examples of these leaps:

(a) Economics Part I is unusual in being taken after one year, and this fact weighed heavily with the Faculty Board in its decision to ask for declassing. Paragraph 2 of the fly-sheet actually draws attention to the one-year character of Economics Part I, where the authors kindly tell the Faculty Board how the subject should be taught. But paragraph 4 says 'If the Regent House acquiesce in these proposals we shall soon be told that the arguments for them apply with equal weight to other particular triposes.' This may of course be *said* by irresponsible people, but one can hardly imagine a *Faculty Board* using the argument to support a proposal to declass a two-year Part I; and the General Board would surely point out the *non-sequitur* if it did. The fly-sheet, however, proceeds as if the declassing of a single one-year Part I inevitably means the declassing of all Part I's.

(b) The same fourth paragraph also deftly slides the discussion from 'classing in Part I' to 'classing in examinations', and so implies (without of course producing any evidence) that declassing will spread inevitably to all Part II's as well.

Thus a small experiment in the Economics Faculty is held out as a threat to the very survival of the system of classing in the university as a whole. I invite the members of the Regent House to judge the realism of this picture, remembering that declassing has *not* been proposed for Economics Part II, because the Faculty Board believes that classing in its final examination brings considerable net advantages.

The more serious matter is, however, the unsupported assumption in the fly-sheet that declassing in Economics Part I will lead to 'uniform mediocrity' amongst the students. This type of 'argument' seems to me no more convincing than the objections to the Faculty Board's proposals about dissertations in 1972–73, which experience has now shown to be wholly erroneous: I am fortified in my scepticism by the fact that declassing of the first year examination in Oxford produced no such result. And indeed the fly-sheet itself seems quite uncertain about the reactions of candidates to declassing: paragraph 3 doubts whether the strain on Part I candidates would be reduced 'given the detailed information which would be supplied to the candidates' tutors'; paragraph 4 on the other hand implies that they will ignore their tutors' reactions and seek no more than 'uniform mediocrity' . . .

W. B. Reddaway, March 1976.

In the event, these particular proposals were rejected by a vote of the university at large, but others were accepted, and Reddaway's role in helping to formulate and in arguing them was a key one.

X

One paradox mentioned at the beginning—why the left-wing economists of the *CJE* invited Reddaway to be their patron, and why he accepted—has an uncomplicated answer. Many younger heterodox economists in Cambridge were as dissatisfied with pure theory of the Cambridge kind (from Joan Robinson and her colleagues) as they were with the abstractions of general equilibrium theory. They regarded Reddaway's scepticism about economic theory and his emphasis on empirical and policy analysis as much more helpful. They also shared his distrust of the over-use of mathematical and econometric techniques. Reddaway for his part was not concerned with ideology, but with the fact that these people were doing economics in much the same way as he was doing it himself.

I hope I have managed to show the unorthodoxy of Reddaway's approach to economics. His own studies demonstrate that high quality research can be done without using mathematical equations and inferential econometrics. Like Keynes, Reddaway believed in using economic analysis to improve the world. He was an astringent intellectual who was not afraid to ask what he called 'idiot boy' questions and had the courage to say that the emperor frequently had no clothes. He had less time for economic theory than Keynes, but this was because he thought that Keynes had provided much of what macroeconomic theory was needed. What was required was not more beautiful abstractions, but answers, perhaps rough, to real-world questions.

Reddaway thus regarded economics as an empirical, evidence-based subject, which, through economic policy, should help improve the world. In his view, mathematics could sometimes help but, more often than not, it obfuscated economic reality. Currently, the academic economics profession is dominated by a priori theorising and deductive modelling. Greater attention to Reddaway's legacy to economics, to its research methods and to teaching would greatly contribute to rebalancing the subject.

XI

Brian Reddaway died in Cambridge after a short illness on 23 July 2002. After his retirement from the Chair of Political Economy at the University of Cambridge in 1980, he continued to be active as an economist and as economic adviser to many developing country governments, and gave lectures at the Faculty well into his 80s. He also frequently visited his extended family in Australia, the USA and elsewhere in the world during his post-retirement period. In September 2001, he visited Crowborough to meet his newborn great-granddaughter Bethan.

AJIT SINGH
University of Cambridge

Note. The author is grateful to Tony Atkinson, Jo Bradley, Geoff Harcourt, Ron Smith, John Toye, Geoffrey Whittington, Frank Wilkinson, Adrian Wood and Ann Zammit for helpful comments. The author alone is responsible for the views expressed and any errors that remain.

MARJORIE REEVES

Marjorie Ethel Reeves
1905–2003

Marjorie Reeves was born on 17 July 1905 in the village of Bratton, under the Wiltshire Downs, the second daughter of Robert Reeves and Edith Whitaker. Both families were prominent in the local Baptist congregation. Her father's family owned and ran a successful iron works in the village, making agricultural and other machinery and providing steady employment for local men throughout the nineteenth and early twentieth centuries. Her mother's family, the Whitakers, could trace its continuous presence in Bratton from 1576. For more than two hundred years, this family showed a recognisable and recurring concern with the things of the mind. It produced a succession of vigorous long-lived women, who hoarded and preserved family papers, diaries, verses, children's books and games. In three sharply perceptive and historically detached books *Sheep-bell & Ploughshare: the story of two village families* (1978), *The Diaries of Jeffery Whitaker, schoolmaster of Bratton, 1739–1741* (1989) and *Pursuing the Muses: female education and Nonconformist culture, 1700–1900* (1997), Marjorie Reeves made effective and sympathetic use of this material, and of the living memories of her own and earlier generations to construct a remarkable picture of aspects of Wiltshire life. The village of Bratton was important in the formation of Marjorie's historical perception. She used to recall how, as a child, 'I could climb to the top of the hill above my village, and, sitting there, say "Now I can see what I belong to. I can see all its parts. I can see it all at once."'[1] One of her earliest memories was of the mass departure from

---

[1] 'Persons and Individuals', *Illuminatio*, 2:1 (Feb. 1948) 9.

Proceedings of the British Academy, **138**, 309–318. © The British Academy 2006.

Bratton of those local men, many of them her father's employees, who had enlisted in the army at the beginning of the Great War.

For her secondary education Marjorie was sent to the Girls' High School at Trowbridge. In those days of quiet roads, she regularly cycled to school 'with a book propped up on the handle-bars'. These were years of extensive reading, and of early engagement with historical issues. Learning about Oliver Cromwell, she used to recall, had convinced her that she herself was 'a natural Roundhead'.

In 1923 she went up to St Hugh's College, Oxford, where one of her tutors was Cecilia M. Ady, through whose teaching she had her first introduction to the history of Italy. The Oxford School of Modern History was at that time still in the Stubbesian mould, in which all undergraduates studied 'the continuous history of England' and in which constitutional law and political institutions took a central place. There was, however, a celebrated Special Subject on Dante. In Marjorie Reeves the study of Dante sparked an interest, which was to last throughout her life, in the poetic expression of visionary ideas, and the historical implications of their power.

She took a First in 1926 and, having decided upon a career in teaching, followed this immediately with the newly introduced Diploma in Education. Her first post was as a schoolteacher at the Roan School for Girls, Greenwich. Her second, between 1932 and 1938, was a lecturership in History at St Gabriel's Teachers' Training College, Camberwell. She remembered the Camberwell experience as highly stimulating, because of the way in which an able Principal recruited 'wild and unconventional colleagues, who between them succeeded in training excellent teachers for the desperately poorly equipped schools of South East London'. During the 1930s, worried by alarming developments in the Third Reich, she had already begun to speak and to write publicly about the danger of totalitarian ideologies, and about the responsibility of teachers at all levels to define and to defend Christian liberal values. She had also worked out a plan for a series of new-style historical books for schoolchildren, attractive, accessible, and strictly based on documentary material. The plan had to be shelved on the outbreak of war, but it surfaced in the post-war years as the celebrated *Then and There* series published by Longmans, for which she was to remain for many years managing editor. For this, and for her many other activities in promoting a serious approach to historical questions among the general public, she was later awarded the Medlicott Medal of the Historical Association.

When she embarked on her teaching career, her mind was still turning again and again to questions provoked by her study of Dante. She determined to find for herself a research topic in medieval Italian history, and in 1929 registered at Westfield College. Within a few weeks she had chanced upon Émile Gebhart's *L'Italie Mystique. Histoire de la Renaissance Religieuse au Moyen Age* and found there an essay on the subject which (as it turned out) was to engage her intellectual attention for the rest of her long life, namely the Abbot Joachim of Fiore. As she recognised at the time, this was an unfashionable subject to pick in 1929. She recalled that one of her contemporaries commented 'That outlandish subject won't assist your career. You should have chosen something like "The Wardrobe under Edward II".'[2] She was intrigued by what she had read about Joachim himself, and—above all—by the fact that his main works had all been printed in Venice in the early sixteenth century. Why, she asked herself, should the visionary out-pourings of a remote twelfth-century Biblical exegete have been of such interest over three hundred years later to sober Augustinian divines? She soon discovered that these Augustinians were not alone in their interest in Joachim, and that long before and long after the episode of the Venetian editions of the 1520s 'tracks led off in all directions', towards controversies central to the theology and spirituality of the entire later Middle Ages, and the period of the Protestant and Catholic Reformations: St Bonaventure had been impelled to take a view on the merits and dangers of Joachim's teachings. Joachim's ideas had also possessed a powerful attraction for some Lutherans, and for some members of the Society of Jesus. Marjorie Reeves came to focus her enquiries less upon the twelfth century than upon the wider question of Joachim's lasting influence. Her thesis, examined in 1932 by Sir Maurice Powicke and Canon Claude Jenkins, was entitled 'Studies in the reputation and influence of the Abbot Joachim of Fiore, chiefly in the fifteenth and sixteenth centuries'. 'They were polite in their comments', she was to recall, 'but later I realised that they thought the whole subject rather marginal.' In 1932, she herself had some qualms, although not on the same score. She wondered whether she would convince the reader of the central historical importance of ideas as unfamiliar and strange as the ones she had been dealing with. In the preface to the thesis she wrote: 'To treat the fantastic as history may well require explanation. Most of the prophetic material upon which these studies are based . . . is bizarre, fantastic; it seems, in itself, to be quite

[2] Unless otherwise indicated, all the quotations from Marjorie Reeves are taken from her auto-biographical article 'A Sixty-Year Pilgrimage with the Abbot Joachim', *Florensia. Bollettino del Centro Internazinale di Studi Gioachimitti*, anno VI (1992), pp. 7–32.

worthless . . . But . . . one must recognize beneath the groundwork of normal political life, a far more general subsoil of prophetic belief, long since crumbled into superstition, than the rationalist is wont to admit.'

The thesis remained unpublished. During the 1930s Marjorie Reeves turned her attention, as we have seen, to politics and to the education of the young. In 1938 she returned to Oxford as Tutor in History to the Society of Oxford Home Students. She was one of the small band of scholars who kept alive the Oxford Faculty of Modern History during the Second World War, and at the same time she was actively involved in the transformation of the Society of Home Students, first into a permanent Private Hall of the University, and eventually into full collegiate status as St Anne's College. From 1951 to 1967 she was the college's Vice-Principal, giving sterling service to the college throughout its first great building phase, and coming up with a succession of good ideas for its welfare. One of these, widely copied since, and almost certainly no longer remembered as her innovation, was the establishment of the very first 'Middle Common Room' for postgraduate students.

Marjorie Reeves remained Senior History Tutor at St Anne's until her retirement in 1974. Her invigorating and challenging tutorials, her direct kindness, her integrity, and her often sharply radical concern with the live issues of the day inspired affection and respect in generations of undergraduates, not only members of St Anne's but those men and women from other colleges whom she taught, or who attended the fresh and combative seminars she ran under the aegis of the Student Christian Movement, then in its liberal-modernist heyday. On her retirement from her university post and college tutorship she was made an Honorary Fellow of St Anne's College. A similar honour was extended to her by her old college, St Hugh's. In 1979 she brought out *St Anne's College Oxford. An Informal History 1879–1979*. Characteristically, this elegant and entertaining essay is meticulously documented and fair-minded, as well as being refreshingly independent. It was written to coincide with a centenary appeal, just before the debate which resulted in the College being one of the first two women's colleges to open its doors to men as well as to women, as Fellows, as postgraduates and as undergraduates. This was a development which Marjorie Reeves wholeheartedly supported.

In the post-war years (1947–65) she made a valuable contribution to public policy-making. She was early a member of the Schools' Broadcasting Council, and from 1947 to 1961 of the Central Advisory Council of the Ministry of Education. She sat on the 1961–4 Robbins Committee on Higher Education which resulted in the establishment of the first post-war wave of new universities including York, Lancaster, Sussex, Essex, Warwick, East Anglia and Kent. She published in 1965 *Eighteen Plus: Unity and Diversity in Higher Education*, and in 1988 *The Crisis in Higher Education: Competence, Delight and the Common Good*. She continued to follow with keen interest the further expansion of university education in the eighties and nineties. She had independent and progressive views on the ethical and social value of widening of opportunity, as well as some shrewd ideas on how best to cope with the financial difficulties involved in translating this aspiration into practice.

To give so much space to the public achievements of Marjorie Reeves would have fitted well with her own estimate of the short-term usefulness of her activities. It is time to return, however to the long and productive decades of her scholarly work, suspended during the years 1932–42, but resumed thereafter with unremitting vigour and success until the early years of the twenty-first century. It was in her scholarly work that she produced her most deeply considered insights, informed always by rigorous textual interpretation and by awareness of the powerful historical effects of institutions of authority. Marjorie Reeves was jolted back into the mainstream of scholarly enquiry by a chance event: Nicolai Rubinstein, knowing of her interest in Joachim, drew to her attention an article by Fritz Saxl, published in 1942. Here Saxl mentioned that Otto Pächt believed that a hitherto unstudied Oxford manuscript full of elaborate apocalyptic figures almost certainly had a Joachimist reference and probably a Joachimist provenance. The very day she received Rubinstein's letter, Marjorie Reeves went to the Bodleian full of curiosity and anticipation, and ordered up the manuscript, Corpus Christi College MS 255A. She later recalled that 'The idea of a lost set of *figurae* by Joachim had been buzzing in my mind for some time, partly because of strange figures in the Venetian editions, partly because the Franciscan Salimbene referred to a *Liber Figurarum*.' She set about making a careful step-by-step comparison of the pictures in the Corpus manuscript with the text of Salimbene's *Cronica*. 'The correspondences, both in concepts and in details, were extraordinary. The figures fitted the Abbot's idea like a glove.' She was now convinced that the Corpus manuscript was undoubtedly the 'lost' work which Salimbene had entitled the *Liber Figurarum*. Without delay she resolved to produce an edition, with the collaboration of Beatrice Hirsch-Reich. The project was still in its early stages, when, as Marjorie Reeves recalled, 'international barriers were lifted at the end of the war, and European scholarship breathed again. We then learnt that Monsignor Leone Tondelli had discovered another finely illuminated copy of the *Liber Figurarum* in Reggio Emilia and had published an edition of it in 1939.' 'Comparison showed close correspondence between the two manuscripts, but also significant variations. The Oxford manuscript appeared to be the earlier by half-a-century or more, and it had four important *figurae* missing from the Reggio copy.' Learning of this, Monsignor Tondelli encouraged Marjorie Reeves and Beatrice Hirsch-Reich to proceed, in cooperation with himself, on a new critical edition of the *Liber Figurarum*. It was eventually published in 1972.

In 1950, for the first time ever, Marjorie Reeves was able to get away from her teaching duties and to enjoy a term's sabbatical leave in Italy. The experience of visiting Europe, so soon after the end of the war, was a liberating one, and proved to be a catalyst, a second turning point, in the progress of her studies. It enabled her to meet European scholars, including Tondelli, and it furnished her with a rich store of fresh documentary evidence, which amplified and transformed the questions she had first raised in the thesis of 1932. Treasures turned up in every library she visited—the Vatican, the Biblioteca Nazionale in Naples, Santa Croce and Santa Maria Novella in Florence, the Marciana in Venice, the Antoniana in Padua, and University Library in Pavia. Many years later she could still vividly recall the sense of excitement and the feeling of 'standing at a point where half a dozen promising paths led off in different directions'.

Soon after her return from Italy she published a long article on the Corpus manuscript[3] followed by a succession of articles in which she sought to identify and to explore the Joachimist element in the preoccupation with prophetic spirituality shown by a wide variety of religious writers between 1300 and 1700.[4] This work was summed up decisively in her book: *The Influence of Prophecy in the Later Middle Ages*, published in 1969.

Certain problems about prophetic writing in general, and about the Joachimist component in particular, engaged her attention at this time. Were those late medieval commentators who had condemned Joachim's ideas as dangerous to the authority of the Catholic Church right? How

---

[3] 'The *Liber Figurarum* of Joachim of Fiore', *Medieval and Renaissance Studies*, 2 (1950), 57–81.
[4] 'Joachimist Expectations in the Order of Augustinian Hermits', *Recherches de Théologie ancienne et médiévale*, 22 (1958), 111–41, 'The Originality and Influence of Joachim of Fiore', *Traditio*, 36 (1980), 302–4, and 'The Abbot Joachim and the Society of Jesus', *Medieval and Renaissance Studies*, 5 (1961), 163–81.

radical was Joachim's *transitus* to the Third Age to be? she enquired. Did the logic of his coming new age lead inevitably to the conclusion that the institutions and authorities of the second *status* had to be abrogated? This she regarded as 'The crucial question underlying all Joachimist studies' and her answer to it was uncompromising. She found herself in disagreement with those scholars who regarded Joachim's teachings as intentionally destructive of established ecclesiastical authority. She argued that for Joachim, and for those of his followers who had understood his message, 'the Church of St Peter would endure to the end of time, although the *vita activa* of Peter had to be superseded by the *vita contemplativa* of John'. This interpretation allowed one to account for the lasting appeal of the so-called 'Pope Prophecies' (*Vaticinia de summis pontificibus*). She concluded that their appeal lay in their intrinsically paradoxical form: 'the hermit of the rocks is to become the instrument of profound spiritual reform but only when the papal electors have raised him to the highest office in the institutional Church'.

Was Joachim a millenarian? She argued that he was not. 'Joachim's Age of the Spirit was not a sudden supernatural state of blessedness imposed from above, such as many millenarians dreamed of, but the fulfilment of an internal logic in history, the cue to which lay in the divine activity which operated throughout the whole time-process.'

Why were Joachim's ideas so influential for so long? She claimed that 'his belief that the agents of divinely orchestrated change were to be human institutions and individuals' gave his teachings a kind of political attraction in all kinds of different circumstances. 'The particular agencies could become outmoded but the concept was infinitely adaptable and continued to grip the imagination of succeeding generations.'

A question she confessed herself unable to resolve was the debt of Dante to Joachim. In the case of the *Three Eagles*, and the *Trinitarian Circles* Dante's borrowing of Joachim's figurative imagery seemed certain — 'but this evidence supplies no clear proof that Dante saw the future in Joachimist terms'.

> In one important respect — the future role he assigns to the Roman Emperor — he clearly differed radically from Joachim. Yet the affinities between the two, in their interpretation of history as God's providential design and their search for figural signs of this purpose haunted my mind. In the use both made of the biblical figure Zorobabel at the end of the first *status*, I believed I had found evidence that Dante had actually been reading Joachim's *Liber de Concordia*. However this conjecture has so far not met with support: The relationship between these two medieval Italians remains problematical.

By 1980, the whole international landscape of Joachimist studies had changed; the Abbot and his disciples had finally 'come in out of the cold'. As she tells us: 'It was becoming fashionable to find the Abbot's mark in all kinds of places.' A two-volume work of enormous sweep published in 1978 and 1980 was that of Cardinal de Lubac, *La posterité spirituelle de Joachim de Fiore* which brought the story right up to the present day. 'In this work he surveyed in a magnificent sweep all possible inheritors of Joachim's perspective.' In an important article[5] Marjorie Reeves expressed her scepticism about a good many of these claims. Works were not to be described as 'Joachimist' unless there was 'direct evidence that their writers had direct knowledge of the Abbot or had read his works'. They had to show a precise debt to his trinitarian ideas, to use his special number-symbolism (five+seven=twelve), and to utilise Biblical figural symbols in his particular way. Simply to believe that history had three stages was, in her view, not sufficient at all. She strove hard to keep her feet on the ground, and insisted that Joachim should not be given credit—or blame—for any old prophetic visionary stuff.

In this new climate of receptivity to the idea that prophecy had been a pervasive mode of looking at the past and future of the human race, she drew on her own early work to demonstrate—with stern rigour— that among a whole host of attitudes not directly attributable to Joachimist texts, and indeed inconsistent with his teachings, there were authentic examples of the transmission of specifically Joachimist ideas. The routes of transmission of spurious and genuine Joachimist writings were many. For example, 'Collections of pre-Reformation writings made by Protestant apologists for polemical attacks on Catholicism often contained Joachimist material.' Prominent participants in the Catholic Reformation, such as the Jesuit Daniel Papebroch, also used for their own purposes the Joachimist idea of the *viri intellectuales* who would appear in the third age.

Marjorie Reeves was awarded a D.Litt. by Oxford University and became a Fellow of the British Academy in 1974. In 1980 a Festschrift was published in her honour, edited by Ann Williams, under the title *Prophecy and Millenarianism*. This volume included an evaluation by Sir Richard Southern of her work as an historian, and a tribute by William Lamont to her talents as a teacher. It also brought together essays by fourteen others, among them several of her collaborators and pupils. The extraordinarily broad ramifications of the study of prophetic his-

[5] 'The Originality and Influence of Joachim of Fiore', *Traditio*, 36 (1980), 307–8, 310–15.

tory can clearly be seen in this volume, and the outline of her particular scholarly role in the field shows through with diamond sharpness.

In the 1980s Marjorie Reeves collaborated with a Yeats specialist, Warwick Gould, to produce *Joachim of Fiore and the Myth of the Eternal Evangel in the Nineteenth Century* (Oxford, 1987). 'It was exciting', she wrote, 'because the nineteenth-century perspective on the twelfth-century seer was so utterly different from the medieval and renaissance images of him. Here were thinkers, in the main radicals, who had broken with the established church, yet still sought for a religious basis for their visionary society of the future.' Nineteenth-century figures fascinated by Joachim— and surprisingly well-acquainted with some of his ideas—included Mazzini, Renan, Matthew Arnold, George Eliot, George Sand. Janacek wrote a cantata based upon an 1891 poem by the Czech poet Vrchlicky, on Joachim's *Eternal Evangel*. A revised and enlarged edition entitled *Joachim of Fiore and the Myth of the Eternal Evangel in the Nineteenth and Twentieth Centuries* appeared in 2001. It took the story up to Yeats, Joyce and D. H. Lawrence.

It was in 1992 also, that her final work in the field appeared, in a collaborative volume of essays, which she conceived, planned and edited, and to which she contributed an introduction and two new essays, *Prophetic Rome in the High Renaissance Period* (1992). The volume seeks to show how in the early sixteenth century Joachimist visions of the future had a powerful appeal in the world of high international politics: would the world see a Golden Age heralded by an Angelic Pope and a Last World Emperor, or with the coming of Antichrist, would it all end in fire and blood? She alluded to the establishment of the *Centro Internazionale di Studi Gioachimiti* at S. Giovanni in Fiore, and to the congresses and publications it sponsors. 'A major task [before the scholars involved] is the promotion of modern editions of Joachim's works.' 'The Abbot may be in the process of becoming a new modern myth but this does not lessen the obligation laid on scholars to get as close to the original figure as can be achieved by meticulous work on the texts.'

Between 1992 and her death in 2003 Marjorie Reeves continued, despite increasing physical infirmity, to show her all her old alertness and intellectual vigour. She continued to take great pleasure in music, taking her friends regularly to concerts in the Sheldonian, even if it became increasingly difficult for her to get to Glyndebourne. She was often present at College guest nights, and visitors to her house in Norham Road were grilled, as always, on their own current scholarly activities, and on their reactions to topical issues of the day. She died on 27 November

2003, aged 98. In his address at her memorial service, Canon Brian
Mountford, Vicar of the Oxford University Church of St Mary the
Virgin, recalled that she had been for more than fifty years a regular member of that congregation and only a few weeks before her death 'she
presided at the launch in Oxford of a collection of essays and memoirs by
various hands, in which she had had an editorial role. It is entitled *St
Mary the Virgin University Church Oxford: the dynamics of a congregation
in a century of change 1900–2000.*' The present writer has a vivid recol-
lection of that occasion, in which Marjorie, in the nave, discoursed to the
assembled company, battling on despite considerable distraction from the
sound of choir practice in the chancel. It was an entirely characteristic
performance, lively, vigorous and undeterred.

Marjorie Reeves was a fluent public speaker, much in demand as a par-
ticipator in conferences in Europe and the United States. Especially after
her retirement, she travelled all over the world. In 1975 she spent a semes-
ter at Columbia University, New York; in 1977 she was Distinguished
Professor in Medieval Studies at the University of California, Berkeley.
One of her most cherished honours, because of its West Country associations, was the honorary degree awarded her by the University of Bath.
Another was the award of honorary citizenship of Joachim's native town
in Calabria, in recognition of the fame she had brought to that city by
securing scholarly acceptance for the importance of Joachim's historical
role. In 1996 she was made CBE for services to history. She belonged to a
generation the like of which we will not see again.

GILLIAN LEWIS
St Anne's College, Oxford

MARTIN ROBERTSON

Charles Martin Robertson
1911–2004

MARTIN ROBERTSON was born in Pangbourne on 11 September 1911, the first child of Donald Robertson, who had been appointed that year to an Assistant Lectureship in Classics at Trinity College, Cambridge, and Petica (née Coursolles Jones). The family, including his brother Giles who was born in 1913, lived in Huntingdon Road in Cambridge, moving after the First World War to Bateman Street overlooking the Botanic Gardens. Although Donald wanted his sons to follow him at Westminster School, Petica, a strong personality who ran a salon for the literary and artistic personalities of the day, wished them to stay at home, and, after a time at a prep school, they attended The Leys School in Cambridge. Martin (he was always 'Martin', never 'Charles', to his parents and his children) learned to read early and is reputed to have read from the newspaper, when four years old, to the noted Cambridge mathematician G. H. Hardy. His love of literature was deep and abiding, but he was not a practical boy nor good at physical pursuits. His father loved riding and arranged for Martin to have riding lessons; Martin did not like the instructor and the lessons were not a success. He found his father rather oppressive and felt that he was an inferior reproduction of him. Whether he would have fared better at the piano is unknown, as Petica decided that Giles was the musical one and denied Martin the chance. He never learned to drive but enjoyed cycling (in his late sixties, on retirement from his Oxford chair and moving house to Cambridge, he cycled all the way from the one to the other).

In 1930, on leaving The Leys and before starting to read for a Classics degree at Trinity, Martin was able to spend some months in Greece—this was a major step in his search for a career. At that time the Director of

Proceedings of the British Academy, **138**, 321–335. © The British Academy 2006.

the British School of Archaeology at Athens was Humfry Payne who was initiating the excavation of Perachora, a small archaic site on the north side of the Gulf of Corinth. Martin was enraptured by Greece and by Greek art and archaeology, he was taken under the director's wing, and the road to his future career was laid down. He returned to England and began his undergraduate life as a Pensioner at Trinity where his father had recently been appointed the Regius Professor of Greek. One can only guess at the effect so close a connection had on the young man. His start was not auspicious; he himself confesses that he did not do well in his first year and was awarded a Second in Part 1. However, by Part 2 he was well into his stride; he became a Research Scholar (alongside David Hinks, Dale Trendall and Enoch Powell) and then a Senior Scholar in his final year, gaining a First in Part 2.

In 1934 he returned to his beloved Greece as a student of the British School and his two years there were a defining time. Humfry Payne gave him the task of working on the later excavation material unearthed on the island of Ithaca by members of the School who, in searching for evidence of Odysseus, were less interested in the later Iron Age remains. This was perhaps too heavy a burden, the fruits of which were not published until 1948, but he flourished. He was attracted to the study of Greek vase-painting which at that time was being revolutionised by the work of John Beazley, the Lincoln Professor of Classical Archaeology and Art at Oxford. His fellow students at that time were ones who, like Robertson, later made names for themselves in academia, including John and Robert Cook, Tom Dunbabin, Nick Hammond, Romilly Jenkins and 'Peter' Megaw. His connection with the British School lasted most of his working life; he had a number of papers published in the *Annual of the British School at Athens.* He returned to the School as Visiting Fellow in 1957–8 and was Chairman of its Council from 1959–68.

Martin unconsciously assumed that he would follow an academic career. He applied for a fellowship at Trinity for which competitors had to submit written work. His examiner misunderstood the nature of the system and Martin's submission (on the Ithaca material) was diverted to John Beazley in Oxford who was already backing another applicant (Dale Trendall). Martin was not successful, more to his father's disappointment than to his own. However, Humfry Payne's early death in his mid-thirties and Martin's failure in his bid for a fellowship made 1936 a depressing year. In September he moved to the position of Assistant Keeper in the Department of Greek and Roman Antiquities in the British Museum but was unsettled by the closed and factional environment he found in the museum at that time. His initial task was to work on the early Greek pottery from Al Mina in Syria that had come to the museum from Sir Leonard Woolley's excavations of 1936 and 1937; his report on the vases was published in 1940.

It was in the later 1930s that the scandal of the unauthorised cleaning of the Parthenon sculptures rocked the British Museum, and two senior members of staff were dismissed. Martin remained as the only junior Assistant Keeper, as he had had no connection with whatever misdemeanours had taken place. Nonetheless he lost some years of seniority. The arrival of two newcomers improved the atmosphere. Denys Haynes, who had also been a student at Trinity and already had a position at the Victoria and Albert Museum, was appointed as a second Assistant Keeper, and a life-long friendship developed between the two men. More importantly for the future of the department, Professor Bernard Ashmole, who held the Yates Chair of Classical Art and Archaeology at University College, London, was now employed part-time to run the department, and Robertson later spoke of his own 'precious apprenticeship' under him (*Between Archaeology and Art History, An Inaugural Lecture delivered before the University of Oxford on 15 November 1962*, p. 21). In August 1939 Martin was sent out to represent the British Museum at a Classical conference in Berlin but was summoned back just before war was declared. Contingency plans for removing the collections from the museum had already been adumbrated in 1933, but it was not until 23 August 1939 that a directive was issued instructing the staff to set about the backbreaking task of moving the material out of the museum, to London Underground stations and to country houses.

While still a student at the British School, Martin had had a short article on a skyphos by the Pan Painter published in *The Journal of Hellenic Studies* for 1935; it was an earnest of his later work, a mature beginning. During the pre-war years at the British Museum, besides his work on the Al Mina material, he published a few articles on objects in the museum and on new acquisitions. However, his detailed reviews in *JHS* for 1937 of Diepolder's *Der Penthesilea-Maler* and Rumpf's *Sakonides* in the 'Bilder Griechischer Vasen' series and later his review of Beazley's *Attic Red-figure Vase-painters* in the *Classical Review* for 1943 indicated the direction he had chosen to go and the progress he had already made in his study of Attic vase-painting. The seeds of his future harvest had been planted.

Martin's war years were a mixture of mind-numbing boredom and only slightly more interesting service abroad. After abortive training for the Signals and an equally unsuccessful transfer to the Intelligence Corps and preparation for work at Bletchley Park, he was eventually initiated into the Secret Service. Alan Wace, a leading classical archaeologist who had for some years been excavating the Bronze Age palace at Mycenae, where he was refining Schliemann's earlier work, asked for Martin's presence in Cairo where he was attached to the British Embassy as an undercover agent. His arrival there followed soon after Rommel's defeat at El Alamein in late 1942 and the advance of the allies across North Africa. Nonetheless, though quieter and less crucial than when the German troops had been approaching, Cairo was not a safe place, and Martin found the whole episode demoralising as he was merely used as a clerk. In the winter of 1943–4 he was sent to Naples (by mistake for Athens), and here too there was little for him to do, so he wrote a pantomime that contained satires on his colleagues (he was equally at home compiling political, social and literary satire). A colleague in Naples at that time who remembers the pantomime, recalls that one line ran 'it was rush hour in the brothel; a woman's work is never done' and can still dimly picture a chorus kicking their legs in the air and singing a ditty 'Language, Truth and Logic'. Towards the end of the war he was transferred to Salonica where he had a miserable time but also a memorable encounter with his childhood friend Kim Philby, then a senior figure in British intelligence. His acquaintance with Philby was obvious and caused consternation among the others there, who concluded that he was being asked to spy on them on Philby's behalf. Martin attributed a period of home leave to their desire to appease him.

The war produced both sorrow and joy. His mother, a woman of strong pacifist beliefs who worked for the WVS, was killed in early 1941 in a stray air-raid on Cambridge; she was on air-raid warden's duty. The following year, when Martin was a trainee for the Intelligence Corps, he married Cecil (née Spring Rice) whom he had known as a family friend; their marriage took place in Hammersmith Register Office. Lucy, their first child, was born after Martin had been posted to Cairo and Stephen, their second, when he was back in Salonica. Cecil, having worked in the Registrar General's Office, spent her time as a young mother at Iken (Suffolk), south of Snape and not far from Aldeburgh, where her own mother, Margie, was running a nursery school for evacuees.

After his war service, Martin's return in 1946 found him assisting in moving the British Museum material back in place again. Two years later Ashmole resigned from the Yates Chair at University College, London, and worked full-time at the museum; Martin took over the chair the same year. During his time at UCL Classical Studies were particularly strong, with Tom Webster (Greek), Otto Skutsch (Latin), Eric Turner (Papyrology), Arnaldo Momigliano (Ancient History) and Oswald Szemerényi (Comparative Philology); at the early stages of distinguished careers were Robert Browning, David Furley and Eric Handley. It is with his move to UCL that Martin's work on Greek pottery and on Classical art in general gathered momentum. He was unsure whether he would take to lecturing but found it congenial. His inaugural lecture, delivered in 1949 and entitled 'Why study Greek art?' (it was typical of Martin that it was couched as a question—in a later lecture in 1986 (*Papers on the Amasis Painter and his World* (1987), p. 14) he confessed 'I do like mulling the questions over') was a statement of his belief in the need to study Greek art as art, with the eye of the connoisseur, a belief that he continued to hold throughout his life. The labour-intensive lecturing programme that Martin laid down for himself found him dealing with the whole history of Greek and Roman art, and the detailed preparation he needed to carry out for those lectures formed the foundation of his major work on the history of Greek art published nearly thirty years later. Although Martin enjoyed teaching, he was not a natural lecturer; he needed to make sure that his undergraduate audience understood that what he was saying was by no means incontrovertible but was hedged about by uncertainties. His students realised that here was a scholar who cared for the accuracy of what he was proposing, but this did not always make for easy listening. With postgraduates who came to discuss their research he showed a more relaxed manner that was refreshing. His research during his time at UCL showed that he was building on the foundations laid in the 1930s. An early article on the origins of the Berlin Painter (*JHS,* 70 (1950)) revealed his fine eye for attribution that never deserted him, and he returned to the same painter a few years later (*American Journal of Archaeology,* 62 (1958)). He demonstrated how the Gorgos cup that had been found in the Athenian Agora could be the Berlin Painter's earliest extant work, following an attribution made by Lucy Talcott, and the article was a masterly study of a cup that has teased students of red-figure vase-painting from the moment of its discovery. He also wrote on Roman wall-painting. Obviously his need to cover the whole of classical art for his students was paying dividends.

Martin had been demobbed in 1946, and from the end of the war he and Cecil returned to living in St Peter's Square in Hammersmith in a house which Cecil's mother had given them. Over the next decade their family was increased with the births of Matthew (1949), Catherine (1950), Dominick (1952) and a little later Thomas (1958). Lucy recalls her father being very much a family man; at a time when fathers could be rather distant figures, Martin took his children to museums and on walks on which he was tolerant of dawdling, told them stories and read to them from a range that stretched from *Just William* books to James Joyce's *Ulysses*. His father, when explaining to his second wife, Margaret, how to recognise Martin, had described him as the man with 'a child under each arm'. With Margie's help, Martin and Cecil were able to manage holidays without the children, and they both took delight, Cecil particularly, in assisting at the creation of the Aldeburgh Festival and became friends with Benjamin Britten and Peter Pears. They were also members of the CND.

Having already brought to publication the Ithaca and Al Mina pottery that others had excavated, in 1955 he found himself charged with another task of editing unpublished material, and it was not the last occasion on which he was called to do this service. He agreed to take over the editorship of the second volume of the Perachora findings when the untimely death of Tom Dunbabin left the publication without its editor. His preface to the volume is dated 1958, an indication of the complex work that had been needed in collating the contributions of various scholars; the book appeared in 1962. During the time he was editing this volume he was working on the text of his first book, *Greek Painting* (1959), a Skira volume with coloured photographs tipped in to the text. It followed Pallottino's *Etruscan Painting* and Maiuri's *Roman Painting* in the same series, and there were fears that the colours might be as lurid as the illustrations in those volumes. The fears were unfounded, and his choice of illustrations was bold. Robertson aimed to use as many of the media as were extant (painted metopes, altars, sarcophagi, mosaics, as well as the vase-paintings on which scholars must depend) to recreate an idea of the wall and panel paintings that have not survived. The text showed the acute observation and stylistic charm that characterise all of Robertson's writings.

In the later 1950s Martin and Cecil considered moving out of St Peter's Square. Martin enjoyed his work at UCL, but neither he nor Cecil was finding central London to their liking. However in 1961, before they brought this plan to reality, Martin was appointed to the Chair of Classical Archaeology and Art in Oxford, once again in succession to Bernard Ashmole who at the end of his career had taken over that position for a brief period after Sir John Beazley's retirement in 1956. Martin spent a year resident in Lincoln College, with Cecil still in London. Eventually, they moved to Sheepstead House at Marcham, near Abingdon, and most days Martin cycled the ten miles or so from there to his office in the Ashmolean. The cycling was enjoyable in summer but dangerous in the dark evenings of winter, and there were numerous times when, dazzled by headlights, he finished up in a ditch. The house itself, which had been built on a grand scale in the nineteenth century for the Morland Brewery family, was solid but dilapidated; tales of decay with fungus emerging from the walls when it rained are fondly remembered by the children. Cecil, who always welcomed new projects, relished the chance of restoring the property; it became a much loved home.

The Oxford years were particularly happy ones for Martin. In his inaugural lecture (*Between Archaeology and Art History*) delivered at the end of 1962, he disclaimed with characteristic modesty his entitlement to be considered 'either an archaeologist or quite an historian of art' but then added that he did not think it mattered when he reviewed the work of the previous holders of the chair. He saw connoisseurship as 'the right and true end of studying art' but was worried to what extent one could write a history of classical art. There is some irony in the fact that he went on to do just that, and the result was a triumph. He voiced his distrust of a conventional and schematic development in classical art and preferred the more organic progress that the study of individual painters had started to provide. He confessed an antipathy to fixed dates and admitted that he was 'a loose, imprecise dater' ('Early Greek Mosaics' in *Macedonia and Greece in Late Classical and Early Hellenistic Times* (1982), p. 246). Indeed, the main thrust of his Oxford inaugural was to endorse the work of Sir John Beazley in differentiating painters of Attic black-figure and red-figure vases, and thus advancing vase-painting 'from a branch of archaeology to a branch of art-history'. His assertion towards the end of the lecture that 'treasure-hunting is in itself a good' was not politically correct then, still less is it so now, but Robertson valued beauty for itself and all his writings bear this out. A characteristic element in the lecture is the way in which Robertson, like Beazley, made reference to the Italian painters of the Renaissance in his search for parallels to Athenian vase-painters, an approach of which he was fond, but on occasion he misjudged the connection between the two crafts. Martin's brother, Giles, who after an unhappy time at Oxford became a Professor of Fine Art at Edinburgh University, was himself an expert on Renaissance painting, particularly Bellini, and with the two brothers maintaining a close friendship all their lives, it was pleasing to see Martin recognising an echo of classical sculpture in a Bellini painting (*Burlington Magazine*, 121 (1979)).

Martin's publications in the first decade of his tenure of the chair show him working in various areas of classical archaeology. As well as his continued work on the painters and subjects of Attic pottery, he also wrote a brilliant account of early Greek mosaics (*JHS*, 85 (1965)), using the newly discovered material from the Greek excavations at Pella in Macedonia as the basis for a wider investigation. A brief treatment of the Parthenon sculptures in a supplementary volume to *Greece and Rome*, 10 (1963) that celebrated the dedication of the Athena Parthenos twenty-four centuries earlier, was to lead to a fuller treatment of the frieze in a volume of 1975 and to the chapter in the *History of Greek Art* of the same year. At the end of the decade Martin found himself once more helping to prepare an unfinished work for publication. Sir John Beazley died in 1970, and his work on updating and re-ordering his vase-painter lists in the second edition of his *Attic Red-figure Vase-painters* of 1963 was still not ready for publication. Martin, along with Dietrich von Bothmer of the Metropolitan Museum of Art, New York, worked on what came to be called *Paralipomena* published in 1971. Martin never wavered in his adherence to Beazley's principles and he spent time defending and explaining them. The tide was beginning to turn against both the validity of the method and the prominence given to the painter's role. Towards the end of his review of the second edition of Beazley's *Attic Red-figure Vase-painters* in *JHS* for 1965, Martin had already asked '[w]here do we go from here?' and after 1970 he saw clearly the difficulties that lay ahead now that the subject had lost its major figure. He also highlighted the problem that was endemic in Beazley's approach—the spectrum of talent from the quality pieces to the hack work. His Munich lecture 'Beazley and after' of 1976, his contribution to the Beazley Centenary conference in Oxford in 1985, his chapter in Spivey and Rasmussen's *Looking at Greek Vases* (1991) and his Berlin lecture to the Euphronios Colloquium in 1991 were, in a way, a spirited rearguard action.

The excellence of his *History of Greek Art* was recognised as soon as it was published in 1975, and it has continued to hold its place in English-language scholarship. It was the culmination of years of patient research that had started when Martin embraced the teaching of the history of the subject nearly thirty years earlier. Reviewers remarked on the way in which the book was both a personal study of Greek art and also a comprehensive treatment of the whole field. Through its measured structure and the grace and power of its style, it shows the author at the peak of his talent.

Life at Sheepstead House was full. The children were growing apace. In the 1960s Lucy read for a degree in Classics, both Stephen and Matthew for degrees in Mathematics—all at Cambridge. Catherine read

Modern Languages at Warwick University and at Goldsmiths. Dominick rebelled in the period of rebellion and at the age of 16 took himself off from Westminster School to Spain. He was inveigled back, and many years later he became a mature student at the Southern Oregon University but had no desire for an academic life. Thomas chose rock music and fashioned a successful career under the name of Thomas Dolby. Meanwhile, Martin continued at Lincoln and Cecil taught mathematics at St Helen's and St Katharine's in Abingdon and became deputy head. In such a hectic atmosphere it is not to be wondered at that Martin and Cecil, deep in their own work, found themselves living semi-separate lives.

The year for retirement, 1978, arrived, and it was decided that they should move to Cambridge. Sheepstead House was sold but before a move was possible the Robertson family lodged in the Clockhouse, in the grounds of Sheepstead. It was clear to Cecil that with advancing years they would need a house near the centre of Cambridge, and although the change from a rural retreat to the vibration and pollution of Parker Street was extreme, the choice was a good one. Martin continued his research and Cecil her teaching. In 1968–9 Martin had been a member of the Princeton Institute for Advanced Study, and in 1980 he made the first of his visits to the Getty Museum in Malibu as Guest Scholar, a connection he renewed in 1988 and at other times and which led to the publication of a fine series of rich and detailed studies of the red-figure work, mainly fragmentary, that was being bought for the museum: Euphronios, the Kleophrades Painter, the Berlin Painter, Douris, the Pan Painter. He was in demand for help with the publication of newly excavated material (1981 Kition) and museum collections (1987 Liverpool). 1982 saw Martin in Basel speaking at the prestigious Parthenon Congress and in the same year he was honoured with a Festschrift, *The Eye of Greece*, a small collection of important papers that pleased him immensely. But the new decade was soon to cast dark shadows. In 1984 as a result of an accident in the garden of the Parker Street house Cecil fell to her death. A few years later Martin's brother, Giles, also died.

In 1985 a conference to celebrate the centenary of the birth of Sir John Beazley was held in London and Oxford. Martin spoke at the Oxford meeting and faced the attack that was gathering ground against Beazley's method and influence. He was willing to acknowledge that there was merit in some of the newer approaches and admitted that he had been enabled to see more clearly than he had before that there was an important interaction between metalwork and pottery, but he refused to believe that the long and strong tradition of pottery-making that Athens had enjoyed was hijacked by the workers in metal. He forcefully maintained his allegiance to the principles which had guided him throughout his career.

It was at this time that he met Louise Berge again. She had been one of his postgraduate students at Oxford in the late 1960s when she, together with her small children, had accompanied her husband, a physicist from the Lawrence Radiation Laboratory in Berkeley. Louise was a mathematician but had also taken an MA degree in classical archaeology at Berkeley. So she began to work under Martin's guidance on the Athenian red-figure painter Myson. They corresponded in the years that followed, and in 1985, with Martin a widower and Louise in a troubled marriage, their friendship was renewed. Martin visited the States on a number of occasions over the next few years. By 1988 friendship had 'developed into love and the need to be together' (personal letter 10 Mar. 1988). The wedding took place that same year, and they enjoyed sixteen years of happy marriage in which Louise helped him with his work and nursed him through his illnesses.

During these years Martin continued to research and publish his results and to review other scholars' books: a catalogue of the vases in the Lady Lever Art Gallery, work on the archaic marble sculptures from Aegina, articles in honour or memory of colleagues, and lectures at conferences in Athens, at the Getty (to follow the exhibition on the Amasis Painter that had been mounted in New York, Toledo and Los Angeles to honour Sir John Beazley), at the University of Texas at Austin, and in Berlin. All the time he was working on the book which stands next in importance to his *History of Greek Art. The Art of Vase-painting in Classical Athens* (1992) is the culmination of a lifetime's devotion to the study of Athenian vase-painting in the sixth, fifth and fourth centuries: black-figure, red-figure and white-ground. It is in a sense an account of the subject that expands, explains and deepens an early study that Beazley himself had published in 1918, *Attic Red-figured Vases in American Museums*. But Martin's book was much fuller and incorporated the vastly enlarged understanding that he himself had helped to bring about.

Martin's contribution to our understanding of Greek vase-painting covered all major aspects of the subject. His expert eye sorted out the attribution of old and new material; he wrestled with the problem of the meaning of the word *epoiesen* (= 'made') and on what occasions it could count as a personal 'signature' and when it might refer to the workshop as a whole. His reading of classical literature gave him a wide understanding of Greek myths and he was able to make subtle connections between the stories in the texts and the images the vases carried—Europa, Sarpedon, Troilos, Talos, Kyknos and many others. Similarly, his desire to recreate the monumental paintings that are all lost took him to a close reading of Pausanias. He kept abreast of new papyrus publications, mainly of archaic poetry, and he threaded the fragmentary narratives in Stesichoros and Ibykos with the vase-paintings that illustrate the same themes. The powerful fragment of Archilochos (PColon 7511) moved him to produce his own verse translation.

The 1990s were difficult years for Martin, and also for Louise. In 1994 Martin contracted Guillain-Barré Syndrome, a painful inflammation of the nervous system. Martin joked that GBS was usually known as GBH, and there is no doubt about the harm it did him. There were times when he despaired of his life and of his ability, or indeed his wish, to resist the disease. A few years later he was struck by myasthenia gravis, and the battle began again. Louise nursed him through those dark days and nights and furnished him with loving care and attention. However, these years were not all full of gloom. He was cheered by a new pastime: watching films on video or TV, particular favourites being Claude Berri's 'Le maître d'école' and 'When Harry met Sally', and visits from old students and colleagues were tiring but uplifting. When his health allowed, Martin and Louise recuperated by taking cruises, some to the far north; on one of these they toured St Petersburg, and Martin was at last able to see on display the splendid collection of Greek vases that during the nineteenth century the Hermitage had bought from Italian collectors—a late view of pottery that he had written about unseen. A particularly nostalgic cruise to Greece in 1994 found Martin returning to Perachora which he had first visited more than sixty years earlier.

Martin was elected a Fellow of the British Academy in 1967, and other honours were to follow: in 1978 he was made an Hon. D.Litt. at Queen's University, Belfast; in 1980 both University College, London, and Lincoln College, Oxford, elected him an Honorary Fellow. In 1985 he was made an Honorary Member of the Archaeological Institute of America, and two years later Trinity College, Cambridge, elected him an Honorary Fellow (this rise to 'Olympian heights' would have especially pleased his father). The same year he was awarded the Kenyon Medal by the British Academy.

Martin's reading of poetry was wide and comprehensive: Dante, Icelandic sagas, Chinese stories, and from his teenage years his own poetry testified to his need to express his feelings and thoughts in sensitive

language and showed how he loved and respected words. The volumes
that were published in book form (*Crooked Connections* (1970), *For
Rachel* (1972), *A Hot Bath at Bedtime* (1977), *The Sleeping Beauty's
Prince* (1977)) contain the poems that 'satisfy me enough to make me
want to preserve them' and are written in a personal style on private and
public themes, with a few translations. (Many of his published and
unpublished poems are available on a handsome website compiled by
Stephen Robertson and his son: http://rtnl.org.uk/now_and_then). The
title poem of one collection, 'A Hot Bath at Bedtime', is given the alternative title of 'The Necessity of Purgatory' and expresses his humanist
stance.

> Heaven I don't covet.
> Timeless nothing's enough.
> I feel so dirty though.
> I should like to believe God
> will have me on the mat
> to tell Him and myself
> everywhere I went wrong.
> Then, all the dirt out,
> admit me to the furnace.
> After that, nothing.

Martin was a man of personal gentleness and intellectual acuity. The
modern world moved too fast for him. He was inexpert in the simplest
technology; the typewriter did not work in the way he wished, the carriage
return was an unknown luxury and many was the time that the typed line
continued beyond its allotted span. His handwriting was notable for its
illegibility—he was one of those academics whose penmanship defies
their own attempts at decipherment.

In 1989 Martin compiled an obituary for the *Proceedings of the
British Academy* of the life of his friend Bernard Ashmole who had died
the previous year and under whose aegis his own working career had truly
started. In the first paragraph he writes of him as 'always himself, and it
was a very good self to be'. A fitting tribute to repeat for Martin himself.
He died on 26 December 2004.

BRIAN A. SPARKES
University of Southampton

Note. I am particularly grateful to Martin's wife, Louise, and to his children, especially Lucy and Stephen, for the assistance they have afforded me in the preparation of this obituary. It was also helpful to have the opportunity to watch an interview of Martin recounting his life, filmed by members of his family in 1995. I also received support and advice from John Boardman, Sue Boothby, Eric Handley, Sybille Haynes, Jody Maxmin and Dyfri Williams. The Commemoration held on 19 April 2005 in the Institute of Archaeology at University College, London, provided fresh help and insight.

Publications

There follows a list of Martin Robertson's published writings that complete the list compiled by Jody Maxmin and published in his Festschrift, *The Eye of Greece: Studies in the Art of Athens*, edited by Donna Kurtz and Brian Sparkes (Cambridge, 1982), pp. 183–8.

1979:
Review of G. B. Waywell, *The Free-Standing Sculptures of the Mausoleum at Halicarnassus* (BMP, 1978) in *The Burlington Magazine*, 121, 182–3.
1981:
'Euphronios at the Getty' in *The J. Paul Getty Museum Journal*, 9, 23–34.
'Kition: the Attic black-figure and red-figure pottery' in V. Karageorghis *et al.*, *Excavations at Kition IV: the non-Cypriote Pottery* (Cyprus: Department of Antiquities), pp. 51–74.
1982:
'Beazley's use of terms' in *Beazley Addenda*, compiled by L. Burn and R. Glynn (Oxford, Oxford University Press for The British Academy), pp. xi–xviii.
'Lekythion and Autolekythos' in *The Journal of Hellenic Studies*, 102, 234.
'A red-figure krater: South Italian or Etruscan' in *Oxford Journal of Archaeology*, 1, 179–85.
'Early Greek Mosaic' in *Macedonia and Greece in Late Classical and Early Hellenistic Times* (*Studies in the History of Art, 10*, National Gallery of Art, Washington), pp. 241–9.
'Le arti in Magna Grecia' in *Megale Hellas, nome e immagine, Atti del ventunesimo convegno di studi sulla Magna Graecia, Taranto, 2–5 ottobre 1981* (Taranto: Istituto per la Storia e l'Archaeologia della Magna Grecia), pp. 187–203.
'Le arti in Magna Grecia' in *Magna Graecia*, 17 (Jan.–Feb. 1982), 1–6 (a reprint of the previous with some illustrations).
1983:
'Fragments of a dinos and a cup fragment by the Kleophrades Painter' in *Occasional Papers on Antiquities 1, Greek Vases 1* (The J. Paul Getty Museum), pp. 51–4.
'The Berlin Painter at the Getty Museum and Some Others' in *Occasional Papers on Antiquities 1, Greek Vases 1* (The J. Paul Getty Museum), pp. 55–72.
1984:
'The South Metopes: Theseus and Daidalos' in E. Berger (ed.), *Parthenon-Kongress Basel* (Mainz), pp. 206–8.

1985:
'Beazley and Attic vase-painting' in D. Kurtz (ed.), *Beazley and Oxford* (Oxford, Oxford University Committee for Archaeology, Monograph No. 10), pp. 19–30.
1986:
'Two Pelikai by the Pan Painter' in *Occasional Papers on Antiquities 2, Greek Vases 3* (The J. Paul Getty Museum), pp. 71–90.
1987:
Catalogue of the Greek, Etruscan and Roman Vases in the Lady Lever Art Gallery, Port Sunlight (published for the National Museums and Galleries on Merseyside by Liverpool University Press).
'The state of Attic vase-painting in the mid sixth century' in M. True (ed.), *Papers on the Amasis Painter and his World* (Malibu, The J Paul Getty Museum), pp. 13–28.
1988:
'Sarpedon brought home' in J. H. Betts, J. T. Hooker and J. R. Green (eds.), *Studies in Honour of T. B. L. Webster 2* (Bristol), pp. 109–120.
'Corn and Wine on a Vase by the Pan Painter' in *Praktika tou XII Diethnous Synedriou Klasikes Archaiologias, Athens 4–10 September 1983*, Vol. 2, pp. 186–92.
(with Martha Ohly-Dumm) 'Aigina, Aphaia-Tempel XII. Archaic marble sculptures other than architectural' in *Archäologischer Anzeiger*, pp. 405–21.
1989:
'Bernard Ashmole 1894–1988' in *Proceedings of the British Academy*, 75, 313–28.
1990:
'Troilos and Polyxene: Notes on a changing legend' in J. P. Descoeudres (ed.), *Eumousia, Ceramic and Iconographic Studies in honour of Alexander Cambitoglou* (*Mediterranean Archaeology* Supplement 1), pp. 63–70.
'Beazley's use of terms' in *Beazley Addenda* (2nd edn.) compiled by T. H. Carpenter with T. Mannack and M. Mendonca (Oxford, Oxford University Press for The British Academy), pp. xii–xx.
1991:
'A fragmentary phiale by Douris' in *Occasional Papers on Antiquities 7, Greek Vases 5* (The J. Paul Getty Museum), pp. 75–98.
'Adopting an approach. 1' in T. Rasmussen and N. Spivey (eds.), *Looking at Greek Vases* (Cambridge), pp. 1–12.
'The Pioneers in Context' in I. Wehgartner (ed.), *Euphronios und Seine Zeit, Kolloquium in Berlin 19.20 April 1991* (Berlin: Staatliche Museen zu Berlin, Antikensammlung), pp. 132–9.
1992:
The Art of Vase-painting in Classical Athens (Cambridge).
'Europa and others: nostalgia in late fifth century Athenian vase-painting' in H. Froning, T. Hölscher and H. Mielsch (eds.), *Kotinos, Festschrift für Erika Simon* (Mainz), pp. 237–40.
1993:
'What is "Hellenistic" about Hellenistic Art?' in P. Green (ed.), *Hellenistic History and Culture* (Berkeley), pp. 67–110.
1995:
'Menelaus and Helen at Troy' in J. B. Carter and S. P. Morris (eds.), *The Ages of Homer: a Tribute to Emily Townsend Vermeule* (Austin), pp. 431–6.

1998:

'A note on Epiktetos and Douris' in G. Capecchi *et al.* (eds.), *In Memoria di Enrico Paribeni* (Rome), pp. 363–6.

2000:

'Thoughts on the Marsyas Painter and his Panathenaics' in G. R. Tsetskhladze, A. J. N. W Prag and A. M. Snodgrass, *Periplous, Papers on Classical Art and Archaeology presented to Sir John Boardman* (London), p. 244.

2002:

'Victoria Domestica' in A. J. Clark and J. Gaunt (eds.), with B. Gilman, *Essays in Honor of Dietrich von Bothmer* (Amsterdam, Allard Pierson Museum), p. 283.

CONRAD RUSSELL   *Derry Moore*

Conrad Sebastian Robert Russell
1937–2004

CONRAD RUSSELL, THE FIFTH EARL RUSSELL, historian of sixteenth and seventeenth-century Britain, was born on 15 April 1937. He was the younger son of the mathematician, philosopher, political activist and Nobel prize winner Bertrand Russell, OM, FRS. In 1931 Bertrand became the third Earl Russell, inheriting the title created in 1861 for his grandfather Lord John Russell, proponent of the 1832 Great Reform Act and twice prime minister. Bertrand was an admirer of the novelist Joseph Conrad, and in 1921 wrote to him to ask permission to name his first son John Conrad. The author died in 1924, but Russell also gave the name to his second son, intending that (unlike John) he should be known by it. Conrad's mother was Bertrand's third wife, the striking redhead Patricia Spence, always known as 'Peter', an Oxford undergraduate hired originally as a summer holiday governess who later became Bertrand's secretary. They married in January 1936, after Bertrand and his second wife, the feminist Dora Black, concluded an acrimonious divorce triggered by his leaving her for Peter in 1932. Peter was still in her twenties, while Bertrand was already 64. Conrad was born in April 1937 and spent his first year in Kidlington near Oxford, where his father told at least one visitor, Lady Constance Malleson (the actress Colette O'Niel), that the baby was 'the spitting image of my grandmother Stanley' [of Alderley].[1]

In autumn 1938 Conrad and his parents moved to the University of Chicago where Bertrand had been offered a one-year professorship. Subsequently they moved to the University College of Los Angeles,

---

[1] Ray Monk, *Bertrand Russell, The Spirit of Solitude* (London, 1996), p. 611; Ronald Clark, *The Life of Bertrand Russell* (London, 1975), pp. 459, 463.

Proceedings of the British Academy, **138**, 339–359. © The British Academy 2006.

together with John and Kate, the much older children of Bertrand's second marriage, both educated at American universities. Some of their time
in California was idyllic, but problems arose with the president of UCLA
and they moved on to City College of New York. The college found itself
bitterly attacked for appointing a notorious atheist, and the post was
withdrawn. Bertrand was saved from destitution by the offer of a lectureship at the Barnes Foundation, but this too went wrong. To American
eyes, Bertrand was cold and aloof while Peter was prickly, insisting on
being addressed as Lady Russell although her husband did not use his
title. Feeling snubbed, Dr Albert Barnes withdrew the post, and although
Bertrand successfully brought suit for breach of contract, for a time the
family lived in isolation in a primitive three-roomed cottage with barely
enough money for basic sustenance.

These upheavals put the Russells' already uneven marriage under considerable strain, especially as they were both homesick and worried about
the situation in wartime England. However, Bertrand delighted in his son.
'Conrad is the joy of our lives, partly by his merits partly because he
doesn't know there is a war on', he wrote in December 1939. Photographs
taken in 1940 show a fair-haired, sturdy little boy laughing and holding
his parents' hands as they stroll around Los Angeles. Playing with his
model train set, Conrad's concentrated focus on the track is already
evocative of his expression in adulthood. His mis-pronunciation "diddy"
instead of Daddy became the family term for Bertrand. In 1941 in
Pennsylvania, Bertrand described him as 'very happy to be in the country, where he can wander about freely', adding in 1943 that 'Conrad flour-
ishes exceedingly, he is very tall, very healthy and very intelligent'. Yet
problems were beginning to emerge: 'Conrad gets into trouble with other
children for speaking English instead of American and is worried by
American nationalism which is very pervasive.'[2] In 1944, Bertrand
accepted a five-year fellowship at Trinity College, Cambridge, and crossed
the Atlantic on a Liberty ship, while his wife and son returned on the
overcrowded *Queen Mary*. After a difficult period when the only accommodation available for Peter and Conrad was a squalid boarding-house,
Bertrand bought a property in Babraham Road, filling it with unwieldy
furniture acquired earlier from Wittgenstein. The Cambridge ladies did
not call. They had encountered the same ostracism in Kidlington: dons'

---

[2] See photographs 40–2, reproduced in Clark, *Russell*. Nicholas Griffin (ed.), *Selected Letters of Bertrand Russell: The Public Years 1914–1970* (London and New York, 2001), pp. 369, 380, 387, 395–6.

wives did not consider them respectable. Unsurprisingly, Peter hated Cambridge, but Conrad enjoyed his mixed day-school and fell in love with the architecture. 'He gave the Master his considered opinion of the college Library (built by Wren!)' reported Bertrand.

Throughout Conrad's early years the influence of his father was immense, even overpowering. Bertrand could be a remote husband and father, and his study was out of bounds to everyone. 'This rule was so sacred', Conrad remembered, 'that I did not venture to break in until I was eight. When I went in, with my heart in my mouth, my father was covering pages with an endless succession of mathematical symbols. When the door opened he simply continued working and, after what seemed an age, I withdrew crestfallen wondering whether he had ever known that I had been in the room.'[3] However, Bertrand treated the boy as an equal whose ideas deserved attention. He taught him precision of thought and language, and from this rigorous parental training, Conrad emerged as someone who enjoyed discussion and was always ready to give careful consideration to any reasonable viewpoint.

The Russells' marriage deteriorated further and in the winter of 1946 Peter attempted suicide. Gradually she recovered and they spent a family summer in North Wales, purchasing a house near Ffestiniog. 'This place is perfect for Conrad who has learned to swim and dive and is practising rock-climbing', enthused Bertrand. A neighbour and close friend, the writer Rupert Crawshay-Williams, observed Conrad enjoying his own skill in pronouncing lengthy Welsh place-names: 'he is the perfect intellectual's son: enormous and cherished vocabulary'. Conrad quickly picked up new ideas. He listened to the grown-ups describing an experiment on behavioural conditioning. A pike (a voracious eater of minnows) is separated from them by a glass plate inserted into his tank, against which he bangs in vain. When the glass is removed, the minnows come within reach but the pike does nothing. Conrad immediately exclaimed, 'The minnows had stopped being eatables and become bump-my-noses.' Another neighbour, Michael Burn, writer and journalist on *The Times,* overheard what he characterised as 'Conrad's gift for a dismissive truth'. An admirer of Bertrand Russell arrived to pay tribute, and found the child digging in the sandpit. 'What are you doing, my little man?' the

[3] Clark, *Russell*, pp. 490–1: Griffin, *Selected Letters*, p. 404; *The Autobiography of Bertrand Russell 1944–67*, vol. 3 (London, 1969), pp. 15–16.

visitor enquired well-meaningly. 'I am minding my own business', came the withering reply.[4]

Conrad went to Dartington Hall as a boarder in autumn 1946, but did not enjoy it. At home the situation did not improve, and by late March 1949 Peter was in the London Clinic. In April, Bertrand and Conrad were invited by friends to stay in Taormina, Sicily, and went off without her. Peter turned up unexpectedly, and an immense upheaval followed, as she suspected Bertrand of reviving his old affair with Colette O'Niel. Peter woke Conrad up one morning and abruptly told him she was leaving by taxi and never wished to see Bertrand again. Conrad and his father travelled home a week later, but the family crisis left him traumatised. Bertrand hoped Conrad was growing calmer, but there were further incidents in which the boy demanded an apology from Colette. 'He is inclined to hysteria', wrote Bertrand. Conrad was living with his mother, fearful that she might again attempt suicide, but he spent a final summer holiday with Bertrand in Wales in 1949. Well into his adult life, Conrad struggled with a misplaced but heavy sense of guilt that he had been asleep and hence not quick enough to prevent Peter's furious departure from Taormina. He could do little for at least the first hour of every morning, feeling haunted by the final scenes of his parents' marriage. Bertrand regretted the damage. 'The worry, weariness and disgust of the sordid quarrel with Peter, and the terrible injury to Conrad, have left me half-dead emotionally', he wrote shortly afterwards. The Ffestiniog house legally belonged to Peter, who sold it. Bertrand was made OM in 1949 and was awarded the Nobel prize for literature in 1950. By November 1952 the divorce from Peter was finalised, and she gained custody of Conrad, who had won a King's scholarship at Eton in autumn 1950. 'I do not see him' wrote Bertrand sadly, although he continued to pay for Conrad's education and holidays.[5]

Initially Conrad was not socially at ease at Eton. His father was an earl, but the descendants of Lord John Russell had none of the wealth of the dukes of Bedford and his unconventional upbringing distanced him from upper-class society. In his last term, autumn 1954, he was Keeper of the College Wall (captain of the college scholars in the Eton wall game), which gave him some gratifying cachet. At Eton he acquired his lifelong

[4] Griffin, *Selected Letters*, p. 416; Rupert Crawshay-Williams, *Russell Remembered* (Oxford, 1970), pp. 35–6. I am grateful to Michael Burn for personal correspondence.
[5] *Autobiography of Bertrand Russell* (vol. 3), pp. 50, 71. Russell wholly omitted the Taormina crisis from his autobiography but it can be reconstructed from his letters. Griffin, *Selected Letters*, pp. 433–4, 438–40, 443, 471.

love of cricket, cited as his recreation in *Who's Who*, together with swimming, enjoyed originally in Wales. Conrad swam regularly until he was well into his sixties, both on holiday in the Mediterranean and in Hampstead Heath ponds. School holidays with his mother were stressful. In childhood, Bertrand had been terrified of his grandmother who warned him of hereditary madness in the Russell family, and Peter repeatedly told Conrad that Bertrand was mad. In 1954 his older half-brother John was diagnosed as schizophrenic and never fully recovered. As a result of all this upheaval, in his teenage years Conrad experienced periods of deep depression and perturbation.

In 1955 he went up to Merton College, Oxford, where he read Modern History under three inspiring tutors, Ralph Davis, Roger Highfield and John Roberts. He made many friends, and even played rugby in the Merton second XV, later remarking that it had been 'quite a shock' to find that people genuinely liked him. Joining the Labour party in 1956, he organised the Oxford contingent which went to the Trafalgar Square demonstration against Suez. He distributed a preliminary circular that instructed participants, 'Ties will be worn on this occasion, preferably Old Etonian'. He was a founder-member of the Oxford CND group, emulating Bertrand who early in 1958 became the national president. Conrad also campaigned with Paul Foot to allow women to join the Oxford Union, which endeared him to many female undergraduates. Tall, with bony features and a fine head of unruly hair, 'the Hon. Con' was a striking figure around the university.[6]

Conrad graduated with a First in Modern History in 1958, and undertook research into the early seventeenth century, but after two years he had not made much progress with the expected D.Phil. The lack of what was becoming the standard entry qualification for the academic profession had some long-term detrimental effects, but in autumn 1960 he was appointed as a lecturer at Bedford College, University of London. In 1962 he took his Oxford MA and also married Elizabeth Sanders, one of his students. Both of them delighted to tell the story of their engagement. Elizabeth was a beautiful and vivacious undergraduate with many admirers. Having on one occasion received two different proposals of marriage, she went in some confusion to consult her tutor. Conrad listened courteously. 'Oh', he said at the end, smoking thoughtfully for some time, 'I had rather hoped that you would marry *me*'. She accepted. Her practicality and sunny good temper complemented and ameliorated Conrad's intense

---

[6] Obituaries especially *The Independent*, 16 Oct. 2004, p. 56, and personal knowledge.

intellectualism and inability to cope with much of ordinary life—a trait perhaps passed on from Bertrand, famously unable even to make himself a cup of tea. However, in deference to the strict attitudes of the Principal of Bedford (the oldest women's college in the university, which did not accept male undergraduates until 1965) Elizabeth moved to Westfield College to complete her degree. Conrad thought this was splendid: she would have tutorials on late medieval history with May McKisack. The notably happy union with Elizabeth helped him to overcome the traumas of his early life. Aware of his profound emotional debt to his wife, he later listed 'uxoriousness' among his recreations. As he grew older Conrad was increasingly conscious, as he said, that theirs was the first marriage in the Russell family since 1864 to last 'till death do us part'.

Emboldened perhaps by settling into a profession, and encouraged by his marriage, Conrad moved to reconcile himself with his very elderly father. In 1952 Bertrand had married his fourth wife, the American Edith Finch, and in late 1955 they moved to Plas Penrhyn, a Regency house on the Portmeirion peninsula. In June 1967 Bertrand wrote to his daughter Kate, 'I got yesterday a letter from Conrad, saying he wants to make friends again, and I have sent a friendly answer.'[7] Conrad enjoyed visiting Plas Penrhyn, with its fine views of Snowdon, the estuary and the sea. He took Elizabeth to meet Bertrand and Edith there early in 1968, and later in May he made a two-sentence speech at Bertrand's 96th birthday party, celebrated with champagne and lots of caviar, a present from Russian admirers. Elizabeth was pregnant, so she remained in London, but Crawshay-Williams described a lively conversation. Bertrand produced a sociological query: when did it cease to be immoral to travel on a Sunday? 'Conrad's already very well-packed memory produced a beautifully relevant story, about the Warden of a Cambridge college who was approached in the 1890s by a travel agency wanting to arrange a Sunday excursion from London to the college. In his reply the Warden said: The Warden is convinced that your proposal is as unwelcome to the Almighty as it is to the Warden himself.' Conrad was present at his father's last birthday party in May 1969, a small family affair which included Elizabeth with Nicholas, age seven months, as the youngest guest, as Bertrand proudly recorded.[8] Conrad fondly recalled the times spent with

---

[7] Clark, *Russell*, p. 552; Griffin, *Selected Letters*, p. 612.
[8] Crawshay-Williams, *Russell Remembered*, pp. 153–4; Griffin, *Selected Letters*, p. 624; Ray Monk, *Bertrand Russell 1927–1970: The Ghost of Madness* (London, 2000), p. 499, erroneously dates Conrad's reconciliation with his father to Christmas 1968.

his father. 'I remember him reaching the top of Cnicht when he was 77 and I was 11, and our climbing powers were approximately equal, and I remember him at 95, swinging over the steps to the balcony, for the sheer delight of the view of Snowdon in the afternoon sun.' Visits to North Wales to see the friends he had made there continued long after Bertrand's death in February 1970.[9] The reconciliation with his adored but intimidating parent had been another great step in Conrad's search for self-stability, but it came at a high price. His mother cut him off completely and they ceased to be even on speaking terms.

The History department of Bedford College was housed in St John's Lodge, Regents Park, a handsome Regency villa, and on one occasion Conrad was appointed Fire and Safety Officer. His finest moment came when he personally tested the safety device installed to evacuate the upper floors. Slowly, the cigarette-smoking Conrad was lowered in a sling past the windows of colleagues (whose tutorials were inevitably disrupted as he hove into view), before coming gently to rest on the lawn. Elected as a Fellow of the Royal Historical Society in 1971, Conrad was promoted to a London University readership in 1974, and in the following year he became one of the convenors of the Tudor–Stuart seminar held at the University of London's Institute of Historical Research. This brought him into regular contact with Professor Joel Hurstfield, who had succeeded Sir John Neale as the senior convenor. Both Conrad and Elizabeth were great devotees of the IHR and never missed the Monday seminar. Elizabeth worked for a time as Hurstfield's research assistant, and she made the seminar a much friendlier place, introducing herself to postgraduates and visiting academics and then presenting them to senior members. In discussion, her astute but refreshingly straightforward questions encouraged others to speak up instead of cowering in the background. For historians in the colleges of London University, scattered across one of the world's largest cities, the logistical problems of meeting regularly to discuss their subject might prove insuperable without the IHR. As a result, the Monday seminar acquired immense intellectual significance for Conrad and many others.

In 1979 Conrad moved to Yale to succeed Professor Jack Hexter, who had made the university the leading American institution for the study of seventeenth-century British parliamentary history. The move did not prove wholly successful as the family found difficulty settling in. Their neighbourhood was unwelcoming, and the two boys Nicholas and John

[9] Clark, *Russell*, p. 50. Information in a private letter from Michael Burn.

experienced problems in transferring to the American educational system. Conrad was regarded by Yale undergraduates as a figure of notable English exoticism, although he also inspired some of them to go on to graduate work in his specialist field. One of them, Lori Anne Ferrell, recalls the terrifying treatment meted out to those who arrived late to class. Even in mid-sentence, Conrad would stop speaking, gaze at the offender and enquire in tones of great civility and concern whether the student 'had a course syllabus yet'—no matter how far into the academic year it was. Stories about him abounded. In part because of his distinctive accent and bearing, he was one of those singular teachers about whom students become obsessed. Most of the colourful anecdotes were entirely fabricated, as Professor Ferrell discovered when, some years later, she asked Conrad about them.[10] Yet they arose from an undergraduate appreciation of his relentless focus on ideas, his Russell background and his outstanding academic abilities.

Conrad particularly valued the facilities of the Yale Center for Parliamentary History, with its wealth of microfilm and transcripts of manuscripts, especially the unrivalled collection of unpublished parliamentary diaries. Researchers could compare different accounts of crucial debates without the toil and expense of going round scattered English repositories and transcribing each diary in turn. His five years of reading at the Center were vital in laying the foundations for much of his later work, and he formed a high regard for colleagues there such as Dr Maija Jansson and Dr William Bidwell, who were generous with their vast expertise. He found other aspects of American society less congenial, not least the food, which he characterised as 'insubstantial'. Conrad's tastes were for well-cooked meat, two vegetables (preferably soggy) and roast potatoes swimming in fat. He loved dishes such as toad in the hole and apple crumble and could not abide pasta or salads. He smoked throughout meals and took several teaspoonfuls of white sugar in his coffee. It was a mystery to his friends that despite this dreadful diet he never put on any weight.

After five years at Yale, Conrad returned to Britain in 1984, succeeding his old friend Joel Hurstfield in the Astor Professorship of British History at University College, London. He gave an outstanding inaugural lecture in March 1985, entitled 'The British problem and the English

---

[10] Private correspondence with Professor Lori Anne Ferrell of Claremont Graduate University, California.

civil war', which indicated the direction in which his ideas were moving.[11] Conrad was a well-known figure in the wider university. At the London History Board's annual meeting to scrutinise Finals papers, he would make achingly funny suggestions for the more precise rewording of questions, revealing hitherto-unsuspected *doubles entendres* while looking both innocent and inscrutable throughout the discussion. At the Final Examiners' meeting, he scrupulously explained how he had arrived at his own marks (which were often at variance with those of his co-examiners). He spoke regularly at the History Faculty Board, once proposing that instead of devising new courses, we should simply continue to teach what we already knew, until we had all completed the various books and articles on which we were currently engaged. Only after that, would it be worth our while to turn to 'novelties'. There was a strong sense that Conrad was aware that this admirable proposal would not find favour with higher authority. Meanwhile, his academic reputation was growing and he was invited to deliver the Ford Lectures at Oxford in the winter of 1988. They were gratifyingly well-attended and subsequently published with a dedication to the Warden and Fellows of Merton, whose hospitality Conrad had enjoyed during his time as Ford's Lecturer.[12] Closer to home, the 1980s saw many changes in the organisation of London University, and he was strongly opposed to moves breaking up the traditional federal structure of collaborative teaching and examining. This caused friction at University College, and in 1990 Conrad transferred to King's College as Professor of British History. He delivered another incisive inaugural lecture in 1991, 'The Scottish party in English Parliaments, 1640–42, or the myth of the English Revolution', later published in *Historical Research*. He was also elected a Fellow of the British Academy in 1991 and remained at King's until his retirement in 2002, when he became a Visiting Professor in the department.

After returning from Yale, Conrad was delighted to be back in the Institute of Historical Research. For research students and junior colleagues, the Tudor–Stuart seminar with Conrad at its head played a formative role in their intellectual development. Discussions repeatedly underscored the value of archival research. Frequently Conrad would bring out the importance of a crucial reference in a way that its discoverer had not fully appreciated. He had a remarkable memory and could

---

[11] Reprinted in Conrad Russell, *Unrevolutionary England 1603–1642* (London, 1990), pp. 231–52.

[12] Conrad Russell, *The Causes of the English Civil War* (Oxford, 1990).

quote at length from other documents to give point and context to new material. His enthusiasm was contagious. History was not only an academic pursuit of great rigour, but also a pleasure shared between like-minded friends. In lighter moments Conrad might be moved to perform renditions of noted seventeenth-century orators: Sir Edward Coke made some memorable guest appearances. Members of the seminar also found that Conrad read not merely for his own research but also for theirs. Many of us cherish a sheaf of notecards in his spiky handwriting offering choice morsels from archives as diverse as the Phelips MSS in the Somerset Record Office and the Carreg-lwyd MSS in the National Library of Wales. Conrad particularly enjoyed the summer term, when steadily increasing numbers of friends from North American universities would trickle across the Atlantic to appear in the IHR common room for tea before joining in the seminar. In this way, his own years at Yale, although relatively brief, played an important part in supporting a wide circle of Anglo-American historians who exchanged ideas and insights. There were amicable disagreements, but those whose research was influenced by their visits to London paid tribute to the impact of encountering Conrad's work and his generosity in sharing his knowledge.

Unfailingly courteous to seminar guests, Conrad was nevertheless a formidable presence. His increasingly crumpled appearance was at odds with his aristocratic profile and distinguished stoop. Speakers who over-ran their time found, alarmingly, that he would slowly pull out his heavy silver pocket watch (inherited from Bertrand) and silently slide it across the table towards them. Occasionally his comments were disconcertingly opaque, obliging junior convenors to feign incomprehension in order to elicit a specific point the speaker could attempt to answer. We also learned to decode. After a thin paper, Conrad would opine that it was very interesting but he would require more evidence. After a bad paper, he would require *much* more evidence. Good papers got a word of thanks, an opening question, and then an immediate invitation to the seminar to plunge into detailed discussion which lasted three-quarters of an hour. Conrad also thought that the conversation over drinks and dinner afterwards was a valuable aspect of academic enquiry, and encouraged people not to rush away. Since otherwise he was not particularly sociable, going out to seminar dinners was probably the only way most historians came to know him personally. Conversation tended to focus on his current research project, to the exclusion of other subjects. Once, returning from California at the beginning of the autumn term, I related how I had found myself caught up in a serious earthquake. After a moment of mild interest Conrad deflected discussion to the events of autumn 1641, which to him were far more immediate. The real pleasure for the dinner party was in seeing how his mind worked, how he isolated key problems, and how he would probe various possibilities until he arrived at a historical solution which satisfied him. He dedicated his last great book, *The Fall of the British Monarchies 1637–1642*, 'To the Members, Past, Present, and Future, of the Tudor and Stuart Seminar at the Institute of Historical Research' and in the preface thanked the current members, who had 'supplied some forty pairs of spectacles to peruse almost every problem' encountered in his research and writing.[13] The unpretentious retirement dinner that the seminar held in the local Spaghetti House (Elizabeth's choice) in his honour in June 2002 was, he said, one of the proudest events of his life. The speaker that evening was Professor Linda Levy Peck of George Washington University, then President of the North American Conference on British Studies, who began her paper by paying tribute to Conrad's Anglo-American career. Former members of the seminar came from far and wide, both to drink his health and to thank him for the unforgettable stimulus of participating in discussions.

Throughout his academic career, Conrad was a devoted tutor and his students felt the vibrancy of engaging directly with a historian who was posing new questions in his own field. Dr Jacqueline Eales came up to Bedford College in 1972. She found Conrad attentive to the youthful ideas she floated, but also firm in insisting on proof as well as fashionable theories. In a kindly manner he would intone, 'An interesting idea. I have been looking for the evidence for that for some time. Do let me know when you find it.'[14] Postgraduate students sensed his intense motivation, as he communicated a sense of excitement about the subject. They learned that there were big historical questions still awaiting an answer, and that their own archival research might provide the key to the problem. Conrad was also attentive to the need for pastoral care in the History departments in which he taught. On his retirement, the head of department, Dr Arthur Burns, paid tribute to his efforts for King's students as a whole. He was never too busy to offer good advice and practical assistance on a whole range of student welfare issues.[15] He often took time to have lunch with a student who wanted to talk. In 1993 he came to the defence of Austin Donnellan, an undergraduate in the King's History

---

[13] Conrad Russell, *The Fall of the British Monarchies 1637–1642* (Oxford, 1991), pp. ix–x.
[14] *The Times*, 3 Dec. 2004, 'Lives Remembered', p. 63.
[15] *Comment* (the magazine of King's College, London), Nov. 2004, p. 15.

department accused of 'date rape' by a fellow-student. The college authorities (acting, it must be said, in accordance with the current received wisdom on handling these contentious matters) urged Donnellan to withdraw from his degree course, thereby tacitly admitting guilt. Instead Conrad took Donnellan's side against a college tribunal, encouraging him to fight for his innocence. The case went to the Old Bailey and Donnellan was acquitted. Conrad himself became something of a celebrity; the donnish, chain-smoking nobleman was widely quoted in the press when he made pertinent comments about the effects of the sexual revolution. 'When I was an undergraduate I think women could afford to say "No" when they meant "Yes". Now they can't. The more freedom a woman has, the plainer her sexual signalling has got to be.' Equally characteristic was his gently astringent aside, 'I think a woman who takes all her clothes off and gets into a man's bed is perhaps . . . unwise.'[16]

The Donnellan case was very public, but much of his good work with students was done out of the limelight. Conrad summed up his philosophy in a passage entitled 'The advice that I would give to the young', originally published in December 2003. It carries the echo of his speaking voice.

> If one is asked to play Polonius, it is best to begin where he did: 'To thine own self be true'. Your right to self-respect comes from being a human being: take it for granted and enjoy it. Being you is the only thing at which you will always be the best in the world. What you think is the only thing about which you will always know more than anyone else. You are the best judge of what you want— but good judges think twice. Remember you always look better than you do in the mirror. Expressions make faces, and a woman looking in the mirror is looking for faults. The face you see will be far less warm and attractive than the face seen by anybody that you like. If you do badly in an examination, remember that, even if the examiner was flawless, it was only your performance on the day. Exams are a cup-tie, and the winner one day may not be the winner another. Never let them write you off, and never write yourself off.[17]

Conrad must have said that before, dozens of times, to students disappointed with their examination results.

If we turn to the Russell historical oeuvre, it is immediately apparent that it was very concentrated in its range of interests. As a postgraduate, Conrad became dissatisfied with the usual list of 'The causes of the English Civil War', because, as he later commented, 'They did not appear

---

[16] Obituary in the *Daily Telegraph*, 15 Oct. 2004, p. 29.
[17] The passage, taken from *Country Life*, Dec. 2003, was reprinted on p. 13 of the programme for the Service of Thanksgiving for the Life and Work of Professor the Earl Russell, held at St Margaret's Westminster on 14 June 2005, and read by Susan Kramer, MP.

to be anchored by any logical link with the events which led up to it.' He added, 'It took me thirty years to come to terms with this insight.'[18] In the 1960s he wrote articles on aspects of the political and legal history of the period which struck him as problematical. Among them 'The Ship Money judgements of Bramston and Davenport' and 'The theory of treason in the trial of Strafford' were widely cited.[19] In 1971 he published his first book, *The Crisis of Parliaments: English History 1509–1660*, in the 'Short Oxford History of the Modern World' series.[20] It achieved considerable success as a thought-provoking university text book, as well as appealing to the general reader. More articles followed, one of them contributed to a volume edited by Conrad and entitled *The Origins of the English Civil War*. 'Parliament and the King's finances' challengingly argued that 'we have over-rated both the powers and the ambitions of early seventeenth-century parliaments', an insight which underlay all Conrad's later work. The volume was well received since it showcased much current research. 'The New Look has arrived', opined Sir Geoffrey Elton.[21] In 1976 the iconoclastic 'Parliamentary History in Perspective, 1603–1629' appeared in the journal *History*, attacking any notion of historical inevitability in the outbreak of civil war. Instead, Conrad argued that in the early seventeenth century, Parliament was not yet a powerful institution, but rather an irregular event. There was no division into two clearly defined 'sides', Crown and Opposition, but a fluid political scene in which men divided unpredictably according to the specific issue under debate, without prior ideological or party commitments. So, as late as 1629 and even 1637, there was no reason to assume that war would be the outcome of political disagreement.

The book that really made Conrad's name was his brilliant 1979 monograph, *Parliaments and English Politics 1621–1629*. 'Revisionism', as it became known by the late 1970s, was a very disparate phenomenon, advanced by a group of historians who did not all agree. It was not so much a programme as a collection of negative propositions. Probably the most important was its rejection of any dialectical framework for history and consequently its suspicion of any 'clash of opposites', either economic or cultural, as the mechanism of change. In English political and

[18] From the web-site of the History Department, King's College, London, quoted in *Comment*, Nov. 2004, p. 15.

[19] *English Historical Review*, 77 (1962), 312–18; *EHR*, 80 (1965), 30–50.

[20] Conrad Russell, *The Crisis of Parliaments* (Oxford, 1971).

[21] Conrad Russell (ed.), *The Origins of the English Civil War* (London, 1973), p. 92; G. R. Elton, review of *Origins of the English Civil War* in *Historical Journal*, 17 (1974), 213–15.

parliamentary history, a pioneering Cambridge thesis of 1953 by J. N. Ball, on the parliamentary career of Sir John Eliot, was followed in 1978 by *Faction and Parliament*, a ground-breaking collection of essays (including one by Dr Ball) edited by Kevin Sharpe.[22] The exploration of similar themes by H. G. Koenigsberger and Sir John Elliott had long impressed Conrad by their emphasis on the concept of multiple monarchies and their problems, so relevant to the British experience in the early seventeenth century. Despite the undoubted differences, Conrad later wrote that 'all versions of revisionism, like all brands of whisky, enjoyed certain broad similarities'.[23] He particularly attacked the twin contentions that the explanation for the political crisis of the 1640s lay in long-term social and economic change, and that as a result, the breakdown of the English polity was both pre-determined and unavoidable. Conrad's points emerged from his detailed account of the parliaments of the 1620s, since he insisted that the search for causes or explanations, before establishing the story, was premature and pointless. The course of events was worthy of study in its own right, and vital in avoiding the dangers of hindsight. Few historians had appreciated the extent to which the steady discovery of additional primary sources was undermining the chronological history of England from 1603 to 1660 written by the great Victorian historian S. R. Gardiner, whose magisterial volumes were still regarded as the essential starting-point for research. Conrad embarked on the ambitious project of constructing a new political narrative. He also pointed to the significant fact that outside Westminster, where they formed part of the legislature, most members of the Lords and the Commons were hard-working members of their local or county executive. These day-to-day duties took up much more of their time than did their service in relatively brief parliamentary sessions. Such multi-faceted men could not easily be encased in the twin straitjackets of 'government' and 'opposition'. This perception allowed him to incorporate a full understanding of the pioneering regional and county studies that were preoccupying other historians such as Alan Everitt and John Morrill. In his preface Conrad paid tribute to Elizabeth, who 'evening after evening', had listened to his reading of his drafts: the final version owed 'as much to her questions as it does to my research'.[24] His conclusion was that as inflation eroded the value of the Crown's income, and as the costs of military action spiralled

---

[22] Conrad Russell, *Parliaments and English Politics 1621–1629* (Oxford, 1979); Kevin Sharpe (ed.), *Faction and Parliament: Essays on Early Stuart History* (Oxford, 1978).
[23] Russell, *Unrevolutionary England*, p. ix.
[24] Russell, *Parliaments and English Politics*, p. vi.

steadily upward, the localist outlook of most members of Parliament, in both Lords and Commons, made them unwilling and unable to comprehend the genuine problems faced by royal government, particularly in a period of widespread Continental warfare which might threaten English interests. This was the real 'functional breakdown' (a phrase borrowed from Gerald Aylmer), rather than the classic Whig explanation of a House of Commons aggressively defending English liberties or the neo-Marxist depiction of a class struggle inexorably leading to victory for the rising 'middling sort'.

After reworking the 1620s, Conrad spent the next twelve years tackling the 'Everest' as he described it, of the origins of the civil war. Three books resulted. His collected essays, *Unrevolutionary England 1603–1642* was published in 1990 and included articles written in the 1980s. It also brought to a wider readership 'The Catholic Wind', published originally in a collection of essays not widely noticed. This posited the imaginary scenario that James II had defeated William III in 1688, and explored typical historical 'explanations' for the victory. Provocatively, Conrad argued that 'James II . . . was always on a winning wicket', with Europe-wide trends, such as the decline of representative assemblies and the triumph of resurgent Counter-Reformation catholicism, uniting to make King James not a fugitive would-be absolutist, but 'the first of the Enlightened Despots'. It was all the more lively since Conrad's ancestor Edward Russell was one of the seven who had offered the throne to William in 1688. A *jeu d'esprit*, the piece nevertheless devastatingly demonstrated that once the historian knows the outcome, it is all too easy to excavate supposedly 'deep-seated' and 'long-term' forces.

Also published in 1990 was *The Causes of the English Civil War*, a revised version of the Ford Lectures. It outlined a structural analysis reaching back to the Henrician Reformation, emphasising how growing religious division, not merely between protestantism and catholicism but also between various branches of protestantism, steadily permeated political conflict. It described the difficulties of Stuart rule over multiple kingdoms, where every problem was exacerbated by increasingly inadequate royal revenues. In many ways the book offered some conclusions to the whole project of Conrad's research on the causes of political breakdown in the first half of the seventeenth century. Yet it is not easy to read, immensely allusive and suggestive rather than clearly constructed, with a sense that sometimes the author saw his argument as provisional and debatable rather than wholly convincing. It also revealed Conrad's relative lack of interest in areas such as cultural, intellectual and literary history, and the history of the court, which other scholars increasingly deployed to illuminate late Elizabethan and early Stuart society. More satisfactory was the magisterial account of *The Fall of the British Monarchies 1637–1642,* published in 1991. An extraordinary work of detailed research incorporating large amounts of new primary material, the book demonstrated Conrad's mastery of the day-by-day account, devoid of all hindsight. It also substantiated a new view of Charles I, already sketched in *The Causes of the English Civil War.* Instead of the cultivated, devout but ineffectual monarch of standard textbooks, here was an opinionated king at the centre of politics, an active protagonist in events, with a distinctive cluster of attitudes and personal characteristics (not least his devotion to his wife and children) that proved crucial in shaping outcomes. The book revealed how fruitfully Conrad had read the work of the new 'British' school of historians, including his friend Dr Jenny Wormald who particularly emphasised the unexpected impact of Scottish kingship and Scottish political ideas after 1603. The central theme was precisely what the title suggested: that it was the novel and perhaps insoluble problem of managing a multiple *British,* not solely English, monarchy that explained the outbreak of war in 1642. The Scots rebelled first, the Irish next, so the English were the last of Charles I's subjects to defy him. After 1637, the clash between Charles and the Scottish Covenanters destabilised the dynastic union established by James I in 1603, but perhaps more significantly, the outbreak of revolt in Ireland in late autumn 1641 destroyed the king's increasingly hopeful option of a dissolution of the Parliament. By summer 1641 Charles had achieved a nearly successful resolution of the political crisis which began in 1637, thereby winning many men back to his side: but the Irish revolt fractured the emerging consensus and provided the fatal catalyst of conflict. In this interpretation, the civil war might equally be seen as the result of an imperialistic attempt to enforce the political and religious hegemony of England within the British Isles, a theme going back to the early middle ages and continued by Oliver Cromwell. Perhaps most controversial was the claim made by Conrad at the outset, that 'England in 1637 was a country in working order . . . There is very little evidence in 1637 that any significant body of the King's subjects would have wanted to resort to revolution if it had been a practical possibility.'[25] Although critics considered that this approach greatly underestimated the tensions already present within Jacobean and Caroline England, the central argument was

[25] Russell, *The Fall of the British Monarchies,* pp. 1–2.

irrefutable: that it was impossible to explain the events leading up to the outbreak of war if they were seen within an enclosed, wholly English context.

Conrad continued to publish scholarly articles until 2002, the year of his retirement, which was also the year of his festschrift, *Politics, Religion and Popularity,* edited by Thomas Cogswell, Richard Cust and Peter Lake, all of them members of the IHR Tudor–Stuart seminar. In the preface they expressed their appreciation of the magnitude of Conrad's contribution, 'of the scope, ambition and achievement of the intellectual project on which he has been engaged, and which he has in different ways shared with us . . . even where we take issue with him, his work is an unerring guide to where the important issues and questions really are'.[26] With an introductory survey of Conrad's work followed by twelve essays, the book's contents ranged from court masques and sermons under James I, through the cultural and religious impact of visits to London enjoyed by country members of the Commons, to popular preaching and petitioning in the years just before 1642. Conrad was exceptionally moved by this volume which, he said, pleased him as much if not more than any of his own publications. As contributors we felt that the honour was ours. Conrad's last academic work emerged with the publication of the *Oxford Dictionary of National Biography* in 2004. Four penetrating studies of leading seventeenth-century political figures, John Pym, John Hampden, Sir John Eliot and Francis Russell fourth earl of Bedford, displayed once again his mastery of the detailed politics of the period, while never losing a sense of the humanity, dignity and sometimes frailty and inadequacy, of those whose lives and concerns he so deeply understood.

In 1987, Conrad succeeded his half-brother John as the fifth Earl Russell. This led to a separate public career in which he resumed the political involvements of his younger days. As a Labour candidate he had contested South Paddington in the general election of 1966, and even considered giving up academic life and going into politics.[27] Thereafter, however, he became increasingly disenchanted with the party. In 1968 he was expected to stand as the Labour candidate for Mitcham and

[26] Thomas Cogswell, Richard Cust and Peter Lake (eds.), *Politics, Religion and Popularity: Early Stuart Essays in Honour of Conrad Russell* (Cambridge, 2002), p. viii. The volume also contains a valuable reference bibliography of the principal published writings of the honorand, compiled by Richard Cust and Elizabeth Russell.

[27] Professor Blair Worden kindly alerted me to a letter written by Dr Valerie Pearl on 16 Dec. 1966, among the papers of the late Lord Dacre (Hugh Trevor-Roper), relating a conversation in which Conrad told her that he intended in future to pursue a full-time political career.

Beddington, but decided against doing so, partly from pressure of academic work. The recent birth of his first child was also a consideration. Conrad admired Jeremy Thorpe, the leader of the Liberals, and during the election of 1974 he became convinced that British politics would never break free of its class-based slogans until the implementation of proportional representation. Only then, as he wrote later, could the British people 'stop looking for scapegoats and start looking for solutions'. Thorpe's party political broadcast on behalf of the Liberals persuaded Conrad to join the party. Consequently in 1987, on entering the Lords he went to the Liberal whips' office to offer his services,[28] and became Liberal (and later Liberal Democratic) spokesman for social security. Conrad acquired an encyclopaedic knowledge of the working of the social security system, housing benefit and other entitlements for individuals. He put this at the disposal of students and others who appealed to him for help, with great generosity and to very good effect. He mastered the complexities of welfare legislation and argued the cause of single parents, becoming an early critic of the Conservative government's Child Support Agency and foreseeing the inadequacies of its operations. He was also a strong supporter of women's refuges as essential in combating domestic violence. He brought his historical knowledge to bear on the Jobseekers' bill in 1995, pointing out that the legislative provision of a safety net derived from the Elizabethan Poor Law act of 1601, and not the Beveridge Plan. On another occasion he compared the practice of awarding peerages to businessmen who were substantial donors to political parties, to the corrupt sale of peerages in early Stuart England by James I and the Duke of Buckingham. He was a consistent champion of university students. Deeply distressed by the increase in student poverty, which he regarded as one of the most socially retrogressive trends of his lifetime, Conrad campaigned vigorously against the abolition of grants and their replacement by loans. He pointed to the adverse effects of top-up fees, and cited examples from personal knowledge of the paradox of undergraduates so tired by the long hours of work necessary to support themselves at university that they were unable to take full advantage of their expensive education. He also found time to write dozens of letters to the newspapers on these and other themes, and in 1993 published *Academic Freedom*, an attack on ill-conceived policies in higher education. He characterised them as 'a perpetual pressure to cut-price expansion, regardless of academic consequences', which inevitably undermined

---

[28] Michael White, *The Guardian*, 15 Oct. 2004, p. 31.

degree standards.[29] His last book, in 1999, was *An Intelligent Person's Guide to Liberalism*. He argued that the Liberals possessed the longest unbroken political traditions in the country, going back to his great-grandfather Lord John Russell, last of the Whigs. The book was well reviewed and sparked considerable public discussion.

By his sixties, Conrad seemed an increasingly eccentric figure, clad in a baggy old black suit and carrying his voluminous papers around London in supermarket plastic bags. He never mastered email or any other type of information technology, conducting his extensive correspondence by means of an elderly typewriter. On occasion he could be a worryingly erratic judge of people, both historians and politicians. Yet in the Lords he won great respect for his undeviating integrity and easily made friendships across party lines. He was critical of New Labour, and had a low opinion of Tony Blair whom he regarded as more or less a Tory, or even more disdainfully (quoting the spoof sermon in *Beyond the Fringe*) 'a *smooth* man'. In 1996 Conrad was chosen as the 'Highland Park'/*Spectator* Peer of the Year for his combination of learning and parliamentary skill, and he came top in his party when the elections to retain some hereditary peers in the Lords were held in 1999. He refused to defend the privileges of the 'hereditaries', but was committed to the Lords' role in scrutinising legislation and tempering the excesses of a government that could rely on a large majority in the Commons. He repeatedly opposed the growing use of broadly drafted 'skeleton bills' which governments could subsequently expand by regulation, a procedure which tended to reduce parliamentary debate to an irrelevance.[30] He served as president of the Electoral Reform Society and was a trustee of the John Stuart Mill Institute, as well as of the History of Parliament Trust. He was very conscious of his family's political inheritance. He drew the attention of visitors to Westminster to the statue of Lord John Russell in the lobby (where he often suggested his guests should meet him), and to the Victorian wall-painting of Lord Russell, condemned for treason by Charles II, bidding farewell to his stalwart wife Rachel. Serving in the Lords was another way in which Conrad reclaimed his Russell family background and his painful early years. He regarded himself as a champion of traditional Whig values, particularly the Whigs' detestation of abuses of power. He was an acknowledged expert on the history of the Upper House and frequently used historical quotations in his speeches.

[29] Conrad Russell, *Academic Freedom* (London, 1993), p. 107.
[30] Obituaries in *The Times* and *The Independent*.

Occasionally he lost his audience completely, but on form, he could be electrifying. On 4 May 2004, already ill, Conrad went to the Lords to fight against the asylum and immigration bill, in which he quoted the seventeenth-century Sir Thomas Wentworth's ringing denunciation, 'God deliver us from this arbitrary government.'[31] In the last year of his life, as a widower he found the House a comfort, almost a second family.

Sadly, Elizabeth suffered from cancer of the lung, which after an operation and a hopeful period of remission was followed by a fatal brain cancer in 2003. Her death left Conrad bereft, but gallantly, he attended the IHR Tudor–Stuart seminar on the evening of her funeral service. We stood in silence to honour her memory and share Conrad's grief. His already precarious health worsened; his emphysema increased until he was dependent on his oxygen inhaler, and he went into Middlesex Hospital on two occasions suffering from extreme breathlessness. His last academic appearance was at a conference jointly organised by King's College, London, and Somerset House in May 2004, to commemorate the four-hundredth anniversary of the peace treaty between England, Spain and Flanders signed at Somerset House in 1604. His paper, based on the French ambassadors' accounts, contained many flashes of the old brilliance. His last speech in the House of Lords was on 15 September, a three-minute intervention which deplored the English lack of interest in constitutional affairs.[32] It contained three historical references. Conrad died in hospital on 14 October 2004. The memorial service, held at St Margaret's Westminster on 14 June 2005, brought large numbers of historians, politicians, journalists and friends together to pay tribute. The Liberal Democrat shadow minister Baroness Hamwee recalled his cheery singing to other members of the party of a personally adapted song, 'Lloyd George *jailed* my father'.[33] Charles Kennedy, the Liberal Democrat party leader who attended the service, had already spoken to the press in praise of Conrad's contribution to the development of Liberalism in Britain, adding that he had found him 'a personal, political and intellectual rock of support'.[34] Dr David Starkey outlined Conrad's achievements as a historian and emphasised his kindness as a friend. The fund which Conrad founded to commemorate Elizabeth has been

---

[31] *The Guardian*, 15 Oct. 2004, p. 31.

[32] *The Independent*, 16 Oct. 2004, p. 56.

[33] Bertrand's unfounded and inflammatory suggestion that American troops would be used as strike-breakers in Britain led to a jail sentence in Brixton between May and September 1918. Clark, *Russell*, pp. 338–53.

[34] *The Guardian*, 15 Oct. 2004, p. 3.

relaunched as the Conrad and Elizabeth Russell Fund, and has become a general hardship fund for graduate students at the Institute of Historical Research, University of London. It is a fitting tribute to Conrad's achievements as a historian and to his lifelong concern for the welfare of young researchers in history.

PAULINE CROFT
Royal Holloway, University of London

Note. I am grateful for information and personal reminiscences from many friends and colleagues in the University of London and elsewhere. I thank the Library, Eton College, for helpfully responding to my queries about Conrad's schooldays. I have also drawn on the informative (but occasionally inaccurate) obituaries which appeared in *The Times*, 15 October 2004, *The Daily Telegraph*, 15 October 2004, *The Guardian*, 15 October 2004, *The Herald* (Glasgow), 16 October 2004, and *The Independent*, 16 October 2004.

ARNOLD TAYLOR   *Society of Antiquaries of London*

Arnold Joseph Taylor
1911–2002

ARNOLD TAYLOR, or Joe as he was known to some, was a medieval scholar, archaeologist and architectural historian, who spent his working career in the public service within the Ancient Monuments Inspectorate. An international expert on castles and, in particular, the authority on the North Wales castles of Edward I, he was not restricted in his interests in medieval buildings as a whole. Nor did Taylor study castles solely as monuments to medieval military architecture. He was fascinated by their construction, who designed and built them, where the materials and craftsmen came from, and how this side of the work was organised. To do this he combined study of the standing remains with intensive documentary research. There were two other main strands to his professional life; his wider career in the Ancient Monuments Inspectorate, first in the Office of Works and ultimately in the Department of the Environment, and second, his service to the Society of Antiquaries of London.

Arnold came from a long line of schoolmasters. Three generations of Taylors were consecutively headmasters of Sir Walter St John's Grammar School for Boys, Battersea, London. Arnold's father was in post from 1932 to 1946. His mother was also a teacher. Arnold was born on 24 July 1911 at the family home, 36 High Street, Battersea. This was reputedly within earshot of Bow Bells, and he was to remain a committed Londoner. He was particularly delighted to be made a Freeman of the City in 1959.

From 1922 to 1930 Arnold was educated at Merchant Taylors' School, at that time situated in the City of London, where matters historical were an early fascination for him. Together with fellow sixth-formers he contributed to *Merchant Taylors' School—its Origin, History and Present*

Proceedings of the British Academy, **138**, 363–381. © The British Academy 2006.

Surroundings (1929). His chapter was on 'The Priory of St. John, Clerkenwell, and the Order of the Hospital of St. John of Jerusalem in England'. He had already contributed to the school magazine, in the same year, on the Diary of Henry Machyn and on the Palace of Bridewell.[1] The following year (1929), there were short pieces on 'Merchant Taylors' and the Great Fire', and demonstrating his long-standing religious beliefs, a review of *Hymns and Prayers for Use at Merchant Taylors' School* and School Prayer Books.[2]

It was at Merchant Taylors' that Arnold met his lifelong friend, Reg Adams, who later accompanied him to St John's College, Oxford. Adams, indeed, collaborated with Arnold in some of the latter's early archaeological investigations during 1932, particularly in the roof space above the Hall. 'This involved preparing an extension cable from the pendant lamp socket over my [Reg Adams's] bed to the louver from which access to the roof of the Hall was possible, a somewhat dangerous activity for amateur electricians in a fire-risk building, but the results are now part of Arnold's historical discoveries.' Arnold became President of the University Archaeological Society with 'A Medieval Roof in St. John's College' as his Presidential lecture in June 1932.[3] The development of the buildings of St John's was a major interest, together with survivals from the earlier Cistercian college of St Bernard, eventually incorporated into St John's. This study was included as Appendix XVI, 'The Building of St. Bernard's College and Subsequent Developments' in W. H. Stevenson and H. E, Salter, *The Early History of St. John's College.*[4]

Upon graduating with a second-class degree in modern history, Arnold followed the family tradition of teaching by joining Chard School, Somerset, as an assistant master in 1934, after taking the Diploma in Education. He had not been there long when an advertisement for a vacancy in the Ancient Monuments Inspectorate appeared offering an opening to a career that matched his chief interests. Bryan O'Neil, also an old Merchant Taylors' and St John's man, having been promoted to be Inspector of Ancient Monuments for Wales, sought advice from his former college tutor, A. L. Poole, on filling the resultant vacancy for assistant inspector. Taylor was recommended, approached and invited to apply. Yet this was a difficult personal decision for Arnold in which he felt it necessary to take advice from his father, who in fact

---

[1] *The Taylorian,* 51 (1929), 150–3; 252–4.
[2] *The Taylorian*, 52 (1930), 171–3; 194–6; 231–5.
[3] *British Archaeological Journal*, NS, 38 (1933), 278–92.
[4] *Oxford Historical Society*, NS, 1 (1939), 93–110.

had no hesitation in encouraging his son to apply. Arnold's subsequent appointment led him to the Office of Works in 1935.

An early task was to oversee archaeological work at Minster Lovell Hall, Oxfordshire. This ruined fifteenth-century manor house had just come into the care of the Office. Arnold's analysis of the ruin was published in 1939.[5] He also became aware of the former alien priory of Minster Lovell. Nothing remained of this small house dependent on Ivry Abbey, but its origins involved Arnold in fieldwork by bicycle in France, and associated documentary research at the Archives Départementales. This resulted in an article in *Oxoniensia*.[6] Documentary research occupied much of his spare time in the years immediately before the Second World War. His transcription of the *Records of the Barony and Honour of the Rape of Lewes 1265–6,* together with appendices relating to later court and account rolls, were published by the Sussex Record Society.[7]

At the beginning of the war he was retained within the Office of Works and engaged in establishing office accommodation for the civil servants being dispersed from London into the provinces. While this prevented his immediate desire to be on more active service, it was an opportunity for him to marry Patricia Katharine Guilbride, a twenty-year old Canadian working in London, on 19 April 1940. She had earlier helped him in the preparation for his Sussex Record Society publication, particularly in the compilation of the index and checking the proofs, which he acknowledged in the preface. He was then living at Seaford, Sussex, and already a Fellow of the Royal Historical Society.

Taylor's historical and archaeological standing during the late 1930s was now sufficient for him to be proposed for fellowship of the Society of Antiquaries of London by O'Neil in May 1941. His 'blue paper' was impressively signed, not only by colleagues in the Office of Works but by leading antiquaries in Wales and by English historians. In the citation he was described as a member of the Council of the British Archaeological Association. He had joined the Association 1932, while still an undergraduate at St John's, and was a member of its Council in 1938. As well as his various articles in archaeological journals, the 'Records of the Barony and Honour of the Rape of Lewes' was given prominence. By now his address was 12 Thornton Hill, Wimbledon. He was duly elected a Fellow on 26 March 1942 immediately prior to war service.

[5] *Minster Lovell Hall* (official guidebook) (HM Stationery Office, 1939).
[6] *Oxoniensia*, 2 (1937), 103–17.
[7] *Sussex Record Society*, 44 (1939).

He joined the RAF and was trained as an intelligence officer in the aerial photographic interpretation branch. Being based at the training establishment at RAF Medmenham put him in fairly easy bicycle reach of London and home. He was eventually posted to Algiers and, briefly, to Tunis, before arriving in Italy. Here he was to study aerial photographs involving counting the numbers of aircraft on enemy airfields, and later analysing German convoys over the Alps. In some respects this was a most fortunate posting since he was able to visit many Italian historic towns during his short periods of leave. Significantly, while travelling back to England prior to demobilisation in 1946, his train took him through Switzerland past a castle, subsequently identified as Saillon in the Vallais, 'whose very stance', as he later wrote, had seemed to him even from a mile away to have an affinity of form and line with Conwy Castle, different in scale as the two might be. This experience was prescient as a precursor for his future researches. Stimulated by this acute observation, Taylor was later able to point to other direct similarities between the Edwardian castles in Wales and the Savoyard castles in the mountains around Lake Geneva. The helicoidal putlog holes (spiralling scaffold sockets) that provided ramped access for the builders, making it much easier to carry up materials during construction, was, for example, a technique that impressed itself on him and which he was to observe in some of the English castles in Wales.

Returning after the war to the Office, now in the Ministry of Works, in 1946, he found that Bryan O'Neil had become Chief Inspector of Ancient Monuments. Arnold was now promoted to O'Neil's former position as Inspector for Wales. This was to involve him in all aspects of ancient monument protection, conservation and interpretation over the next eight years as well as providing opportunities for research into castles and town walls. In the course of this time he wrote ten official guidebooks to Welsh monuments, He was also more broadly involved in Welsh history and archaeology, publishing a wide range of articles in various Welsh national and local society journals such as one on 'Usk Castle and the Pipe Roll of 1188'.[8] Another early publication was on Montgomery town wall (1947)[9] and 'A Note on Walter of Hereford, Builder of Caernarfon Castle' (1949),[10] though it later seemed that Walter was more master mason than 'architect'. This note was to be later qualified by Arnold's seminal study in

---

[8] *Archaeologia Cambrensis*, 99 (1947), 249–55.
[9] Ibid., 281–3.
[10] *Transactions of the Caernarvonshire Historical Society*, 9 (1948), 16–19.

1950 of the career of Master James of St George.[11] He was, however, not restricted to the study of castles. When the Cambrian Archaeological Association published its centenary volume, *A Hundred Years of Welsh Archaeology* (1949), Arnold contributed an article on 'The Greater Monastic Houses', which included a résumé of the consolidation of their ruins that had resulted from their coming into state care. His reputation as a historian led him to be elected Vice-President of the Flintshire Historical Society in 1953. A significant contribution was 'Castle-building in Wales in the later thirteenth century: the prelude to construction', written in homage to his mentor and predecessor in Wales, Bryan O'Neil.[12] Later, in 1969, Taylor was to become President of the Cambrian Archaeological Association. At a more official level, between 1956 and 1983 Taylor served as a Commissioner of the Royal Commission on Ancient and Historical Monuments (Wales and Monmouthshire). He was awarded an honorary doctorate of the University of Wales in 1970.

These years in Wales were dominated in an academic sense by the figure of Master James of St George, and this thirteenth-century master mason's role in the design and construction of the Edwardian castles in North Wales. Taylor records that as far back as 1937 he had noted the earliest references to Master James as '*magister operacionum Regis in Wallia*'.

Master James was indeed already known in the literature. J. E. Morris in 1901 had considered that he was the 'chief architect and designer' of Edward's castles.[13] Later, Sir Charles Peers thought that St George was the master mason of Rhuddlan, Harlech and Beaumaris but omitted others in the series.[14] Douglas Simpson argued that St George was not a master mason at all, still less an architect, but rather an administrator who supervised the financial aspects of these undertakings.[15] To Taylor it was desirable that their architectural authorship should be firmly established.

Taylor's paper 'Master James of St. George' (1950) was to do just that, and in fact anticipated his excursions to Switzerland and Savoy. It was achieved by researching predominantly in the English and Welsh sources at the Public Record Office for references to the construction of the North Wales castles in the various royal accounts. Arnold was already

---

[11] *English Historical Review*, 65 (1950), 433–57.

[12] *Studies in Building History: essays in recognition of the work of B. H. St J. O'Neil* (London, 1961), pp. 104–33.

[13] J. E. Morris, *The Welsh Wars of Edward the First* (Oxford, 1901), p. 145.

[14] *Transactions of the Honourable Society of Cymmrodorion*, 1915–16, 28, 29.

[15] *Transactions of the Anglesey Antiquarian Society and Field Club*, 1928, 41.

aware of Master James at Yverdon Castle in Savoy, and other clues that anticipated his services as Edward I's architect and military engineer. This paper was subsequently reprinted without alteration in *Studies in Castles and Castle-Building* (1985) but with ten pages of addenda and corrigenda keeping abreast with subsequent research during the thirty years interval.[16] Taylor's prolonged study of this influential castle designer eventually saw him awarded the Médaille d'Honneur de la Ville de Saint Georges-d'Espéranche in 1988.

By carefully comparing the North Wales castles one with another and noting some of their particular features, Taylor was to identify five constructional or architectural elements that were not, to his knowledge, paralleled in other English or Welsh castles, and were therefore likely to be directly derived from a Continental source. These, and the identity and previous whereabouts of Master James of St George, led to a dual purpose: to search, on the one hand, for architectural parallels and, on the other, for authentic sources for dating them, which might also throw light on the overriding problem of authorship. He thus set out from England in the autumn of 1950, as he was later to record in the Albert Reckett lecture given to the British Academy in 1977.[17] He added that the journey owed something of its inspiration to T. E. Lawrence's *Crusader Castles* (1936), a copy of which had been given to him in 1949 by E. T. Leeds, sometime Keeper of the Ashmolean Museum, Oxford, and a good friend to both Lawrence and Taylor. The perception of the link between Wales and Savoy was influenced by the latter's geographical situation, and to the close family relationship between Edward I and Savoy's ruling Count Philip. The Savoy archives at Turin certainly seemed to demand urgent investigation. Initially, however, Arnold disappointedly felt he had drawn a blank in his first visit to Turin, and he returned to Switzerland to study the castles of Grandson, Chillon, Yverdon and Champvent.

Similarities were found between the ground plan of Champvent and Yverdon with Flint Castle; also the accommodation on the principal floor appeared to have matched, almost exactly, that of Edward and Eleanor's apartments at Conwy. At Chillon, 'surely beyond doubt were the ancestors I was seeking of the Harlech fenestration'. The documentary 'breakthrough' came on 22 September in the University Library at Lausanne. 'This day's work has made it clear to me', he quotes from his diary, 'that

---

[16] 'Castle-Building in Wales in the Later Thirteenth Century: the Prelude to Construction', Arnold Taylor, *Studies in Castles and Castle-Building* (London, 1985), pp. 99–128.
[17] *Proceedings of the British Academy*, 63 (1977), 265–92.

I must go back to Turin, tedious journey as it will be, and look at the "comptes savoyardes" for myself to see how much early stuff there really is there.' 'It sounds like a forgotten era to recall that at 3.37 a.m. the next morning I was leaving Lausanne on the Orient Express for Arona, bound once more for Turin. The next 3½ days . . . were as productive of crucial sources as any I have ever spent.' They pointed to the presence of Master James then working under his father, Master John, at Yverdon. Later there were payments to him at Chillon in 1266–7. That St Georges-d'Espéranche in the Viennois, south-east of Lyon was coming to the fore in the early 1270s with the building there of a new 'palace' castle by Count Philip gave rise to the possibility that it might be from *this* St Georges that the Master James who made his debut in English records in 1278 took his local surname. A visit to Saillon, like that to Chillon, at once revealed examples of the architectural parallels Arnold was seeking for Harlech, and Conwy.

The next major step in Taylor's examination of Master James's architectural career was a detailed study of the Castle of St Georges-d'Espéranche.[18] A year after the trial run to Switzerland in 1950, the help of a Leverhulme travel grant enabled him to return and devote a whole month to exploring other parts of Savoy and other archives. The significance of St Georges-d'Espéranche enforced itself upon him.

The new castle built at St Georges for Count Philip of Savoy in the 1270s was expressly termed his *palacium*. It was Count Philip's latest and favourite creation. It had a particular interest for Anglo-Savoy relations, for it was here on 25 June 1273 that Count Philip of Savoy rendered homage to his great-nephew, the as yet uncrowned King Edward I. At the time the castle was so new that parts of it were still under construction, so that Edward and his circle, themselves shortly to be engaged in castle building on a very large scale, actually saw it in building. The documents demonstrated that Master James was associated with it and there was architectural evidence, which made the ascription of St Georges to Master James 'very likely indeed'. Arnold recognised that 'We have here conditions which might play a part in the transference, in this matter of castle-building, of ideas from the Continent to north Wales.' Elsewhere, the suggestion was put forward that it was from St Georges-d'Espéranche that this Master James took his name, it having been either his birth-place or the professional headquarters from which he set out for England and to which, in his new sphere, he looked back as his home. There was

[18] *Antiquaries Journal*, 33 (1953), 33–47.

similarity between the castles of St Georges and Yverdon, and between
Flint, Rhuddlan, Aberystwyth, Conwy, Harlech and Beaumaris. There
was the exceptional use of octagonal towers at St Georges, contrasting
with the characteristic round towers employed at other contemporary
castles in the Viennois. Arnold went on to argue that 'in north Wales as
in Savoy not only do we have a unified group of castles in which round
towers are the rule and polygonal towers the exception, namely at
Caernarfon, which has something in common with that of the Savoy
exception, namely St. Georges'. For Caernarfon was essentially intended
as a palace of the English principality of Wales, the formal official seat of
the prince's government and it may be that in some way similar ideas
underlie the distinctive treatment accorded to both buildings. Arnold had
written separately on the date of Caernarfon Castle.[19] His purpose was to
examine afresh certain of the early documents on which the previously
accepted dating was based, and to reconsider, where this seemed desirable, interpretations of them that had been put forward by Sir Charles
Peers. The following year saw the publication of 'Building at Caernarfon
and Beaumaris in 1295–6'.[20]

The idiosyncratic elements of the royal castles were thus traced back
to Savoy in regular solitary visits, and later incorporated into family holidays. He would drive long distances often with just a bunch of grapes on
the passenger seat for refreshment. As Peter Curnow has said, 'Those who
have been passengers with Arnold Taylor will know that these journeys
were not for the faint-hearted.'[21] He was moved to examine the archives
of the Counts of Savoy (relatives of Edward I) finding further evidence
that Edward had chosen Master James of St George, to be architect and
master-builder for his great military project in Wales. This research in
1960 led to essays demonstrating additional close associations between
England and Savoy: 'A Letter from Lewis of Savoy to Edward I'[22] and
'Count Amadeus of Savoy's Visit to England in 1292'.[23]

The various links between Wales and Savoy were summed up in the
Albert Reckitt Archaeological Lecture in 1977.[24] In this lecture Arnold
referred to Sir Goronwy Edwards's paper to the British Academy in 1953
on the subject of 'Edward I's Castle-Building in Wales' setting out the

---

[19] *Antiquity*, 26, no. 101 (1952), 25–34.
[20] *Bulletin of the Board of Celtic Studies*, 15 (1953), 25–34.
[21] *Études de castellologie médiévale*, 21 (2004), 3–4.
[22] *English Historical Review*, 68 (1953), 33–47.
[23] *Archaeologia*, 106 (1979), 123–32.
[24] See above, n. 17.

documentary evidence for the creation of eight new royal castles in Mid and North Wales between 1277 and 1295.[25] 'The study broke new ground', Arnold claimed, 'in that it was the first time the building of these great works had been considered as a single state enterprise, costing so much money, requiring the recruitment and movement of so much labour, calling for special expedients of finance, and taking this or that number of years to carry through.' Arnold went on to say that for a long time he had been pursuing one aspect which Sir Goronwy specifically excluded, namely the architecture of the castles and in particular their authorship and affinities.

In his lecture Arnold made the point that

> I have stated elsewhere [*Kings Works*] the grounds for believing that the real explanation of the differences between Caernarfon and Flint, Rhuddlan, Conway, Harlech and Beaumaris lies in the king's intention that Caernarfon should be a palace castle reflecting in its symbolism its own Roman origins and using the likeness of the Theodosian walls of Constantinople to invoke the imperial theme.

Taylor was the first to suggest that the banded walls of Caernarfon were inspired by the walls of Constantinople, reflecting the legend that the Emperor Constantine had been born in the town where his father had been a legionary.

The authorship of the North Wales castles and the parallels and associations with Savoy was followed by a detailed analysis of their construction and the organisation of the works in 'Castle-building in Wales in the later thirteenth century: the prelude to construction'.[26] In this essay Arnold recorded his indebtedness to O'Neil who had given every encouragement to the documentary study of these castles.

> O'Neil realized the need for a full recourse to original sources in unravelling the building history of the great medieval monuments whose custody became increasingly his concern . . . He accordingly gave full scope for record research wherever it might be expected to further the right understanding of the buildings in his charge. Especially was this so in regard to castles, always the holders of a foremost place in his interests.

Here, Taylor considered some of the indispensable preliminaries to the building of the castles, namely the administrative planning, the organisation of labour and the supply of materials, which were the foundations of medieval building achievement. This detailed analysis, supported by

---

[25] *Proceedings of the British Academy*, 32 (1953), 15–81.
[26] *Studies in Building History*, pp. 104–33.

distribution maps which had been compiled before 1961, anticipated the more comprehensive account of Edward I's castles in 'The King's Works in Wales, 1277–1330'.[27] As a scholar, Taylor, an obituarist was to write, 'was exact and cautious, requiring an unimpeachable array of evidence before reaching a verdict. He had a prodigious, almost photographic memory for physical details.' His tenacity in scouring the remnants of damaged Exchequer Rolls in the Public Record Office for scraps of evidence pertaining to castle construction was to impress his collaborator, Howard Colvin, who had been commissioned in 1951 as General Editor of *The History of the King's Works*. It was inevitable that Arnold, already an authority on Welsh castles, was one of the contributors along with R. Allen Brown and Colvin himself. As well as chapter VI, Arnold contributed to some of the appendices dealing with expenditure, and to Harlech Castle in particular, as well as notes on Savoyard and other foreign craftsmen employed by Edward I in Wales. Arnold's chapter was later reprinted separately under his own name.[28]

Already, in a more general context, Arnold had contributed the chapter on 'Military Architecture' in *Medieval England* where he summarised the current state of knowledge on the development of castles.[29] *The History of the King's Works,* however, was the climax of Taylor's writings on the North Wales castles, though there were later essays on particular aspects. And then there were the official guide-books, five in all, which went through innumerable printings and several editions. As a tail piece in 1995, came 'The Town and Castle of Conwy: Preservation and Interpretation'.[30] This he explained was a note which summarised and expanded one of the short papers communicated to the Society of Antiquaries on 23 February 1995 under the title of 'New Thoughts on Some Castles in Wales'.

Leaving aside his academic achievements in Wales, Arnold's most visible memorial lies in the glorious walls of Conwy, where through patient negotiation and diplomacy he secured the removal of numerous sheds and scrap metal yards built against the outside of the walls, including the local fire station, so that the walls could be appreciated in their full medieval splendour. However, with the work complete, the whole grand effect was threatened by the construction of the new North Wales Expressway, which was planned to be carried across the river below the

[27] H. M. Colvin (ed.), *The History of the King's Works* (London, 1963), I, 293–408; II, 127–40.
[28] A. J. Taylor, *The King's Works in Wales 1277–1300* (London, 1974).
[29] Austin Lane Poole (ed.), *Medieval England* (Oxford, 1958) I, 98–127.
[30] *Antiquaries Journal*, 75 (1995), 339–63.

castle on a bridge of grotesque ugliness dwarfing in scale the castle and the town walls. Taylor was not a man to be hobbled by his political or Civil Service masters, important as the road was held to be economically, and both before and after his retirement, he put his full energy into ensuring that the road was set out of sight in a tunnel. This he chronicled in his Presidential Anniversary Addresses to the Society of Antiquaries and photographically in his final 1995 paper.

As has already been said, Arnold's academic interests went beyond castles and Wales. Of papers on ecclesiastical subjects, 'The Cloister of Vale Royal Abbey',[31] was an early example in 1949. 'Evidence for a Pre-Conquest Origin for the Chapels in Hastings and Pevensey Castles',[32] 'Royal Alms and Oblations in the Later Thirteenth Century',[33] and 'Edward I and the Shrine of St Thomas of Canterbury',[34] were just a few which he felt deserved to be included in his *Studies in Castles and Castle-Building* (1985).[35]

To return to his official career in the Inspectorate, this was to change dramatically with the sudden and premature death of Bryan O'Neil in October 1954. He was succeeded as Chief Inspector by P. K. Baillie Reynolds. A new post of Assistant Chief Inspector was created shortly afterwards and filled by Taylor. While he still retained an interest in Welsh matters and more widely in England, Arnold was now largely London based. This had an advantage for the preparation of the first two *King's Works* volumes. It made possible research in the Public Record Office, Chancery Lane, most afternoons and allowed the coordination of the work of the Ancient Monuments drawing office in the preparations of plans for the volumes and of individuals who were contributing in various ways.

The preparation for the *King's Works* also included fieldwork. While studying the records for Calais, it has been said that Taylor and Howard Colvin had been puzzled by references to crosses on the town walls.[36] Reckoning themselves the first Englishmen to study the Calais fortifications since the sixteenth century, they found an intact stretch of

[31] *Journal of the Chester and North Wales Architectural, Archaeological and Historical Society*, 35 (1949).
[32] *European Castle Studies: Château Gaillard III* (1981).
[33] F. G. Emmison and R. Stephens (eds.), *Tribute to an Antiquary: Essays Presented to Marc Fitch by his Friends* (1976).
[34] *Journal of the British Archaeological Association*, 132 (1979).
[35] Arnold Taylor, *Studies in Castles and Castle-Building* (London, 1985).
[36] *The Times*, 14 Nov. 2002.

the defensive wall with crosses formed of characteristic English flush-flintwork marking the length of each sentry patrol. Much later, Arnold was to be the first to identify the mysterious castle of Belrem illustrated in the Bayeux Tapestry, showing that it corresponded to earthworks of the motte and bailey castle that he had observed at Beaurain in Artois.[37]

The retirement of Baillie Reynolds in 1961 saw Taylor's promotion to Chief Inspector of Ancient Monuments and Historic Buildings, a post he was to hold until 1972, first within the Ministry of Public Buildings and Works and later in the former Ministry's new guise as the Department of the Environment. This was a time when the responsibilities of the post and the Inspectorate as a whole were widening and the general archaeo-logical discipline was expanding. The traditional diet of castles and abbeys had changed. In this new role he maintained rigorous standards. The business of the department he believed was to identify, describe, pre-serve and transmit to posterity the physical relics of the past in its stew-ardship, without embellishment, addition or encroachment. The former Permanent Secretary of the old Ministry of Works wrote in his Foreword to Arnold's Festschrift.

> Those who complain of the inadequate complement of the Inspectorate should look back and then realise how much is owed to Arnold Taylor for the size and status of the Inspectorate today. It is the case that his years as Chief Inspector were seminal in the development of today's Inspectorate, including not least the development of the Ancient Monuments laboratory. Furthermore it fell to him to lead the Inspectorate into the new world of amalgamation with the Historic Buildings organisation of the former Ministry of Housing: an amalgamation which for years had proclaimed itself as a necessary development in the admin-istration of these matters . . . Arnold Taylor was among the more distinguished of the line of Chief Inspectors of Ancient Monuments.[38]

His period as Chief Inspector encompassed rapid archaeological expansion and an enlargement of duties and functions. In his last ten years of service he was responsible for leading the Inspectorate into this wider role and succeeded in maintaining the traditional identity of the Inspectorate; its professional standards, philosophy and its corporate sense remained unaltered. During the 1960s the archaeology of the coun-tryside was under enormous threat from the plough, motorway construc-tion and quarrying as never before, while historic town centres were gutted for redevelopment. The concept of rescue archaeology, that is the salvaging of information for understanding the past by excavation, and

---

[37] See below, n. 46.
[38] M. R. Apted, R. Gilyard-Beer and A. D. Saunders (eds.), *Ancient Monuments and Their Interpretation, Essays presented to A. J. Taylor* (Chichester, 1977).

the recording of standing structures that were being destroyed, became an urgent matter. This was first recognised by O'Neil during the Second World War as a counterpart to the physical protection of sites and monuments, but the mechanics for achieving this on any scale were inadequate at the time. Arnold saw that it was essential to achieve greater input from the Inspectorate to match and support the efforts of independent archaeologists. Three new posts were created to cover the three main periods— prehistoric, Romano-British and medieval. These inspectors were to be engaged on rescue archaeological excavations full time, and, what was revolutionary for the Ministry, the crucial task of bringing the results to publication, was part of their duties. As the rate of destruction accelerated, particularly in urban areas, pressure from the archaeological profession for greater resources grew during the late 1960s and early 1970s and became increasingly political. Arnold felt overwhelmed by this pressure, and regretted the political lobbying, as it pushed the department into unforeseen territory.

On the other hand, new areas of involvement such as industrial archaeology, which was then becoming recognised as a legitimate discipline, and whose remains needed protection and, in selective cases, preservation were more congenial. The maintenance of country houses, and historic buildings generally, was recognised by government, and the identification of cases for consideration by the newly created Historic Buildings Council formed another area of responsibility for the Inspectorate. Following closely behind were the problems of redundant churches, and by the time of his retirement, the grant aiding of churches in use was another new step. Taylor and the department were therefore at the centre of new pressures demanding increased public expenditure and additional specialist staff. In all this he proved an effective and generous leader, stimulating and encouraging younger colleagues.

Arnold Taylor retired as Chief Inspector in 1972 and on the occasion of a farewell dinner, his colleagues announced their intention of publishing a volume of essays in his honour. This appeared in 1977 under the title of *Ancient Monuments and Their Interpretation: Essays presented to A. J. Taylor*.[39] It is unusual among Festschriften in that all the contributors, whether from Wales, Scotland or England, adhered to a central theme: the work, philosophy, and methods of the Inspectorate as it existed at the time. The volume also contained a bibliography of Taylor's publications, consisting of 105 titles, covering the years 1929–76. Unusually for someone outside the mainstream of academic life he was, in the year of his

---

[39] See above, n. 38.

retirement, elected to the Fellowship of the British Academy. The award of the CBE in the previous year marked his place among official honours.

After his retirement, he continued to act in an advisory capacity to government. He was a member of all three Ancient Monuments Boards— England 1973–82; Scotland 1974–9; and Wales 1974–82. He also served on parallel bodies as a Commissioner, first on the Royal Commission for Ancient and Historical Monuments (Wales and Monmouthshire) 1956–83 and on the Royal Commission for the Historical Monuments (England) 1963–78.

He was a committed member of the Church of England and his concern for the future and preservation of England's medieval churches and cathedrals was another important feature of his life. In 1942, following the destruction caused by bombing in London, he produced a pamphlet entitled 'Friends of the City Churches: Statement of Policy'. His friend Reg Adams records that together they visited most of the City churches and observed the post-war development of their roles within the 'square mile'. Proposals for change without due respect for tradition met with opposition which 'we were both anxious to support'. Arnold's research and publications respecting ecclesiastical buildings and subjects were a continuing process from his days at Merchant Taylors'.

In later life, he was able to put this to active and practical service towards the preservation of churches through membership of the Cathedrals Advisory Committee (1964–80). He served on the Advisory Board for Redundant Churches at a time of increasing concern for the number of churches across the country being demolished on the grounds that they were of no historic or architectural interest. It was during his chairmanship (1975–7) that the first grants for historic churches were announced. More locally, he was on the Westminster Abbey Advisory Panel from 1979 to 1992.

With his familiarity with archives in France, Italy, Switzerland and elsewhere in Europe, Taylor was international in outlook. It was therefore appropriate for him to be invited to join a small group of architectural historians who individually represented most West European countries. The International Burgens Institute (IBI) was formed during the late 1940s. There was a strong scientific base which produced an annual *Bulletin* to which Arnold contributed in 1966 with a paper on 'The rehabilitation of castles in the country districts in England and Wales'.[40] It

---

[40] *Bulletin de l'Institut International des Châteaux Historiques,* No. 22, 71–4.

was a cultured association of like-minded scholars, who met annually in different countries to discuss broad castle themes.

In May 1962, a conference gathered at Les Andelys at the foot of Château Gaillard as the first public showing of the recently created Centre for Medieval Archaeological Research of the University of Caen. Michel de Boüard, its director, who was then excavating the Château of Caen, had invited the participants, choosing from among archaeologists, historians, architects and inspectors of ancient monuments those who had distinguished themselves by their excavations or writings in medieval castle research. The choice of Château Gaillard, recently restored, was symbolic.

Dr Joseph Decaëns has recalled the creation of this European institution and his personal memories of one of its founders and pioneers.

> I can visualise him on 30th May 1962, a little before the start of the first conference at Les Andelys on a very Norman morning when spring dithers between cold showers and lovely sunny intervals. He was wearing a big raincoat, which made him seem even taller. Armed with his camera before everyone else, he had already climbed the hill to look at Richard the Lionheart's fortress on his own, in peace and quiet. I saw him coming out of a steeply sloping path. It was impossible not to be struck by his very British elegance, his natural air of distinction and the kind smile which lit up his face.

Decaëns went on to describe the Conference and the details of its creation.

> In 1962 Arnold Taylor already had a long career behind him as Inspector of Ancient Monuments. He was renowned for his great knowledge of buildings, his vigour and the quality of his documentary research. At the Les Andelys conference he found a special friendship with Michel de Boüard, which never faltered. During the final session of the conference, on the proposal of A. Herrnbrodt, it was decided unanimously to continue the meeting in regular conferences which would take place every two years under the name of Château Gaillard Conferences in different parts of Europe to advance castellology—the word was invented that very day. Thus in 1962, was born almost spontaneously a European scholarly institution. It has lasted for more than forty years, always equally successfully, without, however, comprising statutes or rigid rules: it was governed by genuine customary law! Arnold Taylor was immediately appointed to represent Great Britain in the group of five individuals around Michel de Boüard given the responsibility of ensuring liaison between researchers, archaeologists and amateur enthusiasts, and arranging future conferences. This group became the liaison committee and later the permanent Château Gaillard Committee. Nowadays, the conferences are held in turn in European countries. The second conference was held in Germany (Büderich 1964). Arnold Taylor organised the third at Battle, Sussex, in 1966, on the very site of the Battle of Hastings and on its nine hundredth anniversary. It was a great success both in

the proceedings, whose quality is attested in the beautifully published volume[41] and in the excursions and visits to ancient monuments that were so carefully chosen and arranged. In 1980, Arnold was awarded an honorary doctorate by the University of Caen. The last time Arnold Taylor was seen in Normandy was in 1990, at the unveiling of the plaque in honour of Michel de Boüard at the Château of Caen, President Colloque International du Château Gaillard. In spite of his age and health problems Arnold wanted to pay his tribute to his friend who had died a year earlier.

Decaëns added a final tribute to Arnold, which is more telling since it comes from a foreigner:

> All those who read and appreciated his writings will never forget him. He will be remembered for his great courtesy, his kindness, his urbanity but also for his accurate and penetrating observation of machinery and monuments, his chronological analysis of buildings and his reliable and deep knowledge of texts and history.[42]

Another important component of Arnold's life was the Society of Antiquaries of London. Having been elected a Fellow during the war at the age of 31, he was elected to its Council in 1955–6 and again in 1963. From then on he maintained steady progress in holding the major offices: Vice-President 1963–4, Honorary Secretary 1964–70, Director 1970–5 and finally President 1975–8.

His first Anniversary Address to the Society as President on 29 April 1976[43] is revealing of the man:

> If filial piety to an *alma mater* is not out of place on such an occasion, may I say that one of the special pleasures you have given me, a Londoner born and bred, by electing me as your thirty-third President, is the thought that there is one thing which Peter Le Neve (the first President, chosen in 1707) and I and no other two Presidents have in common: we were nursed upon the self-same hill, though admittedly the nursing of the 1670s and the 1920s took place on opposite sides of the Walbrook. I find another source of pleasure, and indeed pride, in reflecting that the occupant of this chair in the days when I made my first three visits to these rooms in 1932 was also my predecessor as Chief Inspector: and if it is to the first Inspector of Ancient Monuments, Pitt Rivers, that we look back as the father of modern field archaeology, it is the second, Sir Charles Peers, successively Secretary, Director, and President of the Antiquaries from 1908 to 1934, who deserves to be remembered as the initiator of Britain's approach to the conservation of standing monuments, an approach which has brought renown to this branch of the public service and set the standards which

[41] *Château Gaillard: European Castle Studies*, III Conference at Battle, Sussex, 19–24 September1966 (Chichester, 1969).
[42] *Château Gaillard: European Castle Studies*, 21 (2004), pp. 5–6.
[43] *The Antiquaries Journal*, 56, part 1 (1976), 1–10.

are still its guide today. It is not a little sobering to glance back over the line of outstanding Presidents who over the last forty years and more have come after, to realize one has known them all, and now to find oneself following on in their distinguished company. But pride is quickly overtaken by humility, and I have no words to thank you for having chosen me as their successor. I do not need to tell you I am no archaeologist in the earthier sense of that term; most of my digging has been done in the Round Room in Chancery Lane and places like it in this and other lands. But I think I can say, with John Aubrey, that 'I was inclined by my Genius from my childhood, to the love of antiquities: and my Fate dropt me in a countrey most suitable for such enquiries'. I can only add that I will do my utmost to preserve, enhance, and hand on undiminished the heritage that you have entrusted to me.

Arnold recorded that it was in the previous year (1975),

ironically European Architectural Heritage Year, when the longest Public Inquiry yet seen took place into objections to a new road scheme which saw the District Council of Aberconwy, engaged in combat with the Welsh Office in a determined defence of the setting and amenity of Conwy Castle and Town Walls, no less, against their threatened obliteration by the ill-conceived and stubbornly pressed proposals of the Welsh Office.

Arnold accepted the local authority's invitation to appear as their principal archaeological and historical witness along with many other Fellows of the Society and on behalf of other bodies. The process was described and illustrated in his final paper of 1995.[44]

Taylor was finally awarded the Society's Gold Medal for distinguished services to archaeology in 1988. The then President, Michael Robbins's citation deserves to be quoted in full.

In recognition of his work in two adjacent areas: the practical problems of conserving ancient monuments, throughout his distinguished service which culminated in appointment as Chief Inspector of Ancient Monuments; and, second, his outstanding contribution to knowledge derived from the combined study of evidence from physical remains and from documentary sources. In particular, for his investigation of the records of the process by which the north Welsh castles of Edward I came into existence has sharply illuminated many aspects— technical, financial and economic and personal—of this important group of fortresses, several of them, as he has written, 'buildings of surpassing architectural and scenic beauty'. And he has enlivened the impersonality of the account books by tracing the careers of the master masons, especially by establishing the importance of Master James of St George—from St Georges d'Espéranche in Savoy. But his concerns have not been bounded by Wales: Merchant Taylors' School, Sussex, London and Middlesex, the Channel Islands, Normandy, Sicily, the international Château Gaillard conferences are all within the range

[44] *The Antiquaries Journal*, 75 (1995), 339–63.

of Arnold Taylor's inquiring mind and activity, backed by his skill at connecting things apparently far apart as Caernarfon and Constantinople. In 1976 his score of recorded publications was 105, not out, and he goes on adding to it. Arnold Taylor has combined skill and enthusiasm as conserver, researcher, and interpreter at the highest level in all three departments: and he devotes time and effort to one of his recreations, which he lists as 'resisting iconoclasts'. There can be no one who has proved more worthy to receive the Society's gold medal.[45]

Active membership of other national archaeological societies, and the holding of offices in them, included the Royal Archaeological Institute as well as his first love, the British Archaeological Association. Winner of its Reginald Taylor Prize in 1949, he was its President in 1993. He was President of the Cambrian Archaeological Association (1969). He had won its C. T. Clark Prize in 1956. He was President of the Society for Medieval Archaeology (1972–5). Among more local societies he was President of the Surrey Archaeological Society (1979) after serving as President of the London and Middlesex Archaeological Society (1971–4). Another of his interests was English place-names and he was Vice-President of that Society in 1953.

After formal retirement, his scholarly activity did not slow as he got older. Publication of source materials, monographs on castles, historical and archaeological articles added to a bibliography that was already extensive. In 1991 he took part in the Battle conference, where he paid tribute to R. Allen Brown, his long-standing friend and collaborator, recently deceased. Arnold's Memorial Lecture, entitled 'Belrem', was a profound analysis of the caption above scenes 6–7–8 of the Bayeux Tapestry. He identified Belrem with the motte and bailey castle of Beaurain-Sur-Canche on the banks of Ponthieu, which he had visited and photographed himself.[46]

Taylor had produced many articles in learned journals and guide-books often on subjects which were not castle related. It has been observed that he did not publish the 'great book' but his contribution lay in key articles many of which he consolidated in his *Studies in Castles and Castle Building* (1985). This was in addition to *King's Castles in Wales,* which was a reprint of his chapters in *The History of the King's Works.* The former he described as 'a by-product of a career spent in a once much respected government service now broken up in the supposed interest of "profitability"'.

---

[45] *The Antiquaries Journal*, 68, part 1 (1988), 1–2.
[46] *Anglo-Norman Studies*, *Proceedings of the Battle Conference 1991* (Woodbridge, 1992), 1–23.

Arnold's final entry amongst his recreations in *Who's Who* was 'resisting iconoclasts'. This he achieved in no small measure with the victory over the Conwy Expressway bridge. He successfully resisted the authorities at the Tower of London, who wished to convert the partially filled moat into a car park. Closer to home he fought the addition of a coffee/meeting room to his local church at Chiddingfold. It was an issue which split the village but Arnold stuck fast to his principles.

He maintained the family links with Walter St John's School and was President of its Old Boys Association (1969). He was also a member of the Sir Walter St John's Schools Trust. Lydiard Tregoze was the Wiltshire seat of the St John family, one of whom, Sir Walter, founded the school in Battersea which carries his name. The house fell into disrepair until bought by Swindon Corporation in 1943. Arnold was one of the 'Friends of Lydiard Tregoze'. Similarly he retained his association with the Old Boys of Merchant Taylors' School, becoming President of the Old Merchant Taylors' Society (1985–6).

His personal life revolved round his family of Patricia and their son John and daughter Kate. For much of his working career they lived in Teddington, moving out to Chiddingfold, Surrey, after retirement. Music and reading figured strongly in his interests. One of his great delights was attending meetings of the Cocked Hat Club, a dining society of the Antiquaries, whose whimsical procedures, conversation and outings gave him great pleasure and companionship. A gentle person, sometimes quizzical, on occasions quietly obstinate, in private Taylor was apt to undervalue his achievements. But while modest about himself he was also singularly free from academic jealousy. To his junior colleagues he was a kindly and sympathetic superior and they repaid him with affection and loyalty. Other scholars benefited from his constant and unselfish readiness to share his erudition.

It was a personal tragedy that in later life progressive blindness and deafness made his last years wretched. He never really recovered from a fall, which led to a fractured shoulder, arm and hip. He was to die of old age in a nursing home on 24 October 2002, aged 91, never really believing the extent of his life's achievements and the respect in which he was held in the academic world.

ANDREW SAUNDERS

KATHLEEN TILLOTSON   *Lotte Meitner-Graf*

Kathleen Mary Tillotson
1906–2001

KATHLEEN TILLOTSON, née Constable, was born on 3 April 1906 of Quaker parents in Berwick-on-Tweed where she and her two younger siblings, Denis and Jean, passed their early childhood. Her father, Eric Arthur Constable, a graduate of the University of Durham, was a journalist on *The Berwick Advertiser.* It was thanks to him, she gratefully recorded in the preface to her *Novels of the Eighteen-Forties,* 'that I grew up among the classics of the last century'. Her mother, Catherine Hannah Davidson, was born in Fritchley, Derbyshire. She attended The Mount School in York and subsequently studied at the University College of Aberystwyth. After his First World War service in the Friends' Ambulance Unit, where one of his colleagues was F. R. Leavis, Eric Constable moved his family to Birmingham where he had obtained a job on *The Birmingham Gazette.* His wife, who had herself become a journalist during the war, was for many years editor of *The Birmingham Soroptimist.* Kathleen Constable's Quaker upbringing and education, first at Ackworth School in Pontefract and subsequently at The Mount, exercised a profound and lasting influence upon her, instilling into her a high regard for truthfulness in all aspects of life, concern for the welfare of others, modesty about her own achievements, a preference for plain living, and a marked distaste for all forms of self-promotion.

In 1924, she went up to Somerville College, Oxford, as an Exhibitioner to read English. Her tutors were Charlotte Young and Helen Darbishire, the eminent Wordsworth and Milton scholar of whom she was in after years to write a warmly appreciative memoir for *The Dictionary of National Biography.* In it she recalled that Helen Darbishire 'was quick to recognise and foster any genuine response to literature, however

Proceedings of the British Academy, **139**, 385–397. © The British Academy 2006.

immature', and commented on how the 'slow-growing, durable influence' of her teaching was 'sustained by the continuing example of her own disciplined and disinterested scholarship', a phrase that very much applied to Kathleen herself. She had a distinguished undergraduate career, winning a major university prize, the Charles Oldham Scholarship for Shakespeare Studies, in 1926 and the next year was awarded a first-class honours degree in English, and was elected to Somerville's Shaw Lefevre Scholarship. She then enrolled in the B.Litt. course, recently reorganised by David Nichol Smith, Percy Simpson and others so that it now included courses in textual criticism, bibliography, palaeography and the history of English scholarship. Among her fellow-students were three who, like herself, were destined for great scholarly distinction, namely John Butt, J. B. Leishman, and her future husband, Geoffrey Tillotson. During the B.Litt. course she had become particularly interested in Elizabethan poetry and her thesis took the form of a variorum text of Drayton's sonnets with a critical study of the differences. She was awarded the degree in 1929, having also held the post of Assistant Lecturer in English at Somerville during the last year of her course.

Between 1923 and 1928 she reviewed regularly for *The Birmingham Gazette*. All her life she was a keen theatre-goer (a list she compiled of books read during 1922–3 included numerous plays) and, at a memorial gathering held at the University of London to celebrate her life and work, Professor Richard Cave recalled that no fringe theatre venue in London had been so obscurely located as to deter her from seeking it out if, for example, it was staging a play by Harley Granville Barker whose work she greatly admired. For the *Gazette* in the 1920s she reviewed many Birmingham Rep productions as well as others by the New Shakespeare Company at Stratford. At the Rep she saw some outstanding actors, for example Laurence Olivier whose Uncle Vanya she described as 'a performance of great beauty and power'. On a Stratford production of *Coriolanus* she commented, having found the music somewhat intrusive, 'The orchestra needs to be very reticent in the Roman plays.' Among her numerous literary reviews was one of Virginia Woolf's *A Room of One's Own* which she called 'a brilliant, beautiful and important book', and another of a volume of Chesterton's poetry, the boisterousness of which delighted her. 'There is not enough shouting poetry nowadays,' she wrote, 'not enough of the gusto that is to be found in our ballads and in Byron and Browning.'

She began teaching part-time at Bedford College for Women, University of London, in 1929 and had a 'room of her own' in the basement of a house in Bedford Square, Bloomsbury, that was mostly divided into bed-sits. Bloomsbury landladies had at that time, she later recalled, a reputation for 'dubious morals' but hers was eminently respectable. For some time she continued to teach part-time in Oxford also, both at Somerville (where she began a close and lifelong friendship with Mary Lascelles, who was Tutor in English there from 1931) and at St Hilda's. But already by 1930, she said later, she had begun to feel herself to be a Londoner who did some teaching in Oxford rather than an Oxonian doing some teaching in London (among her papers is a letter of this period from Charlotte Young at Somerville begging her not to commit herself to London, now that she has had her 'Bohemian fling', since there was a strong likelihood that she would shortly have a good chance of getting a Somerville Fellowship). During the politically troubled decade that followed, her left-wing sympathies led her to join some of the London protest marches and demonstrations like those stirred up by the Spanish Civil War and the Italian invasion of Abyssinia (it was at an earlier such march in Birmingham, she later recalled, that she had first noticed how the police used horses to break up a crowd). Life was not all work and politics, however. She was, for example, a founder member of the London Film Society, which had been organised by Professor Jack Isaacs of Queen Mary College to show screenings of avant-garde Continental films, and she was to retain a great interest in film in later years. Both she and Geoffrey Tillotson became great Antonioni aficionados in the 1960s and as a Fellow of the British Academy she was a strong supporter of the move to bring film studies within the purview of that body.

John Butt took up a full-time post at Bedford in 1930 and in the following year Geoffrey Tillotson was appointed to an Assistant Lectureship in English at University College, London. Kathleen and Geoffrey fell in love and their marriage in 1933 was the beginning of an ideal partnership which proved to be for both of them a deep and unfailing source of happiness and mutual support, both personal and professional, that continued unabated until Geoffrey's untimely death in 1969. They began housekeeping in the basement flat in Bedford Square before moving first to Millman Street and then to Tanza Road, Hampstead. The happiness of their private life was greatly enhanced by their two adopted sons, Edmund and Henry.

Kathleen's work on Drayton had brought her to the notice of the American scholar J. William Hebel and she became good friends with him and his wife. Hebel was working on a full-scale scholarly edition of Drayton's works, three volumes of which were published by the

Shakespeare Head Press before his unexpected death in 1934. Kathleen was asked by the publisher, and by Hebel's widow, to complete the edition, working jointly with Bernard Newdigate. Hebel had finished all the textual editing but introductions and annotation remained to be supplied for all the poems so far published, i.e., Drayton's entire oeuvre apart from the *Poly-Olbion*. Kathleen undertook this large and taxing task while Newdigate undertook the annotation of *Poly-Olbion* and the writing of Drayton's life with which Hebel had planned to conclude the edition. Her work appeared as Volume 5 of the Shakespeare Head Drayton in 1941 and may be called truly magisterial. Her crisply authoritative introductions are thoroughly illuminating in their detailed contextualisation and analysis of the poem in question while the formidable range of scholarly knowledge—historical, Biblical, literary—so succinctly deployed in the explanatory notes looks forward to what John Carey was to call the 'sumptuous rigour' of her annotation in Volume 4 of the Pilgrim Edition of Dickens's letters. Her outstanding achievement in the Drayton volume was recognised in 1943 by the award of the British Academy's Rose Mary Crawshay Prize.

In 1936 F. P. Wilson, 'the most learned Elizabethan scholar of his generation' (*DNB*), became Hildred Carlisle Professor of English at Bedford and three years later Kathleen was at last appointed to a full-time lectureship there. At the same time came the Second World War and the evacuation of Bedford College to Cambridge where Kathleen with her mane of beautiful red hair was a striking figure as she cycled around the streets with baby Edmund safely stowed in the bicycle's basket. Her wartime visits to London, where Geoffrey was working at the Ministry of Aircraft Production, are commemorated in his poem 'Homage to Tennyson, 1940', dedicated to her and published in his *Criticism and the Nineteenth Century* (1951). The poem was inspired by an episode that occurred during an air raid when she had acceded to his wish to hear her read some Tennyson to him (Geoffrey always loved the sound of her voice which he described as contralto).

With Bedford re-established in Regent's Park after the War, Una Ellis-Fermor succeeded Wilson as Hildred Carlisle Professor in 1947 and Kathleen Tillotson was promoted to a University Readership. By this time the focus of her research interests had moved away from the literature of the sixteenth century to that of the nineteenth, and in 1954 the Clarendon Press published her *Novels of the Eighteen-Forties*, based on a series of intercollegiate lectures given in 1949. At this time in Britain (the situation was very different in the United States) university English departments were paying scant attention to Victorian literature. At Cambridge F. R. Leavis had, in 1948, famously and influentially excluded from his 'Great Tradition' of the English novel all early and mid-Victorian novelists apart from George Eliot (with just one novel by Dickens, *Hard Times*, being allowed in, as an appendix). Meanwhile, at Oxford the undergraduate syllabus simply stopped at 1830, Lord David Cecil's *Early Victorian Novelists*, published in 1934, being still the standard work of reference for those interested in the subject. When touching on the 'social problem' novel of the early Victorian period, Kathleen had to go even further back, and to another country, to find any substantial earlier discussion of the genre. Louis Cazamian's *Le Roman Social en Angleterre* (1904) was, she noted, 'still the standard survey of the field'.[1] Her own book was hailed by the *TLS* as 'the most distinguished contribution so far to the animated new discussion of the Victorians'.[2] The first half of the book, called 'Introductory', consists of a survey, exhilarating in its width and depth, of the fiction published in this decade, demonstrating why it was such a fruitful and important one for the development of the English novel—how, for example, writers in the 1840s enjoyed much greater freedom with regard to choice of subject-matter than they did in the later decades of Victoria's reign. This formed part of Kathleen's contention that the time had come 'to break up "the Victorian novel" into manageable fragments . . . by concentrating upon a decade or so at a time'.

> Replaced in their original context of time and opinion, the novels may be found to make better sense, to take on new values to us, which modify or substantiate the old. At the same time, in attempting to recover something of the contemporary eye, the perspective of distance need not be rejected. My ultimate purpose has been to learn more about particular novels and their time, and about the novel as a 'kind', by looking rather more closely than has been customary at the novels of an early decade, the eighteen-forties.[3]

One of the most impressive and enlightening features of the book is the great extent to which it draws upon the work of nineteenth-century critics and reviewers and indeed it may be said to have initiated that whole process of rediscovering the critical discourse of the Victorians which so much enriched our understanding and appreciation of their literature during the second half of the twentieth century. Routledge's

---

[1] *Novels of the Eighteen-Forties* (Oxford, 1954), p. 123.
[2] *TLS*, 23 July 1954, p. 472.
[3] *Novels of the Eighteen-Forties*, p. 1.

valuable 'Critical Heritage' series (for which Geoffrey Tillotson, together with Donald Hawes, edited the Thackeray volume) provides a notable illustration of this process.

The second part of *Novels of the Eighteen-Forties* focuses on particular novels. Dickens's *Dombey and Son*, Gaskell's *Mary Barton*, Thackeray's *Vanity Fair* and Charlotte Brontë's *Jane Eyre* are all closely and illuminatingly studied in their biographical and historical context. The whole book is written throughout in that beautifully clear style, uniting precision with elegance and with feeling (also showing the same remarkable facility for apt and witty quotation that was such a feature of her conversation), that characterises all Kathleen's prose, even down to such things as her comment on a highly impressionistic piece of work by a student who had clearly not done his or her homework: 'an ingenious and imaginative essay untrammelled as it is by the burden of fact'.[4]

In 1956 she was invited to deliver the British Academy Warton Lecture on English Poetry and chose as her theme 'Matthew Arnold and Carlyle'. The lecture took the form of a sensitive and rewarding investigation of Arnold's complex response to the poetic qualities of Carlyle's writing and of the effect this had had upon his own poetry. Arnold, like Tennyson, and indeed Carlyle (as poet rather than as prophet), was one of her abiding enthusiasms and by 1956 she had already published in *The Review of English Studies* two substantial exploratory studies of his work, 'Yes: in the Sea of Life' (1952), and 'Rugby 1850: Arnold, Clough, Walrond and *In Memoriam*' (1953). The former essay was singled out for particular praise by Professor Barbara Hardy when speaking of Kathleen as a critic of poetry at the University of London memorial celebration. It was, she said, an outstanding example of literary scholarship combined with textual comprehension and appreciation, 'a model of scholarship which has sensibility'.

Kathleen's discussion of *Dombey and Son* in *Novels of the Eighteen-Forties* makes detailed reference to Dickens's preliminary outline of the novel and his 'number-plans', that is, working notes for the monthly numbers in which it was originally published. Three years earlier an essay entitled '*Dombey and Son*: Design and Execution' had appeared in *Essays and Studies*, jointly written by Kathleen and John Butt (who had moved to a chair at Durham University in 1946). This represented the first-fruits of their shared interest in studying the genesis and textual history of

---

[4] Quoted by Dr Geoff Britton in his tribute to K.T. at the celebration of her life and work held at the Institute of English Studies, University of London, 28 Sept. 2001.

Dickens's novels through scrutiny of the documentary evidence in the form of the surviving manuscripts, number-plans and corrected proofs. All this material had lain, principally in the Forster Collection at the Victoria and Albert Museum, virtually undisturbed by Dickens students until now when Butt and Tillotson (and also Sylvère Monod, a French scholar, working independently) began to investigate it. Butt and Tillotson's ground-breaking *Dickens at Work*, published by Methuen in 1957, opened up a whole new area of Dickens studies, one that revealed him as a much finer craftsman and a more painstaking artist than had ever been previously recognised. In their introduction the authors observe that 'despite some excellent interpretative criticism and much zealous biographical enquiry, Dickens studies have hardly passed beyond the early nineteenth-century phase of Shakespeare studies; while the study of his text seems arrested in the early eighteenth century'. The allusion to 'zealous biographical enquiry' is a nice glance at the Ellen Ternan scandal, as is also Kathleen's comment at the end of her chapter on *Pickwick Papers*: 'with *Pickwick*, Dickens embarked upon his lifelong love-affair with his reading public; which, when all is said, is by far the most interesting love-affair of his life'.

Butt and Tillotson identified the need for a full critical edition of Dickens's novels which should take account of all surviving manuscript material and corrected proofs as well as all editions published, whether in serial or volume form, during Dickens's lifetime and in which he might be supposed to have had a hand. In 1958 Oxford University Press committed itself to the project by appointing them to be Joint General Editors of the Clarendon Dickens. In 1958 also Kathleen Tillotson succeeded Una Ellis-Fermor as Hildred Carlisle Professor at Bedford College and in the following year delivered her outstanding inaugural lecture, 'The Tale and the Teller', a thoughtful and wide-ranging (as well as very entertaining) consideration of the richly varied uses made of the author's voice by the Victorian novelists. Characteristic of Kathleen was the peroration in which she urged the merits of William de Morgan, a Victorian novelist *après la lettre,* so to speak, and now in her view unjustly neglected. Another novelist who, for obvious reasons given its theme, figures prominently in the lecture is Thackeray, whose work was a particular enthusiasm of Geoffrey Tillotson's (his *Thackeray the Novelist* had appeared in 1954 and his 'Critical Heritage' volume has already been mentioned). The great Thackeray biographer and editor of his letters Gordon N. Ray was one of the Tillotsons' closest American friends, another being Gordon S. Haight, the editor of George Eliot's letters. In 1963 the Tillotsons collaborated on the Riverside Edition of *Vanity Fair* with Kathleen contributing, in the second half of the Introduction, a fascinatingly detailed history of the planning and writing of the novel, as well as exemplary annotation of the text itself. In the same year she made a notable contribution to the study of another mutual favourite of hers and Geoffrey's in her James Bryce Memorial Lecture at Somerville. The lecture, 'Tennyson's Serial Poem', is a fascinating account of the genesis of *The Idylls of the King* which she describes as a 'life-work', long meditated and 'slowly perfected' by the poet, 'taking shape partly in sight of his readers' so that the process 'may fairly be called serial publication though of an uncommon kind'.[5] Two years later Somerville elected her to an Honorary Fellowship. It was in 1965, also, that she was elected a Fellow of the British Academy and published, jointly with Geoffrey Tillotson, a collection of their reviews and essays entitled *Mid-Victorian Studies*. Included in this volume was Kathleen's massively researched and highly enlightening essay 'Donne's Poetry in the Nineteenth Century', first published six years earlier in a volume honouring F. P. Wilson. The year 1965 also saw the completion of the first volume of the Clarendon Dickens, and was very much a year of honours and achievements for Kathleen but it was greatly saddened for her towards its close by the death of John Butt. And only four years later she suffered a still more grievous loss when Geoffrey Tillotson also died, after a short illness from which he had been confidently expected to recover. In her preface to his posthumously published *View of Victorian Literature*, which she prepared for the press, she movingly refers to this expectation as 'not groundless but unfulfilled'.

Kathleen served as a member of the Council of the British Academy from 1968 to 1971 and as Vice-President from 1968 to 1969. She was also very active for many years in nominating people to give the Warton Lecture and also the Chatterton Lecture on Poetry. Peter Brown, former Secretary of the Academy, remembers her as 'a steely person, of great charm but strong resolve' who 'always put us right when we did wrong'.

Her work with John Butt on the Clarendon Dickens proceeded steadily from the late 1950s onwards. Their grand project was to establish a critical text of each novel, 'free from the numerous corruptions that disfigure modern reprints' and with an apparatus of variants that should record Dickens's progressive revision of the text, 'accompanied by all

[5] 'Tennyson's Serial Poem' was reprinted in Geoffrey and Kathleen Tillotson, *Mid-Victorian Studies* (London, 1965), pp. 80–109. I quote from the opening words of the lecture. The volume also includes her Bedford College Inaugural Lecture.

such assistance as Dickens himself supplied in the shape of prefaces, descriptive headlines, illustrations and cover designs from the wrappers of the monthly part-issues, which often foreshadow the drift of the novel as Dickens originally conceived it'.[6] The first volume in the series, *Oliver Twist*, appeared in late 1965, shortly after Butt's death. Kathleen had chosen to edit this novel herself in view of its peculiarly complex bibliographical and textual history, some aspects of which she had explored in a 1962 lecture to the Bibliographical Society.[7] She subsequently made some notable discoveries concerning the novel's textual history, showing that the first American edition must have been partly printed from uncorrected proofs. As for other textual witnesses, the manuscript survives only in part while the many editions printed during Dickens's lifetime range from the instalments in *Bentley's Miscellany* (1837–9) to the Charles Dickens Edition of 1867. Kathleen's choice of the very extensively revised (even with regard to its system of punctuation) monthly-part edition of 1846 for her copy-text caused some controversy but in the Introduction to her edition she makes what would seem to be an irrefutable case for choosing this particular text based upon the argument that until 1846 'Dickens was still writing his novel'. Eight further novels were to appear in the Clarendon Dickens during her lifetime, either under her sole General Editorship, or under that of herself and Professor James Kinsley, whose sudden death in 1984 left his *Pickwick Papers* edition to be completed by her (she also contributed a fine obituary of him to the *Proceedings of the British Academy*). All the Clarendon volume editors testify warmly in their respective acknowledgements to the prodigious amount of invaluable advice, information and general support received by them from her at all stages of their work. One of them, Dr Elizabeth Brennan, editor of *The Old Curiosity Shop*, speaking at the memorial gathering, referred to her as 'a marvellously selfless general editor' who 'shared our joy in what we brought to light'. Even after Professor Pamela Dalziel had, to Kathleen's great satisfaction, succeeded her as General Editor in 1997, she continued to take a close interest in the progress of the series (of which seven further volumes are currently in active preparation).

The other great scholarly enterprise with which Kathleen Tillotson's name will be forever associated is the Pilgrim Edition (from Volume 8 called The British Academy Pilgrim Edition) of Dickens's letters. This

---

[6] 'Preface by the General Editors' (1965), first printed in the Clarendon *Oliver Twist*, published a few months after John Butt's death.
[7] '*Oliver Twist* in Three Volumes', *The Library*, 5th series, 18 (1963), 113–32.

project was initiated by Humphry House, 'the pioneer of modern literary-historical scholarship of Dickens'.[8] Kathleen was deeply involved in the project from the start as a member of the original editorial board and from her vast knowledge of Victorian literature and Victorian literary and social history made a huge contribution to the detailed historical and biographical annotation of the letters. This annotation, evoking as it does 'the Dickens world' in all its tumultuous detail, was quickly seen to be one of the great glories of the Edition. She enjoyed a particularly close personal and working relationship with Humphry's widow Madeline House whose death in 1978 was a great sorrow to her. Volume 4 of the Letters, published in 1977, was edited solely by Kathleen, with her long-time and much-valued research assistant Nina Burgis (a considerable Victorian scholar in her own right) as Associate Editor. From 1981 onwards she was one of the General Editors and in 1988 the British Academy awarded her the Rose Mary Crawshay Prize for the second time in respect of her work for the edition. For the last four volumes (1997–2001) she acted as Consultant Editor and continued to be very much involved in the work in spite of increasing health problems, which had necessitated her moving into a retirement home in 1996. Here, at Guinness Court in St John's Wood, she embarked upon what was to her a deeply pleasurable re-reading of the whole of Henry James, and in the afternoons received a constant flow of visitors. Among the most regular of these was Margaret Brown (Assistant Editor for Pilgrim Vols. 9–11 and Associate Editor for Vol. 12), whose visits were a continuation of the almost weekly editorial meetings she had been having with Kathleen for the previous twelve years or so. Writing about her in *The Times* for 13 June 2001, Margaret Brown gives a memorable description of one of her very last visits to Guinness Court: 'In March, almost blind and very frail, she insisted on hearing a piece of annotation in which she was particularly interested, and gave her opinion with her usual deep insight and sharpness of mind undiminished.' In the final volume of the Edition, proofs of which Kathleen had seen, or which had been read to her, the Pilgrim Editors say of the volumes, for which she had been Consultant, that 'her authority, knowledge, and insistence on the truth, are evident on every page'. She died very peacefully on 3 June 2001.

Her work on Dickens for both Clarendon and Pilgrim was the primary concern of Kathleen's scholarly life from the late 1950s onwards,

---

[8] Robert Newsom, entry for House in *The Oxford Reader's Companion to Dickens* (Oxford, 1999).

fuelled as her work on Dickens had always been by her admiration of, and unending delight in, his art which no amount of familiarity with his writings could ever diminish. She was a long-serving Vice-President of the Dickens Fellowship as well as a much-valued contributor to the Fellowship's journal *The Dickensian* and in 1970, the centenary year of Dickens's death, she gave the first of a series of lectures organised by the Fellowship at the Royal Society of Arts. Entitled 'The Middle Years from the *Carol* to *Copperfield*', it is a masterly and thoroughly illuminating study of a crucial period of Dickens's artistic development, seen as 'a series of turning points, pauses, as it were, at crossroads; and at the same time an underlying, perhaps unconscious, sureness of direction'.[9] But, if Dickens was her prime concern, she was also generous with the time and support she gave to bodies concerned to promote the knowledge and enjoyment of other writers whose work mattered greatly to her. For twenty-five years she was very much a working member of the Wordsworth Trust, an activity which linked with the passion she and Geoffrey shared for walking in the Lake District where, accordingly, most of their brief vacations were spent (in London they rejoiced to live on the edge of Hampstead Heath, another part of England very close to their hearts). She was also an active member of the Charlotte M. Yonge Society and a Vice-President of the Brontë Society, twice delivering the latter society's Annual Lecture (1966 and 1986). But it would probably be fair to say that it was above all Tennyson, first read by her with a child's enthralled delight at the tender age of seven, who claimed her allegiance next after Dickens. She was a leading member of the Tennyson Society, giving the Annual Tennyson Lecture (on Tennyson and Browning) in 1974 and the Tennyson Memorial Address in 1983. For many years she served on the Society's Publications Committee along with Professor Leonee Ormond, who vividly recalled at the London University memorial gathering her 'down-to-earth response to anything that seemed to her pretentious or sub-standard', something that was very much in keeping with her bedrock belief that a scholar's first duty was to his or her subject.

Kathleen Tillotson retired from the Hildred Carlisle Professorship at Bedford in 1971, having spent thirteen years as an extremely hard-working, conscientious and caring Head of Department. She was sometimes perceived as rather an austere and remote, indeed rather formidable figure, especially by those who had perhaps never experienced the warmth of her

---

[9] Published in *Dickens Memorial Lectures*, a supplement to the September 1970 issue of *The Dickensian*, The Dickens Fellowship (London, 1970).

wonderful smile, or her own special brand of dry humour, or her zestful enjoyment of unmalicious professional gossip (nothing pleased her more than to surprise people with news items of which they were ignorant). At times her manner could certainly be acerbic, and even brusque, but it was remarkable how many acts of personal kindness on her part were recalled by former colleagues and students at the celebration of her life and work, and how warmly many of them spoke of the extent to which she invariably concerned herself with every student as an individual. Her prodigious memory meant that she never forgot any of them and indeed kept in touch with a surprisingly large number long after they had graduated. This can be seen from her carefully preserved correspondence files which are now deposited, with her other papers and those of Geoffrey Tillotson, in the archives of the Royal Holloway College, University of London. Bedford was very much at the centre of her life and it was a great sadness to her, as well as a source of anger against those governmental policies towards the universities which had brought about the event, when her college ceased to exist as a separate entity within London University and was merged with Royal Holloway.

Retirement from administrative and teaching duties meant, of course, that she had more time for her work on the Clarendon Dickens and the Pilgrim Letters, and her unmistakeable figure with its crown of snow-white hair was to be seen almost every day working away at her accustomed desk in the old North Library of the British Museum. If not there, she was most probably to be found delving into the stacks at her beloved London Library, or else at one of the auction houses, meticulously checking the texts of any unpublished Dickens letters that happened to be coming up for sale. She was also able to devote more time to her work for the various literary trusts and societies already mentioned. Moreover, she continued, as long as she was able to do so, her long-standing service as a board member of the Theodora Bosanquet Trust, which provides bursaries for women graduate students. Like her great loyalty to Bedford College, and to the University Women's Club, her years of devoted work for the Bosanquet testified to her lifelong strong sense of solidarity with other women engaged in higher education.

Kathleen Tillotson was the recipient of many honours during the course of her long and distinguished career. Some of these have been already mentioned, others followed after her retirement from Bedford. She was awarded an honorary doctorate by the Queen's University, Belfast, in 1972, and by the University of Oxford in 1982 and by the University of London also in 1982. She was made an OBE in 1983 (raised to CBE in 1991), and was elected a Fellow of the Royal Society of Literature in 1984. Most richly deserved were all of these honours for she was without doubt one of the greatest and most influential, not to say inspirational, scholars working in the field of English literature during the second half of the twentieth century.

MICHAEL SLATER
Birkbeck College, University of London

Note. For help in compiling this memoir my thanks are due to Pauline Adams, Librarian and Archivist at Somerville College, Oxford; Margaret Brown; Professor Pamela Dalziel; Anna Davin and Henry Tillotson (especially for providing me with a copy of the tape made of the speeches given at the meeting to celebrate Kathleen Tillotson's life and work at the University of London on 28 September 2001); Shirley Dixon, Project Archivist working on the Geoffrey and Kathleen Tillotson Papers at the Royal Holloway College, University of London; and Professor Donald Hawes.

GLANMOR WILLIAMS

Glanmor Williams
1920–2005

IT IS A WELL-KNOWN FACT that adult males born in Wales are the shortest
in Britain, and on a good day Glanmor Williams measured just over five
feet in his stockinged feet. But physical stature has never mattered to the
natives of Dowlais, and this Lilliputian man, by dint of intellectual brilliance, far-sighted vision and exceptional personal charm, achieved tow-
ering eminence in the field of Welsh historical studies. At most gatherings
he cut a compelling figure, and he was particularly adept at turning his
smallness to advantage. Having famously written in the preface to his first
big book that the work had 'like Topsy, "just growed"', it amused him
thereafter to reproach nature for denying him the same opportunity.[1]
When he was chairman of the Broadcasting Council for Wales in the late
1960s, he impishly confessed never to have been able to see eye to eye with
the impossibly tall Controller of the BBC in Wales, Alun Oldfield-Davies.
On another occasion there was much mirth in the Williams household
when a reporter described him in the *Evening News* as a 'pint-sized but
very eloquent professor of history'.[2] Few Welsh scholars in the modern
era have served their profession, university and country as admirably as
this diminutive giant and the flourishing condition of Welsh historical
studies during the last half century is in considerable measure attributable to his influence. Yet, in spite of his unrivalled standing as a Welsh historian and the weight of honours he accumulated over the years, he
remained unspoiled by his academic successes and public achievements,

---

[1] Glanmor Williams, *The Welsh Church from Conquest to Reformation* (Cardiff, 1962), p. vii.
[2] N[ational] L[ibrary] of W[ales], Glanmor Williams Diaries, 17 July 1969.

Proceedings of the British Academy, **138**, 401–423. © The British Academy 2006.

It is to his great credit that he remained, without side or pretence, a humble man, the quintessential 'little boy from Dowlais' ('*bachan bech o Ddowlish*').

By friends and colleagues alike, Glanmor Williams was known as Glan, and his charming autobiography, published in 2002, is pervaded with a burning sense of pride in, and affection for, his birthplace.[3] He was born on 5 May 1920 in Dowlais, Glamorgan, the only son of Daniel and Ceinwen Williams, both of whom were of rural stock but were also Dowlais-born. His appearance was a surprise to his parents, who had fully expected a girl, but they showered affection on him and swiftly detected his precociousness. Bringing up children in a community scarred by deprivation and suffering was a daunting prospect, though the working people of Dowlais prided themselves on their ability to work wonders through sheer hard work and sacrifice. Built by the Guest family, Dowlais held—and still holds—an iconic position in the history of the industrial revolution in Wales. But when the furnaces of the steelworks which had traditionally lit up the sky at night with a red glow were closed down in 1930, over 3,000 men were consigned to the dole queues and the region became ravaged by unemployment, deprivation and out-migration. 'See Dowlais and sigh',[4] murmured the poet Idris Davies as he witnessed malnourished people scrabbling for coal on the slag tips or kicking their heels on street corners. People now lived more in dread of the workhouse than of the might of the Guests. Yet, despite the privations, Glanmor experienced a happy and fulfilling childhood and, as was the case for many Victorian and Edwardian writers, 'the remembrance of [his] childhood and [his] youth was the sweetest of pleasures'.[5] Blessed with an unusually retentive memory, he recalled the humorous banter of colliers as they trudged in their heavy hobnailed boots through the town, the bike rides to local reservoirs, and the picnics in rural Breconshire during hot summer months. But what struck him most forcibly was the warmth, altruism and courage of the industrial *gwerin*, the proletariat who endured probably the most lamentable economic crisis since the Black Death. Even though another diminutive Dowlais-born historian, Gwyn A. Williams, would have us believe that there were reds under every bed in 'dismal

[3] Glanmor Williams, *A Life* (Cardiff, 2002), chap. 1. See also idem, 'Eira Ddoe: Cofio Dowlais', *Taliesin*, 69 (1990), 12–19.
[4] Dafydd Johnston (ed.), *The Complete Poems of Idris Davies* (Cardiff, 1994), p. 127.
[5] Christopher Parker, *The English Idea of History from Coleridge to Collingwood* (Aldershot, 1988), p. 119.

Dowlais' during this malaise,[6] the democratic socialism espoused by Glanmor was clearly the prevailing gospel in this community. His admiration for the selfless humanity of common people knew no bounds and it deeply affected his values as a historian and his own moral and intellectual development. When he wrote on the Tudor period he rather liked using George Owen's depiction of the lower orders as 'the general and common sort of people' and he strongly empathised with them.[7] Many years later, when he received the coveted medal of the Honourable Society of Cymmrodorion, he wrote: 'May we always have an ear delicately attuned to the still small voice of our common humanity.'[8]

Although Glanmor's parents began life with few advantages and were not well-educated in the formal sense, they were determined to ensure that he was properly fed, clothed and schooled. Badly shaken on three separate occasions by accidents in the pits, his father abandoned his mandrel and hobnail boots to become an insurance agent and, subsequently, a factory worker. Even though he earned little more than dole money, he was an omnivorous and intelligent reader who plied his son with books. Music and tales from the past figured prominently on the hearth and, on his grandfather's knee, Glanmor was regaled with stories of local heroes like Ifor Bach, Dic Penderyn, Lewsyn yr Heliwr, Henry Richard and Keir Hardie, and was more than once reminded that British governments had a long and unsavoury reputation for dispatching troops into industrial South Wales and shooting innocent people. From an early age, therefore, Glanmor assimilated an interpretation of the working-class political tradition which, though partial, was a formative influence on his thinking. His Christian upbringing also planted within him a profound understanding of the way in which spiritual values underpinned moral virtue, social justice and good neighbourliness. He became a devout Baptist chapelgoer and, although English was increasingly viewed in this multiethnic society as the language of 'getting on',[9] his Welsh-speaking parents introduced him to the extraordinarily lively and well-attended

---

[6] Gwyn A. Williams, *Fishers of Men: Stories towards an Autobiography* (Llandysul, 1996), pp. 11–24. For the contrasting careers and values of these two strikingly different Dowlais-born historians, see Geraint H. Jenkins, 'Dau Fachan Bech o Ddowlish', in Hywel Teifi Edwards (ed.), *Merthyr a Thaf* (Llandysul, 2001), pp. 192–226.

[7] Glanmor Williams, *The General and Common Sort of People 1540–1640* (University of Exeter, 1977).

[8] Glanmor Williams, 'History and Creation', *Book News from Wales*, Winter (1991), 4–5.

[9] Geraint H. Jenkins and Mari A. Williams (eds.), *'Let's Do Our Best for the Ancient Tongue': The Welsh Language in the Twentieth Century* (Cardiff, 2000), *passim*.

eisteddfodau, singing festivals and soirées (complete with jellies and blancmanges) which were part of the cultural fabric of Nonconformist life. At one stage he thought that he might become a Baptist minister. The poet Dyfnallt Morgan, whose impressive *pryddest* '*Y Llen*' (The Veil) was a commentary on how English became the lingua franca in the Merthyr area, recalled hearing Glanmor at the age of eight reciting Welsh prose and poetry for an hour and a half in Calfaria chapel on Dowlais Top.[10] When he was sixteen, his prize-winning essay '*Dowlais fel yr Eos*' (Dowlais like the Nightingale), was published on St David's Day in the *Western Mail*.[11] A few months earlier King Edward VIII had visited Dowlais and, visibly shocked by the dereliction and suffering, he reputedly said 'something must be done'.[12] In the event, nothing was done. The government turned a blind eye to the economic malaise and the sovereign abdicated the throne in order to marry his American mistress. Meanwhile, Glanmor resolved to repay his debt to his parents by pursuing his studies at school with renewed zeal. Over his whole life he possessed a strong desire to succeed.

In 1937, armed with a battery of scholarships and glowing references gained at Cyfarthfa Castle Grammar School, he went to the University College of Wales, Aberystwyth, to read History and Welsh. Like many of his age, he was the first member of the family to enter higher education. He was immediately struck by the heart-warming *esprit de corps* which prevailed among the *c.*700 students, and his years at 'the College by the Sea' proved to be among the happiest of his life. Aberystwyth was no cultural backwater. Its vigorous Welsh-language activities had never been more thriving, and when invited speakers such as Vera Brittain, Jan Masaryk, Josiah Stamp and Albert Schweitzer arrived they were bowled over by the 'Aber spirit'. Glanmor appreciated 'the spontaneous camaraderie, the happy we're-all-one-family attitude of Aber students'[13] and partook fully in their time-honoured habits—kicking the bar, quadding, hoaxes, ambushes, and mock funerals—as well as figuring fleetingly in the college soccer side in 1938–9. Nicknamed 'Twinkle Toes', he became the Welsh-language editor of the student magazine, *The Dragon*, in 1940 and

[10] Dyfnallt Morgan, '. . . Deigryn am a fu': Atgofion am Ddowlais 1917–1935', *Taliesin*, 71 (1990), 47; Tomos Morgan (ed.), *Rhywbeth i'w Ddweud: Detholiad o Waith Dyfnallt Morgan* (Llandysul, 2003).
[11] *Western Mail*, 1 March 1937.
[12] Ted Rowlands, '*Something Must be Done': South Wales v Whitehall 1921–1951* (Merthyr, 2000).
[13] *The Dragon*, 64, no. 3 (1942), p. 2.

also President of the Celtic Society. When he was elected President of the Students' Representative Council in 1941 his speeches were so enthralling that one student claimed: 'My religion is Glanmor Williams, and it's a lot of other people's religion, too, if only they had the honesty to admit it.'[14] Fully aware that education was a precious asset not to be wasted, he worked like a beaver and gained a richly deserved first in History and Welsh. To his dismay, luminaries within the Department of Welsh were so preoccupied with philology, which did not greatly interest him, that his creative gifts were not allowed to blossom. Outside the Department of History, lectures were to be endured rather than enjoyed, and the scholar who left the deepest imprint on him was Professor E. A. Lewis, a distinguished economic historian who had long captured the affection of students by storming to victory in the annual staff race and who, in Glanmor's case, awakened his interest in Tudor Wales. As all self-respecting Welsh scholars should, Glanmor fell in love with the unparalleled resources of the National Library of Wales, and it was with great sorrow that he learned of the sudden death of E. A. Lewis on the Aberystwyth golf course in January 1942. He was mortified, too, when he failed a medical examination to gain admittance into the armed forces. An active member of the OTC, unlike close friends like Dyfnallt Morgan and Emyr Humphreys, he did not hold deeply moral pacifist convictions. But even though he was released from war duties, the experiences of the times meant that there were no funds or opportunities for him to pursue research, a grievous setback which was only partly mitigated by his appointment in 1942 as a teacher of History, Welsh and a little French at Merthyr Intermediate School.

His prospects of an academic career took a turn for the better in 1945 when he was appointed temporary assistant lecturer in History at the University College of Wales, Swansea, where he was given a room in Singleton Abbey, a neo-Gothic pile which had been home to the youngest constituent member of the federal university since 1920. He immediately found life at Swansea—both academic and social—so congenial and fulfilling that he stayed in this 'ugly-lovely town' for the rest of his life. On 6 April 1946 he married Margaret Fay Davies, a native of Cardiff and a fellow History student at Aberystwyth, who had taken up a post as a history teacher at Gowerton Grammar School for Girls. Fay was an ideal partner for him: lively, resourceful, independent and yet caring, she supported him through thick and thin over a marriage which lasted for

---

[14] Ibid., 63, no. 2 (1941), p. 27.

nearly fifty-nine years. Glanmor often maintained that his debt to her was beyond redemption and he readily acknowledged her support as a copy-editor, indexer, proof-reader and confidante. It was she who urged him to persevere at a time when he was struggling to cope with unfamiliar man-uscripts for his master's degree on Bishop Richard Davies, one of the most influential and energetic Protestant reformers in Elizabeth's reign, and he reciprocated by supervising her well-regarded thesis on the Society of Friends in Glamorgan.[15] Their lives were further enriched when their daughter Margaret (March 1952), and son Huw (December 1953) were born, and they subsequently derived great pleasure from being in the company of their four grandchildren, Daniel, Elinor, Nia and Eleri, on whom they lavished affection. Swansea suited Glanmor perfectly and he was proud of his adopted town. He served on the magistrates' bench, became a director of the Dillwyn (later Swansea) Building Society, and joined the executive committee of the Swansea Festival of Music and Arts. Those of us who sat at his feet in the sixties were aware that this hec-tically busy and many-sided figure had his fingers in a large number of pies, and had we been told that he was also Lord Mayor of Swansea, manager of Swansea Town (as it then was) Football Club, and Governor of Swansea prison we would have accepted it as the plain, unvarnished truth. His abiding love for Swansea was evinced in the illustrated history of the city which he was pleased to edit and publish in 1990.[16]

From the outset, Glanmor was eager to make his mark in the groves of academe. Not many Welsh scholars in their late twenties would have dared to demolish, courteously yet firmly, one of Saunders Lewis's misbegotten theories about Protestant history on the pages of *Y Traethodydd.*[17] David B. Quinn, his head of department, thought highly of him, so much so that his lectureship was made permanent and, as his publications began to flow, John Scott Fulton, who had replaced the rather languid Charles Edwards as Principal, saw promise in him and raised him to a senior lectureship in 1952. Fulton's critics believed that his aim was to make Swansea a 'Balliol by the sea' and he certainly embarked on active, large-scale expansion. Glanmor was invited to prepare a blueprint for the future study of Welsh history at the college and, even though his own research interests fell in the early modern period, he was prescient enough

[15] M. Fay Williams, 'The Society of Friends in Glamorgan, 1654–1900', MA thesis (Wales, 1950).
[16] Glanmor Williams (ed.), *Swansea: An Illustrated History* (Swansea, 1990).
[17] Glanmor Williams, 'Cipdrem arall ar y "ddamcaniaeth eglwysig Brotestannaidd"', *Y Traethodydd*, 16 (1948), 19–57.

to call for investment in the modern period.[18] When David Quinn was appointed to the chair of modern history at Liverpool, an unexpected opportunity arose for him to implement these future lines of inquiry. In 1957, amid some controversy, Glanmor was appointed to the chair by the college council even though both Fulton and Quinn had favoured his rival, Charles Mowat. Hurt, but not embittered, by this unfortunate episode, Glanmor resolved to prove his critics wrong. In retrospect we can appreciate that hardly ever has an appointment associated with Welsh history had such beneficial consequences. He remained the senior professor of history at Swansea until 1982.

Glanmor's inaugural lecture, entitled 'History in a Modern University', delivered in January 1959, is a model of its kind and should be required reading for every apprentice historian. Mindful of Fulton's plans for dynamic expansion, he set out very clearly a manifesto for the study of the social history of Wales and urged the college not to neglect its opportunity to exploit what was likely to prove to be an enormously rich and exciting field:

> Historians are no longer wedded to the idea that sovereign states are the supreme end-product of the historical process or that they and the relations between them are the only phenomena worthy of a historian's attention. For that matter there is nothing sacrosanct about the history of a nation either. But it is an interesting and rewarding subject, particularly when you trace down the centuries the subtle and elusive problem of how an ancient and distinctive social and cultural ethos is maintained or modified within a wider political framework. It is one that not unnaturally has a strong appeal for those who belong to that nation. But the justification for Welsh history, or any other history, is not that it bolsters patriotism or national consciousness. It is the sober historical fact that the Welsh have a history of their own which, despite its close links with that of other British peoples, is in marked respects different. It cannot be understood as a regional fag-end of the history of England. Its connecting-thread is not political or constitutional history but social development.[19]

No previous Welsh historian had spoken in these terms, and this statement of intent not only caught the imagination but also came at a propitious moment. Under Fulton's successor, J. H. Parry, a highly distinguished historian, a major new development programme produced new buildings, disciplines and faculties on the campus. With enhanced resources to hand, Glanmor, in the words of the college historian, assembled 'a veritable

---

[18] Neil Evans, '"When Men and Mountains Meet": Historians' Explanation of the History of Wales, 1890–1970', *Welsh History Review*, 22, no. 2 (2004), 246–8.

[19] Glanmor Williams, *History in a Modern University* (Swansea, 1959), p. 22.

constellation of historical scholarship'.[20] He surrounded himself with
high quality teachers and researchers with a strong interest in the history
of Wales. Llandysul-born Alun Davies was lured from a Readership at the
London School of Economics to fill a new chair of modern history, while
Ieuan Gwynedd Jones, a miner's son and a former railway signalman, was
persuaded to abandon his studies of Stuart parliaments in favour of the
social history of nineteenth-century Wales. Young minds brought fresh
ideas and energies. From Oxford came Kenneth O. Morgan (Oriel), Rees
Davies (Merton) and Prys Morgan (Jesus), John Davies was a product of
Cambridge, and Ralph A. Griffiths was a graduate of Bristol. In the full-
ness of time, each of these became immensely productive and attained
international standing in Clio's vineyard. When some of them moved on,
Glanmor replenished his department with social historians like David
Jones, David Howell and Peter Stead. His reputation as a talent spotter
was unrivalled and, as the study of Welsh history acquired impetus and
prestige, even teachers whose principal teaching and research interests
lay elsewhere were persuaded to throw in their pennyworth. Neville
Masterman wrote a biography of Tom Ellis, Muriel Chamberlain investigated the Welsh in Canada, and David Walker (who was, in this writer's
view, the finest lecturer in the department) published a highly regarded
textbook on medieval Wales.

These fruitful developments coincided with the post-Robbins years of
student expansion. 'More will mean worse', cried Kingsley Amis, lecturer
in English at Swansea, without ever indicating whether he was referring
to student numbers or his own novels. But historians with a flair for
teaching and a desire to encourage innovative postgraduate work welcomed the influx of a new generation of working-class students and
braced themselves to face the full impact of what Alun Davies called
'those twin giants, Bulge and Trend'.[21] Leading by precept and example,
Glanmor blossomed as a strategist and a policy-maker. Under his benign
eye, students realised that, far from being dead and buried, the Welsh past
was alive and pregnant with possibilities. History 'from below' became
particularly inviting, and grappling with -isms like capitalism, Calvinism
and socialism in a Welsh context opened up new vistas. At the same time
Glanmor insisted that the history of Wales should never be viewed or
taught in isolation, and he could never be persuaded that ring-fencing
autonomous departments of Welsh history within the federal university

---

[20] David Dykes, *The University College of Swansea: An Illustrated History* (Stroud, 1992), p. 187.
[21] Alun Davies, *Modern History in a University* (Swansea, 1961), pp. 3–4.

was the only sure-fire way of protecting the interests of the subject, though the ebbing fortunes of Welsh history at Swansea following his retirement would appear to suggest that in this instance he was misguided. At any rate, he and his colleagues established a far more progressive and stimulating syllabus at Swansea than that found in most other British universities, and their labour bore fruit in the form of robust postgraduate schools. Glanmor's great achievement was to place the study of Welsh history in its rightful place within broader academic and intellectual studies.

Glanmor delighted in the company of students and readily won their trust and admiration. More than any other Welsh remembrancer, he radiated a sense of enjoyment while pursuing his scholarly tasks and in the classroom, and although some of the more morose students would have liked more histrionics and tired of his 'three causes and four results' approach the majority marvelled at the way in which he threaded his way through the centuries with such assurance and verve. He was punctilious in marking essays and scripts, and his beautifully neat handwriting was a wonder to behold. Though seldom one to lose his temper (at least not in public), he was not averse to showing his displeasure whenever students misbehaved in classrooms or failed to meet required scholarly standards. Always reacting to unreasonable demands with conspicuous good sense and moderation, he served as one of the first masters of the two new Singleton halls—Sibly and Lewis Jones—in 1961–2. Even though he heartily disliked administrative chores, his appointment as the first dean of a new faculty of economic and social studies in 1964 enabled him to promote the interdisciplinary approaches he favoured. Although it was not a role that he relished, as Vice-Principal of the college in 1975–8 he made a valuable contribution to the smooth and efficient running of the institution. And whenever things went awry, his perennially cheerful and obliging departmental secretary, Mrs P. M. Thomas (whom staff and students adored), was there to rescue him.

Although Glanmor took a lively interest in the university and college gossip which filtered through the corridors, he had little patience with the machinations of other senior historians elsewhere and would not on any account be a party to their intrigue. On one occasion he was plainly shocked to discover evidence of 'the fine Italian conspiratorial hand of D[avid] W[illiams]',[22] the founding father of modern Welsh history, and he privately condemned the examples of bias and sentiment which ran deep in the constituent institutions of the University of Wales. It would

---

[22] NLW, Glanmor Williams Diaries, 4 April 1967.

have been remarkable, of course, had he not used his own considerable clout to further the careers of those who were gifted and dear to him, but he realised that the key to success in the murky world of college intrigue lay in thorough preparation. At meetings and interviews, especially those which he chaired, no single member was better prepared or more alive to possible outcomes. As a result, Glanmor not only retained his uncompromising integrity but also always remained one step ahead of colleagues, rivals and enemies.

In order to promote his subject, Glanmor was also determined to take advantage of the opportunities provide by the federal University. Defederalists believed that the administrative machinery of the University of Wales resulted in duplication, delay and frustration. To some extent, this was true, but Glanmor knew full well that the institution was inextricably bound up with a sense of nationhood and that some of its central organs, especially the Board of Celtic Studies, could help him to fulfil his mission. First elected to the History and Law Committee in 1948, he remained a member of the Board for over forty years. Virtually all his books were published by the University of Wales Press and, as he confessed in 1991, 'the University of Wales has been to me an Abraham's bosom and there I have lain content and secure'.[23] Although the Board of Celtic Studies was hampered by lack of funds, Glanmor also detected a lack of vision and energy. As far as Welsh history was concerned, there was no single learned journal which specialised in the field and this meant that the subject was not only poorly understood but also lacked an international profile. Although the idea of establishing a Welsh historical journal was first mooted in 1954 by Glyn Roberts, Professor of Welsh History at Bangor, one suspects that Glanmor was the principal driving force behind this notion during the late fifties. He was elected editor of the *Welsh History Review* in October 1957, the first issue of which emerged in 1960. The launching of this attractive scholarly journal was a major turning point in Welsh historical studies and it remains to this day the principal flagship of the profession. In June 1966 Glanmor yielded the editorial reins to Kenneth O. Morgan and Ralph A. Griffiths who, over a period of thirty-eight years, kept the 'bright and steadily burning lamp of scholarship' shining within its covers.[24]

---

[23] See his address on the occasion of the award of the Cymmrodorion medal, *Trans. Honourable Society of Cymmrodorion* (1991), 25.

[24] Ieuan Gwynedd Jones and Glanmor Williams, 'The Castor and Pollux of Welsh History', in R. R. Davies and Geraint H. Jenkins (eds.), *From Medieval to Modern Wales: Historical Essays in Honour of Kenneth O. Morgan and Ralph A. Griffiths* (Cardiff, 2004), p. 12.

By this stage he was also thinking about how best to bring the work of postgraduates and other young researchers into the public domain and how to broaden access to the Welsh past. 'No N. Y. resolutions', he wrote in his diary on 1 January 1967, 'but plenty of aspirations.'[25] The lumbering machinery of the History and Law Committee was cranked into action once more and in its quinquennial proposals in 1972 it declared its intention of sponsoring a series of monographs based on the best postgraduate theses in Welsh history and also a series of six volumes on the History of Wales. As one might expect, there were dissenting voices on the committee but, tiring of aimless talk and procrastination, Glanmor offered the members a clear sense of direction and a set of achievable targets. The committee grasped the nettle and appointed Glanmor, Ralph A. Griffiths and Kenneth O. Morgan editors of a series entitled 'Studies in Welsh History'. Beginning in 1977 with the publication of F. G. Cowley's *The Monastic Order in South Wales, 1066–1349*, this series of monographs disseminated more widely than ever before the research findings of young scholars. Its chronological range was impressive—from the medieval governance of Gwynedd to work and social conflict in Merthyr and from the Bute family to the Welsh in Scranton—and by the end of the second millennium twenty volumes had been published. The second major enterprise—a multi-volume 'History of Wales' published jointly by the Clarendon Press and the University of Wales Press—brought more than its share of vexations. Doubting Thomases maintained that the time was not ripe for a full-scale series, but Glanmor relentlessly pursued the matter, arguing that it was both practicable and desirable for the Welsh to have their own authoritative, standard history from the earliest times onwards. Once more his opponents caved in and thus was born another major undertaking with which his name became associated as general editor. In the event, some of the selected authors fell by the wayside and, at the time of writing, two volumes still remain outstanding, but the four substantial volumes published by 1987 vindicated Glanmor by providing a wide-ranging and stimulating guide to the social and political development of Wales through the centuries.[26] Each of these initiatives is a striking example of how an eloquent, single-minded

[25] NLW, Glanmor Williams Diaries, 1 Jan. 1967.
[26] Kenneth O. Morgan, *Rebirth of a Nation: Wales 1880–1980* (Oxford, 1981); R. R. Davies, *Conquest, Co-existence and Change: Wales 1063–1415* (Oxford, 1987); Glanmor Williams, *Recovery, Reorientation and Reformation: Wales c.1415–1642* (Oxford, 1987); Geraint H. Jenkins, *The Foundations of Modern Wales: Wales 1642–1780* (Oxford, 1987).

individual was able to bring a sense of unity and purpose to the mission of Welsh historians.

Such demanding enterprises would have over-taxed the strength of most mortals, but Glanmor also had another bold and onerous plan under way relating to the county of Glamorgan. Just as he transformed the prospects of the national history of Wales, so did he strive to recover the deep historical roots of his native shire. Glamorgan mattered deeply to him and he knew that its history lay at the heart of the making of modern Wales. As early as 1947 he had been one of the founders of the journal *Gower* and had served it well as joint editor and contributor. He was also chiefly responsible for establishing *Morgannwg*, the journal of the Glamorgan Local History Society, editing its first three numbers and subsequently becoming the Society's Vice-President and President. This paved the way for a much more challenging venture in 1960 as the general editor (and saviour) of the long-standing but incomplete Glamorgan County History. First conceived in 1931, this project had just one volume to its name at that stage, published as long ago as 1936. With his wife Fay as his assistant, Glanmor breathed new life into this moribund undertaking by adding it to his editorial portfolio. Some of his friends believed that he had taken leave of his senses, but Glanmor did not believe that regional and local history were peripheral matters of no concern to the professional historian. As a proud Glamorgan citizen, moreover, his sense of public duty prompted him to drive the programme forward with all the rigour and energy he could muster. He appointed five editors for each of the remaining volumes, not all of whom, regrettably, fulfilled their remit. Although he had every right to feel badly let down, he persevered and whenever untoward circumstances prevented individual contributors from honouring their promises he either stepped into the breach or recruited able substitutes. He greeted the arrival of the final volume, published in time for the centenary of the founding of the Glamorgan County Council in 1989, with a profound sense of delight and relief. In total the six volumes, weighing fifteen kilograms, were probably heavier than the general editor himself, and the whole undertaking could easily have sent a lesser man to an early grave. By any standards, it was a magnificent achievement.

This proud son and grandson of a collier was also the guiding hand in the late 1960s behind an innovative coalfield research project established at Swansea and funded by the Social Sciences Research Council. Time was of the essence: the severe contraction of the coal industry in south Wales meant that valuable historical material was in danger of vanishing forever. By assembling a 'small but hyper-active team of postgraduate students'[27] and supervising their work, Glanmor helped to rescue and collect a diverse range of personal and institutional records, which became the core of the newly established South Wales Coalfield Archive at the college library. It was a proud moment in his life when the South Wales Miners' Library was opened at Hendrefoelan House, Swansea, in October 1973.[28] This new resource provided an enormous fillip to the newly founded Society for the Study of Welsh Labour History, whose journal *Llafur* (founded in 1972) provided opportunities for students of Welsh social and labour history to publish their findings and for people from all walks of life to benefit from them. Once more a coherent programme of action had borne rich fruit.

Yet, Glanmor's international reputation as a scholar rests mainly on his unrivalled expertise as an early modern historian, and the importance and influence of his work on the late medieval and Tudor period in particular can hardly be overestimated. As a church historian bent on making sense of the past, he pondered long and hard over the nature of historical knowledge, over issues such as truth and objectivity, and over his own duty as a practising Christian to recreate the past in 'as full, accurate, reasonable and impartial' manner as could be expected.[29] Although the pain of living in a post-Christian society and of witnessing the decline of chapelgoing left a profound mark on him, he was sensible of the responsibility of analysing and indeed celebrating the 'ancient privilege and great honour' (to quote Bishop Richard Davies) which constituted the spiritual patrimony of the Welsh. From around 1950 onwards he set himself the task of writing a major study of the Reformation in Wales. It soon dawned on him, however, that he could not hope to do justice to this decisive event without understanding the nature of the Church in late medieval Wales. His friends warned him that since the sources were patchy and inadequate this might prove to be a minefield for an innocent trespasser. Others reminded him that medieval scholars were prone to be precious and proprietorial about their field of study. But, as we have seen, Glanmor could never resist a challenge and, with the help of a Leverhulme fellowship in 1956–7, he turned himself into a medievalist by

---

[27] Glanmor Williams, 'Dr Joseph Gross and the Standing Conference for the History of the South Wales Valleys', *Merthyr Historian*, 15 (2003), 6.

[28] Merfyn Jones, 'The Swansea Project', *Llafur*, 1, no. 1 (1972), 33–4; Hywel Francis, 'An Educational Citadel: The South Wales Miners' Library', *Welsh Historian*, no. 11 (1989), 19–22.

[29] Glanmor Williams, *Cymru a'r Gorffennol: Côr o Leisiau* (Llandysul, 2000), p. 55.

embarking on a major research programme into the ecclesiastical history of Wales between 1282 and 1517, an undertaking which culminated in his superlative book, *The Welsh Church from Conquest to Reformation* (1962), in which he displayed a magisterial grasp of the sources and of the period. Glanmor had always had a deep feeling for literature and he was the first professional Welsh historian (if we discount Ambrose Bebb) to use literary evidence as a means of shedding light on the broad religious and social background of the period and of weaving this material into the narrative in a wholly satisfying way. Reviewers in Wales were agreed that it was a scrupulously fair and open-minded volume, while David Knowles, the Benedictine monk and historian, who was probably the best qualified scholar outside Wales to pass judgement, pronounced it 'a great book . . . planned on an ample scale and executed in masterly fashion'.[30] No more seminal work in the field of Welsh historical scholarship had been published since J. E. Lloyd's *History of Wales from the Earliest Times to the Edwardian Conquest* (1911). A revised edition of Glanmor's tour de force was published in 1976 and it remains one of the bedrocks of Welsh historiography. It is a book that will surely live forever.

A stream of more modest studies and articles on the Reformation then followed which highlighted the efforts of a small but determined band of Welsh Protestant reformers and humanists to promote the religious welfare of their compatriots, strengthen their native tongue, and preserve their own sense of national identity in the post-Union era. His collection of essays, *Welsh Reformation Essays* (1967), bolstered his reputation further by disposing of hoary myths, stressing the central role of the vernacular language in religion, and imprinting on the mind pithy sayings such as the description of Reformation historiography as 'the dog that hasn't barked' and the depiction of pre-Methodist times as 'not an age of torpor but an age of gestation'.[31] With characteristic impatience, G. R. Elton expressed his hope that the compendium would prove to be a harbinger rather than a substitute for the proposed major study: 'The big book is eagerly awaited.'[32] No one in Wales doubted that the work would arrive and that it would be worth waiting for, but not until his premature retirement in 1982 was Glanmor able to devote adequate time for

---

[30] *History*, 48, no. 164 (1963), 359–60. For other complimentary reviews, see A. H. Dodd in *Archaeologia Cambrensis*, 112 (1963), 193–4 and T. Jones Pierce in *Welsh History Review*, 2, no. 1 (1964), 95–7.
[31] Glanmor Williams, *Welsh Reformation Essays* (Cardiff, 1967), pp. 11, 29.
[32] In his review of *Welsh Reformation Essays* in *Welsh History Review*, 4, no. 3 (1969), 306–7.

this monumental work. In the meantime, appetites were whetted by studies of Reformation historiography and of the complex but fascinating interplay between the language, religion and nationality of Wales, a trio of forces which acted as an active and powerful leaven in the lump. The sheer sweep of some of his essays was astonishing, none more so than the 30,000-word chapter, entitled 'Fire on Cambria's Altar', which was published in *The Welsh and their Religion* (1991), a remarkable analysis of the development of the Christian religion in Wales from Roman times to the modern decline in church membership. One of Glanmor's chief assets was his unerring ability to see the big picture. This broad canvas was evident in his compelling account of the post-Glyndŵr era, the effects of the Acts of Union, and the opportunities presented by the Reformation and the Renaissance, all of which were major themes in the awkwardly titled *Recovery, Reorientation and Reformation: Wales c.1415–1642* (1987), which was his contribution to the 'History of Wales' series. Then, as promised, in 1997 came the culmination of scholarly work stretching over nearly half a century, the beautifully written and handsomely produced *Wales and the Reformation* (1997), the first substantial study of how the Welsh were set on the path which made them a fervid Protestant people. He was, of course, acutely aware that the Reformation in Wales was not an event but a process which came of age in the eighteenth century, but his last big book brought out very clearly the momentous significance of the 1563 Act and the ensuing translation of the Bible into Welsh in the long and arduous task of winning hearts and minds. Nevertheless, it would be fair to say that the freshness which characterised *The Welsh Church* was not replicated here, partly because Glanmor's conclusions had been rehearsed by him in earlier, shorter works and also partly because he had not been able to familiarise himself with some of the wider shifts in Reformation historiography. Yet, this eagerly awaited volume (440 printed pages by a septuagenarian) was respectfully and heartily received by his many admirers in the academic world and among the public at large.

In the space available, it is impossible to do full justice to the sheer range and quality of Glanmor's published output. Charting the *longue durée* held no terrors for him, and he could move backwards and forwards in time with apparently effortless ease. He wrote about monumental inscriptions, castle-building, prophetic myths, the Union with England, printing presses, the Welsh gentry, early Puritans and Dissenters, educational movements and patriotic sentiment in its diverse forms. His excursions into the modern period were not as rare as some have believed, and his beautifully written early essay on the idea of nationality on Wales,[33] for instance, opened up new areas of research, as did his edited volume, *Merthyr Politics: The Making of a Working-Class Tradition* (1966). He was among the first to recognise the critical influence of the industrial revolution and radical Nonconformity in the shaping of modern Wales. Popular books like those on Owain Glyndŵr and Henry Tudor were matched by studies of David Rees, Joseph Harris (Gomer) and Samuel Roberts, Llanbryn-mair, each of which was unpretentious and readable.[34] A conscious stylist, he was totally at ease in addressing a popular audience as well as the scholarly community, and he had an uncanny knack of bringing fresh eyes to old problems. As his extensive bibliography reveals, not a year went by without a Welsh-language publication or review appearing under his name.[35] Since he always insisted that speaking or writing in Welsh did not come naturally to him, it stands greatly to his credit that he published far more Welsh-language books, articles and reviews than did many academics who had been specially appointed in other colleges to teach and publish in Welsh. He never forgot his parents' insistence that he should '*wilia Cwmbreg*' (speak Welsh) and he felt a keen sense of obligation to close friends in Departments of Welsh such as Henry Lewis, T. J. Morgan, J. E. Caerwyn Williams and Stephen J. Williams. He most certainly did not share the anti-Welsh language animus which prevailed in several Welsh colleges and he treated Richard Cobb's judgement on scholarly publishing through the medium of Welsh as 'a foolish and wasteful exercise undertaken by second-rate minds' with the contempt it deserved.[36] Glanmor's Welsh-language biography of Richard Davies, published in 1953, won the Ellis Griffith Prize awarded by the Board of Celtic Studies for the best scholarly work of the year.[37] Sixth-form pupils and university graduates had cause to be grateful for the abbreviated, but highly readable, Welsh-language version of *The*

[33] Glanmor Williams, 'The Idea of Nationality in Wales', *Cambridge Journal*, 7, no. 3 (1953), 145–58. See also idem, 'Seiliau Optimistiaeth y Radicaliaid yng Nghymru', *Efrydiau Athronyddol*, 15 (1952), 45–55.

[34] Glanmor Williams, *Owen Glendower* (Oxford, 1967); idem, *Owain Glyndŵr* (Cardiff, 1993); idem, *Harri Tudur a Chymru: Henry Tudor and Wales* (Cardiff, 1985); idem, *David Rees, Llanelli: Detholion o'i Waith* (Caerdydd, 1950); idem, 'Gomer: Sylfaenydd ein llenyddiaeth gyfnodol', *Trans. Honourable Society of Cymmrodorion* (1982), 111–33; idem, *Samuel Roberts, Llanbrynmair* (Caerdydd, 1950).

[35] For an appraisal, see Geraint H. Jenkins, 'Bachgen Bach o Ddowlais: Yr Athro Emeritws Syr Glanmor Williams', *Y Traethodydd*, 160, no. 675 (2005), 197–212.

[36] *Y Faner*, 4, 11, 18 Sept. 1981.

[37] Glanmor Williams, *Bywyd ac Amserau'r Esgob Richard Davies* (Caerdydd, 1953).

Welsh Church published in 1968,[38] while *Grym Tafodau Tân* (1984), a sparkling collection of essays designed to show how Wales bred a galaxy of preachers, poets and prose writers whose profound spiritual experiences had been expressed through the 'power of fiery tongues', was rewarded with a Welsh Arts Council prize for literature.[39] Another set of wide-ranging essays on politics and religion in *Cymru a'r Gorffennol: Côr o Leisiau* (2000) was couched in the limpid vein associated with one of his heroes, R. T. Jenkins: 'clear to me, and clear to my readers'.[40] In English and in Welsh, Glanmor was a born communicator, and the enduring value of his work lies in his writings.

With characteristic selflessness, Glanmor placed his services and expertise at the disposal of many institutions and bodies within Wales and beyond. Indeed, it is remarkable that he found time to play such an active part in the public life of his country. He served the University of Wales well, spearheading the mission of the Board of Celtic Studies as its chairman for over twenty years, contributing valuably both as a member of the Management Committee and as a contributor to the pioneering research projects of the Centre for Advanced Welsh and Celtic Studies, and regularly enriching the portfolio of the University of Wales Press. His alma mater was pleased to elect him Vice-President in 1986, an office he held for a decade. Aware of his reputation for wisdom and moderation, public bodies jostled for his services as chairman. He particularly enjoyed assuming the chairmanship of the committee of the National Folk Museum at St Fagans since its mission focused closely on the travails of common people, their social practices and beliefs. The Pantyfedwen Trust, a dispenser of charitable funds, was delighted with his performance as chairman between 1973 and 1979, while from 1978 to 1981 the Welsh Arts Council benefited enormously from his long experience of cultural initiatives. He served on the councils of the National Library of Wales, the National Museum of Wales and the Honourable Society of Cymmrodorion. The Cambrian Archaeological Association elected him President in 1980. His expertise in manuscripts and love of books made him an ideal member of the board of the British Library from 1972 to 1980 and the chairman of its Advisory Council from 1979 to 1985. During this period, too, he gave unstinting service to the Advisory

---

[38] Glanmor Williams and T. M. Bassett, *Yr Eglwys yng Nghymru o'r Goncwest hyd at y Diwygiad Protestannaidd* (Caerdydd, 1968).
[39] Glanmor Williams, *Grym Tafodau Tân: Ysgrifau Hanesyddol ar Grefydd a Diwylliant* (Llandysul, 1984).
[40] Williams, *Cymru a'r Gorffennol*, p. 214.

Council of the Public Record Office in Chancery Lane. As a member of the Historic Buildings Council and of Cadw, and as chairman of the Royal Commission on Ancient and Historical Monuments in Wales, he not only deepened his own knowledge and appreciation of the Welsh landscape and its architectural heritage but also, in the company of knowledgeable and enthusiastic experts, he actively promoted seminal research programmes. Even when the agenda was gritty and unappetising, his wise head and 'gift of equanimity'[41] served him well on these occasions, though he could be extremely forthright in reminding those archaeologists, historians, lexicographers and librarians who had a record of poor delivery of their public duty.

Glanmor's reputation as an efficient administrator and a man of vision spread into government circles. When Welsh-language issues came to the fore in the wake of the formation of the Welsh Language Society in 1962, he was one of three appointees to a commission (1963–5) which produced the celebrated Hughes Parry Report on the Legal Status of the Welsh Language. The crux of the matter was the extent to which Welsh was judged to be an appropriate medium for law and government, a vexed issue which had exercised Welsh patriots since the Acts of Union. At the time, the commission's recommendations—that Welsh should have equal validity with English—was accepted as a practical compromise[42] and only with hindsight has it been viewed as an inadequate response to a complex problem. When the Welsh Language Act, which was based on the concept of 'equal validity', was published in 1967 it provoked a hostile response and, as Lord Prys Davies recently pointed out, its fundamental weakness was that it lacked teeth.[43] Relishing the controversies of these turbulent times, in 1965 Glanmor became chairman of the Broadcasting Council for Wales and a governor of the BBC. In his early days as an academic he had been a frequent broadcaster on the Welsh Home Service of the BBC and, as someone who understood the significance of the printed book, he was also deeply aware of the revolutionary effects of the modern media. Eager to act as an ambassador for Wales in what was a highly Londoncentric institution, he soon discovered that tussles for key strategic posts within the corporation resembled fights pursued under

[41] A phrase used by Peter Roberts, who presented him for the Cymmrodorion medal in 1991. *Trans. Honourable Society of Cymmrodorion* (1991), 19.
[42] See, for instance, the comments of Alwyn D. Rees in 'Statws yr Iaith Gymraeg', *Barn*, Dec. 1965, editorial.
[43] Gwilym Prys Davies, 'The Legal Status of the Welsh Language in the Twentieth Century' in Jenkins and Williams (eds.), *'Let's Do Our Best for the Ancient Tongue'*, p. 243.

bedclothes.[44] The Council thrived under his stewardship and he remained absolutely determined never to allow the post of Controller to fall into the hands of a non-Welsh speaker. These were volatile times in Wales and broadcasters were in a vulnerable position as the campaigns of the Free Wales Army, the Anti-Investiture Campaign Committee and the Movement for the Defence of Wales gathered strength. Glanmor especially enjoyed telling of the dressing down he received at the hands of George Thomas, an unpleasant bully who was Secretary of State for Wales at that time. Infuriated by the coverage afforded by the BBC to Welsh-language and anti-investiture protests, Thomas summoned the chairman to his office and barked: 'I'll tell the prime minister about you.'[45] As a long-standing, if diminutive, magistrate, Glanmor was hardly quaking in his boots and he retained his office until 1971. Mandarins in the Welsh Office became extremely fond of him and when, as founding President of the Association of History Teachers in Wales, he led a delegation to the Welsh Office in 1988 on behalf of the cause of a separate history curriculum for Wales he charmed them once more by arguing that the most expeditious way of protecting the distinctive cultural heritage of the Welsh was by appealing 'to them and their children through the medium of their long and valiant history'.[46] Even stony-faced public servants who were hostile to things Welsh found themselves melting in his presence.

Not surprisingly, this brilliant scholar, wordsmith, administrator and public servant was showered with richly deserved honours, all of which gave him great delight and satisfaction. He received honorary fellowships at Swansea (1988), Aberystwyth (1993) and Carmarthen (1996), and the University of Wales, which had already awarded him a D.Litt. for *The Welsh Church* in 1963, conferred upon him an honorary LL.D. in 1998. In October 1991, in the company of the Anglo-Welsh scholar Professor Gwyn Jones, and the artist Kyffin Williams, he was presented at the National Library of Wales with the coveted medal of the Honourable Society of Cymmrodorion. Elected a Fellow of the Royal Historical Society in 1954, he served as Vice-President from 1979 to 1983. The Society of Antiquaries elected him a Fellow in 1970 and the ultimate scholarly accolade arrived in 1986 when he was elected a Fellow of the British

---

[44] Glanmor Williams, 'Fighting under the Bed Clothes', in Patrick Hannan (ed.), *Wales in Vision: The People and Politics of Television* (BBC Wales, 1990), pp. 146–52.

[45] Williams, *A Life*, p. 139.

[46] Glanmor Williams, 'All Our Yesterdays', *Welsh Historian*, no. 11 (1989), 5.

Academy, whose section meetings he attended faithfully. The state recognised his status as an elder statesman and as the dominant figure within his profession by awarding him a CBE in 1981, and in 1995 he was raised to a knighthood 'for services to the history, culture and heritage of Wales'. Never was there a more deserving recipient. Other, more personal, tokens of gratitude moved him deeply. On his retirement, four of his colleagues edited a Festschrift in his honour, a valedictory greeting 'to salute his remarkable services to scholarly and other activities in Wales'.[47] But nothing gave him greater joy than to be made a freeman of the Borough of Merthyr Tydfil in 2002.

Small but solidly built, Glanmor was fortunate to remain physically healthy and active for most of his life and he was blessed with sufficient energy to keep many irons in the fire, all of which seemed to stay hot and alive. Routine was important to him, and the phrase 'Down to College early' recurs frequently in his diaries (which he presumably kept with an eye to history). He discharged his extraordinarily wide range of academic, public and social duties with conscientious care and never shirked taking painful decisions. He loved conversation, discourse and argument, and seldom failed to get his own way. Following his retirement in 1982 his intellectual energy remained undiminished, and although computers never impinged on his life, his battered typewriter was seldom allowed a moment's peace. Even though writing came easier to him than it does to most scholars, he took immense pains with his style and much drafting and fine tuning was undertaken before he declared himself satisfied. All his published writings are distinguished by clarity and elegance. He was invited to deliver a wide range of prestigious public lectures in Wales and beyond, and his inimitable high-pitched voice, which tended to move up an octave as he warmed to his theme, made his presentations all the more memorable. He was much in demand as an extra-mural lecturer, and in day-schools and conferences his discussions with mature students and sixth-form pupils kept his mind alert and sharp. After he had delivered the John Rhys Memorial Lecture in 1983, Sir Owen Chadwick, President of the British Academy, wrote to thank him warmly: 'there was not an instant, yesterday, in which my attention was not gripped'.[48] Late in his career he made a valuable contribution as an associate editor of the *Oxford Dictionary of National Biography*, just as he had done in his entries for *The*

[47] R. R. Davies *et al.* (eds.), *Welsh Society and Nationhood: Historical Essays presented to Glanmor Williams* (Cardiff, 1984).
[48] I am grateful to Lady Williams for allowing me to see a copy of this letter in Sir Glanmor Williams's private papers.

Dictionary of Welsh Biography down to 1940 (1959) over three decades earlier.

Glanmor liked people and always emphasised their qualities rather than their shortcomings. He enjoyed being with students who, for their part, found that the warmth of his friendship immediately broke down barriers. Requests for help from strangers were never left unanswered and authors, great and small, benefited enormously from his words of encouragement and his rigorous appraisal of their work. He fired the imagination of scores of amateur historians and local enthusiasts, and cared for them as if they were his own children. His great friend and colleague, Ieuan Gwynedd Jones, rightly praised his 'almost prodigal readiness to assist others'.[49] Dr T. G. Davies, a well regarded historian of health and medicine in Wales, once estimated that at one stage Glanmor had read over a quarter of a million words on his behalf. Countless other writers have sincerely recorded in prefaces and acknowledgements their special debt of gratitude to him. His generosity of spirit was also manifest in his myriad scholarly reviews, and he served for over two decades as a conspicuously fair-minded weekly reviewer of historical and political works for the *Western Mail*. A witty man, with a lively sense of fun, he was a brilliant raconteur who possessed an exhaustible fund of anecdotes and reminiscences which he would recount with the relish of a Celtic *cyfarwydd*. His gift for parody entertained even those who were his victims, for there was no malice in Glanmor and he bore no grudges. The photograph of him which accompanies this memoir captures the wonderful twinkle in his eyes. A brisk walker, he visited the Gower and the Swansea Valley at every opportunity and marvelled at the beauty of the Welsh landscape and the variety of its natural habitats. He had an ear for classical music— Mozart and Beethoven were his favourite composers—and his home in Grosvenor Road, Sketty, rang daily to the sound of concertos, quartets, sonatas and symphonies. In the light of all these personal qualities and diverse interests, it is a relief to report that he was weak at mathematics and no great shakes as a cricketer.

Glanmor gave the outward impression of being an extrovert. Sunny, warm and gregarious, he radiated genial good humour and affability. But he was also an intensely private man, given to moods of introspection and melancholy. The unexpected death of his mother in the spring of 1970 was a grievous blow to this only child (his father had died earlier at the

---

[49] Ieuan Gwynedd Jones, 'Glanmor Williams', in Davies *et al.* (eds.), *Welsh Society and Nationhood*, p. 3.

age of sixty-one) and one from which he never truly recovered. Sleep never came easily to him and he was often assailed by bouts of pessimism and what Aneurin Bevan used to call the invasion of doubt. His Christian convictions remained strong, and the lecture which he delivered to the Welsh Baptist Union on '*Grym Ddoe a Gobaith Yfory*' (Yesterday's Power and Tomorrow's Hope) in August 1977 offers telling insights into his religiosity.[50] He remained a faithful member (and a deacon) of Capel Gomer, Swansea, at a time when it felt the heat of competition from rival faiths and from Mammon. But he nursed deep misgivings about the quality of his written work and the imperfections within them, especially his Welsh-language compositions. The arrival of one of his books, fresh from the press, used to fill him with gloom. 'I was reading through the printed work [*The Reformation in Wales*] this evening', he wrote in September 1997, 'and I *still* can't make up my mind whether it's really good.'[51] Although generous, perhaps overly so, in his praise to fellow historians, he was hypercritical of himself. Given his stature as the doyen of Welsh historians, such modesty and uncertainty are all the more inexplicable. In public, of course, he gave no hint of the anguish this caused him, nor indeed of the sleepless nights he spent fretting about the propensity of the Welsh to commit self-inflicted wounds or about wider issues like global poverty, the prevalence of war, and damage to the environment. There were also tensions in his mind regarding the potential conflict of interest arising from his strong attachment to a common British culture and his genuine desire, expressed implicitly in a good deal of his written work, to see the separate identity of the Welsh people flourish.

Glanmor continued to study, write and lecture until shortly before his death. His last public engagement, delivered in his eighty-fifth year, was a poignant occasion. On 7 February 2005 he travelled to Oxford to deliver a lecture at the Schools on 'Oxford, London, Ewenni and Rome: A Tudor Welshman's Odyssey' to mark the retirement of his ailing former colleague, Sir Rees Davies, who, alas, passed away a few months later. It proved to be a bravura performance which drew warm and prolonged applause for this 'smiling cherub', as one admiring member of the audience called him. Glanmor's own personal odyssey came to an end shortly afterwards. After a brief illness, his long, rich and fulfilling life ended on 24 February 2005. The fact that hundreds of people from all walks of life came to pay their respects at Swansea Crematorium showed that he had

[50] Glanmor Williams, 'Grym Ddoe a Gobaith Yfory', *Seren Cymru*, Aug. 1977, 61–71.
[51] NLW, Glanmor Williams Diaries, 8 Sept. 1997.

touched the lives of many of his countrymen. Fittingly, his ashes were scattered on the Gower in his beloved Glamorgan. His memory will be cherished by everyone who was privileged to know him and wherever the study of the history of Wales is undertaken.

GERAINT H. JENKINS
Fellow of the Academy

Note. In preparing this memoir I have been greatly assisted by personal communications, both oral and written, from Dr T. G. Davies, Professor Ralph A. Griffiths, Professor Gareth Elwyn Jones, Professor Prys Morgan, Mrs P. M. Thomas, Dr David Walker and, most of all, from Lady Williams and her children, Margaret and Huw. I am deeply grateful to them all. A volume of essays in memory of Glanmor Williams is being prepared by several of his former colleagues and pupils.